Machine Gunners
on the Western Front

Machine Gunners on the Western Front

The Emma Gees

Herbert W. McBride

The Canadian "Emma Gees"

C. S. Grafton

LEONAUR

Machine Gunners on the Western Front
The Emma Gees
by Herbert W. McBride
The Canadian "Emma Gees"
by C. S. Grafton

FIRST EDITION

First published under the titles
The Emma Gees
and
The Canadian "Emma Gees"

Leonaur is an imprint
of Oakpast Ltd

Copyright in this form © 2014 Oakpast Ltd

ISBN: 978-1-78282-263-9 (hardcover)
ISBN: 978-1-78282-264-6 (softcover)

http://www.leonaur.com

Publisher's Notes

The views expressed in this book are not necessarily those of the publisher.

Contents

The Emma Gees   7

The Canadian "Emma Gees"   137

The Emma Gees

Contents

Introduction	13
New Names For Old Letters	15
Headed For the Kaiser	17
Straight to the Front	23
In the Midst of a Battlefield	33
Eight Days In	42
At Captain's Post	49
Our Own Cheerful Fashion	56
Sniper's Barn	60
Getting the Flag	69
Hunting Huns	75
A Fine Day For Murder	83
Without Hope of Reward	87
The War in the Air	93
The Battle of St. Eloi	97
Fourteen Days' Fighting	105
Blighty and Back	113
Out In Front Fighting	117
Down an Out—For a While	130

To The Memory of
William Emmanuel Bouchard
Lance-Corporal
Machine Gun Section
Twenty-first Canadian Infantry
Battalion
Killed in Action, at Courcellette
September 15th 1916

In Flanders' fields the crosses stand—
Strange harvest for a fertile land!
Where once the wheat and barley grew,
With scarlet poppies running through.
This year the poppies bloom to greet
Not oats nor barley nor white wheat,
But only crosses, row by row,
Where stalwart reapers used to go.
Harvest in Flanders—Louise Driscoll

Introduction

When the final history of this war is written, it is doubtful if any other name will so appeal to the Canadian as Ypres and the Ypres Salient; every foot of which is hallowed ground to French, Belgians, British and Colonials alike; not a yard of which has not been consecrated to the cause of human liberty and baptized in the blood of democracy.

Here the tattered remnants of that glorious "contemptible little army," in October, 1914, checked the first great onrush of the vandal hordes and saved the channel ports, the loss of which would have been far more serious than the capture of Paris and might, conceivably, have proved the decisive factor in bringing about a Prussian victory in the war.

Here the first Canadian troops to fight on the soil of Europe, the Princess Pat's, received their trial by fire and came through it with untarnished name, and here, also, the First Canadian Contingent withstood the terrible ordeal of poison gas in April, 1915, and, outnumbered four to one, with flank exposed and without any artillery support worthy of mention, hurled back, time after time, the flower of the Prussian Army, and, in the words of the Commanding General of all the British troops: "saved the situation."

Here, too, as was fitting, we received our baptism of fire (Second Canadian Division), as did also the third when it came over.

For more than a year this salient was the home of the Canadian soldier and Langemarck, St. Julien, Hill 60, St. Eloi, Hooge, and a host of other names in this sector, have been emblazoned, in letters of fire, on his escutcheon.

Baffled in his attempts to capture the city of Ypres, the Hun began systematically to destroy it, turning his heaviest guns on the two most prominent structures: The Halles (Cloth Hall), and St. Martin's Cathedral, two of the grandest architectural monuments in Europe. Now there was no military significance in this; it was simply an exhibition of unbridled rage and savagery. With Rheims Cathedral, and hundreds of lesser churches and *châteaux*, these ruins will be perpetual monuments to the wanton ruthlessness of German *kultur*.

When we first went there the towers of both these structures were still standing and formed landmarks that could be seen for miles. Gradually, under the continued bombardment, they melted away until, when I last passed through the martyred city, nothing but small bits of shattered wall could be seen, rising but a few feet above the surrounding piles of broken stones.

Glorious Ypres! Probably never again will you become the city of more than two hundred thousand, whose "Red-coated *Burghers*" won the day at Courtrai, against the trained army of the Count d'Artois; possibly never again achieve the commercial prominence enjoyed but four short years since; but your name will be forever remembered in the hearts of men from all the far ends of the earth where liberty and justice prevail.

H. W. McB.

New Names For Old Letters

When reading messages sent by any "visual" method of signalling, such as flags, heliograph or lamp, it is necessary for the receiver to keep his eyes steadily fixed upon the sender, probably using binoculars or telescope, which makes it difficult, if not impossible, for him to write down each letter as it comes, and as this is absolutely required in military work, where nearly everything is in code or cipher, the services of a second man are needed to write down the letters as the first calls them off.

As many letters of the alphabet have sounds more or less similar, such as "S" and "F," "M" and "N" and "D" and "T," many mistakes have occurred. Therefore, the ingenuity of the signaller was called upon to invent names for certain of the letters most commonly confused. Below is a list of the ones which are now officially recognised:

A	pronounced	ack
B	"	beer
D	"	don
M	"	emma
P	"	pip
S	"	esses
T	"	ock
V	"	vick
Z	"	zed

The last is, of course, the usual pronunciation of this letter in England and Canada, but, as it may be unfamiliar to some readers, I have included it.

After a short time all soldiers get the habit of using these designations in ordinary conversation. For instance, one will say: "I am going over to 'esses-pip seven,'" meaning "Supporting Point No. 7," or, in stating the time for any event, "ack-emma" is a.m. and "pip-emma" p.m.

As the first ten letters of the alphabet are also used to represent numerals in certain methods of signalling, some peculiar combinations occur, as, for instance: "N-ack-beer" meaning trench "N-12," or "O-don" for "O-4."

"Ack-pip-emma" is the assistant provost marshal, whom everybody hates, while just "pip-emma" is the paymaster, who is always welcome.

Thus, the machine gunner is an "Emma Gee" throughout the army.

CHAPTER 1

Headed For the Kaiser

The following somewhat disjointed narrative, written at the solicitation of numerous friends, follows the general course of my experience as a member of the Machine Gun Section of the Twenty-first Canadian Infantry Battalion. Compiled from letters written from the front, supplemented by notes and maps and an occasional short dissertation covering some phase of present-day warfare and its weapons and methods, it is offered in the hope that, despite its utter lack of literary merit, it may prove of interest to those who are about to engage in the "great adventure" or who have relatives and friends "over there." The only virtue claimed for the story is that it is all literally true: every place, name and date being authentic. The maps shown are exact reproductions of front-line trench maps made from airplane photographs. They have never before been published in this country.

I am sorry I can not truthfully say that the early reports of German atrocities, or the news of Belgium's wanton invasion impelled me to fly to Canada to enlist and offer my life in the cause of humanity.

No, it was simply that I wanted to find out what a "regular war" was like. It looked as though there was going to be a good scrap on and I didn't want to miss it. I had been a conscientious student of the "war-game" for a good many years and was anxious to get some real first-hand information. I got what I was looking for, all right.

The preliminaries can be briefly summarized. The battalion mobilised at Kingston, Ontario, October 19th, 1914, and spent the winter training at that place. The training was of the general character established by long custom but included more target practise and more and longer route marches than usual. The two things we really learned were how to march and how to shoot, both of which accomplishments stood us in good stead at a later date.

Leaving Kingston May 5th, 1915, we sailed from Montreal the following morning on the *Metagama*, a splendid ship of about twelve thousand tons. We had as company on board, several hospital units, including about one hundred and fifty Nursing Sisters, all togged up in their natty blue uniforms and wearing the two stars of First "Leftenant," which rank they hold. And, believe me, they deserve it, too. Of course they were immediately nicknamed the "Bluebirds." Many's the man in that crowd who has since had cause to bless those same bluebirds in the hospitals of France and England.

We ran into ice at the mouth of the St. Lawrence and for two days were constantly in sight of bergs. It was a beautiful spectacle but I'm afraid we did not properly appreciate it. We remembered the *Titanic*.

Then we got word by wireless that the *Lusitania* had been torpedoed. I think an effort was made to suppress this news but it soon ran throughout the ship. Personally, I did not believe it. I had had plenty of experience of "soldier stories," which start from nowhere and amount to nothing, and besides, I could not believe that any nation that laid any claims to civilization would permit or commit such an outrage. I began to believe it however when, next day, we received orders to go down in the hold and get out all our guns and mount them on deck. We had six guns; two more than the usual allotment for a battalion; two having been presented to our commanding officer, Lieutenant-Colonel (now Brigadier-General) W. St. Pierre Hughes, by old associates in Canada, just a few days before our departure.

Two of the guns were mounted on the forward deck, two on the flying bridge and two on the aft bridge. I'm not sure, to this day, just what we expected to do against a submarine with those machine guns, but at any rate they seemed to give an additional feeling of security to the others on board and of course we machine gunners put up an awful bluff to persuade them that we could sink any U-boat without the least difficulty. Of one thing we were sure. Being a troop ship we could expect no mercy from an enemy and we were at least prepared to make it hot for any of them who came fooling around within range provided they came to the surface. I was with the forward guns and, as we had several days of pretty rough weather, it was a wet job.

Our wireless was continually cracking and sputtering so I suppose the skipper was getting his sailing orders from the Admiralty as we changed direction several times a day. We had no convoying war-ships and sighted but few boats, mostly Norwegian sailing vessels, until, one night about nine o'clock, several dark slim shadows came slipping up out of the blackness and established themselves in front, on both flanks and behind us. We gunners had been warned by the captain to look out for something of the kind, but I can assure anyone who has not been through the experience that the sigh of relief which went up from those gun crews was sincere and deep. We were running without lights, of course, and none but the crew was allowed on deck. The destroyers (for such they were), were also perfectly dark and we could barely discern their outlines as they glided silently along, accommodating their pace to ours.

Just before sunrise we dropped anchor inside Plymouth breakwater. This was a surprise, as we had expected to land at Liverpool or Bristol. But you may depend on it, no one made any complaint; any port in England looked good to us. A few hours later we moved into the harbor and tied up at Devonport Dock where we lay all day, unloading cargo. Right next to us was a big transport just about to sail for the Dardanelles. The Dublin Fusiliers were aboard her and they gave us a cheer as we came in. Poor devils, they had a rough time of it down there; but I guess by this time they think the same about us; so we'll call it square.

It rained all day, but we finally got everything off the ship and on the trains and pulled out about dark. No one knew where we were going. The only training camp we had heard of in England was Salisbury Plain and what we had heard of that place did not make any of us anxious to see it. The First Canadian Division had been there and the reports they sent home were anything but encouraging. Our men were nearly all native-born Canadians and "Yankees," and they cracked many a joke about the little English "carriages," but they soon learned to respect the pulling power of the engines. We made ourselves as comfortable as possible with eight in a compartment, each man with his full kit, and soon after daylight the train stopped and we were told to get out. The name of the station was Westerhanger but that did not tell us anything.

The native Britishers we had in our crowd were mostly from "north of the Tweed" so what could they be expected to know about Kent. For Kent it was, sure enough, and after a march of some two or three miles we found ourselves "at home" in West Sandling Camp. And how proudly we marched up the long hill and past the Brigade Headquarters, our pipers skirling their heartiest and the drummers beating as never before. For we were on exhibition and we knew it. The roads were lined with soldiers and they cheered and cheered as we came marching in. We were tired, our loads were heavy and the mud was deep, but never a man in that column would have traded his place for the most luxurious comforts at home.

There came a time when we hated that hill and that camp as the devil hates holy water, but that Sunday morning, marching into a British camp, with British soldiers, eager to keep right on across the channel and clean up Kaiser Bill and feeling as though we were able to do it, single-handed—why, the meanest private in the Twenty-first Canadians considered himself just a little bit better than any one else on earth.

Thus we came to our home in England, where we worked and sweated and swore for four solid months before we were considered fit to take our place in the firing-line. All that time, from the top of Tolsford Hill, just at the edge of our camp, we could see France, "the promised land"; we could hear the big guns nearly every night, and we, in our ignorance, could not understand why we were not allowed to go over and settle the whole business. We marched all over Southern England. I *know* I have slept under every hedgerow in Kent. We dug trenches one day and filled them up the next. We made bombs and learned to throw them. We mastered every kind of signalling from semaphore to wireless, and we nearly wore out the old Roman stone roads hiking all the way from Hythe to Canterbury. We carried those old Colt guns and heavy tripods far enough to have taken us to Bagdad and back.

But, oh, man! what a tough lot of soldiers it made of us. Without just that seasoning we would never have been able to make even the first two days' marches when we finally did go across. The weaklings fell by the wayside and were replaced until, when the "great day" came and we embarked for France, I verily believe that that battalion, and especially the "Emma Gees," was about the toughest lot of soldiers who ever went to war.

(Emma Gee is signaller's lingo for M. G., meaning machine gunner.)

It must not be inferred that our four months in England were all work and worry. Personally, I derived great pleasure from them. We were right in the midst of a lot of old and interesting places which figure largely in the early history of England. Within a mile of our camp was Saltwood Castle, built in 499 by the Romans and enlarged by the Normans. It was here that the conspirators met to plan the assassination of Thomas à Becket at Canterbury, only sixteen miles away, and which we had ample opportunities to visit. Hythe, one of the ancient "Cinque Ports," was but a mile or so distant, with its old church dating from the time of Ethelbert, King of Kent. In its crypt are the bones of several hundred persons which have been there since the time of the Crusaders, and in the church, proper, are arms and armour of some of the old timers who went on those same Crusades. Among numerous tablets on the walls is one:

> To the memory of Captain Robert Furnis, Commanding H. M. S. *Queen Charlotte*: killed at the Battle of Lake Erie: 1813—Perry's victory.

About three miles away was "Monk's Horton, Horton Park and Horton Priory," the latter church dating from the twelfth century and remaining just about as it was when it was built. Then there was Lympne Castle, another Roman stronghold; Cæsar's Plain and Cæsar's Camp, where Julius is said to have spent some time on his memorable expedition to England; and, within easy reach by bicycle, Hastings and Battle Abbey where William the Norman defeated Harold and conquered England. The very roads over which we marched were, many of them, built by the Romans. Every little town and hamlet through which we passed has a history running back for hundreds of years. We took our noon rest one day in the yard of the famous "Chequers Inn," on the road to Canterbury. We camped one night in Hatch Park, where the deer scampered about in great droves. On Sundays we could charter one of the big "rubber-neck" autos and make the round trip to Margate, Ramsgate, Broadstairs, Deal and Dover.

But, just the same, when we were told, positively, that we were going to leave, there were no tears shed. We had gone over there to fight and nothing else would satisfy us.

FRENCH HOTCHKISS GUN FIRING AT AEROPLANE

Chapter 2

Straight to the Front

The Machine Gun Section, having its own transport, travelled *via* Southampton, as there were better facilities for loading horses and wagons there than at the ports from which the remainder of the troops embarked. After we had everything aboard ship it was an even bet among the crowd as to whether we were going to France, the Dardanelles or Mesopotamia. There were other ships there, loading just as we were, some of which were known to be destined for the eastern theatre; so how could we know? As a matter of fact, our officers did not know any more about it than the men.

On the dock I discovered a box containing blank postcards given out by "The Missions to Seamen." I wrote one to my mother and stuck it in a mail-box, on the chance that it *might* go through. I had no stamps and didn't really expect it to be taken up, but someone "with a heart" inscribed on it "O. H. M. S.," and, sure enough, On His Majesty's Service it went, straight to Indianapolis.

After having everything nicely stowed in the hold, Sandy McNab and I had to go down and dig out a couple of guns to mount on deck. It required quite a lot of acrobatic stunts to get down in the first place and then to get the guns and ammunition up, but we managed to finish the job just before dark and got the guns mounted, mine on the starboard and Sandy's on the port side, before we steamed out. It was a black drizzly night and the cold wind cut like a knife, but we "stood to" until dawn, expecting anything or nothing. After an hour or so we didn't care much what happened.

Everything was dark, not a light showing aboard ship or elsewhere until, about midnight, I saw a glow on the horizon, nearly dead ahead. As the ship's lookouts said nothing, I did likewise, but I assure you I was mightily puzzled. I knew we could not be near enough to shore

POST CARD.

SOUTHAMPTON PAID SEP 14

Mrs. Ida S. McBride
1434 Park Ave
Indianapolis,
Indiana
U. S. A.

POSTCARD

to see a lighthouse and, anyway, there was too much light for any ordinary shore signal. I finally concluded that it must be a ship burning and wondered what we would do about it, but the thing gradually took on the appearance of a gigantic Christmas tree and then I felt sure that I was going "plumb nutty." I sneaked over to McNab's side and found him in about the same frame of mind. We were both too proud to ask questions, so we simply stood there and watched—what do you suppose?—*a hospital ship!* lighted from water line to truck with hundreds of electric lights; strings of them running from masthead to mast-head and dozens along the sides, fitted with reflectors to throw the light down so as to show the broad green stripe which is prescribed by the Geneva Convention. Then we both laughed. Little did we think then that we would both be coming back to "Blighty" on just such a ship; Sandy within a few weeks and I more than a year later.

Before daylight we picked up a string of beacons, red and white, and dropped anchor. As soon as it was light we could see the harbour of Le Havre. I had been there before and recognized it quickly enough. Then we knew that France was our destination.

After waiting for the proper stage of the tide, the anchor was weighed, and with a lot of fussy little tugs buzzing about, now pushing at one end and then scurrying around to give a pull at the other, we finally tied up to the dock at our appointed place and prepared to disembark. The docks were thronged with men, mostly in some sort of uniform and all busy. Many of the French soldiers were wearing the old uniforms of blue and red, while others were clothed in corduroy. The new "horizon blue" had not yet been adopted. There were many English soldiers, mostly elderly men of the so-called "Navvie's Battalions," but among all the others, was quite a number whose uniform was the subject for much speculation until someone happened to notice that they were always working in groups and were, invariably, accompanied by a *poilu* carrying a rifle with bayonet fixed. It was our first sight of German prisoners and it gave us a genuine thrill. The war was coming closer to us every minute.

Disembarking was nothing more than common, every-day, hard labour, relieved, occasionally, by the antics of some of the horses that did not want to go down the steep narrow gangway. It was the devil's own job to get them aboard in the first place and equally difficult to persuade them to go ashore. Such perversity, I have noticed, is not confined to horses: the average soldier can give exhibitions of it that would shame the wildest mustang.

We had been living, since leaving Sandling, on "bully beef" and biscuits, but here on the dock we found one of those wonderful little coffee canteens, maintained and operated by one of the many thousands of noble English women who, from the beginning of the war, have managed, God knows how, always to be at the right place at the right time, to cheer the soldier on his way; working, apparently, night and day, to hand out a cup of hot coffee or tea or chocolate to any tired and dirty Tommy who happened to come along. If you have any money, you pay a penny; if you are broke, it doesn't make the least bit of difference; you get your coffee just the same, and the smile that always accompanies the service is as cheerful and genuine in the one case as in the other. Many women of the oldest and most aristocratic families of England have given, and are still giving, not only their money but their personal labor to this work; making sandwiches, boiling tea, yes, and washing the dishes, too, day after day and month after month. You do not often hear of them; they are too busy to advertise. But Tommy knows and I venture the assertion that no single sentence or "slogan" has been as often used among the soldiers in France as "God bless the women."

So we finally got everything off, wagons loaded and teams hitched up, and about mid-afternoon made our way through the quaint old city to a "rest camp" on the outskirts where we had time to wash and shave and eat another biscuit before we received orders that we were to march, at midnight, and entrain at Station No.—. It commenced to rain about this time and never let up until we had entrained the next morning.

That was a night of horrors. Sloshing through the mud, over unknown roads and streets, soaked to the skin. Oh! well, it was a very good initiation for what was to follow, all right, all right.

Polite language is not adequate to describe the loading of our train: getting all the wagons on the dinky little flat-cars and the horses aboard. The horses fared better than the men for, while they were only eight to a car, we were forty or more; and in the same kind of cars, too. They look like our ordinary cattle cars but are only about one-half as big. Forty men, with full equipment, have some difficulty to crowd into one, let alone to sit or lie down. And, of course, everything we had was soaked through. When I come to think of it, the strangest thing about the whole business was that there were no genuine complaints. The usual "grousing," of course, without which no soldier could remain healthy, but I never heard a word that could have been taken to indicate that any one was really unhappy. While we were loading, our cooks had managed to make up a good lot of hot tea and that helped some. We also got an issue of cheese and more bully and biscuits and, after filling up on these, everybody joined in a "sing-song" which continued for hours.

This subject of soldier's songs would make an interesting study for a psychologist. Not being versed in this science I can only note some of the peculiarities which impressed me from time to time.

The first thing that one notices is the fact that the so-called soldier's songs, written by our multitudinous army of "popular" song-smiths to catch the fleeting-fancy of the patriotically aroused populace, are conspicuous by their absence. No matter how great a popularity they may achieve among the home-folk and even the embryo soldiers, during the early days of their training, they seldom survive long enough to become popular with the soldiers in the field. When in training, far away from the field of battle, soldiers appear very fond of all the "Go get the Kaiser" and "On to Berlin" stuff and are not at all averse to complimenting themselves on their heroism and invincibility, with specific declarations of what they are going to do. Sort of "Oh, what a brave boy I am," you know. But as they come closer to the real business of war, while their enthusiasm and determination may be not a whit less, they become more reserved and less prone to self-advertisements; so, as they *must* sing something, they fall back on the old-timers, such as *Annie Laurie* or *My Old Kentucky Home* when they feel particularly sentimental, and for marching songs, any nonsensical music-hall jingle with a "swing" to it will serve.

Our crowd was what might be called "a regular singing bunch" and had a large and varied repertoire, including everything from religious hymns to many of that class of peculiar soldier's songs which although vividly expressive and appropriate to the occasion are, unfortunately, not for publication. Among the most popular were *The Tulip and the Rose, Michigan* and *There's a Long, Long Trail Awinding*, together with several local compositions set to such airs as *John Brown's Body* and *British Grenadiers*. You might hear *Onward, Christian Soldier* sandwiched between some of the worst of the "bad ones" or *Calvary* followed by *The Buccaneers*. You never heard that last one, and never will, unless you "go for a soldier."

I've heard men singing doleful songs, such as *I Want to Go Home*, when everything was bright and cheerful with no sign of war, and I have heard them, in the midst of the most deadly combat, shouting one of Harry Lauder's favourites, as *I Love a Lassie*. I once saw a long line "going over the top" in the gray of the morning, and when they had got lined up, outside the wire, and started on their plodding journey which is the "charge" of now-a-days, one waved to his neighbour who happened to be on a slight ridge above him and sang out: "You tak the High Road an' I'll tak the Low Road." And immediately the song spread up and down the line; even above the tremendous roar of the guns you could hear that battalion going into action to the tune of *Loch Lomond*.

So, you see, there is a difference between "songs about soldiers" and "soldier's songs," the latter being the ones he sings because they appeal to his fancy and the former including the long and constantly growing list of cheaply-sentimental airs intended for home consumption. The difference between the two classes is as great as that between war as it really is and war as the people at home think it is. This is a difference which will never be understood by any excepting those who have been over there. Those so unfortunate as to be unable to learn it at first hand will be forever ignorant of the real meaning of war. There is no language which can adequately describe it; no artist can paint it; no imagination can conceive it. It is just short of the knowledge of one who has died and returned to life. So, by all means, let us have songs if they serve to cheer or amuse any one, whether at home or abroad.

It will probably do the soldier no harm to have people think he is a "little tin god on wheels" any more than it will hurt him to be belittled by the sickly mollycoddling name of "Sammie," no matter how deeply he resents it. It is astonishing to me that our newspapers persist in the use of this appellation in the face of the fact, which they should know, that it is obnoxious to the American soldier himself. Would they call a Canadian or Australian or Scotch soldier a "Tommy"? If they do, I advise them to hide out and do it by telephone. Such sobriquets, to be of any real value, must come spontaneously; perhaps by accident; possibly conferred by an enemy. They can never be "invented."

But, to get back to our story. This country through which we passed is an historical pageant,—from the very port of Harfleur, which figures largely in the stories of both Norman and English invasion, all the way up the valley of the Seine. Who could see Rouen, for the first time, without experiencing a thrill of sentiment as the memories of Jeanne d'Arc, Rollo the Norman, Duke William, Harold and many others come forth from their hiding-places in the back of one's brain? Although we passed through without a stop, we could see the wonderful cathedral and the hospice on the hill and, crossing the river, we had a fleeting glimpse of the delightful little village of St. Adrien, with its curious church, cut out of the face of the chalk cliff; where the maidens come to pray the good Saint Bonaventure to send them a husband within the year.

On, past the field of Crécy, across the Somme which was to us only a name at that time but to become "an experience" at a later date, we made our slow progress across northern France. At a certain junction we were joined by the rest of the battalion which had travelled from England by a different and shorter route.

In the early hours of the morning we came to our stopping place, St. Omer, which was then the headquarters of the British Expeditionary Force in France. We did not tarry, however, but before daylight were on the march—eastward. We stopped for a couple of hours, near some little town, long enough to make tea, and then went on again. This was the hardest day we had had. Everyone was overloaded, as a new soldier always is, and, moreover, our packs and clothing had not dried and we were carrying forty or fifty pounds of water in addition to the regulation sixty-one-pound equipment. Then, too, the roads were of the kind called *pavé*; that is, paved with what we know as cobble-stones or Belgian blocks. On the smooth stone or macadamized roads of England we would not have minded it so much, but this kind of going was new to us: ankles were continually turning, our iron-shod soles eternally slipping on the knobbed surface of the cobbles and, take it all in all, I consider it the hardest march I have ever done, and I have made forty-eight miles in one day over the snow in the Northwest, too.

About dark we were halted at a farm and told that we were to go into bivouac and would probably remain there for a week or more. Now, one characteristic of the good machine gunner is that he is always about two jumps ahead of the other fellow, so, there being a big barn with lots of clean straw in it, we just naturally took possession while the rest of the troops were patiently waiting for the quartermaster to assign them to billets. Of course we had a fight on our hands a little later but, by a compromise which let the signallers and scouts come in with us, we were enabled to hang on to the best part of the place. From names inscribed on the beams we learned that the Princess Pat's had once occupied the same place, and from the people who lived there we heard tales of how the Germans had carried off all their stock when they made their first great advance. All this was the next day, however, as we were too tired even to eat that night; we simply dropped on the straw and slept.

Next morning was bright and fair and everybody got busy, drying kits, overhauling and cleaning the guns and ammunition and fixing up our quarters for the promised week's rest. About four o'clock in the afternoon we were ordered to form up and march to a place about two miles distant, where, we were told, General Alderson, commander-in-chief of the Canadians, was to give us a little talk.

We arrived at the appointed place ahead of time, and while we were lying about waiting we had our first glimpse of real war. It was a long way off and high up in the air but it was a thrilling sight for us. A couple of German airplanes were being shelled by some of our anti-aircraft guns, and as we watched the numerous shell-bursts, apparently close to the planes, we expected, every moment, to see the flyers come tumbling down. However, none was hit and they went on their way. It was only later we learned that it is the rarest thing in the world for an airplane to be brought down by guns from the ground. I suppose I have seen several hundred thousand shots fired at them and have yet to see one hit by a shell from an "Archie" and only one by machine-gun fire from the ground. The majority of planes destroyed are shot down by machine guns in combat with other flyers.

When the general finally came, he looked us over and told us what a fine body of troops we appeared to be, and just for that, he was going to let us go right into the front line, instead of putting us through the usual preliminary stages in reserve and support. Of course we felt properly "swelled up" about it and considered it a great compliment. We did not know, what we now know, that they were about to start the big offensive which is known as the Battle of Loos and that the British had not enough troops in France to be able to afford such luxuries as reserves. It was a case of everybody get in and "get your feet wet."

As we were to march at daybreak, we had a busy night getting our scattered belongings together and repacked. This was our first experience of what shortly became a common occurrence and we soon learned that, in the field, a soldier never knows one day where he will be the next, and thus he is always "expecting the unexpected."

We moved out at dawn and had another heart-breaking march as the weather had turned very warm. Through Hazebrouck and nu-

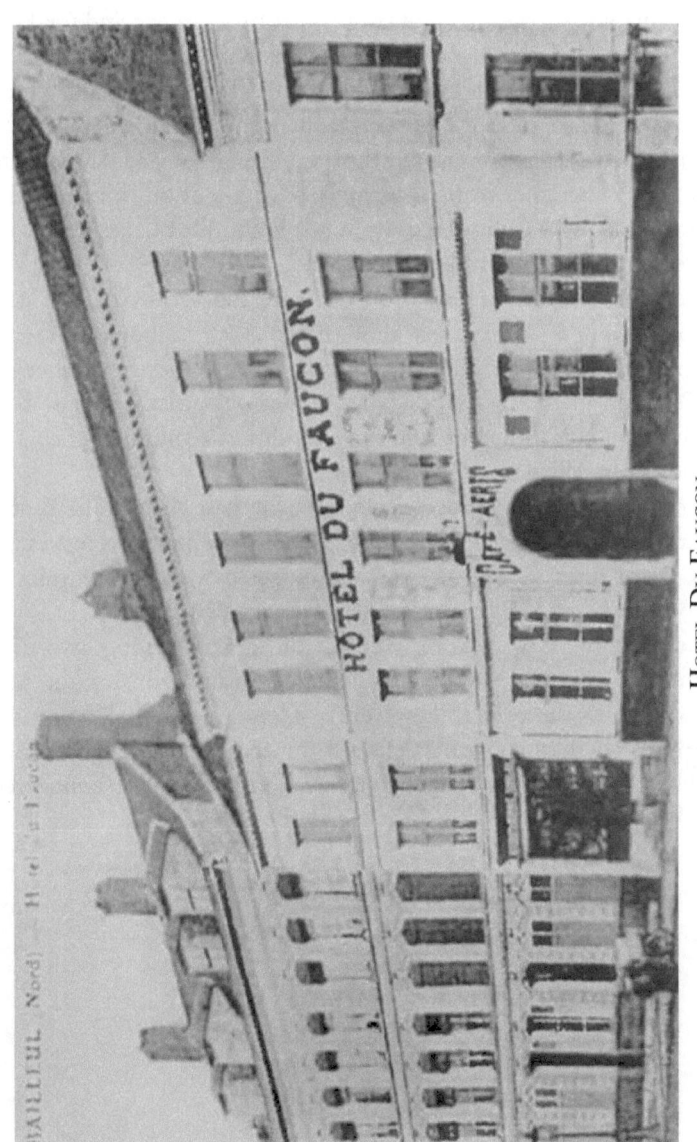

Hôtel Du Fauçon

merous small towns we continued our eastward way to Bailleul, stopping there for an hour's rest. Our section happened to be right in the market square so had a good opportunity to see some of the principal points of interest in this famous and ancient city. The Hotel de Ville with its curious weather-vane of twelfth-century vintage and the Hotel Fauçon particularly interested me: the former because I had read of it and the latter because it had real beer on ice. This is the place which Bairnsfather speaks of as the hotel at which one could live and go to war every day and I afterward did that very thing, for one day; leaving the front-line trenches in the morning, having a good dinner at the Fauçon and being back in the front line at night. That happened to be Thanksgiving Day; November 25, 1915.

After our rest we continued on our way and arrived at the little town of Dranoutre, in Flanders, about five o'clock in the evening and went into bivouac. On this day's march we saw more evidence of war. Here and there a grave beside the road; occasionally a house that showed the effect of shell or rifle fire and, almost continually, firing at airplanes, both Allied and German.

At our camp we found detachments of the East Kents (The Buffs), and the Second East Surrey Regiment, from whom we were to take over a sector of the line. They said that it was comparatively quiet at that point but had been pretty rough a few months earlier.

The Machine Gun Section went in the next morning, two days ahead of the infantry, and the East Surreys remained during the two days to show us the ropes. They were a splendid lot of soldiers and I am sorry to say that when they left us it was to go to Loos, where they were badly cut up at the Hohenzollern redoubt. We never connected up with them again.

CHAPTER 3

In the Midst of a Battlefield

It was a bright warm Sunday morning, that nineteenth day of September, when we made our first trip to the front-line trenches. Only the Number Ones, lance corporals, of each gun went in ahead, the guns and remainder of the section to come up after dark. I was a "lance-jack" at that time, in charge of No. 6 gun; and had a crew of the youngest boys in the section, two of whom were under seventeen when they enlisted and not one of whom was twenty at that time. Subsequent events proved them to be the equals of any in the whole section; a section of which a general officer afterward wrote: "I consider it the best in France." They were strong and healthy, keen observers, always ready for any duty and during all the time I was with them I never saw one of them weaken. They played the game right up to the finish, in fair weather and foul, during the easy times and the "rough," each until his appointed time came to "go West."

One, in particular, named Bouchard, a boy who enlisted when but sixteen, developed into the brightest and most efficient machine gunner I have ever known. His zeal and eagerness to learn so impressed me that it became my greatest pleasure to give him all the assistance in my power, and, despite the difference in our ages, there grew up between us such a friendship as can only be achieved between kindred spirits sharing the vicissitudes of war. Small of stature and slight of frame, it was only by sheer grit and determination that he was able to endure the terrible strain of that first winter. At times, when the mud was nearly waist deep, he would throw away his overcoat, blanket and other personal effects, but never would he give up his beloved gun. When trenches were absolutely impassable he would climb up on top, scorning bullets and shells, intent on the one job in hand—to get to his appointed station without delay. He was a constant source of inspiration to all of us, often inciting the older heads to undertake and achieve the apparently impossible by daring them to follow his lead.

Our sector was made up of what were then known as the "C" trenches, running north from the Neuve Eglise-Messines road and directly between Wulverghem and Messines. To the south of the road was the Douve River and just beyond that "Plugstreet" (Ploegstert). There had been some very hard fighting all along the Messines Ridge during the preceding year, but for several months things had been quiet. Now, by "quiet" I do not mean that there was any cessation of hostilities for there is always artillery firing and sniping going on, with a fair amount of rifle grenade and trench-mortar activity. It simply means that there is no attempt being made, by either side, to attack in force and to capture and hold captured ground.

Our route, that first morning, was rather a roundabout one, by way of Lindhoek, taken, as explained by our guide, because it was less exposed to enemy observation than a much shorter road which we used when moving at night. When a short distance out from town, we passed in front of one of our howitzer batteries which decided that then was just the proper time to cut loose with a salvo, right over our heads. We were not more than fifty yards from the guns and the result was that we were all "scared stiff," to say nothing of being almost deafened. This appears to be a characteristic and never-ending joke with artillerymen and so we soon learned to "spot" their emplacements and go behind them, when possible.

At all cross-roads ("*Kruisstraat*," in Flemish), sentries were stationed who acted as guides and also gave warning of the approach of enemy aircraft. At a long blast of the whistle every person was supposed to stop and not make a move until the signal "all clear," indicated by two blasts, was given. It appears that, while the airmen have no difficulty in seeing moving objects on the ground it is next to impossible for them to locate stationary ones.

As we progressed, the signs of war were multiplied. Numerous graves along the road, each marked by a cross, houses and barns torn by shells, a bridge and railroad track blown up and trees shattered and rent, until, finally, everything was desolation. When we arrived at Wulverghem, we had our first sight of a really "ruined" town. Of course we saw many worse ones later, but at that time, we could not conceive more complete destruction than had been wrought here by the German shells. Every building had been hit, perhaps several times; some had one or more walls standing, while many were totally destroyed

Light Vickers Gun in Action Against Aircraft.

and were nothing but piles of broken brick and mortar. Part of the church tower remained and one hand of the clock still hung to the side facing the German lines. This seemed to aggravate the boche as, every day, he would send from a dozen to forty or fifty shells over, all seemingly directed at the church tower.

As Messines Ridge is now "ours" I think there can be no objection to my going into details about our dispositions. Our Battalion Headquarters was located in the St. Quentin Cabaret, about two hundred yards south of Wulverghem and we had a supporting gun, with infantry, at Souvenir Farm and also at a redoubt near by, called "S-5." Our front-line guns were distributed from the Neuve Eglise road to the northern end of our battalion frontage, about "C-3."

These numbers refer to certain locations on the map, and the cabarets are not exactly such as one is accustomed to seeing in American cities. They are, or were, inns, such as in England would be called public houses and in America, road houses. In Flemish they are *herbergs*, but these happened to bear French names, hence were called cabarets. One can not help wondering at the indiscriminate manner in which French and Flemish names are used in this corner of the world. Neuve Eglise, Bailleul, Dranoutre and Locre are all mixed up with Wolverghem, Ploegstert, Wytschaete and Lindhoek: Ypres and Dickebusch are neighbors; while St. Julian and Langemarck lie side by side, as do Groot Vierstraat and LaClytte. Look at a map of West Flanders and the adjoining parts of France and you will see what I mean.

Just as we arrived at the Battalion Headquarters the signal was sounded, "German up," which is the short way of saying that an enemy airplane is approaching, so we were obliged to take cover and remain quiet for some time. We were near a group of farm buildings and, going inside, found that former occupants had left elaborate records of their visits. Among other mural decorations were some rough sketches drawn by Captain Bairnsfather, which afterward became famous as "Fragments from France."

This suggests another interesting field for speculation. Why is it that all men, regardless of race, creed or colour, have an inborn craving to inscribe their names on walls and trees and rocks, especially on walls other than those of their own home? Wherever you go, all over the world, you will find the carved or written record stating that, at such and such a date, John Doe, of Oskaloosa, Iowa, honoured the place with his presence. The buildings of Flanders and France are storehouses of historical records. From them the historian could almost reconstruct the campaigns of the war. Would it not be an interesting task to make a thorough search of all the old buildings and dugouts, just as the archaeologists have been doing in Egypt and all the ancient habitations of mankind? The prehistoric caves of Spain or the cliff dwellings of the Colorado could not be more interesting than a compilation of these records, including the drawings and sketches, some of which are real works of art.

Regimental crests and badges are often shown with the utmost attention to detail and, in one place which we afterward occupied, one of the walls bore an elaborately carved tablet enumerating the campaigns and battles of one of the oldest British line regiments, together with a list of the honours, V. C's. and so on, won by members thereof. On one of the walls at Captain's Post one of my boys, Charlie Wendt, carved a large maple leaf upon which he inscribed the names of all our squad. He was killed a few days later and others at various times and of that whole list, I am the sole survivor. I would give a great deal to have that bit of wall here in my own home.

Meantime, the *Allemand* has gone away and we are free to continue our journey to the front line.

In an orchard behind the house we entered a communication trench and after a few final words of advice from the guide as to the necessity of keeping our heads down wherever the walls were low, started on the mile-long trip. We learned that the trench by which we were going in was named Surrey Lane, in honour of the West Surreys who constructed it. At various points we came upon intersecting trenches, most of which were marked with the name of the point to which they led. One, I remember, was "Wipers Road"; not that it ran all the way to Ypres but led in the direction of that place.

Except for an occasional large shell, whispering overhead, consigned from Kemmel to Warneton or *vice versa,* and the distant muttering of the French guns away to the south, everything was quiet and peaceful, and had it not been for the ruined buildings and torn-up roads it would have been difficult to imagine that we were in the midst of a battlefield.

Passing through all the maze of cross trenches, we finally reached the front line which we found to be what we afterward called a "half-and-half" trench; that is, it was dug down to a depth of perhaps four feet and built up about the same with sand-bags, making it possibly eight feet from the bottom of trench to top of parapet. It was quite dry and clean and comfortable and proved that the Buffs and Surreys had not been loafing during the summer. I'm afraid we did not properly appreciate it at that time, but as I look back over all the time that has passed since, I am compelled to admit that it was the finest bit of trench we ever occupied.

We had no more than arrived in the line than the cook of the first gun crew we struck brought out a "dixie" of tea and an unlimited supply of bread and butter and jam and invited us to fill up. ("Dixie" is the soldier's name for the camp kettle used in the British Army.) Now if you have been paying attention to the story of our movements since leaving England, I think you can readily imagine that we were hungry. These soldiers had been out, some of them, since the beginning of the war and had become inured to all the hardships which are a necessary part of the game, and, splendid fellows that they were, the first thing they thought of was our comfort. From that time on I never met up with any body of British Imperial soldiers who did not show this same consideration and solicitude for the stranger. And they do it so unostentatiously and naturally that they challenge the admiration of all, especially of Colonials such as we, who were, I fear, very apt to forget the little niceties of manner which are inbred in the native Briton.

While we afterward became the best of friends there was never any danger of our becoming "alike." We secretly admired their perfect and unalterable observance of all orders even though we were, at the same time, scheming to evade a lot of those same restrictions which appeared to us to be unnecessary. They, on their part, could not help admitting that the dash and "devil-may-care" spirit shown by our men often accomplished results not otherwise attainable but from the emulation of which they were barred by "traditions." The discipline of the one and the discipline of the other are based on two entirely different modes of life; the former carefully trained to rely on and obey implicitly the orders of any superior officer, while the latter looks only for initial direction, depending upon his own initiative and ingenuity to see him through any trouble that might arise.

From this line we could see the whole valley which separated us from the famous Messines Ridge. The enemy was firmly established on its crest, with his advance lines in the valley and even, at some places, on the sides of the slope below us. The town of Messines, directly opposite, was in plain sight but nearly a mile away, the church and hospice, or infirmary, being conspicuous landmarks on the skyline. Our front lines were from about one hundred and fifty to three hundred yards apart. Numerous ruined farms and cabarets were scattered along the line, sometimes in our territory and sometimes belonging to the enemy. These were, as a rule, converted into redoubts or "strong-points," and defended by both infantry and machine guns. To the northward, within the German lines, was the town of Wytschaete, while we had Mont Kemmel, a prominent hill which gave our artillery good observation all the way from Ypres to "Plugstreet."

Several of the prominent roads within the German lines were in plain sight from our position and, while the artillery devoted considerable attention to harassing the enemy, we were not sufficiently supplied with ammunition at that time to strafe them as was desirable. This was especially true of several "dumps," which is the colloquial word designating the points where the wagons and motor transports deposit ammunition, food and other trench stores and whence they are carried up to the front line by the men. Thus an ammunition dump means a point where ammunition is stored, while a ration dump is a place where the ration carrying parties repair at night to procure the rations for the following day. At some points the field cookers or "rolling kitchens" come up at night and the cooked food is carried from there to the front. One such place at Messines, we called "Cooker's Halt."

The machine gun officer of the outgoing Surreys had begun to develop some ideas of his own as to the feasibility of strafing enemy transports and dumps at night and had selected a tentative position behind a slight crest, about one hundred and fifty yards N. E. of "*In den Kraatenberg Cabaret*" and immediately adjacent to a disused communication trench called "Plum Avenue." Now I had been a crank on long range, indirect fire in England, so I had no difficulty in persuading our M. G. officer to turn this job over to me. We improved the position and also established another one, about one hundred yards down the trench for daylight work against aircraft. In those days the planes would come over at altitudes of two thousand feet and less and we had some splendid opportunities to practise on them. We succeeded in bringing one down with his petrol tank on fire, and we turned back a good many more until they began to fly so high that we could not reach them.

At night, by using information obtained from our artillery and our own forward observers, we were able to cut up a lot of their transports. At first they would drive down to a place called the Barricade, but after we caught them there two or three times they came only to the top of the hill, to "Cooker's Halt." We soon chased them out of that, however, and then I guess poor Fritz had to carry his stuff all the way from behind the ridge. On two occasions we caught large working parties, in broad daylight, and cut them up and dispersed them. Our position in front of the group of buildings (*In den Kraatenberg*) naturally led the enemy to believe that we were using the building for cover, so he shelled the poor inoffensive houses and barns most industriously but never put anything close enough to our real position to do any damage. This taught me a lesson which I put into operation, later on, at Sniper's Barn, with the best of results.

From that time on, strafing was an important part of machine gunnery until, now, together with barrage fire, it comprises about all there is to machine-gun work, proper, for the automatic rifle has taken over the greater part of the front-line offensive work.

French Using an Ordinary Wine Barrel on which a Wagon Wheel is Mounted to Facilitate the Revolving Movement to Any Desired Direction.

CHAPTER 4

Eight Days In

As the subject of machine guns is one of great interest at this time, it may not be amiss to devote a little space to explaining some of the salient features of the most commonly used types.

All automatic arms are divided into classes, as determined by the following characteristics:

1st. Method of applying the power necessary to operate: (gas or recoil).

2nd. Method of supplying ammunition: (belt, magazine or clip).

3rd. Method of cooling: (water or air).

Another well-defined distinction is made between the true machine gun and the automatic rifle; the former being so heavy that it must be mounted on a substantial tripod or other base, while the latter is so light that it may be carried and operated by a single man. Of the former class, the Colt, (35 lbs.), the Vickers, (38 lbs.) and the Maxim, (63 lbs.) may be taken as representative. They are all mounted, for field work, on tripods weighing fifty pounds or more. In the latter class, the Lewis, Benet-Mercie, and Hotchkiss, running from 17 to 25 lbs., are fair examples. They are all equipped with light, skeleton "legs" or tripods, which, by the way, are never used in the field although they are still considered essential for training purposes.

In the gas-operated arms, a small hole is drilled in the underside of the barrel, six to eight inches from the muzzle, so that, when the bullet has passed this point, and during the time it takes it to traverse the remaining few inches to the muzzle, a certain portion of the enclosed gas is forced through this hole, where it is "trapped," in a small "gas-chamber" and its force directed against a piston or lever which, being connected with the necessary working parts of the gun by cams, links or ratchets, performs the functions of removing and ejecting the empty cartridge case, withdrawing a new cartridge from the belt, clip or magazine, and "cocking" the gun: that is, forcing the "hammer" or striker back and compressing its spring. As the pressure generated in the barrel by our ammunition is not less than 50,000 lbs. to the square inch, very little gas is required to do all this.

There must also be sufficient force to compress or coil a strong spring or springs called "main-springs" or retracting springs which, in their turn, force the mechanism forward to its original position, seating the new cartridge in the chamber and releasing the striker, thus firing another shot. This action continues as long as the "trigger" is kept pressed or until the belt or magazine is emptied. The Colt, Benet-Mercie, Hotchkiss and Lewis are in this class. They are all of the air-cooled type.

In the recoil operated guns, the barrel itself is forced to the rear by the "kick," as we commonly call it, and the force applied directly to the working parts, thus performing the same operations above described. The Maxim, Vickers, Vickers-Maxim and Maxim-Nordenfeldt belong to this class. They are all water-cooled, having a water-jacket of sheet metal entirely surrounding the barrel.

All the last-mentioned class, and also the Colt, have the ammunition loaded in belts containing two hundred and fifty rounds each. The Hotchkiss and Benet-Mercie use clips of from twenty to thirty rounds, while the Lewis is fed from a round, flat, pan-shaped magazine holding forty-seven rounds. (For aircraft guns these magazines are made larger; about double this capacity, I think.)

During the early part of the war, before the advent of the Lewis and other automatic rifles, the only machine guns in general use were of the heavy, tripod-mounted type and it was necessary for them to advance with or even ahead of attacking troops. As the guns and tripods were very conspicuous objects they naturally became the especial targets for enemy riflemen and snipers and the casualties among machine gunners ran far above the average for other troops. It was this that caused the Emma Gee sections to be named Suicide Clubs.

Now, however, the Lewis gun, being light and inconspicuous, can be carried by advancing troops and used effectively in the attack without its operators suffering excessively, and at the same time it has been demonstrated that the true machine gun, of the heavier type, mounted on its firm base, can effectively cooperate with the artillery in maintaining protective or other barrages and in delivering harassing fire upon the enemy at points behind his front line. As this fire is, necessarily, over the heads of our own troops, sometimes but a few feet over them, it must be extremely accurate and dependable and it has been proved that guns of the lighter, automatic-rifle type, can not be safely used for this purpose, even when mounted on the heavy tripods of the other guns. This is probably due to the excessive vibration of the lighter barrels.

For the benefit of any who are not familiar with the word, I might say, in passing, that *"barrage"* is a French word meaning a "barrier" or a "dam" and when used in a military sense it means a veritable barrier or wall of fire, where the shells or bullets, or both, are falling so thickly as to make it impossible for any body of troops to go through without suffering great loss.

I know nothing of the Browning gun, as it is a new invention and has never been used in the field. We can only hope that it will prove as good as the Vickers and Lewis which are giving perfect satisfaction on the battlefields of Flanders and France. No real machine gunner expects or requires anything better, but I can not imagine any *one* type of gun that can replace both of them, any more than a single class of artillery can combine the functions of both the light field guns and the heavy howitzers.

The Germans evidently had good spies within our lines as they always knew when we changed over; that is, when we took over a new line. At first they would call out: "Hello, Canadians, how are you," sometimes even naming the battalion. Later on, however, they used much stronger language but they knew who we were, just the same. Their methods of communicating information from our lines were many and very ingenious. For instance, at one time it was learned by our intelligence department that spies were making use of the many windmills to signal messages across the line. They did this by stopping the sails of the mills at certain angles and moving them about from time to time.

When this was discovered the orders went out for all windmills to be stopped in such a position that the arms should always be at an exact forty-five degree angle whenever the mill was not running, with the understanding that failure to observe this regulation would result in our artillery in the immediate vicinity turning their guns on the offending mill. At one place we discovered a large periscope with a heliographic attachment by which a seemingly inoffensive Belgian peasant kept in constant communication with the boche. This periscope was concealed in the chimney of a partially ruined farm building within our lines. At other places underground cables were discovered, with telephones or field telegraph instruments concealed in cellars or old buildings. Carrier pigeons were also much used and, without a doubt, many men passed back and forth between the lines, some of them, as we learned from time to time, regularly enlisted in our armies. At several places we had men shot down and killed by snipers masquerading as farmers, behind our lines. Needless to say, such affairs were promptly attended to, on the spot, *"tout de suite"* as the French say.

So, although that part of the line had been very quiet for a long time, they began at once to give us a reception. While the shelling was as nothing compared to bombardments we went through later, still it gave us an opportunity to make the acquaintance of the various kinds of shells from "whizz-bangs" up to something of about eight-inch calibre.

The first casualty in the battalion was a scout named Boyer who was killed on his initial trip into No Man's Land the first night in the trenches. Next day Starkey decided he could not see enough with a periscope, so took a look over the parapet. Both men are buried in the garden back of the St. Quentin Cabaret together with many from the best and most famous British Line Regiments.

The Emma Gees came out pretty lucky, having but one man seriously wounded. His name was Mangan, a Yankee, who had served in the U. S. Army in the Philippines. He was badly wounded by shrapnel and was sent back to England. We used to hear from him occasionally until about a year later the letters stopped.

After eight days we were relieved by the Twentieth Battalion and went back to Dranoutre for our first "rest." We went by way of Neuve Eglise but, as it was night, we could see but little of that much shot-up city. It commenced to rain before we started out and kept it up until we went back again, four days later. At that time it was customary to carry in and out everything, including ammunition, and we soon learned to dread the days when we had to move. We would have preferred to stay in the front line for a month at a time rather than carry all that heavy stuff in and out so often. However, we managed to get a bath and some clean clothes, which made everybody feel better. We had no regular billets at Dranoutre but rigged up little shelter tents, somewhat similar to those used in the U. S. Army, by lacing two or more rubber sheets together. Our cooking was done by gun crews, somewhat on the order of a lot of Boy Scouts, in that no two crews had the same ideas or used the same methods. My squad dug out a nice little "stove" in a bank, and by covering it with flattened-out biscuit tins and making a pipe of tin cans of various sorts, managed to get along very well. Here we received our first pay since arriving in France; fifteen *francs* each. It doesn't sound like much but, believe me, we made those "*sous*" go a long way and bought lots of little delicacies we could not otherwise have had.

While at Dranoutre we associated with the inhabitants, in the stores and *estaminets*. The Germans had taken of whatever they needed in the way of live stock and foodstuffs, but the town itself happened to be one of the many scattered up and down the line, which had miraculously escaped even an ordinary bombardment.

There were refugees, hundreds of them; from the towns and cities farther to the eastward, whence they had fled with little or nothing besides the clothes on their backs. There were children who had lost their parents; wives who knew not what had become of their husbands, and men whose wives and families were somewhere back in the German-occupied territory. They told of enduring the direst hardships and suffering; of cold and hunger.

Every town behind the lines that had escaped destruction was crowded with these poor homeless people. Every habitable house sheltered all who could find no room to lie on the floor. Those who could, worked on the roads or in the neighbouring fields. Many of the women worked in the military laundries. They all received some assistance from the French Government and from the many charitable societies. When talking with them they would tell their stories in a monotonous sort of way, seldom making any complaint; seeming to think that all these things were to be endured as a matter of course.

I have read all the available reports on the subject of atrocities and have no doubt that they are true, but none ever came under my personal observation.

In the midst of a battle many men do things which would, at other times, fill them with horror. The excitement of combat seems to breed a lust for killing and the sight of blood is like a red flag to a bull. This, unfortunately, is not confined to Germans. One of our officers who had had a brother killed a few days before deliberately shot and killed several unarmed prisoners. He was, himself, killed the same

Quarter of a Franc
Present value about four cents

Half a Franc   Quarter of a Franc
Present value about eight   *"Good for" about four cents*
cents

French Paper War-Money, Issued by the Various Municipalities. Every Town Has its Bank of Issue. There are Practically no Coins in Circulation day. On another occasion, a wounded German, lying in a shell-hole, stabbed and killed one of our wounded and attacked another only to be beaten at his own game and killed with his own knife. A soldier of the Royal Fusiliers, at St. Eloi, was detected by his sergeant in the act of shooting an unarmed prisoner, whereupon the sergeant immediately shot and killed the soldier. I saw this, myself.

But the deliberate shooting of wounded men and stretcher-bearers has been, so far as I know, confined to the Hun. On numerous occasions, some of which are mentioned elsewhere in this story, German snipers deliberately and in cold blood shot down our helpless wounded and the men who were endeavouring to succour them.

CHAPTER 5

At Captain's Post

The Battle of Loos had opened on the twenty-fifth of September and, although it was a considerable distance to the south of us, we had been hearing the continuous rumble of the guns ever since we had come up to the line. It was the first time we had heard "drum-fire," as the French call it. It is such an incessant bombardment, with such a large number of guns, that you can not distinguish any single reports, but the whole makes a continual "rumble," something like the roll of heavy thunder in the distance; never slacking, night or day. I have forgotten just how many days they kept it up, but it was something like two weeks.

To create a diversion, and prevent the enemy from taking troops from other parts of the line to strengthen the attacked point, our artillery, all along the line, was doing its best and our infantry made feint attacks at several places. We had gone back in the line on the first of October and, early the next morning, our brigade, Fourth Canadian, took part in one of these attacks. Our battalion did not go "over the top," but Bouchard and I stuck our gun up on the parapet and helped support the advance, which was made by the Nineteenth Battalion. It was our first experience of that kind and was, to say the least, interesting. The enemy kept up an incessant rifle and machine-gun fire on our position, the bullets were snapping around our heads like a bunch of fire-crackers and the mud was flying everywhere, but that little seventeen-year-old "kid" kept feeding in belts and all the while whooping and laughing like a maniac. It certainly cheered me up to have him there.

The whole thing was over in about twenty minutes but, during that short time, we had learned something which can be learned in no other way—that it is possible for thousands of bullets to come close to you without doing any harm. From that time on, neither Bouchard nor I ever felt the least hesitation about slipping over the parapet at night to "see what we could see."

During this tour we were subjected to considerably more shelling than on the first occasion, and one morning Fritz made a mistake with one of his shells intended for "our farm," as we called the buildings in the rear, and dropped it "*ker-plunk*" right into one of our dugouts. It was a place we had fixed up for cooking, and we were all outside, but it certainly made a mess of our "kitchen furniture." Then they shot up our communication trench until it was positively dangerous to go up and down it for rations and ammunition. Narrow escapes were numerous, but our luck held, and we went out the night of the eighth without having sustained a casualty. The battalion did not fare so well, having quite a number of wounded, but none killed.

That was our last visit to those trenches, as we marched, that night, away to the northward. "Eéps" was the word that went up and down the line, that being the Flemish pronunciation of Ypres, (in French pronounced "Eé-pr" and in Tommy's English, "Wipers"). We had a hard march; in the rain, as usual; and, about daylight, stopped at the town of LaClytte, which was to be the battalion's billeting place for several months. The rest of the battalion remained there a few days, resting, but the Emma Gees went on ahead and took over some support positions at Groot Vierstraat and along the Ypres-Neuve Eglise road. We relieved the King Edward Horse who were acting, as was all the cavalry, as infantry.

My crew, together with Sandy McNab's, was assigned to an old Belgian farm called Captain's Post. The place was pretty well shot up but we managed to clear out enough room to give us very good quarters; by far the best we had had since leaving England. We were some 1,250 yards from the enemy lines but in plain sight of them, hence it was necessary to be very careful not to allow anyone to move about outside the buildings in daytime, nor to make any smoke.

No doubt some one got careless, for about noon the next day we heard the long-drawn-out "*who-o-o-o-i-s-s-s-h*" of a big shell coming. It struck about twenty-five yards behind our building and failed to explode; in soldier's parlance, it was a "dud." We were eating dinner and refused to be disturbed. Then came a steady stream of the big fellows; to the right, to the left, in front of the building and, finally, "smack," right into the house. Altogether, they put thirty-two "five-point-nine" (150 mm.) shells into that one old building and all the damage they

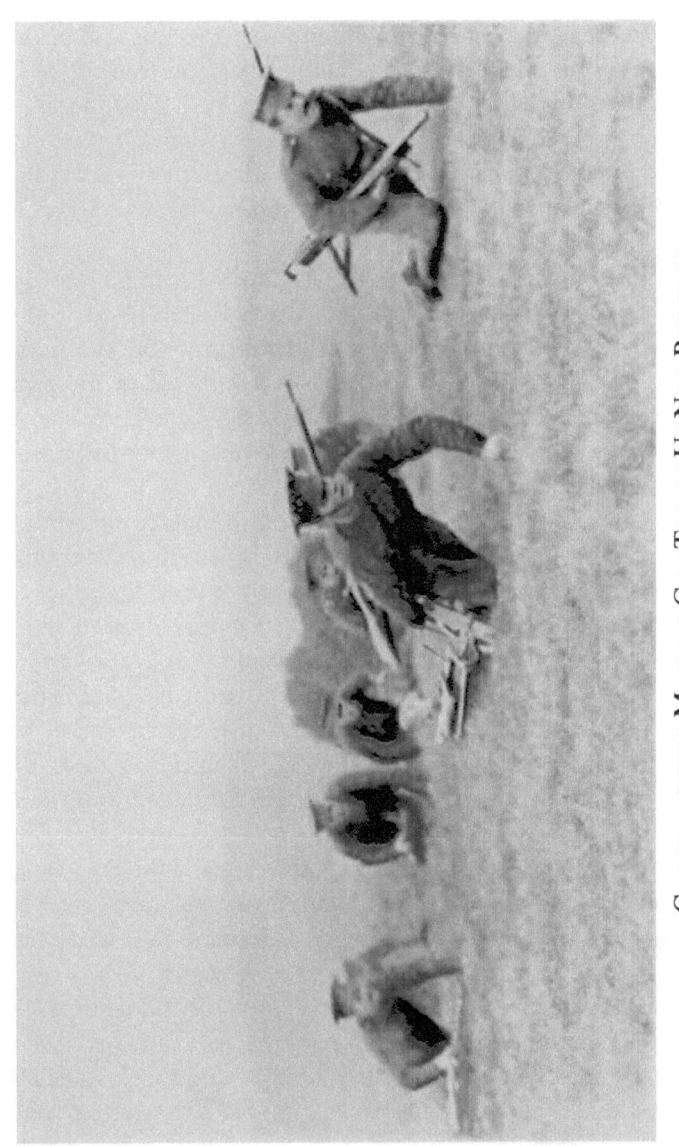

Canadians with Machine Gun Taking Up New Positions.

did was to ruin our dinner by filling the "dixie" with mud. How in the world we escaped has always been a mystery to me, but later on, after other and worse affairs, the men called it "McBride's luck."

They shelled us pretty regularly, after that, sometimes just two or three shells, but on at least one occasion, they evidently had made up their minds to put the place out of business entirely, for they kept up a continuous bombardment, with guns of at least three calibres, for more than an hour. At that time I was a corporal and had twelve men, with two guns at this place, yet, although nearly every one was hit by pieces of brick and mud and covered with dust, not a man was hurt nor a gun injured.

One morning, just after daylight and during a fog, I was up in an old hay-loft where we had a gun, when I heard a cock pheasant "squawking" (that's the only word that describes it), out in front. Looking from the gun position I saw him, standing on the parapet of an abandoned French trench across the road. I could not resist the temptation, so took a shot at him, with the result that we had pheasant stew for dinner that day.

It was a source of never-ceasing wonder to me that the birds and other forms of wild life seemed to be so little affected by the continual noise of guns and shells. So far as I could notice they did not pay the slightest attention to it. Pheasants, partridges and rabbits were numerous at one point in and behind our lines and I have seen them running about, feeding or playing where shells were falling and bursting all about them, without showing any sign of fear. Indeed they were sometimes killed by the shells, especially shrapnel, but those unhit would "carry on" with the business in hand, indifferent to the fate of their companions.

The little robin redbreasts (the English robin and the French *rougegorge*) were abundant, as were the ubiquitous English sparrows, which, sitting out in front on the barbed wire, were often used as targets by men firing experimental shots.

A pair of swallows reared a family of young in a dugout which I once occupied, the nest being within a few feet of my head when I was in my bunk. They would come in and go out through a small hole which we left in the burlap curtain and the old bird would sit on the nest and look at me in such a confidential, unafraid sort of way that she made a friend for life and I would have fought anyone who had attempted to disturb or injure her. But, of course, no such thing was possible. All the men seemed to take a kindly interest in the birds and, except for the occasional shot at the English sparrows (which never hit them, anyhow), they rarely, if ever, molested any of them unless it was for the purpose of getting a meal of pheasant or partridge, which was considered perfectly legitimate although forbidden by "orders." It was all right if you could "get away with it," as the saying is. One morning, after an unusually intense bombardment of a wood called the Bois Carré, I found many dead birds; killed either by direct hits or by the concussion of the heavy shells.

This same morning I watched a pair of magpies who were building a nest in a tree near our station. A shell had struck the tree, below the nest, and had cut it in half while a large branch had lodged just above the nest. The whole thing was swaying dangerously in the light breeze and a strong wind would surely bring it down, but that pair of chattering magpies appeared to be debating whether to continue their work or move elsewhere. One would hop down to the place where the shell had hit and, cocking his head this way and that, would let loose a flow of magpie talk that would bring his mate to him and then they would both investigate, flying to the shattered place, clinging to the bark and picking out splinters and pieces of wood. Then they would go up aloft and consult about the nest itself. I watched them for the better part of an hour when the verdict appeared to be to "take a chance" and go ahead with the building. We left that place soon after and I never learned the final outcome.

At one point, where our lines were about one hundred yards from the enemy, there was a small pond in No Man's Land just outside our wire, and a pair of ducks, teal, I think, made it their home during the entire winter of 1915-16. In spite of the fact that shells were continually falling all around and sometimes bursting squarely in the pond itself, they never showed the least inclination to abandon the place. As this pond was surrounded by a fringe of small willows we often made use of the cover they afforded to make night reconnoissances, but soon learned that it was impossible to approach the pool without alarming the ducks and drawing from them a low scolding note of protest, accompanied by a splashing of water. This was carefully noted and, thereafter, all sentries at that point were especially warned to listen intently for these noises as it would probably mean that an enemy patrol was exploring in the vicinity.

The abandoning of so many of the farms and villages left a great many cats without homes. Nearly every ruined barn or house sheltered one or more of them and they were, as a rule, quite wild. Some, however, had been caught and tamed by the soldiers who made great pets of them. Frequently a soldier would be seen going in or out of the front line with a kitten perched contentedly on top of his pack. There was one big brindle "*madame*" cat who adopted our machine gun outfit when we first went in. She travelled up and down the line but never stayed anywhere except in one of the machine gun emplacements. On bright days she would hop up on top of the parapet and sit there, making her toilet, and then stretch out on the sand-bags for a nap. At this point it was not possible to show a hand or a periscope or any other small object without drawing the fire of some alert boche, but they never shot at the cat I don't know why, superstition, perhaps.

This old cat had two litters of kittens while she was a "member" of our section and they were all grabbed up as soon as weaned, by both officers and men alike. It is simply human nature to want to have a pet of some kind and, as it was forbidden to take dogs into the lines, the soldiers turned to the cats. Of course they were of some use in killing mice, but the real scourge of the trenches, the giant rats, were too big and strong for any cat to tackle. There were literally millions of these rats. At night they appeared to be everywhere. They would eat up any rations that were left within reach and, boldly entering the dug-outs, would run about all over the sleeping men. It is decidedly unpleasant to be awakened to find one of these fellows perched on your chest and "sniff-sniff-sniffing" in your face. The men killed them in all sorts of ways, one of the most popular of which was to stick a bit of cheese on the end of the bayonet and, holding it down along the bottom of the trench, wait until Mr. Rat went after the cheese and then fire the rifle. Needless to say that rat was "*na-poo*," which is soldier-French, meaning "*finis*."

At Captain's Post a cat had a family of kittens, just learning to walk, hidden in a haymow, when we were shelled unmercifully. After the bombardment ceased, upon going up into the mow to inspect the damage, I found them. They were all covered with brick-dust but unhurt. By actual count, no less than five shells had burst within ten feet of the nest in which they were hidden; in fact, the whole place was an utter ruin, yet they came through it untouched. Then, at Sniper's Barn there was a big black cat, wild as a fox, which had a hiding-place somewhere among the ruins of the upper storey. I had a sniping nest, burrowed under a lot of tobacco which had been stored there, and was occupying it one day when the Germans shelled the place.

They put several shells into that part of the building, cutting the legs off the tripod of my telescope and burying the whole works, including myself. But what interested and amused me most was when a shell rooted out that cat and sent it flying down into my quarters, unhurt but so plastered with dust from the bricks and mortar that no one would have ever suspected it of being black. It was an entirely new variety—a red cat. It sat and looked at me for a long time. Disgust, just plain, every-day disgust, was written all over that animal's face. I don't know what would have happened had I not laughed. I simply could not help it, the sight was so funny. With my first shout the cat seemed to "come to" and, with a terrified yowl, sped through a narrow opening and took to the woods.

To change the subject: Many of our men will, doubtless, be comforted to know that in one respect Flanders is like Ireland—there are no snakes.

One of our guns on this line was in the upper story of an old brewery at Vierstraat, about seven hundred yards from my position, and we occasionally exchanged visits. One day, I was down there talking with the boys when a five-inch (sixty pounder) shrapnel shell burst in front of the building, the case coming right on through, into the room where we were. It "scooted," glanced, ricocheted, or whatever you want to call it, all around that room and you never saw such a scampering to get out. It finally stopped, however, and one of the boys dragged it out into the light for an examination. On the side it was branded "BEARDMORE, SCOTLAND." Now, how do you suppose Heinie got that?

CHAPTER 6

Our Own Cheerful Fashion

On October twelfth there was a general attack along our front, to try out some new "smoke bombs" and shells. It was the first time the smoke barrage was used. We took our guns down about half-way to the front line and set them up in hedge-rows and other places where we could sweep the front in case the enemy made a counter-attack and got into our lines. However, we were not needed, so remained spectators of about as pretty a show as I have ever seen. At a given signal, every gun behind our lines dropped smoke shells in a continuous row along the line, just in front of the enemy's parapet. As each shell struck, it burst, sending out great streamers of white smoke that soon became a dense wall through which no one could see. Under cover of this, our bombers advanced, threw hand grenades into the enemy trenches and then retired. No attempt was made to take any part of the line; it was more in the nature of a try-out for the new shells and also for the purpose of harassing the enemy.

Naturally, the boche, expecting a general attack, commenced to shell everything in that part of the country and also opened up a heavy machine-gun and rifle fire, a good deal of which came our way, but no one was hit. On the way back to the barn, Bouchard and I were walking side by side, perhaps three or four feet apart, when a "whizz-bang" came right between us and struck the ground not more than ten feet in front. In nine hundred and ninety-nine cases out of a thousand that would have spelled our finish, but the shell struck on the edge of a little hump, at the side of a ditch, turned sidewise and spun round like a top. We stood there, speechless, fascinated by the peculiar antics of the thing, until it stopped. It was a pretty toy, a 105 mm., painted red and with a beautiful brass fuse-cap. I picked it up but as it was too hot to handle I put on my asbestos gloves, used for changing barrels of machine guns, and carried it "home" where I put it away, intending to get some artilleryman to remove the fuse and explosive so that I might keep it as a souvenir; but a bunch of boys from the Eighteenth Battalion found it, and taking it back to their dug-out at Ridgewood, tried to unload it themselves. Some were killed and several wounded when the thing exploded. I afterward saw one of those who had been wounded and he told me about it.

At this stage of the soldier's career he is always a "souvenir hunter," picking up and carrying around with him all sorts of things, from German bullets to big shells. I was a fiend of the first magnitude and collected enough stuff to stock a museum, only to have to abandon it whenever we moved. I had French rifles, bayonets and other equipment; German ditto and about every size and type of shell and fuse that was used on our front. Whenever we moved I would bury or cache the whole lot, in the hope that I could get back for it some day. But the fever finally wore off, and I got so that I would not even pick up a German helmet. Now, of course, I wish I had some of that stuff to show the folks.

On the fifteenth of October we went into the front line; a line which we, alternating with the Twentieth Battalion, were destined to hold until the following April. About this time the rains set in "for keeps" and we were seldom dry or warm or clean for nearly six months. Mud, mud, nothing but mud—mud without any bottom. We had no trenches, proper; they were simply sand-bag barricades between us and the enemy and it was a continual struggle to keep them built up. They would ooze away like melting butter.

When the deadlock came, in the fall of 1914, and the opposing armies lay entrenched, from the North Sea to Switzerland, it found the Germans occupying the dominating heights, with our forces hanging on, as best they could, to positions on the lower ground.

This was the case at the point where we were located. Our sector (about eleven hundred yards for the battalion frontage) extended from the Voormezeele-Wytschaete road, northward to the bottom of the hill at the top of which was the village of St. Eloi. Directly opposite our left was Piccadilly Farm, located on a hill about ten meters higher than our lines. From there toward the right, the enemy line gradually descended until, at the right of our line, it was only about two meters higher. The distance between the front lines varied from about seventy yards, at the right, to about two hundred and fifty yards at the left. The net result of this situation was that the Germans could dig trenches of considerable depth, draining the water out under their parapets or into two small streams which ran from their lines to ours.

They had a playful habit of damming up these streams until an unusually hard rain would come, when they would open the gates and give us the benefit of the whole dose. I have seen the water in these streams rise seven feet within less than an hour and there were times when in one of our communication trenches it was over a man's head. A soldier of the West York's regiment was drowned in this trench one night.

Under such conditions, it was impossible for us to dig. All we could do was to construct sand-bag parapets or barricades, while our so-called "dugouts" consisted of huts constructed of sand-bags, roofed with corrugated iron and covered with more sand-bags. They afforded protection from shrapnel and small shell fragments, but, of course, not against direct hits from any kind of shells. Even a little "whizz-bang" would go through them as though they were egg-shells. All the earth thereabouts was of the consistency of thick soup and our parapet had a habit of sloughing away just about as fast as we could build it up. As a matter of fact, our communication trenches did become completely obliterated and we had no recourse but to go in and out of the trenches "overland."

At night this was not so bad, although we were continually losing men from stray bullets. But when it was necessary, as it sometimes was, to go in or out in daylight why, it was a cinch that someone was going to get hit, as the enemy had had many good snipers watching for just such opportunities. At one time, for over two weeks more than two hundred yards of our parapet were down, and if you went from one end of the line to the other you must expose yourself to the full view of enemy snipers. My duties required me to cover this stretch of trench at least twice a day.

Our conduct in taking short cuts across the fields when the trenches were knee-deep with mud, was scandalous in the eyes of our neighbours of the Imperial Army, as the troops from the British Isles are known. Quite frequently we were subjected to the most scathing tongue-lashing from officers of the old school, but we won the astonished admiration of the Tommies by our disregard of instructions and advice. I well remember one day when a party of us were going out through the P. & O. communication trench and, finding the mud too deep, we climbed out and walked across the open, whereat an old colonel of some Highland regiment gave us a "beautiful calling."

His discourse was a masterpiece of fluent soldier talk and, as a Scot usually does when excited, he lapsed into the "twa-talk" of his native Hielans. I can remember his last words, which were to the effect that: "Ye daft Cany-deens think ye're awfu' brave but I tell ye the noo it's no bravery; it's sheer stupidity." Of course he was right, but we could not allow the small matter of a bullet or two to stand in the way of our getting out in time for tea, and finally they gave it up in disgust and allowed us to "go to hell in our own cheerful fashion," as they said.

With the assistance of the engineers, we finally succeeded in constructing a new line, slightly in the rear of the old one which was abandoned except for a couple of machine-gun positions and a listening post. We also managed to get out a fairly good barbed-wire entanglement along most of the front. Fritz appeared to be having his troubles, too, so did not bother us much at night. We always got a few shells every day and usually quite a number of rifle grenades and "fish-tail" aerial torpedoes, but they did very little damage. Here was where the mud was our friend, for, unless a shell dropped squarely on the top of you, it would do no harm.

CHAPTER 7

Sniper's Barn

Just as streets and roads must have their names, so must all trenches have official designations. This applies also to localities, farms, crossroads, woods and such places which have no "regular" names or which possess Flemish or French names difficult of pronunciation by the soldiers.

Front-line trenches are usually designated by letters or numbers, running in regular order, from right to left in each sector. Certain important points may have special names. Communication trenches are always given distinctive names. Probably the majority of these names are those of prominent streets and roads in England, especially in London. At Messines we had "Surrey Lane," "Stanley Road" and "Plum Avenue" for communication trenches, while our front line embraced the whole series of "C" trenches.

During the winter we occupied the "N" and "O" front-line trenches, while our communication trenches bore such names as "Poppy Lane," "Bois Carré" (afterward called "Chicory Trench" because it ran through a chicory field), and the "P. & O." so named because it entered the front line at the junction of the "O" and "P" trenches and P. & O. is so much easier to say than O. & P. At St. Eloi, "Convent Lane" and "Queen Victoria Street" were examples of the communication trenches, while the front-line positions were designated by numbers, as elsewhere explained. Originally, they were called the "O" and "R" trenches. Opposite Hill 60 (so named because it is sixty meters above sea level), the numbering method was continued in the front line, while the communication trenches included "Petticoat Lane," "Fleet Street" and "Rat Alley." At various places along the lines you would find "Marble Arch," "Highgate," "Piccadilly Circus," and so on.

Supporting points were generally designated as "S. P. 7" (or other number), or as "Redoubts" with identifying names. In one place we had the "Southern, Eastern and Western" redoubts along the edges of a certain wood.

Sometimes the original Flemish names were retained for the farms, *châteaux* and cross-roads, but more often they would be Anglicized by our map makers. Thus we had "Moated Grange," "Bus House," "Shelley Farm," "Beggar's Rest," "Dead Dog Farm," "Sniper's Barn," "Captain's Post," "Maple Copse," the "White Château" and the "Red Château," "Dead Horse Corner," "White Horse Cellars" and so on, indefinitely. "Scottish Wood" was so named for the London Scottish who made a famous charge there in the early part of the war. Hallebast Corner was changed by the soldier to "Hell-blast" Corner, just as Ypres became "Wipers" and Ploegstert was translated into "Plugstreet." As to the *estaminets*, (drinking places), while many retained their original names, such as "Pomme d'Or," "Repos aux Voyageurs" or "Herberg in der Kruisstraat," such names as "The Pig & Whistle" and "Cheshire Cheese" were not uncommon.

"Shrapnel Corners" and "Suicide Corners" were numerous and had merely a local significance. The names are self-explanatory. "Gordon Farm," where the Gordon Highlanders had stopped for a time, and "School Farm," where we had a bombing and machine-gun school, were other examples. "Hyde Park Corner," afterward changed to "Canada Corner," was an important junction point of the roads back of our lines. "Bedford House" was a name given to a *château* which the Bedfords once occupied. It would require a large book to enumerate them all.

Our line was at the exact spot where the Princess Pat's first went into action and several of them were buried in our trenches, together with many others, both French and English. In fact, it was difficult to dig anywhere for earth to fill sand-bags without uncovering bodies. The whole place was nothing more nor less than one continuous grave. There were a great many crosses, put up by comrades, giving name, date and organization, but hundreds had no mark other than the cross, sometimes inscribed "an unknown soldier," but more often unmarked. Here one of our sergeants found the grave of his brother, who had been serving in the King's Royal Rifles and I noticed another cross near by marked with the name of Meyers, Indianapolis, Indiana, said to have been the first man of the Princess Pat's killed in action.

There was a maze of old French and English trenches, some in front of our line and some behind it and all more or less filled with bodies that had never been buried. Some of the Indian troops had fought here and had left many of their number behind. Whenever it was possible, we buried the bodies, but often they were in such positions that this was impossible and any attempt to do so would only have resulted in further losses. I nearly forgot to mention it; but there were plenty of Germans mixed up with the lot; in one small area, just in front of a farm building, some five hundred yards in our rear, I found eight of them. Inside the building was a dead French soldier who, as we figured it out, had accounted for the eight boches before they got him. This place was called Sniper's Barn.

While our artillery had been considerably increased, it was still far below that of the enemy in number or size of guns, and the ammunition supply was so short that each gun was limited to a very few rounds a day. It was only during the following summer that the English caught up with the Germans in artillery. This, naturally, did not tend to cheer up the men. It was aggravating, to say the least, to have the other fellow sending over "crumps" without limit, and be able to send back nothing but six or eight "whizz-bangs." ("Crump" is the general name for high-explosive shells of from 4.1 up, but the commonest size is the 5.9 or 150 mm.)

> *The reproduction on the opposite page is a section from the map known as Wytschaete. Here are Shelley Farm, White Horse Cellars and St. Eloi, with the British front line shown by faint dashes, crossing the road that runs through White Horse Cellars, at figure 2. The German trenches, indicated by irregular black lines, are close to the British front at this point, but run sharply away down to Piccadilly Farm and beyond on the left. The trenches on this map are corrected to February 20th, 1916. Sniper's Barn that figures so thrillingly in Captain McBride's experiences is shown at the extreme left of the map, only the word Barn appearing.*

Having been so successful at the strafing at Messines, our colonel was anxious that we continue the game here and I was delegated to locate a good position and "go to it." After going over all the ground back of our lines, I decided to try the experiment of placing the gun in a small hedge which ran across the lower end of an old garden or orchard, in front of Sniper's Barn; that is, on the side toward the enemy. It looked rather foolhardy, at first glance, for the place was in plain sight from the German lines and only about five hundred yards

away at the nearest point; but I remembered our experience at our first strafing place and depended on Heinie to jump to the conclusion that we were in the farm buildings, and devote his attention to them. It worked; he "ran true to form," as a race horse man would say, and while we maintained a gun, and sometimes two, in that place for six months, and the boche shot up the barn regularly during all that time, there was never a shell, apparently, directed at our position, and except for an occasional "short," none burst near us.

From there we would shoot, day and night, often, at the first, having our targets where we could "see 'em fall," a very unusual occurrence for a machine gunner, save during a general engagement. Of course we would have to get into the position before daylight and remain until dark as the way to and from it was exposed to view from "across the way."

Here we worked out many of the constantly recurring problems which confront the machine gunner in the field, and which are, as a rule, overlooked or neglected during the preliminary training. As our own soldiers will have to contend with the same conditions, I may mention some of them.

One of the first things we discovered was that while all the small-arms ammunition issued was made pursuant to uniform specifications, furnished by the War Office, a large percentage of it was manufactured in new, hastily equipped factories, by partially trained workmen, and while it was apparently near enough to the standard to pass the tests exacted by the inspectors, only an extremely small proportion would function properly in machine guns or other automatic arms. A few of the old standard brands, made in government arsenals or by the prominent, long-established private manufacturers, could be depended upon at all times, but, unfortunately, these brands were comparatively scarce and hard to get. At least seventy-five *per cent.* of what we received was the product of the small, new and ill-equipped factories, established under the press of war demands, and, while it appeared to work satisfactorily in the ordinary rifles, both Enfield and Ross, it was utterly useless for machine guns.

The difference of a minute fraction of an inch in the thickness of the "rim" would break extractors as fast as they could be replaced, while various other irregularities, so small as to be undiscoverable without the most accurate measurements by delicate micrometers, would cause stoppages and the breaking of different small parts. And, at that time, spare parts were almost unknown, so it required the utmost ingenuity on the part of the gunners to improvise, with what materials could be found on the spot, and with the very few tools at hand, many of the small but all-important parts that go to make up the interior economy of the guns.

All automatically operated firearms are, of necessity, very delicately balanced mechanisms. Whether gas or recoil operated, there must be just sufficient power obtained from the firing of one shot to overcome the normal friction of the working parts, eject the empty cartridge case, withdraw a new cartridge from the belt or magazine, load it properly in the chamber and fire it; continuing this action as long as the trigger, or other firing device, is kept pressed or until the belt or magazine is emptied. Ammunition which does not give the proper amount of pressure or cartridges which, through faulty manufacture, cause an undue amount of friction, either in seating them in the chamber, withdrawing them from the belt or in removing the fired case, will not operate the gun properly and will cause "jams." On the other hand, ammunition which develops too much pressure or creates too little friction, will cause breakages because of the excess jar and hammering of the moving parts.

We utilised parts of cream separators, sewing machines, baby carriages, bicycles and various agricultural implements, found in and around the old Belgian farms, and it soon became common talk that we could make every part of a machine gun excepting the barrel. We learned that there was a certain bolt, a part of the rifle carrier on the French bicycle, which was an exact duplicate of an important part of our guns, so, whenever we found one of those old, broken and abandoned cycles, we would take time to remove this particular part and carry it along for emergencies. This is but one instance of many.

Then, there was the matter of concealing the flash, when firing at night. As the position we occupied was in plain view of the enemy lines, to have fired without some device to prevent the flash being seen would, inevitably, have resulted in a concentration of fire upon us which would have rendered the position untenable. We tried many schemes, from the crude "sand-bag" screen to the most elaborate devices made in the armourer's shops, while back in billets, and finally perfected one which was thoroughly satisfactory. I cannot describe it here, as I hope to see it used by our soldiers in France, but I can say that, out of probably fifty different contrivances made for the same purpose, this was the only one that "filled the bill" from every standpoint.

As most of our firing was done at night, it was necessary to improve the manner of mounting and "laying" the guns as we soon found that the methods taught at the training schools and the lamps and other mechanical devices furnished by the authorities were of no use under actual service conditions.

The various schemes and devices which we originated and elaborated are at the disposal of the proper military authorities in this country but, obviously, can not be described here.

The foreign officers, British and French, who are now in this country acting as instructors and advisers are doing everything in their power to impress upon our officers and men the necessity for keeping up to date in all the various and complicated departments of military training, even to the exclusion of many of the pet ideas of some of the most accomplished instructors in our service schools. The trouble with us is that we have not, and never have had, any machine gunners in the United States Army. By this I mean men skilled in machine gunnery as applied to present-day warfare. The evolution of machine-gun tactics is, perhaps, the most outstanding feature of the whole war. From being, as it was considered four years ago, (at time of first publication), merely an emergency weapon or, as the text-book writers were pleased to call it, "a weapon of opportunity," it has become the most important single weapon in use in any army, not even excepting the artillery. A properly directed machine-gun barrage is far more difficult to traverse than anything the artillery can put down and the combination of artillery and machine guns, working together, whether on the offensive or defensive, represents the highest point ever attained in the effective use of fire in battle.

Our instructors have been technical theorists of the very highest order, basing their theories and working out their problems on the experience furnished by previous wars and of course it is difficult for them to realise that nearly every hypothesis which they have assumed in working out their theories has been proved false. They can not believe that "fire control" of infantry, as taught in the school of fire, has no place in modern trench warfare. It will break the hearts of some of them to learn that the ability to read a map and use a prismatic compass is of far more value than knowledge of the "mil-scale" or "fire-control rule." They will probably be scandalized by the statement, which I make seriously and with full knowledge whereof I speak, that one common shovel and an armful of sand-bags are worth more than all the range-finders that have been or ever will be bought for the use of machine gunners.

Highlanders with a Maxim Gun

Every foot of ground in France, Belgium and Germany has been so thoroughly and accurately mapped that there need be no such thing as estimating ranges. You *know* the range; you do not have to depend on mental or mechanical estimates. And, as machine-gun fire is almost entirely indirect fire, the guns must be laid by using map, compass, protractor and clinometer (quadrant), in exactly the same manner as artillery fire is directed. The average machine gunner will probably go through the whole war without ever seeing a live enemy—excepting prisoners. The various methods of controlling indirect fire by resection, base lines and observation from two or more points are, like the use of an auxiliary aiming point, useless in trench warfare. They are fine in theory and afford much interesting diversion on the training ranges, but when you go to war, why, it can't be done, that's all.

This is a common, plain, hard-headed business proposition: where the only idea is to kill as many of the enemy as possible before he kills you, it has been found that the oldest, crudest and most primitive methods have, in many cases, proved the most effective for the attainment of this end.

Never before has it been of such vital importance to train the individual soldier, whether he be rifleman, bomber, machine gunner or any other specialist, so that he can "carry on" without the direction of an officer. The officer must plan everything in advance; he must look after the health and comfort of his men, see that they are properly equipped and supplied, must station them in their appointed positions, make frequent personal inspections and, finally, lead them in the advance. But in every engagement there comes a time when every man is "on his own," when it is impossible for the officer, if he be still living, to direct the action. The idea that an officer can exercise "fire control" as taught in our service schools, or can personally direct the fire of a number of machine guns, once the action has started, is ridiculous. The limits of one man's sphere of action, at such a time, are extremely small. If the men have been properly instructed, beforehand, and then given a good start, they will do the rest. It is just this ability to assimilate individual instruction that has made the Canadian superior to the native-born Briton. He is better educated, as a rule, has lived a freer and more varied life and, as a result, possesses that initiative and individual ingenuity which are so often necessary at the critical stages of a fight. We have every reason to expect that the American soldier, for these same reasons, will prove to be at least the equal of the Canadian—the finest type of fighting man yet developed by this war.

CHAPTER 8

Getting the Flag

We soon fell into the routine of moving; from front line to support; from support to the front line and back to reserve. For some time these movements were uncertain but we finally settled down to a regular schedule, which was maintained, with few breaks, throughout the winter. When the time came to go into the reserve, the rest of the battalion would go back to LaClytte but the Emma Gees went only to the Vierstraat-Brasserie line before described. From there detachments would alternate in going back to the battalion billets for a bath and clean clothing. Some of us rigged up our own bath house in Captain's Post, so found it unnecessary to go any farther. Personally, there was only one day in three months when I was out of sight of the German lines.

We had comfortable quarters where we were and the towns of Dickebusch and LaClytte had no attractions for me; and as to the battalion billets, they were abominable. They consisted of so-called huts which were simply floors with roofs over them: no walls at all; just a sloping, tent-like roof on top of a rough board floor. Outside, they were partly banked up and plentifully smeared with mud, camouflaged, as it were. The British made it a practise at that time to keep their troops out of the inhabited towns that were within range of the enemy's guns, so as not to give any excuse for shelling them. LaClytte was a very small town of but a few hundred native inhabitants, but Dickebusch, situated about midway between the lines and LaClytte, was a city of several thousands. In both places were hundreds of refugees from the ruined towns to the eastward.

However, it seemed to make little difference to the boche; he shelled both towns, intermittently, killing a number of civilians but very rarely hitting a soldier. Later, in the spring of 1916, they started in to wipe out Dickebusch, and, for all practical purposes, they succeeded. I will speak of this in a later chapter.

Where opposing lines are so close together, say less than one hundred yards apart, and the ground is level and star shells are going up almost continuously, it would seem to be nearly an impossibility for any man or number of men to venture out into No Man's Land without being seen and fired upon by the enemy. But with certain members of each organization it is merely a part of the daily routine. Every night they slip over the parapet and, in small groups, patrol up and down the line, constantly on the alert to prevent any surprise attack by the enemy. But this is not all. There are times, at all points, when it is necessary to put out new barbed wire or repair the old; when large parties of men must go out there and work for hours, within a stone's throw of a vigilant and merciless enemy. Occasionally they are discovered and have trouble, but in the great majority of cases the work is done and everyone gets back unhurt.

How is it done? Simply a matter of training and careful preparation. Every man is rehearsed in his work until he can do it perfectly, quickly and without noise. Materials are carefully checked up and distributed and, each man having a certain specified task and no other, there is no confusion or blundering. They all know that, when a flare goes up near by, they must "freeze" in whatever position they may be. Movements of any kind would be sure to discover them to the enemy lookout, but lacking that movement it is a hundred-to-one shot they will be undetected.

There have been a good many instances where a flag has been planted by the enemy, on his parapets or inside his wire, with a challenge to any one to come over and get it. There was one such opposite our position. Many stories had been told about that flag: The Brandenburgers had it first, then the French got it and passed it along to the English, who relieved them; then the Prussians took it away from the British and had held it ever since; for about a year, in fact. We could see it, plainly enough; a dark blue affair with some sort of a device in yellow in the centre. I often noticed it from our position back at Sniper's Barn and had some rather hazy ideas about going over after it.

One dark rainy night in November, a man in the section named Lucky announced that he was going over to Fritz's line to try to locate a new machine-gun emplacement which we had reason to believe had been recently constructed. He slipped over the parapet where a road ran through our lines and those of the enemy. It was only about seventy yards across at this point.

Working his way through our wire, he crawled along the side of the old disused road, there being a shallow ditch there which afforded a little concealment. The flares were going up frequently and progress was, of course, very slow. At one place the body of a soldier was lying in the ditch and, in trying to roll it out of the way, he pulled off one of the feet. By creeping along, inch by inch, he finally reached the enemy's wire and spent about an hour working through it. Then crawling along the outside of the parapet, stopping often to listen, he soon found the loophole of the new gun emplacement. Taking a sheet of paper which he had brought for the purpose, he fastened it directly below the loophole where it would be in plain sight from our lines but invisible to the occupants of the place. His work done, he was about to start back when he happened to think of that flag and concluded to have a try for it. It was probably a hundred yards or more down the trench from where he then was and it required the utmost care to avoid making a noise as the front of the parapet, as is always the case, was thickly strewn with tin cans and rubbish of all sorts. Lucky had been a big game hunter in Canada, however, and had even stalked the wily moose which is about the last word in "still hunting," so he managed to negotiate the distance without detection and finally reached the flag.

Carefully feeling up along the staff, he discovered that it was anchored with wires which ran into the ground and then he remembered the tales that had been told of how it was attached to a bomb or small mine which would be exploded if the flagstaff were disturbed. That was a common German trick and not at all unlikely in this case, but, after thinking the matter over, he decided to make an attempt to unfasten the wires. This did not take long, after which all that remained was to pull out the staff and "beat it." Taking his pistol in his right hand, to be ready for emergencies, and reaching up with the left, he gave the pole a sharp jerk. Well, there must have been another wire, somewhere, connected up with two "fixed rifles," aimed directly at the stick for, when he pulled on it, two rifle reports rang out and two bullets hit the flagstaff, cutting it off just below his hand which was also slightly cut.

Quickly rolling down into a slight depression he hugged the flag to him and lay quiet, while the Germans, aroused by the shots, immediately opened fire with rifles, which were soon joined by; a machine gun. They could not hit him where he was so he just lay still and waited. Suddenly, without warning, they fired a flare light directly over his head. He told me afterward that was the only time he was really scared. He thought it was a bomb. However that soon passed and the firing having died down, he made his way back to our lines with the flag which he gave to the colonel the next morning. "And they gave him a medal for that."

On another occasion, one of our scouts made his way through the German line and having located a battery in the rear, started back, only to discover that the place where he had come over was now occupied by several soldiers, and, being unable to find another opening, was obliged to hide out and remain inside the enemy's lines all day. The next night he managed to slip back, none the worse for his adventure.

Such things are being done every night and some men consider it the greatest sport in the world to go out alone and spend hours under the lee of a German parapet listening to the Heinies talk. Soon after that, orders were issued in our brigade that no one was to go out alone so when we wanted to prowl around we had to start in pairs. As soon as we were over the parapet we would split and each go his way, to meet later at an appointed place. One man, alone, can get away with a lot of things that would be impossible for two, but we observed the letter, if not the spirit, of the order.

We had cleared out one of the compartments of the big barn at Captain's Post, carefully plugging up all the shell-holes with sand-bags and other materials so that no light could filter through, and there, at night, would build a great fire in the middle of the stone floor and proceed to enjoy ourselves. Usually one or two guns would do a little strafing every night: simply going out into the field in front of the building and setting up the gun in a convenient shell-hole. After a while, from our own observations and from information supplied by the artillery, we occasionally located an enemy battery within range of our guns. Then we would have a regular "strafing party."

Laying all the guns so as to deliver a converging fire on the battery position, we would, as soon as it was dark, open up on them, knowing that they would be moving about in the open and exposed to fire. We could always tell when we had "stung" them, for they would invariably come back at us with a tremendous fire, shooting wildly at everything within our lines in the vain endeavour to locate us. I'll bet we caused them to expend a hundred thousand rounds of perfectly good am-

A Light Vickers Gun in Action

munition in this way, but we never had a man hit while at the game. The German is not much of a hand for night artillery work unless you stir him up, but we could always get a rise out of him, and often did it, just for amusement. This is what is called "getting his wind up." The same thing can be done in the front line by a few men opening up with five or ten rounds, rapid fire, directed just over Heinie's parapet. In nearly every case, he will commence shooting blindly toward our lines: the contagion will spread and, the first thing you know, he will have wasted about a million rounds.

Here, as in most parts of the line, except during an engagement, cooking was done right in the front trenches. The method is to use a brazier made from an old iron bucket, punched full of holes, in which charcoal or coke is burned. As we seldom had charcoal, it was necessary to start the fire before daylight, using wood to ignite the coke which made no smoke but, with careful nursing, could be made to burn all day. The presence of smoke always drew the fire of rifle grenades, trench-mortar shells and even artillery. It was one of our favourite forms of amusement to locate a cook house and shoot it up; and when a shell made a direct hit, if, among the pots and pans flying through the air, we could distinguish a German cap or something that looked like a part of a boche, there was much rejoicing in our lines. Of course it was a game at which two could play and we were not immune by any means.

These little things helped to keep up the interest and break the monotony of the work. About this time the famous Lahore Battery, from the Indian city of that name, was added to the artillery behind our sector; and they appeared not to be restricted in the number of rounds per day which they were permitted to fire. I remember the first time they did any shooting over our heads. It was the day after they had "registered in" that a large working party was discovered on Piccadilly Farm, directly opposite our left. When the F. O. O. (forward observing officer) was informed of it, he had a good look through his periscope binoculars and then called up the Lahore Battery and, without any preliminary ranging shots, ordered "forty rounds per gun." As they had six guns, they poured in the shells at the rate of about one hundred a minute and they certainly did make things fly in and about that farm.

CHAPTER 9

Hunting Huns

During October the casualties in the Machine Gun Section were only three wounded, McNab, Redpath and Jack Lee all getting hit on the same day. They were sent back to England. At that time it was not considered the proper thing for a man to go back if he could, by any means, "carry on" and these three were all bitterly disappointed when they found that they would have to leave the section. There came a time, all too soon, when a "Blighty" was the finest present a man could get; the loss of a few fingers or even a hand or foot being considered not too high a price to pay to get out of hell for a few months.

When the weather was very bad there was but little sniping-going on, so we often went in and out of the lines "overland" in broad daylight. Sunday, November fourteenth, was one such occasion. We had not been relieved until noon by the Twentieth Battalion who had taken a very roundabout way to get in, so I put it up to all my crowd to choose whether we should spend several hours going around or take a chance down the open road. They unanimously decided on the road, so I started out ahead, with instructions for them to follow at about fifty-yard intervals, and in this fashion we walked down at least four hundred yards of open road, every foot of which was in plain sight of the German lines, and got under cover of a small hill without a single shot being fired. From this point it was necessary to cross another small open space but, as it was partly screened by bushes and trees, we did not consider it dangerous.

We had a redoubt concealed in the small hill mentioned and I stopped to arrange about the relief of the gun crew stationed there. The remainder of the party, except Charlie Wendt, continued on their way and soon disappeared in the woods. Charlie stayed a few minutes and then said: "I'll go on ahead, Mac, and wait for you at the Eastern

Redoubt." He started out across the field and I continued my talk with Endersby, who was in charge of the local gun, when, all at once, I heard some one call out: "Oh, Mac," and looked to see Wendt on the ground about one hundred yards away waving his hand to me. Endersby immediately ran to him and I followed as soon as I could drop part of the heavy load I was carrying. On reaching him I found that he had been shot through the abdomen. Just then another bullet snapped beside us, so I told Endersby to get back to the redoubt and telephone for stretcher-bearers, while I bandaged the wound. Charlie remarked: "Well, they got me, but I hope you get about ten of them for me." I assured him that we would and told him to keep his nerve and he would come through all right. He was a very strong, clean-living young man and I really thought he had a chance. He did not think so, saying he was afraid the doctors would have some difficulty in patching up such a hole. He did not cry out nor make the slightest complaint but kept assuring me that "everything is all right."

Meantime, the sniper was keeping up a continuous fire, hitting everything in the neighbourhood but me, at whom he was shooting. It was such a miserable exhibition of marksmanship—only about five hundred yards distant and a bright clear day—that I told Charlie I would be ashamed to have such a poor shot in our outfit. Any American soldier who could qualify as a marksman would scarcely miss such a target and a sharpshooter or expert rifleman would be forever disgraced if he made less than the highest possible score. However, I forgave that fellow; being a German he could not be expected to know how to shoot straight at any range beyond three hundred meters. The shot that hit Charlie was just a "luck shot," but that did not help much.

I tried to drag him along toward a slight depression, but it hurt him so I desisted and waited for the stretcher-bearers. When I saw them approaching I called a warning and had one of them crawl to us with the small trench stretcher, on which we managed to get Charlie into a sheltered place, where they shifted him to a long litter and started out with him. The last thing he said was: "It's all right, Mac; everything is all right; don't you worry."

They did all they could for him while I had to go back and get the machine gun that he had dropped. The fellow across the way showed perseverance, at any rate, and kept up his "*schutzenfest*" as long as I was in sight but without result.

Next day we learned that Charlie had died and was buried at Bailleul. He was not only one of the most popular men in the section, but was the first we had had killed and we all felt very much depressed. I got a permit to go to Bailleul to see whether or not he had been properly buried and there made my first acquaintance with the G. R. C. We had often seen those letters, followed by a number, on the crosses, in trenches, in cemeteries or along the roads, but none knew what they meant. At Bailleul I found the head office of the "Graves Registration Commission" and, within five minutes, knew where Wendt was buried and the number of his grave. This wonderful organization undertakes to furnish a complete record of the burial place of every soldier. Where suitable crosses have not been provided, they furnish one, bearing an aluminium plate showing the name, number, regiment and date of death wherever this information is available. Now they have gone even further and are compiling a photographic record of all known graves so that relatives, writing to the commission, can secure not only a verbal description but an actual photograph of the loved one's grave.

I went back and began to plan ways and means of "getting" Charlie's ten boches, but a day or two later something happened to alter my scheme to a certain extent.

At that time, our ration parties were going out just before daylight, as we had no communication trench and had to cross the open and exposed ground behind our line. The two, who went from one of the guns, however, Dupuis and Lanning, were a little bit late, so that it was light when they started out. About fifty yards down the road was a bend, afterward called the Devil's Elbow. From this point, they were in plain sight from the enemy line and, no sooner had they reached the Elbow than a sniper fired and got Lanning through the lungs. As he fell, Dupuis knelt down to assist, when he received a bullet through the head, killing him instantly.

One of our detachment of stretcher-bearers (composed of the members of our pipe band) was located but a few yards away and, without hesitation, one of the "Scotties" dashed out to help the fallen men. He was instantly shot down, as were three others in succession, who attempted to get to the spot. By this time an officer arrived and prevented more of the men from running out. This officer, by crawling carefully down a shallow ditch alongside the road, managed with the assistance of a sergeant to recover all the bodies. Four were dead and two wounded, one of whom died a few hours later. These stretcher-bearers were unarmed and wore the broad white brassard with the red cross conspicuously displayed on their sleeves. The sniper was only about one hundred yards distant and could not possibly have failed to see this mark.

Then and there I registered a silent vow that these men, to paraphrase Kipling:

> ... *should go to their God in state*:
> *With fifty file of Germans, to open them Heaven's gate.*

Later, I was to see other and worse happenings along that same road, but, at that time, I considered this as about the limit.

The officer who had done such splendid work in recovering the wounded men was himself killed about an hour later, together with one of his sergeants and two men, by a shrapnel shell. He was the first officer we had lost in the battalion, Lieutenant Wilgress, and had been very popular, with officers and men alike.

It was a sad day for us, that twenty-seventh of November, 1915, and yet it was one of those days when "there is nothing to report from the Ypres salient."

Next day I asked and received permission to go back a few miles to a sniper's school, where I got a specially targeted rifle, equipped with the finest kind of a telescopic sight. I only remained long enough to sight it in and get it "zeroed" and was back again in front that same night.

"Zeroing" a rifle is the process of testing it out on a range at known distances and setting the sights to suit one's individual peculiarities of aiming. Having once established the "zero" the marksman can always figure the necessary alterations for other ranges or changed conditions of wind and light.

From that time on, I "lived" in Sniper's Barn. It made no difference whether the battalion was in the front line or in billets, I was there for a purpose and I accomplished it. When the guns were in the front or in support, we had one mounted in the hedge and kept the rifle handy. Bouchard, with a large telescope, and I with my binoculars, scanned everything along the enemy's front and behind his lines. We knew the ranges, to an inch. If one or two men showed, I used the rifle; if a larger number, the machine gun.

Prior to this time, during all the very bad weather, we had ample opportunities to shoot individual Germans from our Sniper's Barn position but had refrained because our own men were also necessarily exposing themselves daily, and to have started a sniping campaign

Canadian Machine Gun Section Getting Their Guns Into Action.

would have done us no particular good and would certainly have resulted in additional deaths on our side. It seems that the troops opposed to us up to this time had been Saxons who were quite well satisfied to leave us alone provided we would do the same by them. Of course we did shoot them occasionally when they became too careless and exposed themselves in groups, but that was perfectly legitimate machine-gun work and taught them a well-needed lesson. Now, however, a different breed of Huns had come in and they had started the dirty work. They were Bavarians alternating with Marines, and we soon learned that for genuine low-down cussedness the Marine had them all beaten, although the Bavarians and Prussians were pretty bad.

When we first began on them it was no unusual occurrence to have from ten to twenty good open shots a day. The ranges averaged about six hundred yards and as I was using a specially targeted Ross rifle, equipped with the latest Warner & Swazey sight, and as I had spent many years in learning the finer points of military rifle shooting, I am very much afraid that some of them got hurt. For about a month we kept it up, the "hunting" getting poorer every day until finally the few German snipers working along the front were safely ensconced in carefully prepared dugouts. A boche cap above the parapet was a rare sight, but we had our hundred, all right; and then some; for, as Bouchard said: "We'd better get a little pay, in advance before they 'bump *us* off.'"

Several times in later days similar events occurred and in each case swift and terrible retribution was meted out to the criminal enemy. They shot down our stretcher-bearers, engaged in their noble work of trying to save the wounded, but we took bloody toll from them whenever this occurred, using unusual methods and taking desperate chances, sometimes, to drive the lesson home.

On one occasion our observers had reported a large gathering of the enemy at a place called Hiele Farm, about eight hundred yards from our position and I had laid two guns on them when, through our telescope, I discovered that it was a burial party assembled in a little cemetery just behind the farm buildings and telephoned to the officer in charge that I did not intend to shoot up any funeral. Within a few minutes came word than an enemy sniper had shot and killed one of our most popular stretcher-bearers and had also fired several shots into the wounded man whom he was bringing in, killing him also. Then, without hesitation, I ordered both guns to open up and we maintained an intermittent fire on that place until long after dark. We could see numbers of Germans lying about on the ground. I have never regretted it.

Then, the day before Christmas, 1915, while the Twentieth Battalion was occupying the front line and we were back in the redoubts of the supporting line, I was up in the gun position at "S-P-7," the redoubt just in rear of the point where the slaughter of November twenty-seventh had taken place, when a boche shell dropped directly in the dug-out which was my home when in the front line. It killed two men, one I remember was named Galloway, and wounded several others. I was so close that I could see everything that happened. One of the wounded was in such bad shape that the only possible chance to save his life was to get him back to a dressing station without delay. The communication trenches were washed out and the only way was down that ill-fated Devil's Elbow road. The officer in command called for volunteers to carry the man out, remarking that, as it was Christmas Eve, he did not think even a German would shoot at a wounded man or unarmed stretcher-bearers.

All hands offered to go and two were chosen. The officer went with them and they started down the road. The minute they reached the fatal bend, where they came in sight of the German lines, a shot rang out and down went the first man. Another shot and the second was down, while a third dropped the officer, who was trying to assist the fallen. I could see each shot strike in the water alongside the road and could tell just about the spot from whence they came so, although we had absolute orders never to fire from that position unless attacked, I immediately swung the gun around and commenced to "fan" that particular spot, at the same time calling to our signaller to get the Sixteenth Battery on the wire and call for S. O. S. fire. (Each yard of enemy line is covered by the guns of some one of our batteries which, when not firing, are kept "laid" on their particular section of parapet.)

Within a few moments the battery opened up but not before at least a half dozen machine guns in our front line had been hoisted upon the parapets and were ripping Heinie's sand-bags across the way. During this proceeding the wounded men were recovered from the road, but, unfortunately, both the volunteer carriers and the man originally wounded had died. The officer, although painfully injured, recovered.

In retaliation for this trick, our heavy guns wiped out at least five hundred yards of German trench. It was the most artistic job of work I have ever seen. From a point approximately two hundred and fifty yards on either side of this murderer's nest we utterly destroyed every vestige of a parapet. How many of the assassins we killed will never be known, but our hearts were filled with unholy joy when we could distinguish bodies or parts of enemy's bodies among the debris thrown up by one of the big 9.2 shells.

CHAPTER 10

A Fine Day For Murder

"Say, kid, want to go sniping?" called out a lank individual as he came over the bridge at "S-P-7" one morning in December, 1915.

The person addressed, a swarthy little boy wearing the uniform and stripe of a lance-corporal of the Twenty-first Canadian Machine Gun Section, took a long careful look around the sky, hastily swallowed a strip of bacon he had in his fingers and as he darted into a little "rabbit-burrow" sort of tunnel, flung back the words; "Hell, yes; this looks like a fine day for a murder." In a few moments he reappeared with a water-bottle and a large chunk of bread. Hastily filling the former from a convenient petrol tin and cramming the latter into his pockets, he walked over to the older man and divested him of some of the paraphernalia with which he was festooned. He took a long case containing a telescope, another carrier holding the tripod, two bandoliers of ammunition and a large haversack.

"How we going in?"

"Straight across," said the sniper.

"Ver-re-well, young-fella-me-lad, if you can stand it I can," said the youngster, for he knew full well that to go from there to Sniper's Barn in broad daylight meant to expose himself to observation from "Germany," only about five hundred yards away, and with a fat chance of playing the part of "the sniper sniped."

Without another word they departed. The sentry on guard at the crossing of the creek volunteered the cheerful hope that they'd get pinked before they got across the field, upon which the boy assured him that he would be drinking real beer in London when the pessimistic sentry was "pushing up the daisies" in Flanders. Crossing the open field to a hedge, they slipped into a shallow remnant of an old French trench, just in time to escape a snapping bullet which was aimed about one second too late. From here they crawled carefully along the hedge, bullets cutting intermittently through the bare branches above them and, at last, came to a small opening that gave entrance to a garden, about one hundred yards from a group of demolished farm buildings. Here they rested for a few minutes, while the bullets continued to "fan" the hedge up which they had come and which led to the buildings.

The boy—"Bou" the other called him—worked his way along the ground to an old cherry tree and was about to lift up a sort of trapdoor at its roots when the other stopped him.

"Never mind the gun," he said, "we'll just wait here until they do their morning strafe and then go into the buildings. I want to try for a few of them over on Piccadilly today and you can't use a machine gun for that. You'll simply have to be the observer, that's all."

Bou came back, lit a cigarette which the other promptly extinguished and then subsided.

"What you think you're going to do; shoot from the farm?" Bou couldn't possibly keep quiet any longer.

"Sure, Mike; why not?"

"Oh, nothing; but do you think we can get away with it?"

"Well, you've been here as long as I have and if you have not figured out the way the boches do things around this place I'm afraid I can't tell you; but I'll try. Now, they saw us come over here, didn't they? And they naturally think we are in the farm buildings. Just as soon as that fellow who was shooting at us can get word to their batteries they will proceed to shoot up the place. After about a dozen direct hits they will feel pretty well satisfied that they have either driven us out or 'na-pooed' us, so that will be our time to get inside and take a shot at this brilliant young Bavarian who will, without a doubt, be looking over the parapet in the hope that he may get a crack at us trying to 'beat it.' I've been wanting to get that guinea for a long time and have a hunch that this is our day. See?"

Before the boy could answer there came a swift "*whit; whit; whit;*" and three "*bang; bang; bangs*" in and above the main building of the farm. Followed several more salvos, finally crashing through the walls and throwing up fountains of brick-dust and earth. After waiting several minutes they worked their way carefully along the hedge and around behind the buildings. Entering the one nearest the road, which was a mere shell with the roof and two walls entirely gone, they crept cautiously across the floor, and dodging the carcass of a cow that lay

Canadian Soldiers in Action with Colt Machine Guns

with its head in an old fireplace, they finally found themselves in a back room. Many bales of tobacco lay piled up on the floor, covered with the litter and wreckage from the upper story. Here the older man uncovered an opening under the tobacco, through which they entered a small chamber, perhaps eight feet square, comparatively clean. At one side of this narrow space lay a figure covered with the well-known blue overcoat of the French soldier.

"Who's your friend?" inquired the youngster.

"I don't know; he was here when I first came; but I think he was the original sniper of Sniper's Barn. Look at that pile of shells beside him."

Near the dead soldier was his rifle and a great pile of empty cartridge cases.

"We'll have to bury him some day: I think he earned it. He's got a hole right through the heart. Must have been here a year: he's all dried up, like a mummy."

While delivering this discourse the sniper had been carefully removing straw and tobacco leaves from an irregular hole in the brick wall. Here he set up the telescope and settled himself to scrutinize that part of the German line which lay directly opposite. After a few minutes' observation he began to clear away another and smaller opening, to the right of and below that where the telescope was set.

"He's there, all right: look just about four o'clock in the 'scope as it stands. See him, right beside that leaning tree? Keep your eye on him while I get my sight set."

In a few seconds, everything ready for action, the tall man sprawled himself on the floor, sling adjusted, piece loaded and cocked, while Bou, now behind the telescope, whispered excitedly: "He's still there and looking right at me. I can see his cap badge. He's one of those damned Marines. Get him, Mac, for God's sake, get him, quick."

"I'll get him, all right," muttered the other as he gingerly poked the muzzle of his rifle through the few remaining straws. "Now watch and see if his hands come up and whether he falls forward or just drops;" with which he slowly pressed the trigger and the shot roared in the small chamber.

"You got him!" shrieked Bou; "I saw his hands come up to his face and he pitched right forward into the trench. Hooray! that's another one for Charlie Wendt."

CHAPTER 11

Without Hope of Reward

All the bandsmen (we had both bagpipe and bugle bands) go into the front line with the other troops. They are unarmed, but equipped with first-aid kits and stretchers. It is their task to administer first aid to all wounded and then to carry or otherwise assist them back to the dressing stations which may be anywhere from a few hundred yards to a mile or more, depending on the ground. When a man is hit while in an exposed place, whether in No Man's Land or behind our lines, it is up to the stretcher-bearers to get to him at the earliest possible moment. I have seen these men, time after time, rush to the assistance of a stricken soldier, knowing full well that they would immediately become the target for snipers' bullets. Personal considerations never appeared to enter their heads. Never, in all my experience, have I seen one of them backward in going to the aid of a wounded man. Often they would spend hours in the effort to bring back to the lines some soldier too badly injured to help himself; and the pity of it was that, on many occasions, after all their self-sacrificing labour, they would be shot down just as they were about to come over the parapet and into the trench.

And all without hope of reward other than the love and admiration of their comrades. There was a time, before this war, when such exploits were considered worth the Victoria Cross. Now, however, they are merely a matter of daily routine. Thousands of men are, every day, performing deeds of valour, which in any other war would have brought the highest decorations, without receiving even so much as an honourable mention. Exposure to fire such as theorists had told us would demoralise any army is merely a part of the day's work. Troops go in and out of the trenches, often under artillery fire that, according to our books, ought to annihilate them, and they do it without thinking it anything unusual or worthy of comment other than perhaps, in answer to a question, to remark: "Oh, yes, they shot us up a bit in the P. & O." or "They handed us a few 'crumps' and 'woolly bears' coming through Ridgewood." ("Woolly bear" is the name given to a large, high explosive shell, with time fuse, which bursts overhead, giving out a dense black smoke, which expands and rolls about in such a manner as to suggest the animal for which it is named.) In fact, nearly all the names invented by the soldier to describe the various projectiles are so apt and expressive as to be self-explanatory.

The "Silent Lizzies," "Sighing Susans" and "Whispering Willies" belong to the class of large calibre, long range naval gun shells which pass over the front line so high that only a sort of whispering sound is heard. The "middle heavies" with percussion fuses, which burst on impact and give out a dense black smoke, have been called "Jack Johnsons" and "coal boxes," but are now usually grouped under the general designation of "crumps," because of the peculiar sound of their explosion. They run all the way from 4.1 inch to 9.2 inch calibres. Some of the very large shells are called "Grandmothers" or "railroad trains." The French call them "marmites," meaning a large cooking pot or kettle. The "whizz-bang" is just exactly what the name would suggest: a small shell of very high velocity, which arrives and bursts with such suddenness as to give no time for taking cover.

Its moral effect exceeds the material in the trenches, but it is deadly along roads or in the open. Gas shells have a peculiar sound, all their own, difficult to describe but never forgotten when once heard. It has been described as a "rumbling" noise, but I think "gurgling" is better. (It's a pity someone can not take a phonograph into the lines and "can" some of these things.) When gas shells land they do not make much noise, having a very small bursting charge; merely sufficient to break the case which contains the gas in liquid form. They are often mistaken, by new troops, for "duds" or "blinds," as we call shells which fail to explode. As soon as the liquid gas is liberated, however, it vaporizes and quickly spreads over a considerable area. There are many kinds, but they can generally be distinguished by the smell. Some are merely lachrymatory or "tear" shells; the gas affecting the eyes in such a manner as to produce constant "weeping" and consequent inability to see clearly. Others, however, are deadly and one good breath will put a man out of action and a couple of "lungfuls" will usually kill him.

About this time, I think it was December 19th, 1915, we had our

British Machine Gun Squad Using Gas Masks

first experience with chlorine gas or "cloud gas" as distinguished from "shell gas." The troops on our immediate left got a pretty bad dose, but, owing to the peculiar formation of the lines and varying air currents, we did not suffer severely from it. The lines in the Ypres salient were so crooked that the enemy rarely attempted to use this form of gas after the first big attack in April, 1915, as it would frequently roll back upon his own troops. Shell gas was constantly used, generally being fired against our positions in the rear; artillery emplacements and such. Being well equipped with gas masks or respirators, we suffered little harm from it.

Christmas, 1915, was a quiet day on our front, both sides being apparently willing to "lay off" for a day. There was no firing of any kind and both our men and the enemy exposed themselves with impunity. Aside from this, however, it was the same as any other day. There was none of the visiting and fraternizing of which we heard so much on the previous Christmas. The Germans opposite us had a number of musical instruments and on that night and on New Year's Eve they almost sang their Teutonic heads off.

January passed quietly. By this time we had become so accustomed to the mud and rain that I doubt if we would have been happy without them. In spite of all the difficulties, we managed to get our rations and *mail* every day. The regular shelling had become a part of our daily life, and the constantly growing list of killed and wounded we accepted without comment. The Machine Gun Section was gradually losing its original members and replacing them by drafts from the infantry companies. It was simply a case of "Conditions continue normal in the Ypres salient," to quote the official reports. We now maintained two strafing guns, shifting about from one position to another whenever an opportunity offered to harass the boche.

That winter, 1915-16, was what they call a "wet winter," that is, it rained continually and rarely got cold enough to freeze. With the exception of a light flurry in late November and a fairly heavy snow about the first of March, we never saw any of the "beautiful." A few times there was frost enough to make thin ice, but never enough to enable us to walk on top of the mud which was from six inches deep in the best parts of the trench to thigh deep in the worst. We had no rubber boots at the start but got some late in the winter.

A peculiar affliction, first noticed during this war, is what is known as "trench feet." Where men are required to remain for long periods standing in cold water and unable to move about to any great extent, the circulation of blood in the lower limbs becomes sluggish and, eventually, stops. The result appears to be exactly the same as that caused by severe frost-bite; in fact it *is* freezing without frost, (I don't know why not, if you can cook with a fireless cooker), and, in severe cases, amputation is necessary.

While the Imperial troops on our flank suffered considerably from this dreaded affliction, we had but few cases, although our position was infinitely worse than theirs, we being in lower ground. Probably the average Canadian is better able to stand the cold and wet than the native-born Briton. We had but one case in the Machine Gun Section and that was not severe.

As a preventive measure, whale oil was issued with positive orders that every man must, at some time during each twenty-four hours, remove his shoes and socks and rub his feet with this oil. I never did think the oil was anything but just an excuse to make the men rub as that in itself would be sufficient to restore the circulation. At any rate, when the oil gave out, we still kept up the rubbing game and there was no noticeable change in the result. Another hitherto unknown disease which developed during that season was what is commonly known as "trench fever." The victim's temperature runs up around one hundred and three and he is affected with lassitude and general debility and it requires from three weeks to a month in hospital to put him in shape for duty. The medical officers use a Greek name for this fever, which, translated, means, "a fever of unknown origin" but the colloquial designation is "G. O. K.," (God only knows). It is rarely, if ever, fatal. I never heard of any one dying of it.

Then there is a sort of skin affection; a "rash," which is said to be caused by eating so much meat, especially fats, without taking sufficient exercise. A few sulphur baths at specially prepared places behind the lines soon eradicate this trouble.

Really dangerous diseases are extremely rare. Typhoid fever is almost unknown, pneumonia is seldom heard of and even rheumatism, which one would naturally expect to be prevalent, is by no means common. The ratio of sickness, from all causes, was far below that in any of the training camps in this country although never, in Canada, England, Flanders or France, did we have as comfortable quarters as are furnished for all the troops here. But we *did* have at all times, plenty of good warm woollen clothing and an abundance of substantial food. Cotton uniforms, underwear or socks are unknown in any army except that of the United States. Perhaps you can find the answer in that statement.

    During February an almost continuous fight was waged for a small length of trench on our left, known as the International Trench, because it changed hands so often. It culminated, March second, with the Battle of the Bluff, by which British troops took and held this line. We were in support, as usual, and suffered rather heavily from shell fire. This was the beginning of the spring offensive, and from that time on we caught it, hot and heavy, for four solid months.

Chapter 12

The War in the Air

From the time we first caught sight of our guns shelling the German airplanes there was rarely a day that we did not see many of them, scouting, bombarding or fighting. At first, as mentioned elsewhere, they flew very low; within easy range of machine-gun fire, but soon began to climb to higher altitudes until, at the time of my departure, most of their work was done from a height of about twelve thousand feet.

There was one of our planes, piloted by a major. I never heard his name but he was known all up and down the line as "The Mad Major." He was a pioneer in all the marvellous evolutions which now form an important part of the airman's training. Side slips, spinning dives, tail slides; all were alike to him. He would go over the enemy lines and circle about, directing the fire of a battery, scorning to notice the fire of the "Archies," (flyers' name for anti-aircraft guns) and when that job was finished, would come home in a series of somersaults, loops and spins which made one dizzy to watch. He was a great joker and frequently, when the shell-bursts were unusually thick around him, would come tumbling down from the sky like a shot pigeon, only to recover at a height of several hundred feet and shoot off in a bee line for the air dome. I've no doubt that the enemy often thought they had "got him," but at last reports he was still there.

I watched the planes for months without seeing one hit and had about concluded that, to make an Irish bull, the only safe place on earth was up in the air, when, one morning, hearing the now familiar "*put-put-put*" of machine guns up above, we looked up to see one of our large observing biplanes engaged with a very small but fast enemy plane. The boche had all the best of it and soon our plane was seen to slip and stagger and begin to descend. The little "wasp" came swoop-

German Aeroplane Trophy—Jules Vedrine Examining the Machine Gun ing down after it, firing all the while until, when a few hundred feet from the ground, our machine turned its nose straight downward and crashed to earth, well behind our lines, both occupants being instantly killed, or perhaps they had already been killed by the bullets. The German thereupon turned and was soon back over his own territory. That same afternoon, another of our machines was shot down, apparently by the same man, just opposite our position, inside the German lines.

Shortly after this, when back in reserve, we watched another fight directly over our heads. This was a pitiful tragedy. One of England's best and most famous flyers, Captain Saunders, had been over the German lines and had engaged and brought down an enemy and then, having exhausted his ammunition, started back "home" for more, but encountered a fast-flying boche who immediately attacked him. Being unable to return the fire, he tried every trick known to the birdman to escape but without avail. He came lower and lower in his evolutions and finally settled into a wide and sweeping spiral. The boche did not come very low as several machine guns and "Archies" opened on him.

The other plane came slowly down in its perfect spiral course and, noticing that the engine was not running, we thought the aviator was intending to make a landing in a large open field toward which he was descending, but when the spiral continued until the tip of one wing touched the ground and crumpled up we knew there was something wrong and ran to the spot, not more than one hundred yards from where we were standing. We got the captain out and found that he had been shot in the head but was still conscious. He died within a short time.

Other of our aviators who had witnessed his first fight furnished the beginning of the story and we could see that in the second engagement he never fired a shot, and every one of his magazines was empty. I examined them myself.

The large, sausage-shaped observation balloons sometimes afford a little diversion. When we were at Dranoutre one of them used to hang over our billeting place. One day an enterprising Hun came flying across and endeavoured to attack it but was driven off by two of our planes.

Again, one of our balloons broke away in a strong wind and started toward Germany. Both the occupants of the basket made safe parachute descents with all their instruments and papers, but the balloon sailed swiftly away. Then the Germans opened on it with every gun in that sector. I feel sure that they fired at least two thousand shots at it. The air around was so filled with the smoke of shell-bursts that it was sometimes difficult to discern the balloon itself. It was late in the evening and the last we saw of the "sausage" it was still travelling eastward, apparently unhit. The joke of the whole thing is that the balloon was never hit and, the wind veering during the night, it returned and came down inside our lines within a few miles of its starting place.

On two occasions Zeppelins came over our lines, evidently returning from raids across the Channel. One time it was night and we could only hear, but not see the air-ship. The other time, during the St. Eloi fight, I saw one, just at daybreak. It was in plain sight but well over the German lines and headed east. No attempt was made to do any bombing of our positions by the Zeppelins although we occasionally received visits from bombing airplanes. The night before I left France, the last time, they dropped several bombs on the village of Ecoviers where I was staying. The only result was the killing of two civilians, the wounding of several others and the wrecking of one of the few whole houses in the town which had often been a victim of shells. Not a soldier was injured.

You have, no doubt, read of cases where bombs have been dropped on or near hospitals, ambulances and so on, and possibly you think that this was intentional on the part of the boche. If so you flatter him. This bomb dropping is, at best, very uncertain business and it would be well-nigh impossible for the most expert flyer to aim at and hit any single building. The fact is that, in nearly every town and city behind the lines, hospitals, ammunition stores and billets are located in close proximity to one another, with probably a railway running near by, so that any attempt to bomb the really important "military" points will necessarily jeopardize the homes of non-combatants—including hospitals. Even the Zeppelins, which are much more stable than an airplane, have never been able to place their bombs with any degree of accuracy.

CHAPTER 13

The Battle of St. Eloi

No one realises better than I the utter futility of attempting to describe a modern battle so that the reader can really understand or visualize it. There are no words in any vocabulary that convey the emotions and thoughts of persons during the long days and nights of horror—of the continual crash of the shells, the melting away or total annihilation of parapets and dugouts; being buried and spattered with mud and blood; with dead and wounded everywhere and, worst of all, the pitiful ravings of those whose nerves have suddenly given way from shell shock. No imagination can grasp it; no picture can more than suggest a small part of it. None who has not had the actual experience can ever understand it. The hospital and ambulance people back at the rear see some of the results, but even they can have no conception of what it is like to be actually in the torment and hellfire *at the front.*

I could not, if I so desired, give an accurate description of the operations in general. I have not the necessary data as to the various troops engaged or local results accomplished. Historians will record all that. My field of description is limited to my field of personal observation, which was not very extensive. I suppose, however, that I saw as much as it was possible for any one person to see, so I shall try to describe that part of the battle of St. Eloi in which it was my fortune to participate.

At the point at the southern end of the Ypres salient, where the line turns sharply to the eastward, stood the village of St. Eloi. It consisted of perhaps fifteen or twenty buildings of the substantial brick and iron construction characteristic of all Flemish towns and was situated at the intersection of the two main roads paved with granite blocks, one running to Ypres and the other through Voormezeele. The village itself, except for two or three outlying buildings, was inside our lines. The portion held by the enemy, however, included a prominent eminence, called the "Mound," which dominated our whole line for a mile or more. This mound had been a bone of contention for more than a year and several desperate attempts had been made to take it; notably in February and in March, 1915, when the Princess Pat's were so terribly cut up and lost their first commanding officer, Colonel Farquhar. All these attempts having failed, our engineers proceeded to drive tunnels and lay mines, six in number, so as to cut off the point of the German salient for a distance of about six hundred yards.

All was completed; mines loaded and ready, and the time for the attack was fixed for daybreak of the twenty-seventh of March. The mines were to be fired simultaneously, followed immediately by an attack, in force, by the Royal Fusiliers, the Northumberland Fusiliers and a battalion of the West Yorkshires. Our brigade (Fourth Canadian) was immediately to the right of the point of attack, but, as the Imperial troops had changed their machine guns for the lighter Lewis automatic rifles to be used with the advancing troops, it was deemed advisable to bring up all available machine guns of the heavier types to support the advance and to resist the inevitable counter-attacks. These guns, twelve in number, were placed at advantageous positions on the flanks of the attacking troops. I was only a sergeant at that time, but, having been an officer, and having had more actual experience in machine-gun work than the others, the direct supervision of these guns was entrusted to me.

> *The map on the opposite page is known as St. Eloi map. It is particularly interesting as showing, very faintly, a great group of mine craters within the British lines. No. 1 can be seen in the lower left section just above the horizontal fold in the map and to the left of the perpendicular. Here the British line comes in at the lower left corner, where it almost immediately branches, passing through figures 44 and 77, joining the main line again at the left and below Shelley Farm. Within this loop are the six enormous mine craters. No. 2 is immediately to the right of figure 96, while 3, 4 and 5 are in a line with it just to the right of the perpendicular fold. The faint dotted line that comes to an apex just below St. Eloi is the British trench known as Queen Victoria Street. This map is made from air photographs dated March 5th, 1916.*

We got all the guns up and in place during the night of the twenty-sixth. In addition, our people brought up a great many trench mor-

tars of different calibres, with enormous quantities of ammunition. We then sat down to wait for the "zero" hour, meaning the time for the show to begin. I took my position at our extreme left, as I wanted to be where I could see everything.

Promptly at the appointed time, the mines were fired and then ensued the most appallingly magnificent sight I have ever witnessed. There was little noise but the very earth appeared to writhe and tremble in agony. Then, slowly, it seemed in the dim light, the ground heaved up and up until, finally, bursting all bonds, earth, trees, buildings, trenches and men went skyward. Immediately followed great clouds of flaming gas, expanding and growing like gigantic red roses suddenly bursting into full bloom. It was an earthquake, followed by a volcanic eruption.

Before the flying debris had reached the ground the Fusiliers were over the top, fighting their way through the jungles of wire and shell craters. The occupation of the mine craters themselves was, of course, unopposed as there was no one there to offer opposition. They kept on, however, meeting the German reinforcements coming up from the rear, fighting them to a standstill and establishing themselves beyond the Mound.

Then all hell broke loose. From the beginning our artillery, machine guns and trench mortars had been maintaining a continuous fire, but the Germans, taken by surprise, were several minutes getting started. When they did open up, however, they gave us the greatest demonstration of accurate and unlimited artillery fire which I, or any of us, for that matter, had ever seen. The air seemed to be literally full of shells bursting like a million fire-flies. Our parapets were blown down in a hundred places and the air was filled with flying sand-bags, iron beams and timbers. A shell struck under the gun by which I was standing and flung gun, tripod, ammunition-box and all, high into the air. Even under such conditions I could not help laughing at the ridiculous sight of that gun as it spun around in the air, with the legs of the tripod sticking stiffly out and the belt of ammunition coiling and uncoiling around it, like a serpent.

The lance-corporal in charge of it looked on, spell-bound, and when it finally came down back of a dug-out, he looked at me with a most peculiar expression and said: "Well, what do you think of that?" Then he jumped up and went after the wreckage and, strange to relate, not a thing was broken. After about twenty minutes of stripping and cleaning he had the gun back on the parapet, shooting away as though nothing had happened. He was an Irishman, named Meeks.

I walked down the trench to get a spare barrel for a gun when a shell struck about ten feet in front, killing a man. I started on and another lit exactly where I had been standing. During that little trip of perhaps fifty yards and back I was knocked down and partly buried no less than four times.

Then the prisoners commenced to come back. They appeared to be glad to get out of it and I don't blame them. When they found that they had to go through the Canadian's lines, however, they held back. They had been told that the Canadians killed all prisoners. (We had heard something of the same kind about the Germans, too.) However, when our cooks came out with "dixies" full of steaming tea, with bread and marmalade sandwiches, they soon became reconciled. Our men made no distinction that morning between captor and captive, serving all alike with everything we had to eat or drink. At one time, however, owing to the congestion in the trench, we were compelled to "shoo" a lot of the prisoners back "overland," to the next support trench. As their artillery was raising merry hell all over that section, they were a bit backward about starting and it required threats and a display of bayonets to get them out of the trench and on their way. It was a funny sight to see them beat it.

There was little in the way of obstacles to impede their progress and I think that several of them came near to establishing new world's records for the distance. When they arrived at the second line they wasted no time in climbing down into it; they went in head-first, like divers going into the water. I don't think any of them was hit during this manoeuvre, at least I did not see any of them fall.

Now, it has come to be an axiom that "any one can take a trench but few can hold one." It is another way of expressing the idea that "it isn't the original cost—it's the upkeep."

It was no trick at all, with the assistance of the mines, to advance our lines to what had been the German third line, but, right there, some one had made a miscalculation. It's a cinch our "higher-ups" did not know how much artillery the Germans had that they could turn on that salient. Our own artillery had been greatly increased and they evidently thought we were at least equal to the enemy in this respect, but, say: the stuff he turned loose on us made our artillery look like pikers. For every "whizz-bang" we sent over he returned about a dozen 5.9's. By that night, nearly all the original attackers were gone and Fritz was back in at least two of the craters.

During the day a good many of us, including all our stretcher-bearers, made many trips through the devastated German trenches, getting out wounded and collecting arms and other plunder. I went up where the Fusiliers were trying to consolidate their position, intending to bring up a few guns if it appeared to be practicable, but abandoned the idea as, in my opinion, they were due to be shelled out within a short time, which proved to be correct. We did dig out and mount a German gun which was used for a while, but I then had it taken, with several others, back to our line. We could do so much more good from our original position by maintaining a continuous barrage to hamper the enemy in getting up supports. From prisoners taken later we learned that our machine-gun barrage was much more effective than that of our artillery. However, as we were obliged to fire from temporary positions, on the parapet and without cover of any kind, it was impossible to prevent the loss of some guns by direct hits from shells. During that night and the next day a Highland brigade came up to relieve the Fusiliers. They included battalions of the Royal Scots and the Gordons.

By this time the Germans had brought up more guns and were keeping up such a terrific fire on our position that it did not seem humanly possible to hold it, but that night a bombing attack by the Fourth Canadian Brigade bombers, reinforced by about two hundred volunteers, retook the craters and re-established our line in a more advanced position than that occupied by the original attackers. This line was thereafter called the Canadian trench to distinguish it from the other, which was called the British trench.

Early next morning we had a chance to see some of the "Kilties" in action with the bayonet, during a counter-attack, which they repulsed. As I remember it, they did very little shooting but jumped out of their trench to meet the attackers with the cold steel. I never saw any lot of soldiers who seemed so utterly determined to wipe out all opposition. They were like wild men; savage and blood-thirsty in the onslaught and, although the Germans must have outnumbered them at least three to one, they never had a chance against those brawny Scots. But few of the boches got back to their own line and no prisoners were taken. We then appreciated the nickname given by the Germans (first applied to Canadian Highlanders at Langemarck, but afterward used to designate all "Kilties"), "The Ladies from Hell."[1]

From that time the Canadians were alone in the fight. The fusiliers,

---

1. *Ladies From Hell* by R. Douglas Pinkerton also published by Leonaur.

having started it, faded away, and the Scots, after a few brief days, likewise vanished and for two months or more St. Eloi was a continuous struggle between the Second Canadian Division and at least four German divisions, including some of the infamous Prussian Guards.

During the next twelve days the fighting was almost uninterrupted. Troops came in and troops went out, but the Emma Gees held on, forever, as it seemed to us. But few remained of the original gun crews who started the engagement. Not all had been killed or wounded, but it had been necessary to relieve some who were utterly exhausted. How I kept going is a mystery to me as it was to others at the time. One thing which probably helped was the fact that I never, for one minute, permitted myself to think of anything except the matter of keeping those guns going. Sentiment I absolutely cast out. I was nothing but a cold-blooded machine. Good friends were killed but I gave them no thought other than to get the bodies out of the trench so that we need not step on them. To tie up and assist wounded was a mere matter of routine. In no other way could I have withstood the awful strain. I was hit, slightly, on several occasions but never severely enough to necessitate my going out.

A dugout in which I had a table where I wrote reports and figured firing data was hit no less than three times while I was in it, finally becoming a total wreck. The fact that I was not killed a hundred times was due to just that many miracles—nothing less. My leather jacket and my tunic were cut to shreds by bits of shell, a bullet went through my cap and another grazed my head so close as to raise a red welt, but that same old "luck" which had become proverbial in the battalion, still held and I was not seriously injured.

Our troubles were not all caused by artillery fire by any means. Fritz had a large and varied assortment of *"Minenwerfer"* with which to entertain us at all hours, day and night. A good many people, even among the soldiers themselves, think that *Minenwerfer* or "Minnie" for short, is the name of the projectile or torpedo, while, as a matter of fact, it is the instrument which throws it; a literal translation being "mine-thrower." In the same way they often speak of the shells thrown by trench mortars as "trench mortars" themselves.

Now the family of "Minnies" is a large one and includes every device, from the ancient types used by the Greeks and Romans, with springs of wood, to the latest and most modern contraption in which the propelling power may be steel springs, compressed air or a small charge of powder. In its smallest form it is simply a "rifle grenade," somewhat similar to a hand grenade or ordinary "bomb," to which is attached a rod of brass or iron which slips down into the bore of the regular service rifle and is fired with a blank cartridge. Other and newer types are without this rod but have vanes or rudders affixed to the rear end which serve to guide the projectile in its flight. These usually have a hole through the centre through which the bullet passes and can thus be used with the regular service ammunition. This whole class, embracing everything from the small "pineapples," fired from the rifle, to the monstrous "aerial torpedoes," are commonly spoken of as "fish-tails."

The shells from the trench mortars proper, and most of the "fish-tail" family, are somewhat similar to ordinary artillery shells in that they are made of steel or iron and designed to burst into small fragments, each of which constitutes a deadly missile. On the other hand, the "mines" thrown by the *Minenwerfer*, are merely light sheet-metal containers for heavy charges of high explosives (T. N. T. or tri-nitro-toluol as a rule), and depend for their effectiveness on the shock and blasting effect of the detonation. They have been increasing in size continually. At first we called them "sausages," then "rum-jars" (they resembled the ordinary one-gallon rum jar in size and shape), then they became "flying pigs" and by this time, I have no doubt, new and still more expressive names have been applied to them.

The havoc created in a trench by one of the large ones passes belief. The strongest dugout is wiped out in a twinkle; whole sections of parapet are obliterated, and where was a strong, well-built wall eight feet or more in height there remains a hole or "crater" fifteen or twenty feet in diameter and several feet deep. Any man who happens to be within this area is, of course, blown to atoms, while frequently men in the near vicinity, but not exposed to the direct blast, are killed instantaneously by the shock. Medical men say that the effect is identical to that known as "caisson sickness," and is caused by the formation of bubbles of carbonic acid gas in the blood vessels. Not being a "*medico*" I can not vouch for this, but you can take it for what it is worth.

In daylight it is not difficult to dodge these devilish things and even at night, if they come one at a time, it is possible to escape the most of them, but when they come over in flocks, as they sometimes do, it is more a matter of luck than anything else.

CHAPTER 14

Fourteen Days' Fighting

By this time there was no doubt of the enemy's superiority in artillery, and to make matters worse, the craters were changing hands daily or even hourly. We never knew, for sure, whether our troops or those of the enemy held any certain crater, except the ones on each end, numbers one and six (we held them throughout the entire two months of fighting), but numbers two, three, four and five were debatable ground for several weeks. On two occasions I made the complete circuit of all the craters at night, going through the Canadian trench and coming back via what had been our original front line. On one of these trips I was accompanied by Captain Congreve, afterward Major Congreve, V. C., (now dead) who was the only staff officer I saw in that sector during all the time we were in the line. Sometimes we met individual German sentries and quick, quiet and accurate work was necessary to avoid detection and probable capture.

I found that a French bayonet, the rapier shape, was a very satisfactory weapon at such times. Trench knives have been invented since and may be an improvement. After leaving me that night Captain Congreve came upon a party of eighty-two Germans, commanded by an officer, who had been cut off in one of the craters for several days, without food or ammunition, and captured them all, single-handed. For this feat he received the Distinguished Service Order and promotion to Major. Later, on the Somme, he continued his brilliant work and won the award of the Victoria Cross, but was killed at Mametz Wood before receiving the decoration, which was given to his widow. He was only twenty-five at the time of his death but had proved himself one of the most enterprising officers in the British Army.

What had been left of the village of St. Eloi when the fight commenced was rapidly disappearing under the hail of shells. Where our

Lewis Gun in Action in Front-Line Trench.

original front line had been there remained but few detached fragments of parapet. For perhaps six hundred yards we were holding on with scattered and isolated groups. At one place, on our immediate left, was a hole in the line at least two hundred yards wide. Time after time the Canadians attacked and retook the craters, only to be literally blown out of them by the ensuing hurricane of shells.

The task of getting out the wounded was heart-breaking. Our own stretcher-bearers worked night and day, but they had suffered many casualties and were unequal to the task. The Border Regiment and the Durham Light Infantry, who occupied our old trenches and were not under heavy fire, sent volunteer carrying parties to assist in the work, so that all were taken out with a minimum of delay. It was impossible to remove the dead and they were buried in shell-holes, where they fell. During the succeeding days many were disinterred by other shells.

Then, the matter of maintaining communication with our supports and the headquarters in the rear was of the utmost importance and our signallers waged a continuous fight, against heavy odds, to keep the wires connected up. It would not be fair to others to specify any particular branch as being better. All who serve in the front line at a time like this are equally entitled to credit. At times, when it is necessary to go out and search for breaks and repair them, the work of the signallers is "extra hazardous," just as is that of the stretcher-bearers when obliged to expose themselves to succour the wounded, or the machine gunner when it is necessary to mount his gun on top of the parapet, within plain sight of the enemy, or the riflemen, bombers and scouts in advancing to the attack.

There can be no fair distinction—they all, taken as a unit, are in a class separated by a wide gulf from those back in supporting or reserve or artillery positions, who, in turn, are separated from the transport and ambulance drivers, who, while occasionally under shell fire, are in the zone of comparative safety, where "people" still live and farm and run stores and estaminets. I would not have you think that I am minimizing the value of the services of these men. Their work is of vital importance to the success of the fighting forces and *must* be done; and I can truly say that in all my experience I have never known them to fail in the performance of their duties.

In this war, as in most others, it is the infantryman who stands the brunt of the fighting. True, he is disguised under many other names, such as rifleman, bomber, automatic rifleman, rifle-grenadier, scout, signaller, sniper, runner or machine gunner but, when you get right down to the bottom of the whole business, he is the fellow who travels on his two feet and actually "goes over and gets 'em." Trenches can be battered to pieces by artillery but they can not be actually "taken" and held by anyone but the plodding, patient, long-suffering "doughboy" or "web-foot" as he is called by the men of the other branches.

At one time, during this period, Sergeant H. Norton-Taylor and four men from our section, held one of the craters for five days, against numerous attacks, and even captured prisoners. They had no food, water or ammunition other than that which they could get from the bodies of dead soldiers in the immediate vicinity. We sent many detachments to relieve them but were unable to locate their position and it was only by accident that they were discovered and relieved by a scouting party of the Nineteenth Battalion which was over on our left. But for this, they might be there now, as they were not the quitting kind.

Norton-Taylor was commissioned and commanded the section at Courcellette, where he was killed, September 15, 1916. He came of a long line of distinguished British officers, his father having been a colonel in the Royal Field Artillery. A brother and a brother-in-law were in the service, one of them losing both feet by a shell. A sister was working in the hospitals in France and another in England. He was a true friend and a gallant officer—every inch a gentleman.

On the night of April tenth we were relieved by the Twentieth Battalion and went out for a rest. I had not laid down to sleep for fourteen days, snatching what rest I could, for fifteen or twenty minutes at a time, leaning against a parapet or propped up in the corner of a traverse. We were only able to get as far as Voormezeele, where we stopped in the ruins of the convent school, and dropping on the stone floor slept like the dead for twenty-four hours. The place was being shelled all this time but none knew or cared. The next night we made our way to where the battalion was in billets, near Renninghelst, where I immediately "flopped" for a straight forty-eight hours' continuous sleep. After that a bath, a shave and general clean-up, supplemented by a good hot "feed," made me as good as new. During that two weeks up in front we had had no warm food, nothing but "bully and biscuits" and, occasionally, a can of "Maconochie," a ration of prepared meat and vegetables, which is excellent when served hot but not very palatable when eaten cold.

We now had the longest rest we had enjoyed since coming over, as we did not go back to the front line until April twentieth. Our Sixth and Fifth Brigades had been in during the time we were out and both had suffered severely in the many counter-attacks, but held on, like true British bulldogs, to what had been our original front line. The craters were lost as it was impossible for any troops to hold them under the devastating fire of the German guns. Nearly every battalion of the Second Canadian Division had retaken one or more of them but, as it only resulted in additional loss of life, it was decided by the higher command to give it up and endeavour to re-establish our front along its original line.

We went in *via* Voormezeele, a town of several thousand inhabitants before the war, now a pile of ruins. From here a *pavé* road ran directly to St. Eloi and there had been two good communication trenches leading up to the front line. We soon discovered however that several things had happened during our absence. On the road to St. Eloi and about five hundred yards behind our front line, had been a Belgian farm called Bus House. (A London omnibus was lying, smashed, in front of it.) This place was now but a pile of brick and timbers. To the left, another group of farm buildings, called Shelley Farm, was in about the same condition, and where St. Eloi had been was nothing but a barren waste.

Not a sign of a house or any part of a house was visible; not a brick remained and even the roads, the fine stone-paved roads, had been obliterated. Where had been hedges or trees there was nothing but a desolate expanse of mud which, from a distance, appeared to be a smooth level plain. For a good six hundred yards back of our front line there was not a shrub or bush or tree nor any landmark of any kind. Every inch of this ground had been churned over and over again by shells. Literally, it was not possible to set foot on a spot which had not been upturned. The whole area was simply a continuation of shell craters, joined and interlocked without a break. Where our communication and support trenches had been it was just the same. No man could have gone over that ground and said: "Here was a house," or "There was a field," or "That was once a road," because house, turnip field and road looked exactly alike. The great granite blocks of the road had been pulverized to dust, and the bricks of the houses had shared a like fate. Even the contour of the ground was changed—ditches, depressions and ridges having been hammered to a uniform elevation.

And every hole was full of water. To traverse this desert one must wade and flounder through liquid mud waist deep and sometimes deeper. Yet it had to be done. We had nine positions up there at each of which a handful of men must be relieved daily; or rather nightly, as it was, obviously, impossible to move about over that open expanse in daylight. Every yard of it was under scrutiny from the German lines and, even at night, owing to the lavish use of star-shells by the enemy, it was a long and slow journey as it was necessary to stop and remain absolutely quiet when a light came near.

The hardest thing about the whole business was to find the men who were to be relieved. There was no path nor road nor landmark of any kind. During the time we were in, it rained continuously and at no time was a star visible. The positions where they were stationed were exactly like the rest of the surrounding country—merely enlarged shell-holes with, perhaps, a fragment of a sand-bag parapet. No lights could be shown, they did not even dare use "Very lights," as our "star-lights" are known. They were not in any regular formation but at irregular intervals along what had been a very crooked line. Fortunately, we had a "natural born" guide on our first trip in and we found them all. After that we managed to "carry on" but not without many slips. It was nothing unusual for a relief party suddenly to find themselves in the German lines and have to work their way out as best they could.

If caught out after dawn one had to lie low in a shell-hole all day, probably under heavy artillery fire, until darkness came and made it possible to return unseen. This trouble was not confined to our side and it was by no means an uncommon occurrence for parties of the enemy to get lost in the same way. Sometimes these adventures resulted in rather sharp bombing engagements. One night a whole platoon of about forty Germans went through a gap in our line and bumped into a strong supporting party of ours at Shelley Farm where they were all captured. They had been looking for one of the craters whose garrison they were to relieve. Individual prisoners were taken nearly every night.

Under the prevailing conditions, it was impossible to take machine guns up, so we depended entirely upon Lewis guns. Fortunately no determined attack was made on us during this time as it is extremely doubtful if we could have held them there. We would, of course, have stopped them a few hundred yards back, at our support line, and I must confess that I had at times a sneaking desire to see them come over and get into that mud so we could move back to comparatively comfortable quarters.

Canadian Machine Gunners Digging Themselves Into Shell-Holes

As we no longer had any trenches, we abandoned the old letter method of designation and simply numbered the various positions. On the first morning in, the gun and crew at No. 14 were blown up by a shell. This was an unlucky position as the same thing had happened there to a crew from the Twentieth Battalion. We then moved that position some fifty yards to one side and had no further trouble.

We alternated with other battalions of the division, going in and out, holding that line and gradually improving it, until, on the twenty-second day of May, while we were back in billets, I was "warned for leave" (a week in England), and little Bouchard, my particular *protégé* and warmest friend, was to go along.

You people who have stayed at home can never realize what "leave" means to a soldier after eight months in the trenches and I, for one, will not attempt the impossible by trying to describe the sensation.

We packed our kits and hiked to Poperinghe, where, after sitting up all night, we took train at four o'clock a.m., arriving at Boulogne about noon and were in "Blighty" by four in the afternoon.

"Oh, ain't it a grand and glorious feeling!"

Chapter 15

Blighty and Back

In London we found things running along about as usual and proceeded to enjoy ourselves. Oh, the luxury of having clean clothes and being able to keep them clean: to sleep in real beds and eat from regular dishes and at white-clothed tables. It seemed almost worth the price we had paid to be able to get so much downright enjoyment out of the merest "necessities" of ordinary civilian life. The theaters were all running and we took in some show every night, but I derived the most satisfaction from taking my young companion around to see the museums and many old historical places in and about London. He was a stranger and I was fairly well acquainted.

But, when the time drew near for us to go back, I began to experience a feeling of depression. While I had not noticed it before, I suppose the cumulative effect of the experiences of the last eight months was beginning to tell on me. I noticed that Bouchard appeared to be in about the same condition. He would sometimes sit for an hour or more, in our room at the Cecil, gazing into space, never uttering a word. Poor boy, while of course he could not *know* that this was to be his last trip, I believe he had a presentiment that such was the case.

I found myself now and then "checking up" my own physical and mental condition. I had been slightly injured several times—two scratches from bullets on my left hand, a bullet in my right elbow, two pieces of shell in my shoulder, a knee-cap knocked loose and a fractured cheek-bone from the fuse-cap of a "whizz-bang." None of these had put me out of action for more than a few hours and I had managed to keep out of the hospital. (I had an instinctive dread of hospitals.) But I knew, right down in my heart, that my nerve was weakening. Thinking over some of the things we had done, I believed I could never do them again. I do not think the man ever lived who would not, eventually, get into this condition. Some men "break" at the first shell that strikes near them, while others will go for months under the heaviest shell fire but, as I have said, it will certainly get them in the end. Of course I did not express any of these feelings to Bouchard, but tried to keep things moving all the time so as to give him little opportunity to worry. But, to tell the truth, I guess I needed the diversion more than he did, for he was the bravest and "gamest" youngster I ever knew.

Before we left France for our week in London I was told by my colonel that I had been recommended for a commission and something or other in the way of a decoration and he suggested that I call upon General Carson, Canadian General in London, and find out about it. I did call at the General's office several times but was unable to see him. It afterward developed that the commission had already been gazetted and I was really and truly a First "Leftenant." I did not hear of it for nearly a month and, during the interval, went through, as a sergeant, one of the hottest times in my whole career.

When our leave was up we, together with hundreds of others, left Victoria Station early one morning for Folkestone and Boulogne and so on, back to Poperinghe, where we arrived just at daybreak the following morning and were welcomed by an early rising boche airman, who dropped about half a dozen bombs, evidently aimed at the railroad station. Fortunately, no one was hit. Then we trudged down the road, kilometre after kilometre, every one gloomy and grouchy, looking for our several units. Ours had moved and we spent the whole day before we located it.

We found the battalion in camp near the town of Dickebusch and soon settled down to the same old routine. They had not been back in the line since we left but had been engaged in some special work in and around this town, about which there is an interesting story.

Dickebusch was a town of several thousand inhabitants and considerable commercial importance, located on the Ypres-Bailleul road, about three and one-half miles directly west of St. Eloi. All troops going into the line anywhere from Wytschaete to Hill 60 were obliged to pass through or very close to it. Just east of the town was a shallow lake or pond, about a mile long and half as broad, called Dickebusch Etang, to cross which it was necessary to follow a narrow causeway, constructed by our engineers. While we continually passed and repassed through the place, we never had any troops actually billeted there, as it was within easy range of the German guns and was still occupied by the native population.

About the time of the St. Eloi affair, however, one of our Brigade Headquarters had been located in a group of buildings at the edge of the town, perfectly camouflaged and concealed from aircraft observation. It had long been suspected that there were spies among the people of this place and that they had effective means of communicating with the enemy, so when Fritz turned his guns on that headquarters, no one was very much surprised, but a determined effort was made to discover the guilty parties. Just what means were used I do not know, but it was learned that several of the prominent citizens, including the mayor or burgomaster, were in on it and they were summarily dealt with.

Following this, German airmen dropped notices into the town, warning all the civilians to get out as they were going to raze it to the ground. Not many would have gone, however, had not our authorities ordered the evacuation. As soon as the people had moved out, our troops proceeded to prepare the buildings for use as billets, reinforcing lower rooms and cellars with iron beams and protecting them with sand-bags. This was the work with which our battalion, and others, had been occupied and was just about completed when, true to their word, the Heinies started in, systematically, to write *"finis"* for Dickebusch. The church had already been pretty well shot up, as well as the surrounding graveyard where many of the tombs and monuments were smashed and the dead thrown from their graves. This blowing up of the dead seems to be a favourite pastime with the gentle Hun. They, the Germans, were now engaged in the demolition of the buildings along the principal streets and were doing it in a very thorough manner.

We had here many demonstrations of a matter about which I have been questioned, times without number, by both military men and civilians, and that is, "What is the effective radius of a shell of a certain calibre?" It is one of the things which our theorists in general, and artillerymen in particular, delight in. Many hours of learned discourse have been devoted to proving, theoretically, that an area of a given size can be made impassable by dropping a certain number of shells on it, at stated intervals. This is all rot. Common sense should teach us better. The plain fact is that it depends entirely upon what the shell strikes. If it falls on soft earth, the effect is merely local and a man within a few feet would be uninjured; while, should it fall on a hard, stone-paved road, pieces might be effective at a distance of half a mile or more.

In the bombing schools we are told that the Mills hand grenade has an effective radius of ten yards, yet one will quite frequently escape unhurt from a dozen of them bursting within this radius and yet may be hit by a fragment from a distance of two hundred yards or more. All these theories are based on the assumption that the ground on a battle-field is level, free from obstructions and of a uniform degree of hardness; not one of which conditions ever exists. A small ditch, a log or stump or a water-filled shell-hole will make so much difference in the effect of the explosion of a shell or bomb that all efforts to prove anything by mathematics is a waste of time. If one is unlucky he will probably get hurt, otherwise not.

CHAPTER 14

Out In Front Fighting

We had been "home" but a few days when we received rush orders to pack up and march toward Ypres. There had been an intense bombardment going on up that way and we soon learned the cause from straggling wounded whom we met coming along the road. It was the second of June, 1916, and the Germans had launched their great surprise attack against the Canadians at Hooge. It was the beginning of what has been called the Third Battle of Ypres, but will probably be recorded in history as the Battle of Sanctuary Wood.

The enemy had gradually increased his customary bombardment and then, assisted by some mines, had swept forward, in broad daylight, overwhelming the defenders of the first and second lines by sheer force of numbers and had only been checked after he had driven through our lines to a depth of at least seven hundred yards over a front of nearly a mile, including the village of Hooge, and was firmly established in a large forest called Sanctuary Wood and in other woods to the south. By the time we had arrived at our reserve lines (called the G. H. Q. or General Headquarters Line), we were diverted and directed to a position on the line just south of the centre of the disturbance where we "dug ourselves in" and held on for four days. Shell fire was about all we got here, but there was plenty of that. The rifle and machine-gun bullets that came our way were not numerous enough to cause any concern although we did lose a few men in that way.

Here the news of the fight filtered through to us. It seemed that the Princess Pat's (unfortunate beggars), had got another cutting-up, together with some of the Mounted Rifles, and Major-General Mercer and Brigadier-General Victor Williams, who had been up in the front line on a tour of inspection, had both been wounded and captured. General Mercer afterward died, in German hands, but General

A Shell Exploding in Front of a Dug-in Machine Gun.

Williams recovered and remains a prisoner. It was said that less than one hundred from each the Pat's and the Fourth C. M. R. came out of the fight.

At this place several of our gun positions were in the grounds of what had been one of the most beautiful *châteaux* in Flanders—the Château Segard, hundreds of years old but kept up in the most modern style until the war came. Now the buildings were but a mass of ruins. Not only this but the grounds had been wonderfully laid out in groves, gardens, moats and fish-ponds with carefully planned walks and drives throughout the whole estate which comprised at least forty acres. There were trees and plants from all over the world; beautiful borders and hedges of sweet-smelling, flowering shrubs and cunningly planned paths through the thickets, ending at some old wondrously carved stone bench with perhaps an arbor covered with climbing rose bushes.

All had felt the blighting touch of the vandal shells. The trees were shattered, the roads and paths torn up, the ponds filled with debris and the beautiful lawn pitted with craters, but in spite of all this devastation, the flowers and trees were making a brave fight to live. I could not but think, as I wandered through this place, how well the little flowers and the mighty oaks typified the spirit of France and Belgium. Sorely stricken they were—wounded unto death; but with that sublime courage and determination which have been the admiration of the world they were resolved that *they should not die.*

Along the main road leading up to the *château* was a charming little chapel, handsomely decorated and appointed. It was the only structure on the estate that had not been struck by a shell. We used it as sleeping quarters for two crews whose guns were located in the immediate vicinity. One night a big shell struck so close as to jar all the saints and apostles from their niches and send them crashing to the floor, but did no other damage.

This same thing happened to us once when we were sleeping in the convent school at Voormezeele, when all the statues on the walls were hurled down upon us by a large shell which struck the building.

The boys used to take these sacred effigies and place them on graves of their dead friends. We were not a very religious bunch but I suppose they thought it might help some—at any rate it proved their good intentions and I never interfered to stop it.

For several days the fighting continued furiously, the Canadians recovering some of the lost ground, including most of Sanctuary Wood, and then things settled down to the old "siege operation." During this time we had many opportunities to watch the splendid work of the men of the ammunition columns taking shells up to the batteries in broad daylight and within plain view of the enemy lines. It was one of the most inspiring sights I have ever witnessed and brought back memories of pictures I had seen of artillery going into action in the old days.

Down the road they would come, on the dead gallop, drivers standing in their stirrups, waving their whips and shouting at the horses, while the limbers bounded crazily over the shell-torn road, the men holding on for dear life and the shells bursting with a continuous roar all about them. It was the sight of a lifetime, and whenever they came past our men would spring out of the trenches and cheer as though mad. Time after time they made the trip and the escapes of some were miraculous. A few were hit, wagons smashed and horses and men killed or wounded, but not many, considering the number of chances they took.

The stories of heroism during that first day's fighting equal anything in history. Batteries were shot down to a man but continued working the guns to the last. One artilleryman, the last of his gun squad, after having one arm shot off at the elbow, continued to load and fire. Then a shell blew off about a foot of the muzzle of the gun but he still kept it going. He was found, lying dead across his gun and a trail of clotted blood showed where he had gone back and forth to the ammunition recess, bringing up shells. One member of the crew remained alive long enough to tell the story.

In another place, in Sanctuary Wood, were two guns known as "sacrifice guns," as they were intended to cover a certain exposed approach in case of an attack and to fight to the finish. How well they carried out their orders may be judged from the fact that every man was killed at the guns, *by German bayonets*, after having shot down many times their own number of the enemy.

Our old friends of the Lahore Battery lost so many men that they were having difficulty in maintaining an effective fire until two of our machine-gun squads volunteered to act as ammunition carriers, which they did for several hours, suffering heavy casualties.

Here occurred the only case of which I have ever heard where one of our medical officers was apparently "murdered." Captain Haight, M. O. of one of our western battalions was reported, on excellent authority, to have been bayoneted and killed while attending the wounded.

While we were here, Major-General Turner, V. C., who was in command of the entire Canadian Corps, paid us a visit. He came up unannounced and accompanied by a lone Staff Captain. I was instructed to act as his guide over our sector. During one trip along an exposed road we found ourselves in the midst of a furious hail of shells. I looked at the general to see if he wanted to take cover (I'm sure the rest of us did); he never "batted an eye" but continued at an even pace, talking, asking questions and stopping here and there to observe some particular point. I overheard one of our men say: "*General* Turner? General *Hell!* he ain't no general; *he's* a reg'lar *soldier.*"

On the night of the sixth we were relieved and, next day, took up our quarters in Dickebusch. The Emma Gees had taken possession of a bank building, about the best in town, and had strengthened it, inside and out, with steel and sand-bags until it looked as though it would withstand any bombardment. Fortunately it was not hit while we were there, although many large shells fell very near; but when I again passed that way, just a week later, I noticed that a big shell had gone through our carefully prepared "bombproof" and completely wrecked it. We only remained a few days and then received orders to go into the front line at Hill 60 (south of Hooge), as an attack was to be made to recover the trenches lost on the second.

As we had never been in the sector it was necessary for the non-commissioned officers to go in a day ahead to locate the gun positions and be able to guide the section in. We went in in daylight (the non-coms.) and found it to be the longest trip we had ever undertaken on such a mission. From Bedford House, on the reserve line, it is at least two miles to the front line, all the way exposed to observation and fire. There had been a little trench tramway but it had been wrecked by shells. By breaking our party up into twos we escaped any severe shelling and the rifle fire was at such long range that we ignored it. Beyond three hundred yards the German's shooting is a joke.

We went over the position which extends from what was known as the Ravine, to a point exactly opposite Hill 60. At some places the lines were less than forty yards apart and it was possible to throw hand grenades back and forth. It required the entire day to familiarize ourselves with the wonderful maze of communication and support trenches at this place, as we had never seen anything like it before. We had become so accustomed to doing without communication trenches that they were a distinct novelty. They, together with the many support trenches, made a perfect labyrinth: like a spider's web, only not quite so regular in form.

> The map on the opposite page is a reproduction of what is known as "Hollebeke Trench Map—Part of Sheet 28." Famous Hill 60 is shown encircled by a contour line, just below Zwarteleen. The road running off at top and left of map leads to Ypres. The black and white line immediately to the right of this army road is the railroad from Ypres to Comines. The fine irregular lines represent the perfect network of main and communication German trenches. Various signs indicate supply dumps, dugouts, mine craters, observation posts, earthworks, mine craters fortified, hedges, fences or ditches, churches, mills, roads, footpaths, entanglements, ground cut up by artillery fire, etc., etc. The British front-line trench is shown very faintly on this reproduction but can be picked up as it passes through the first "e" in Zwarteleen and traced up past the figure 30. At the left of Zwarteleen it can be seen crossing the railroad and army road. This map, as were the others, was carried by Captain McBride and the section shown represents about one-sixth of the total size. It was made from photographs taken by Allied aviators. The blurred line bisecting the map just below figures 35 and 36 is one of the well worn folds in the map.

The next night we moved in. As the battalion was crossing the long open stretch we came under fire from an enemy machine gun and some men were hit. There's no use talking, no other weapon used in the war is as deadly as a machine gun. Where you can walk through an artillery barrage with a few casualties, the well-directed fire of only one machine gun will pile men up as fast as they come along. When one of them catches you in the open the only thing to do is to drop into the nearest hole and stay there until the firing ceases.

We went in on the night of the twelfth and the attack was scheduled for the night of the thirteenth, or rather the morning of the fourteenth, as the preliminary bombardment was to commence at twelve-forty-five and "zero" was one-thirty a.m.

This was the greatest place I have ever seen for rifle grenades and "Minnies." They came over in flocks or shoals and one must be everlastingly on the lookout to dodge them. But we had as many as they and also a lot of Stokes guns which seemed to "put the fear of God" into the boche. They sprung a new "Minnie" here, much larger than any we had seen. It hurled a whale of a shell; not less than one hundred and sixty pounds of pure T. N. T., and what it did to our trenches

and dug-outs was a sin. And the worst of it was, they had it in a hole in a deep railroad cutting at the bottom of Hill 60, where our artillery could not reach it.

At this time we had both the regular machine guns and also a lot of Lewis automatic rifles. Shortly after, the latter were turned over to the infantry companies, while the former were taken into the newly-organized machine gun corps, an entirely separate branch of the service, which was under the direct command of the brigade commander. The guns were distributed along the line in favourable locations for either defence or offense but, as there were no prepared emplacements, the men had but little protection.

Here our work, as at St. Eloi, was to support the advance; in fact, that is the normal function of machine guns in an attack, although the lighter automatic rifles of the Lewis type are usually with the assaulting troops.

Our "Higher Command" had learned a lesson from the St. Eloi experience and had brought up many new batteries, including a fair sprinkling of the "super-heavies" of twelve and fifteen-inch calibres. It has been said, on good authority, that we had more than one thousand guns concentrated on about a thousand yards of trench, or a gun to every yard, and I am perfectly willing to believe it after hearing them all at work. It was our first experience of that delightful situation where we had "superiority of fire" and it made everybody happy. Afterward, on the Somme and Ancre, it had become a permanent condition; but to us, who had been "carrying on" under the overwhelming odds of the German guns, it was a welcome change. It did our hearts good to hear those monster thirteen hundred and fifty pound "babies" coming over our heads with a "*woosh*" and landing in the lines across the way, on Hill 60, where they left marks like mine craters. We could put up with quite a lot just to see that, and although we were suffering considerably from the rifle grenades and the "Minnies," every one appeared to be in a good humour.

With everything ready we waited for the "zero" hour. Exactly at the designated time the artillery opened. It was as though all the hounds of hell were let loose. Such a wailing and screeching and hissing as filled the air, from the eighteen-pounders ("whizz-bangs"), which seemed to just shave our own parapet, to the gigantic missiles from the "How-guns," as the Howitzers are affectionately called, each with its own peculiar noise. The explosions became merged into a continual roaring crash, without pause or break. Then our Stokes guns joined in, and, if there ever was an infernal machine, that is it. Vomiting out shells as fast as they can be fed into its hungry maw; so fast, indeed, that it is possible for seven of them to be in the air at one time, from one gun, at a range of less than four hundred yards, it is the last word in rapid-fire artillery.

Of course the Emma Gees started at the head of the procession and kept up a continuous fire.

Fritz soon began to do the best he could but, what with the noise of our own guns and the bursting shells, we were unable to hear his unless they struck very close. He did give us trouble, though, with that devilish *Minenwerfer* which sent over a wheel-barrow load of high explosive at each shot. He blew the left end of our line "off the map" for a distance of a hundred yards or more and made it untenable—for any one but a machine gunner. The infantry was ordered to evacuate that part and did so, but not the Emma Gees; they stuck until one of the big "terrors," striking alongside, killed and wounded all the crew but one and then he still stuck it, loading and firing until I was able to get a reserve crew up to relieve him. He was a Scot, one of the kind that doesn't know what it means to quit. Here's to you, "Wullie" Shepherd, wherever you are!

The attack was carried off with absolute precision. At one-thirty the barrage lifted and over the boys went, sweeping everything before them, back to the original position and then a little farther for good measure. By daylight they had the new line so well consolidated that Fritz was never able to make a dent in it and the Canadian prestige was once more established.

At the left end of our line, where the *Minenwerfer* had done so much damage, was a mine shaft; one of many in that vicinity which our engineers were driving under Hill 60 (they afterward blew it up), and it seemed as though the boche knew of it and was endeavouring to cave it in with the "Minnies." In fact, they did succeed in partly destroying it, but the sheltering roof at the month of the shaft remained in fair condition, and as it was the only protective covering in that neighbourhood, Bouchard and I were sitting inside, with our feet hanging down the shaft, holding down that end of the line. We had relieved the other crew, or rather I had sent them back about two hundred yards along the trench as a precautionary measure and then, feeling that some one *must* remain to keep lookout, decided to take care of the job myself. The boy, of course, insisted upon staying with me.

The big fellows were coming over with regularity (I nearly said monotonous, but those things never get monotonous), and were bursting too close for comfort. Bou had just made a proposition that we sneak over after dark and try to locate the devil-machine and blow it up, when we heard something moving below us in the mine-shaft, and a moment later a mud-encrusted face came up into the light. With an unusually fluent flow of "language," which sounded strangely familiar to me, two men came up the ladder, and as the first one emerged into the daylight he took a look at me and said: "Hello, Mac; it's a long way to Ft. George, isn't it?" When he had removed some of the dirt from his face I recognized a miner, named McLeod, who had once helped rescue me from the Giscome Rapids and afterward worked for me up in British Columbia. He and his partner had been caught in the shaft and had been a day digging themselves out. After a rest of a few minutes they went their way, down the trench, and I never saw or heard of them again.

During the next hour or two I managed to work around through the wreckage of this part of our line, searching for wounded and making a list of the dead. I found none of the former, all having been removed by their companions when they were ordered to evacuate, but I did find a number of bodies which I examined for identification disks or other marks and made a complete record which I afterward turned in to our Headquarters. This is a custom that is always followed, if possible, so that, in the event that your own troops do not return to that spot, a record will be preserved and relatives notified. If this were not done, many would be reported as "missing" which is, to relatives, far more terrible than the knowledge that death has been swift and sure. This is work in which many chaplains have especially distinguished themselves, often working close behind the advancing lines during a battle; writing last messages for the dying and compiling lists of the dead who may or may not be buried at a later date.

In burying dead on the field, every effort is made so to mark the grave that it may afterward be identified and a proper record obtained for the archives of the Graves Registration Commission. The best way is to write all the data, name, regiment and number together with the date, on a piece of paper, place it in a bottle and stick the bottle, neck down, in the top of the grave. If no bottle is available, the next best way is to write the record on a smooth piece of wood with an ordinary lead pencil which will withstand the action of water far better than ink or indelible pencil.

Lewis Machine Gun Squad Observing with Periscope at Hill 60

Here I had my last talk with Bouchard. He was very anxious to go to college and take an engineering course. I suggested Purdue, but he thought he would find it necessary to spend a year or two at some preparatory school. He had heard me speak of Culver and was very much interested in that place, and when I left it was definitely decided that, should he survive the war, he would spend at least four years at any educational institution I might recommend.

As soon as darkness came our infantry returned, and by working hard all night managed to restore the damaged part of the parapet. I went back to my dug-out for a little sleep and had just made myself comfortable when a six-inch shell struck the place and drove me out, together with a companion, George Paudash, a Chippeway Indian and corporal of our section. We had several Indians, there being two pairs of brothers, all from the same reservation and all of them splendid soldiers.

We had several men hit that night by rifle grenades. I particularly remember two: Flanagan and McFarland. The former was hit in numerous places, some of them really serious, but was most concerned over a little scratch on his face which he was afraid would injure his good-looks. McFarland, just a boy, about eighteen, had his left hand terribly mangled and nearly twenty pieces of metal in other parts of his body, but he laughed and called out: "I've got my Blighty; I've got my Blighty." His brother had been shot through both eyes and totally blinded a short time before. By the merest chance I saw McFarland a few days later, as he was being taken aboard a hospital ship at Boulogne and he then gave me his wrist watch, which had been shattered and driven into the flesh, asking that I send it to his father in Canada: I sent it by registered post, from London, but never heard from it.

The artillery fighting continued for several days and on the night of the eighteenth we were relieved and moved back to Bedford House, in reserve.

Next morning I was summoned to Battalion Headquarters and informed that I had been commissioned and was ordered back to England to act as an instructor in one of the training divisions. Our colonel at this time also received his promotion to brigadier-general and he promised, as soon as he was assigned to a brigade, that he would request I be transferred to his command as brigade machine gun officer. He did, afterward, make an effort to have this done, but it was too late. I had finally got my "long Blighty," and was out.

It was hard to part from that old crowd. I did not know when I would get back, but we all knew, without question, that there would be other faces gone from the ranks before we met again. When I did return, during the Somme campaign, I was attached to another battalion and did not often see the Twenty-first and when I did, I recognized but few of them. They had taken part in the great advance of September fifteenth, which captured Courcellette and numerous other towns—the greatest gain ever made in one day on the Western Front until the recent one at Cambrai—and had helped to add another glorious page to Canada's brilliant record. But the cost was great. Many, oh, so many of the bravest and the best fell that day and among them was "my little boy," Bouchard, killed at the age of eighteen, after two years of service.

Yes; a boy in years, but he worked like a man, fought like a man and, thank God he died like a man—out in front, fighting.

CHAPTER 17

Down an Out—For a While

While the following has no direct connection with the machine guns, and is, really, a part of "another story," I think it fitting that I take this opportunity to render my humble tribute of gratitude and admiration for the splendid work of the British Red Cross Society; and that the reader may fully understand, it is necessary to relate the occurrences which led up to my first hospital experience.

Upon returning to England, I was assigned to a Training Battalion at our old camp—Sandling—but found the work so tedious and monotonous that I requested a transfer to other and more active duties, and soon after was engaged first, in conducting troops to France; then, as a messenger to and from the various headquarters; later, on court-martial work at Rouen and Le Havre; and finally reassigned to the Fourth Canadian Brigade and ordered to the front, during the latter part of the Somme Battle. I was with a party of officers of the Gloucestershire and the "Ox and Bucks" (Oxford and Buckinghamshire) Regiments and through an error on the part of the R. T. O. (railway transportation officer) my transportation order was made out the same as theirs, and the first thing I knew I was away over on the right of our line, opposite Combles, where we joined the French. As there was a fight on, I went in with the "Glosters," and after the fall of Combles made my way up the line until I located my own command, near Courcellette.

Here I heard of the great advance of September fifteenth and also of the death of many of my old friends. Among them, it seemed, Bouchard and his crew had been wiped out by a big shell, but no one had been able to get back to look for them or bury them. I was very busy, but getting all available information as to the spot where they were seen to fall, I managed, at night, to make several trips over the ground, but without result. The spot was near the famous "Sugar Refinery," just outside the village, and as this had been one of the hottest places in the fight, there were many bodies lying around but none that I could recognize.

I had a cross made, bearing the names of all the crew and decided that, at the first opportunity, I would plant it at that spot; and when our whole division was ordered out, on October tenth, I took the cross and made my way up the Bapaume road and across the shell-torn field to the place. The enemy was shelling the road, dropping several heavies near me, so I hastily gathered into a shell-hole the remains of all the dead in the immediate vicinity and covered them up as best I could, then placed the cross firmly in the ground and turned to leave. I had not gone far when a "crump" struck so close as to stun and partly bury me. When I regained my senses I found that I could not see. My eyes, especially the left, had been giving me a great deal of trouble ever since I had been hit on the side of the face by a piece of shell at the time of the Bluff fight, but now they appeared to be entirely out of commission, and were very painful.

I lay there for some time, trying to figure some way out of it, all the time hearing the shells coming over. This gave me an idea. Knowing the direction from which the shells came with relation to the location of the road, I started out to make my way there. Troops were continually passing at night and I would be sure to find assistance.

From that time on my remembrance of things is not clear. I have hazy recollections of falling into a trench, crawling out and getting tangled up in some wire and then, I think I fell into another hole. I do remember, distinctly, talking aloud to myself, as though to another person, and telling him to "get down on your knees and crawl, you damn fool: first thing you know you'll fall into one of those deep holes and break your neck."

Whatever I did after that must have been done instinctively. (Was afterward told that I was found, lying stretched out across the Bapaume road.)

The next thing I knew I suddenly discovered that I was trying to *think* of something. I believe I was conscious. I felt as though I *could* move if I wanted to, but didn't want to. I could see nothing, but that also was of no importance. It was something else that was wrong and it worried me in a vague, half-interested sort of way. One thing was sure—I was dead, all right, and it wasn't half bad. Even if I couldn't see or move or think, I was not suffering any pain or inconvenience,

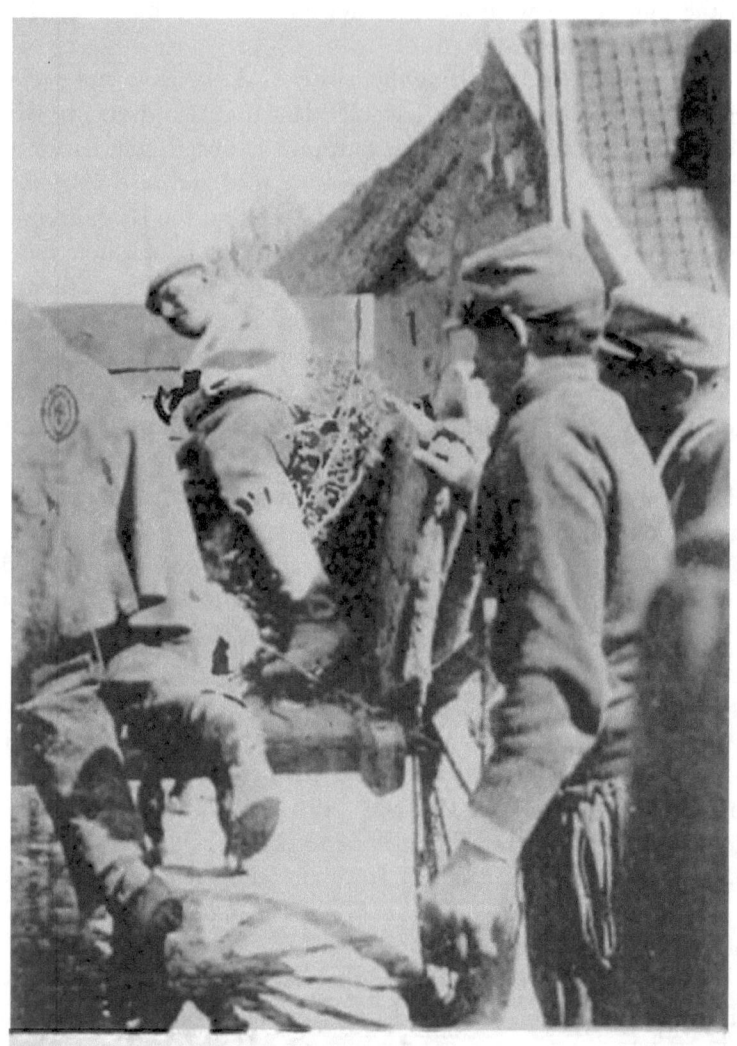

Removing the German wounded from Mont St. Eloi

which was a great relief from "soldiering." Nothing seemed to matter, anyway, and I guess I went to sleep.

I felt, or rather sensed, the presence of others moving about from time to time, but took no interest in the matter until, suddenly, back came the old feeling that something was not right—that there had been a big change in all the affairs of the world—and then, after what seemed hours of struggling with the problem, it came to me like a flash—it was the "quiet" that was bothering me. That was it; there was no noise; and then, my brain becoming clearer all the time, I began to wonder whether I was deaf or whether the war was over. It occurred to me that I might clap my hands or make some movement to find out whether or not I could hear, but the idea was dismissed as involving too much exertion; just as it was too much work to open my eyes to try to see.

Then I *heard* someone come close to me, heard voices, faint and far away they seemed, so I shouted to them (I thought I shouted but it was only a mumbling whisper), and then a voice, low and close at hand, asked me: "Are you awake?"

"Course; what's matter?"

"Nothing is the matter; you're all right now. Don't you think you could eat something?"

I pondered that for some time, but as I was quite comfortable and could not see the sense of dead folks eating, anyhow, I declined and fell asleep again. It was too much trouble to talk, especially to answer questions.

When next I awoke it was different. I actually opened my eyes, or at least one of them, the other being bandaged, and I could see a face looking down at me—a face and a white expanse of something with a brilliant red cross in the centre, and when the face asked me how I felt now and did I think I could eat a little, I grunted something which was intended to assure her that I was feeling all right and was hungry. At any rate, she understood, and disappearing, soon returned with a tray, loaded with things. She first helped me hold up my head while she gave me a tumblerful of hot milk with brandy in it, but that was no good—it would not stay down; so, after a little trouble on that account, she vanished again and came back with a pint bottle of champagne which she opened and fed to me; first a spoonful at a time and then a full glass. That paved the way all right and I was able to eat something, I don't remember just what, but it was good.

By this time I had discovered that I still had all my hands and feet and could move them about. Satisfied on that point, I asked where I was.

"Hospital; but you mustn't talk."

"What hospital; why can't I talk?"

"Number Twelve; but I think you should keep quiet and rest."

"Had plenty rest; where's Number Twelve?"

"St. Pol; but, really, you must go to sleep now."

I went to sleep, wondering how the dickens I happened to be in St. Paul, which was what I understood her to say. (The French spell it differently but pronounce it about the same.)

From that time on, scarcely an hour passed that one of the kindly nurses or sisters did not come in and look to see if I was awake, and if so, could they get me something to eat or drink. It was heaven, all right; or at least, my idea of what heaven should be.

I learned that, although I was disabled on the night of the tenth, I was not picked up until the twelfth and then had been relayed through several dressing stations and hospitals until I landed in Number Twelve General Hospital, at the town of St. Pol. It was a B. R. C. (British Red Cross) institution and was altogether different from my preconceived ideas of hospitals. The day when I first "woke up" was the fifteenth of October, my birthday.

After several days I was put aboard a hospital train and taken to Le Treport, where I was assigned to Lady Murray's Hospital, another B. R. C. place. It had been, before the war, The Golf Hotel, one of the many splendid seaside hotels that have been converted into hospitals. Here, again, I was royally treated. Every wish appeared to be anticipated by the indefatigable and ever-cheerful women and girls, many of them volunteers, members of prominent and even titled families. Lady Murray personally visited every patient at least once a day.

All these ambulances at Le Treport are driven by girls belonging to the V. A. D. I'm not sure whether it means Volunteer Ambulance Department or Volunteer Aid Department, but that is immaterial; they are wonders, whatever name they sail under.

They work all hours, day or night, transferring patients to and from trains and hospitals. They furnished their own uniforms and paid all their own expenses, and for a long time served without any compensation, but I have heard that a small allowance has been made them recently.

The girl who took us down to the train told me that she had been over there two years. I asked her if it was not pretty hard work and she replied: "Oh, sometimes it is hard, when the weather is bad, but we know it is nothing to what the men are doing up in front, so we are glad to be able to do our little bit, wherever we can."

Going down the hill, we passed a big ambulance, filled with wounded, standing alongside the road. A little slip of a girl, who looked as though she weighed about ninety pounds, was changing a tyre and I honestly believe that that tyre and rim weighed as much as she did. Our driver stopped and proffered assistance but the little one declined, remarking that we'd better hurry or she would beat us to the train. As a matter of fact, she was not five minutes after us.

I was in pretty bad shape; could see very little and had an attack of trench fever. As soon as I was able to travel I was sent, with several others, by hospital train to Le Havre, where we went aboard the hospital ship *Carisbrook Castle*, landing at Southampton, and so on to London, where I was lucky enough to draw an assignment to another B. R. C. hospital—Mrs. Pollock's, at 50 Weymouth Street. And here I remained until, passed on by numerous "boards" and subjected to many examinations, I found myself again on the way to France, where I reported the fifth of December—still able to "carry on."

The Canadian "Emma Gees"

Brig.-Gen. R. Brutinel, C.B., C.M.G., D.S.O.
Commanding Canadian Machine Gun Corps, C.E.F.
Advisor Extraordinaire Canadian M. G. Corps. Association

Contents

Preface	143
Introductory	145
Cavalcade—1914-15-16	161
Vimy Ridge	202
Battle of Passchendaele	225
Tense Interlude	247
Motors off Into the Blue	275
Battle of Amiens	293
Drocourt-Queant Line	314
Canal du Nord and Cambria	335
To Mons and Apres le Guerre	358

To the Officers and Men of the Canadian Machine Gun Corps Who Fell In France, this History is Dedicated

Preface

During the Canadian occupation of Bonn, Germany, a Canadian Machine Gun Corps Historical Section was established, in charge of Major Harry Logan, M.C. Capt. Mark Levey was added and with a staff of three or four undertook the task of gathering the necessary data. Moving with Corps Headquarters, the section finally crossed to England and then eventually found itself in Ottawa. Major Logan shortly after resumed his civil occupation and the work was carried on by Capt. Levey until February, 1920. The result of these labours found their way into typewritten script, which, in three volumes, was bound and distributed to six persons. Afterwards another set was subscribed for by other machine gunners interested and again only a few copies were available.

A great many machine gunners who continued on in the militia after the war were not aware of the existence of this history, but as the discussion of the necessity of getting a history written arose from time to time at Canadian M. G. Association meetings, only to be tabled, it was more widely recognized that the History already gathered would be the basis of any further work undertaken.

Upon the disbandment of the C. M. G. C. in 1936, upon reorganisation of the Canadian Militia, it seemed more urgent than ever that something regarding a History should be done.

When the writer first looked over the material collected (it dealt only with battles from Vimy Ridge, where the C. M. G. C. was first authorized) it was recognized that, because of its length, reprinting would run to a sum totally out of reach of available financial resources. The writer, however, believed that the history as it existed could be condensed, given different continuity and narrative structure and as a history could be given abridged form. He therefore volunteered to undertake the task.

Later it seemed only proper that it should be written with a view to having some value to a new generation of machine gunners and so it was necessary to provide a high-lighted background of Machine Gun History.

The Book of the Machine Gun, by Major F.V. Long staff and Capt. A. H. Atteridge, was taken, with the kind permission of the holder of the copyright, Major Longstaff, as the basis of the Introductory Chapter. Many machine gunners of the Great War era were ignorant of the fact that quite an extensive library on machine gunnery of all nations had been written prior to 1914. *The Book of the Machine Gun* may have been followed by many later works, but its general coverage of the Machine Gun s historical background up until 1917, when it was published, still seemed to be adequate today and the tactical principles advocated still as sound as they proved to be during the Great War.

The writer is also indebted to the Historical Section, Department of National Defence, for aid in filling in data from M. G. Company reports dating from the formation of these units down to the Battles of the Somme and including some reports of Hill 70, which latter were missing in the original History.

He recognizes that from a purely History point of view the book will be considered inadequate, but to follow the fortunes, in minute detail, of at least 16 Infantry M. G. Companies from their Battalion Section beginnings and on into their absorption into M. G. Battalions would have required many volumes. Briefly, it seemed more vital that some record should exist, no matter how inadequate, than that the C. M. G. C. should disappear without a trace.

It is hoped, therefore, that this History will be judged by the limitations of finances and space imposed and that if the historical could not be preserved in full detail at least some flavour of the Canadian Machine Gun Corps, its triumphs and vicissitudes, has been retained for those who served and that future machine gunners may derive some value from this account of the Corps phenomenal growth during the war and from incidents in battle, illustrative of the role of the Emma Gees.

July 15th, 1938.

C. S. G.
Timmins, Ont.

CHAPTER 1

Introductory

The genesis of all modern armament is to be found in the simple weapons of antiquity. The siege artillery which shattered the Belgian fortresses barring the immense thrust into Northern France by the German hordes in the Great War was the modern version of the catapult which hurled its huge rocks to crash the thick walls of fortified and beleaguered cities of ancient times. The sling shot of Biblical days was the simple forerunner of the arrow, then the musket and finally the rifle. And it would be perfectly logical to presume that the first of History's Davids to put two or more stones in his sling shot instead of the orthodox one, touched off that inventive spark that was to sputter, flame up, die down and then flame up again and at long last, produce the modern machine gun. You may safely presume also that this innovation caused no end of heated discussion around the tribal fires, if and when they were got going. Indubitably, it would be pointed out that while the intended victim might be made a trifle busier dodging three stones instead of one, the firer had undoubtedly sacrificed something in the way of accuracy.

And if there happened to be a tribal story-teller handy, there also was the beginning of military history. The realms of conjecture and supposition may be left behind at this point. There is historical confirmation of the idea of "multiple missiles." William, Duke of Normandy, threw consternation into the ranks of the sturdy Saxons of our own King Harold and arrows in "sheaves of ten" from a "multiple bow" at the Battle of Hastings. The arrows were discharged simultaneously. The breezes and range saw to it that they were scattered wide enough. It was the first historical bid for a superiority of "fire power" and a saving in man power—the principles of which have actuated the whole evolution of tactical handling of improved armaments right down to this very day. The evolution of the musket and rifle from its bow and arrow origins carried through a lot of centuries. And the "multiple missile" principle was never far behind. Here and there it caught right up. Here and there it lagged—maybe a century behind. The "multiple bow" of the Normans was an adaptation of the bow and arrow.

When gunpowder became a propellant of missiles, the machine gun principle followed right on its heels.

Thus, you have the earliest of machine guns appearing in the 15th century. They were known as "Ribaudequins" or "orgues"—or more plainly organ guns. There were a lot of "stops" in their shattering recitals. It is to be gathered that it was almost as dangerous being the organist as it was the target.

They are mentioned in the histories of sieges in the 15th and 16th centuries and were groups of musket barrels attached to a frame and, ingeniously enough, set off by a matchlock arrangement so that each barrel was fired in succession rather than one loud bang.

The first recorded appearance of the "revolver" principle came in this same 15th century. A revolving butt, however, did not, owing to the lack of precision in boring chambers, fit closely enough to the end of the barrel and the resulting escape of gas quickly wore away the barrel and made them tricky, nasty and dangerous weapons to handle.

However, progress, you may note, was slowly grinding on.

In the 10th century the arrows, you will recall took flight *simultaneously*. Five centuries later, groups of muskets were being fired *in succession*.

There seems to have been a prolonged "stoppage" in the evolution of the machine gun from the 16th century until well on into the 18th.

On May 15th, 1718, there was patented by one James Puckle, in London, a revolving gun. As described in the patent application, this was:

> A portable gun or machine called a defence, that discharges so often and so many bullets and can be so quickly loaden as renders it next to impossible to carry any ship by boarding.

It was also mentioned as another quaint feature of the gun that it was adapted for "shooting square bullets against the Turks and round bullets against Christians."

The Puckle revolving gun, mounted on a tripod of surprisingly advanced design, in appearance is said to have strongly resembled the Gatling.

Before the American Civil War broke out in 1861, there had been a "Requa battery" added to the national armament. It was used in one of the forts at Charleston. It was a multiple barrel weapon with a swinging breech to which was attached a strip of special cartridges, containing both bullet and powder. A hole in the end of each cartridge coincided with a vent in the breech block and these successive vents were connected by a channel filled with black powder. A single percussion cap was used to detonate the priming charge and the barrels were thus discharged in succession and with fair rapidity.

It earned little official notice, but it may have had something to do with inspiring Dr. R. J. Gatling of Chicago, for it was in the next year—1862—that the first of all modern machine guns was invented. It, too, was non-automatic. It consisted of six rifle barrels arranged at equal distances around a shaft which revolved in front of six breech mechanisms, the whole being actuated by a crank on the right side. It was fed from a hopper on top by the force of gravity. In one complete revolution of the barrels around the shaft it fired 10 shots. It was entirely manually operated. It offered continuous fire. With industrious crank-turning it was claimed that 1,200 rounds per minute could be reeled off.

The Gatling was brought out just in time for a few to be used during the Civil War.

And, remarkably enough, they were often operated by employees of the Gatling Gun Company under real conditions of warfare. In the history of arms-selling, most of the "Salesmen of Death" have made mighty sure that they were well out of earshot when t heir merchandise was belching forth destruction. A 10-round salvo from all six barrels seems indicated for these Gatling salesmen. The Gatling's effect on the Civil War produced no immediate echoes in the brooding corridors of Europe's war offices.

Next came, in the mechanical succession of the machine gun, the Montigny *mitrailleuse*, which probably had more far-reaching effects on machine gunnery than its mechanical improvements or departures warranted.

In 1851, M. Montigny, a Belgian engineer, was offered the plans and drawings of a machine gun invention by a compatriot, Captain Fafschamps.

Almost 20 years later, in 1869, the gun, with various improvements, including the adoption of metallic cartridges, was being secretly manufactured in Meudon. On the eve of the outbreak of the Franco-Prussian War the *mitrailleuse* was officially introduced into the French Army. "*Mitraille*" is the word for grape-shot and the new word "*mitrailleuse*," was immediately adopted.

Mechanically, it provided no new principles. Thirty-seven rifled barrels were encased in a wrought-iron tube, looking much like a field gun, even to the mounting. It had a swinging breech-block, allowing for the insertion of a plate of 37 cartridges. The breech-block was then crossed and the gun fired, by the operation of a crank handle.

One complete revolution of this crank handle. in one second, would discharge all 37 barrels. Twelve plates per minute could be fired, thus popping off 444 rounds—which was claimed as a record despite assertions made on behalf of other types of machine guns then in use. It could fire single shots as well.

Now two other types of rifle-calibre machine guns were coming into use. They reverted to the old types of "organ" guns. The first of these was the Nordenfeldt, an invention of a Swedish engineer, Palmerantz. The Gardner followed the Nordenfeldt. The former started with five barrels in 1885, but with improved loading mechanism was ultimately reduced to two.

Up to now all types of guns had been manually operated.

In very short order, however, Mr. (later Sir) Hiram Maxim, an American electrical engineer, was to appear on the scene. In 1883 he applied for the first of a series of patents which were to produce the first automatic-a weapon which, once started, would go on reloading and firing itself as long as pressure was maintained on the firing button-and there was ammunition being fed it.

It is claimed for the Maxim that it is one of the most remarkable inventions ever made, if for no other reason than that the first gun produced was practically perfect and did everything claimed for it. There have been mechanical modifications of the Maxim principles, but in all essentials there have been no real improvements needed.

The first Maxim gun fired between 600 and 700 rounds per minute. Hiram Maxim did not start out to be a gun maker. He had been a successful inventor and was in Europe as the agent of an American electrical concern in the pioneer days of electric lighting. In *My Life*, his autobiography, published in 1915, Sir Hiram recounts a seemingly trivial conversation which led him to explore the field of machine gun making.

In 1881 I visited the Electrical Exhibition in Paris and was made a Chevalier of the Legion of Honour on account of some electrical and chemical work that I had done; and about a year later I was in Vienna, where I met an American Jew, whom I had known in the States. He said: 'Hang your chemistry and electricity. If you wish to make a pile of money, invent something that will enable these Europeans to cut each other's throats with greater facility.' "This made me think of the time when I was only about fourteen years of age and was making drawings for my father of a hand-worked machine gun. I also thought of the powerful kick I got the first time I fired a U. S. military rifle. On my return to Paris I made a very highly finished drawing of an automatic rifle. Happening to meet a Scotchman in Paris, whom I had known in the States, I showed him my drawings. He invited me to come to London. I did so and shortly after I started an experimental shop at 57 Hatton Garden.

There were two patents dated in 1885 which encompassed the form which the Maxim principle and all its modifications was to take.

It was in 1885, too, that the gun was shown at the Inventions Exhibition at South Kensington and that year demonstrations before distinguished visitors, and finally Government trials, resulted in contracts for the manufacture of the gun at the Vickers works in Crayford, Kent. Sir Hiram tells of a gun he invented on request of Lord Wolseley—a gun throwing a long-range projectile which would penetrate barricades and even light armour but yet would stop a rush as effectively as a small gun. The bore was three-quarters on an inch thick. The projectile was made up of lead segments around a steel core, but the real touch of genius came when the gun was to be converted into a short-range blunderbuss. An ingenious device of four cutters bit into the lead segments enough to allow the projectiles to fly apart and act very much like buck-shot out of a super shotgun.

The gun was never used, but out of it came the Pom Pom, a large calibre Maxim gun throwing an explosive shell weighing a little more than a pound. The Hotchkiss, later the machine gun adopted by the French army, followed close on the Maxim trail, as did other forms of automatic guns such as the Colt, Browning, Lewis, Schwarlose (Austrian) and the many other adaptations. In 1905 Capt. von Braun, a well-known German machine gun authority, in his book *Das Maxim*

Maschinengewehr, gives the following statistics of the armies and fleets using the various machine gun systems:

System	Armies	Fleets
Maxim	19	21
Hotchkiss	4	2
Other systems	5	1

Evolution of M. G. Tactics

Two comparatively modern wars, 34 years apart, were to profoundly affect the future of machine guns. The first was the Franco-Prussian War of 1870. The conclusions, largely based on a false premise, drawn from the introduction of the *mitrailleuse* into that sweeping victory for German arms, were to discredit the machine gun and retard the evolution of its tactics for decades. The other war, the Russo-Japanese, which opened in 1904, brought the machine gun a general and startling recognition among the observers of the great and little nations attached to both armies. There was still much groping to be done, however, as the evolution of machine gun tactics ground slowly, but surely, on.

In 1869, as the Montigny *mitrailleuse* was about to be included in the French armament on the eve of the Franco-Prussian War, great secrecy surrounded the actual manufacture of the gun at the Meudon arsenal. Only the officers and men who worked on it were allowed to see or even handle the weapon. Tarpaulins covered the bulky mystery guns as, on mobilisation, they were moved up to the front.

The mystery touch was maintained even among the troops at the front though the French press for some time had been painting fearsome descriptions of the havoc that this new and terrible weapon was going to perform as it mowed down whole battalions of Germans in a matter of mere minutes.

As a matter of fact all this mystery was quite farcical. A British officer, Major Fosbery, had in 1869 included a description of the gun in an article he had contributed to the Royal United Institute's journal on *Mitrailleuses and Their Place in the Wars of the Future*. Major Fosberry, while superintending some of its construction, had suggested improvements which had been carried out in the earlier manufacture of the gun in Belgium. Other nations knew most of the details of its construction.

Therefore it was no surprise to the Germans.

It might well have been a devastating surprise—in effect—had the

French general staff pursued intelligent tactics as an accompaniment to the introduction of the new weapon.

When the French armies were hastily mobilized for the war the *mitrailleuse* immediately displaced a battery in the three-battery group organisation of their artillery.

Ten *mitrailleuses* made up this battery. The extreme range of the *mitrailleuse* was a little over 1,000 yards—just that of their infantry rifle, the *Chassepot*.

Why the French should have substituted the rifle-like fire power of the *mitrailleuse* for a third of their artillery power is best explained by the fact that the tactical use of new rifled field guns—and their longer ranges—was little understood. The French had used them 11 years before against the Italians. But they were still thinking in terms of the smooth bore field pieces, still in use in many European armies. The tactics of the time still indicated that the artillery should go into action on a line with the infantry.

So what seems like incredible folly—and proved so—had some justification.

The application of wrong tactical principles to an improved weapon was not new in 1870 nor, perhaps, will it be avoided in 1970.

The British had made a similar error when the Enfield replaced the old Brown Bess in the Crimean War. Instead of pouring a withering fire into the dense columns of advancing Russians with the longer Enfield range, the British infantry were still thinking in terms of the Brown Bess range. The Enfield fire was the deadlier, but the British suffered needless losses in allowing the Russians to get to Brown Bess range.

The baptism of the *mitrailleuse* came on August 2, 1870, at Saarbruck. The French called it a battle, but it proved to be only a rearguard action fought by a few hundred Prussians in widely extended skirmishing order against a whole French division. With minds aflame from vivid pictures already painted of the havoc to be wrought by "*le infant terrible*" among modern weapons, the Paris correspondents with one accord unsheathed their pencils and wrote furiously of how the new gun had mowed down the Prussians—like corn before a sickle, *mes amis*—and torn wide swathes through the densely packed advancing columns.

It was newspaper fiction which raised, still higher, hopes which were to suffer a corresponding and sickening drop.

At Wisemberg on August 4, 1870, in the mid-morning hours, the *mitrailleuse* was to have its real baptism. The artillery of the German 11th Corps advance guard opened fire on the French position at the Château of Geisberg. *Voila!* a battery of *mitrailleuse* galloped up to make a chattering reply to the Krupp guns, by which they were outranged by many hundreds of yards. The French battery swung into action on a knoll, nicely, and accommodatingly marked by three poplars. With such a fine ranging mark the Prussians got right on the target and a Prussian shell blew up one of the ammunition wagons, mortally wounding General Duoay. Without hope of meeting the German artillery range, the battery had to be quickly withdrawn.

The lesson was not quickly assimilated and in other cases the same tactics were pursued—with equally sad, tragic results.

There cropped up the inevitable exceptions, however, and one came in the same month at Gravelotte on the 18th. There the French moved the *mitrailleuse*s up and placed them in small groups in their infantry firing line.

The German official history in describing the action on the French left at Montigny-le-Grange (an odd coincidence since the *mitrailleuse* was the Montigny) gives the *mitrailleuse* its first real credit mark. It says:

> While the action was thus developing upon the principal line of the battle of the 3rd Division, three battalions of the advanced guard were having a partial engagement in the vicinity of Chautreune. Two companies of the 36th Regiment had been led from Chautreune to the slope which rises from the east, but, as in the wood, they did not succeed in pushing farther forward, for the open ground was entirely under the fire of the French infantry posted in the same wood and in the cluster of trees west of La Folie and Montigny-le-Grange. From this point, notably, a battery of *mitrailleuse*s swept the border north of the cluster of trees, and another battery from the south angle of this cluster held under its fire the clearing which separates it from the Bois des Genivaux. In a short time General von Blumenthal saw the impossibility of an attack upon Le Folie. The position of the 36th Regiment on the open ground afforded it very little shelter against the enemy's musketry and *mitrailleuse*s, so its losses gradually reached a very high figure while the French generally kept themselves defiladed or outside the action of the needle gun.

In the same battle and in the French centre at Bois de la Cusse in front of Amanvillers, the *mitrailleuse* was used with the infantry and a battery coming into action at the right moment led to the capture of the only German guns lost during the war. The Germans had made a few errors of calculation to present this opportunity for the *mitrailleuse*, for the German guns had been pushed forward into dangerous range of the French line, believing this line did not extend to the north of Amanvillers.

The German account of the affair is:

> At this moment the artillery in position on the ridge to the south of the Bois de la Cusse was placed in extremely critical situation. A battery of *mitrailleuses* had debouched in front of d'Amanvillers and fired directly and with excellent range upon the extreme left of the line of Prussian artillery. This point was occupied by the fourth heavy battery already seriously injured by musketry. In a few moments the fire of the *mitrailleuses* so decimated it that several officers, five chiefs of pieces and forty men were disabled and nearly all the horses were killed or wounded. Such was the situation when, suddenly, large detachments of the enemy's infantry rose from a ravine in front of the ridge and threw themselves upon the defenceless battery. Its chiefs, already wounded, succeeded with a few horses still untouched and after desperate efforts in getting two pieces back to the border of the wood, but the rest of the pieces fell into the enemy's possession.

Practically half of the machine gun batteries of the French were captured at Sedan—the other half were beleaguered in Metz with Bazaine's army.

French faith in the *mitrailleuse* persisted to the extent that new guns were manufactured in workshops hastily organised far back on the Loire. Guns were bought abroad, including Gatlings, but trained personnel was almost totally lacking.

It is recorded that at Le Mans, January 1871, there was a very successful use made of the Gatlings in the defence of the plateau of Anvours and the crossings of the River Huisne. They were used intelligently, kept out of sight of the German artillery and burst with surprise effect on enemy infantry. They were used right in the trenches in the French centre.

The Germans had used the machine gun infrequently. They had a type called "*Feld*" and a battery of these guns (four) with the Bavarians at Coulommieres in the Loire campaign, in a 1,000-yard duel with French artillery, quickly silenced their heavier adversaries and later helped repulse three French infantry attacks.

The *mitrailleuse*, unhappily, as the medium of so many high hopes came in for a great deal of undeserved opprobrium from even the French themselves, as a result of the general debacle.

Among foreign military observers, the failures of the *mitrailleuse*s tended almost to obscure its demonstrated possibilities and potentialities when used with some intelligence and within limits which should have been obvious from the outset, it would seem.

The *mitrailleuses* were not quite cast into the outer darkness. It was granted to be a possibly useful weapon within very narrow limits, such as the defence of narrow passes and defiles and the flanking of fortifications. Naval authorities, concerned with power effect and having no wide range of tactical problems to consider, saw its possibilities as a weapon for the fighting tops of warships; in its larger calibres as an anti-torpedo boat armament and equipment for small armed river craft and landing parties.

After 1870, Russia was the first European nation to extensively add machine guns to its armament. Russia had, in fact, made a large purchase in 1871 of Gatlings. The Gatling continued to hold sway. Japan was among the many nations which became good customers.

Innumerable wars, now rated as minor, of the British were to keep the machine gun making a few converts. Lord Chelmsford, after the Zulu War of 1879, was to confirm their good execution against wild frontal charges of the Zulus. He was to emphasize their value in small, isolated posts against numerical odds.

He relates incidents in which the Gatlings figured at Ekowe and again at Ulundi, the first in defence of a *laager* and the other in the centre of a British square. They jammed for one thing. For a short time they committed great execution.

He concludes:

> The Gatlings, however, required too much care in firing and could not be entrusted to any but skilled manipulators. If a machine gun can be invented that may safely be entrusted to infantry soldiers to work and could be fired very much as one grinds an organ, I am satisfied of its great value. They should. however, in my opinion not be attached to artillery, but should

be considered as essentially an infantry weapon and worked by infantry soldiers. So utilised, they might, I feel sure, be used not only in defence but in covering the last stage of an infantry attack upon a position where the troops have ceased firing and are endeavouring to get home with the bayonet.

Thus 10 years after the Franco-Prussian War machine guns were still hampered by the notion that it was a new type of field gun.

In the Soudan and the Burmese War the machine gun earned modest bits of praise.

The Maxim gun was first used by the British troops on the North-West frontier of India. In 1895 they were to do very useful work in the march to the relief of Chitral against the rushes of the Ghazis at the Malakand Pass.

The general trend of British military opinion was to consign the machine gun to work in its colonial outposts, where its magical qualities in the eyes of uncivilized tribes humorously outweighed any serious consideration it might merit in more serious situations.

The machine gun's next demonstration in battle between ranking powers came in the Spanish-American War of 1898. There was a battery of four Gatling guns with General Shafter's army in Cuba, hastily improvised after the American landing. At the Battle of Santiago these guns were sent into the firing line and brought a hail of bullets to bear on the Spaniards entrenched on the crest of San Juan Hill. Three guns fired 6,000 rounds and Lieut. Parker, who commanded the battery, claims that it was this fire that made possible the successful assault on the hill.

Lieut. Parker's *Tactical Organisation and Uses of Machine Guns in the Field*, issued in 1889, even if based on very slight actual experience, was reinforced by an apparently broad knowledge of the world's growing literature on the subject of machine gunnery.

Aside from his prophetic tactical vision, which afterwards was to become uncannily true in many details, he gave some thought to the human element—the type of soldier he thought should man the machine guns of the future. In part he writes:

> The machine gun man must be hot-blooded and dashing. He must have all the verve and *élan* of the best light cavalry, all the resisting power of stolid and immovable infantry. He is not to reason on abstruse theorems, nor approximate difficult ranges; his part is to dash into the hell of musketry, the storm of battle

and to rule that storm by the superior rapidity and accuracy of his fire. The characteristics of the machine gun crew are therefore different from those of the artillery of the future, and it may be added, the artillery of the present. . . . The experience of the battlefield has demonstrated that a greater degree of independent action pertains to the machine guns than is the case with the artillery.

The South African War proved little for—or against—machine guns. The arm was used merely as a supplement to infantry and cavalry. Modern machine gunnery would perhaps—in fact definitely would—have made a great deal of the shifty targets the well-concealed Boer burghers offered. There was a lack of tactical knowledge on the part of the British, a low standard of training in personnel, though here and there exceptional, keen officers were able to do well with their guns. If anything, the machine gun may be considered to have lost further prestige on the *veldt*.

The sporadic bursts of Gatling fire were drowned out by the crackle of musketry fire in the South African scene.

The echo had hardly died away, however, when there came the real dawn—for machine gunnery.

What had happened in two decades before the opening of the Russian-Japanese War had merely been a sort of false dawn, breaking into the murk which spread over the evolution of machine gun tactics after Sedan.

The hostilities in the Far East, opened by Japan without formal declaration of war, found machine guns in considerable numbers on both sides. The Russians had the Maxim; the Japs were using the Hotchkiss. The Russians used eight-gun batteries, while the Japs used six, but the latter, in addition, detailed two-gun sections to the infantry.

Exceptionally heavy losses to the *Czar's* machine gunners at the Battle of the Yalu led the Russians to substitute a tripod for the field gun mounting of their batteries. Thereafter, within the limitations of their own generalship and the steady pressure of circumstances that exerted themselves in a losing campaign, the Russians were to contribute to this nursery of modern machine gun tactics almost as valuable material as the alert Japanese.

The hawk-eyed observers of the Great Powers were with both forces. On the part of most of them, especially the German, the machine gun received as searching analysis as any arm.

General Sir Ian Hamilton, following the campaign, published his *Staff Officer's Scrap-book During the Russo-Japanese War* in two volumes.

These books, valuable as they were, and are, with regard to the development of artillery and infantry fire, made little mention of machine guns. Since a Japanese officer claimed that little general use of the machine gun was made before the Battle of Sha-Ho, the one machine gun incident described by Sir Ian must have struck him as merely a dramatic and isolated episode, though it was to be repeated with valuable variations many, many times later.

Sir Ian wrote:

On October 9th and 10th 1,500 Cossacks, with their battery of horse artillery, attempted nothing decisive but hung about between Penchiho and Chaotao as if waiting for the fall of the former place. On the 11th Prince Kanin with the 2nd Cavalry Brigade and six Hotchkiss machine guns arrived at Chaotao and thus anticipated the Cossacks in making a raid, which everyone here has consistently assumed they must make.... Today (October 12th) at 3 a.m. Prince Kanin marched on Penchiho. At Senkin Pass he had a skirmish and drove the Cossacks back northward. As I had already noted, the Russians in their attack on Penchiho had been trying to envelop the place, and their extreme left had actually worked around along the River Tai-Tsu, due south of the defence line.

Thus on the extreme right the defenders were thrown back like the letter 'S' along the tops of the mountains, whose slopes ran down into the river, whilst the Russians, with their backs to the river and their faces to the north, were half way up the slope, still endeavouring to effect a lodgement on the crest line. After the skirmish of Senkin Pass, the Cossacks fell back as far as the Tai-tsu-ho, where they still interposed between the advancing Japanese cavalry brigade and their own infantry, who on the northern bank were busily engaged with the defenders of Penchiho. On the nearer approach of Prince Kanin, however, the Cossacks shifted their position eastwards, still covering their unconscious infantry so as to forbid the Japanese cavalry from making any attempt to cross the Tai-tsu-ho, but leaving it open for them to occupy some high ground on the southern bank which was in effective rifle range of the Russian camp, which was on the other side of the river.

Prince Kanin is not the sort of man who would miss good chances, and certainly on this occasion he seems to have unhesitatingly seized the ripe gift offered him by fortune. Stealthily manoeuvring his six machine guns into position on a high and broken spur which ran down to the water's edge, he suddenly opened a hellish rain of bullets upon the Russian battalions, who, at half past eleven o'clock, were comfortably eating their dinners. In less than one minute hundreds of these poor fellows were killed, and the rest were flying eastwards in disorder.

Next moment the Hotchkisses were switched on the Russian firing line, who, with their backs to the river and their attention concentrated on Penchiho, were fighting in trenches about halfway up the slope of the mountain. These, before they could realise what had happened, found themselves being pelted with bullets from the rear. No troops could stand such treatment for long and in less than no time the two brigades of Russians which had formed the extreme left of Stackleberg's attack, were in full retreat. Altogether the six machine guns had accounted for, according to the first dispatch, 1,000; according to the second, 1,300 Russians.

The effect of the Manchurian campaign was to open a whole new field of tactics to the machine gun, and of all the nations, Germany was the first to realise it and to reap the most valuable harvest.

Practically every phase of later tactics and even fire direction and control had their foundation in Manchuria. And no role was more emphasized than the value of the machine gun in the offensive. In the last stage of the Battle of Mukden, it has been pointed out, no less than four batteries were used to beat down the fire of a Russian detachment holding the buildings and enclosures of a Chinese farm and under this 24-gun storm the garrison hastily abandoned the position. It was the climax to a growing tendency to the use of massed machine guns.

There in that incident might have been the cradle of machine gun barrage fire, to come later—much later.

The general effect of the war in the Far East was an immense stimulation of thought directed to machine gun and a vast output of literature and resulting study, out of which tactical doctrines began to be formulated in most armies.

Perhaps reports drifting back from the Manchurian battlefields on machine guns interested no German more than the *Kaiser* himself. Soon after Sir Hiram Maxim invented his gun the *Kaiser*, then crown prince, saw it in Berlin. His immediate enthusiasm, temporarily at least, found itself cooled off against the cold, implacable conviction of the German General Staff that the machine gun was useless for a European war. They were sticking stolidly to the post-war convictions of 1870. In 1887 at Queen Victoria's Jubilee, accompanied by a group of German cavalry officers, Crown Prinz Wilhelm paid a visit to the 10th Hussars at Hounslow and so intrigued was he by their machine gun equipment that, on his return, he ordered a gun to be sent over to Germany.

Due in no small measure to the *Kaiser's* personal enthusiasm and interest for and in machine guns, Maxim batteries of four guns were introduced at the German manoeuvres two years later. Out of his own personal pocket Emperor William provided a machine gun of the same type for each of the Dragoon Regiments of the Guard.

German army Field Service Regulations of 1908 indicate to what a high peak of specialisation machine gunnery had been brought in the German Army.

Special regulations as late as 1912 indicate that machine gunners had become a sort of *Corps d'Elite*. The Germans then possessed two different kinds of machine gun batteries—the Machine Gun Company and the Detachment. Companies had been attached to each regiment, corresponding roughly to a British brigade. A six-gun company, it was to work with the regiment normally or be detached, in pairs, to battalions.

The detachment was non-regimental and an independent unit usually attached to cavalry brigades. Motor car detachments had also been formed.

Great Britain lagged considerably behind this procession.

In 1909, however, machine gun sections were given two guns instead of one. Some special courses were given at Hythe. Training seemed to be most haphazard. Officers on the strength of a short machine gun course commanded machine gun sections for a while and then left to take company promotion. If they were enthusiasts they departed to spread a leavening influence in favour of machine guns throughout the service. If they had failed to become enthusiasts, they were distinctly a negative influence. Thus the personal balance swayed.

"The Machine Gun Is a Weapon of Opportunit-ee" probably sang the little band of British machine gun enthusiasts in a Gilbertian refrain.

And they had some reason for song.

Even if they felt that they were isolated outposts, surrounded by conflicting opinion, that opinion was no longer hostile. At its worst, it was hugely—and deplorably—indifferent.

CHAPTER 2

Cavalcade—1914-15-16

It is July—and Canada in July of 1914 was a pleasant land, sweltering in the summer sun but bordered by two mighty oceans, dotted with big and little lakes to which a great part of the vacationing public had repaired for the summer, had spent its two weeks or had annual holidays in prospect.

True, there had been sporadic labour troubles starting in 1913; there was somewhat of a financial stringency being faced. It was being said that perhaps this sprawling young giant of a nation had been too optimistic in its building of vast networks of railways, in its rapid development of huge area into which some of Europe's mightiest nations could be dropped and be lost to sight. There was some feeling of unrest—a sense of vast change portending in the world.

But Canada was on the whole a happy land, offering every contrast in physical features that the mind could envision—and possessing a sense of freedom of movement for which there was every scope.

On June 28th in some little city called Sarajevo, in some little-known province of Bosnia, the Archduke Ferdinand, heir to the throne of the Dual Monarchy, had been assassinated. The papers were full of the incident and its potentially grave implications.

Young Canada had no thought of implications in Europe. It was at that moment too engrossed with the growing dance craze. It had just mastered the tango, which at least had grace, and then all of a sudden had turned to the Turkey Trot, the Bunny Hug and other forms of the dance which sent a shudder through Victorian matrons.

Young Canada had just more sensibly restricted its flaring peg-top trousers and loosened the mirth-provoking restrictions of the hobble skirt.

True, a somewhat older Canada was thinking of more serious

things.

A few years before Canada had refused to vote money for a navy to protect her own shores or a contribution to the British navy. In the controversy over naval matters a strong anti-Imperial trend of thinking was exposed. Signs had been often seen on factories, "No Englishman Need Apply."

A small group of the Conservative Government then in power, including Sir Robert Borden, Prime Minister, and the truculent Sir Sam Hughes, Minister of Militia, had been warning the Dominion that Germany meant war. But Canada had never committed herself to help Britain in war.

In June, under the energetic Hughes regime, the Canadian militia, made more efficient than it had been for years, had held its summer camps. As the militiamen left from various hamlets in their red coats and their white pith helmets they aroused only passing military ardor in the youngsters who watched them depart. Politicians had made the subject of increased militia expenditures the medium of bitter jibes at "this war talk." By the public at large the Canadian militia was looked upon with mild tolerance but little martial pride.

At those militia camps in June there had been perhaps some desultory talk of some war of the future that was sure to come, but it was in generally vague terms. There was more resentment over the fact that Sir Sam Hughes had banned the wet canteen from the camps than there was active dislike and distrust of Kaiser Wilhelm of Germany.

There had been no talk of machine guns as the infantry after their first few days of camp managed to disentangle themselves from forming fours and the more elementary evolutions of drill preparatory to the mimic battle which always climaxed such camps.

Of course they had heard of machine guns but they excited no great amount of curiosity. Few officers or men had even seen a machine gun. The only one officially on record belonged at that time to the 43rd Battalion at Ottawa and officers who had taken courses at Ottawa had been shown the machine gun. It left them unimpressed, one gathers. They had enough troubles of their own with section and platoon drill and with musketry. Bisley each year kept alive the pride of Canadians in their rifle shooting. Whatever the Canadian militia lacked in smartness, discipline and other attributes of efficient military training, its shooting was of a high order.

In fact, few members of the Canadian militia knew that the machine gun had already played a debatable part in Canadian history.

In the Northwest Rebellion of 1885 both the columns of Gen. Middleton and Col. Otter had had Gatling guns, over which Capt. "Gat" Howard, an officer of the regular forces in the United States, exercised control.

George G. Stanley, in his book *The Birth of Western Canada*, in summarising very briefly the actions at Cut Knife Creek and later at Batoche, mentions the Gatlings.

Of Cut Knife Creek he says that Col. Otter's force had not succeeded in surprising the encampment of Chief Poundmaker and his Indians, but they did win the race to Cut Knife Hill as the Indians had discovered their approach at daybreak.

The account says:

> As the Mounted Police and the gunners reached the crest of the hill the Indians fell back into the coulees surrounding it. Taking advantage of the cover thus afforded by the trees and the shrubbery, they worked their way around until they had practically surrounded the troops, and from their concealed positions poured a rapid cross-fire upon the soldiers as they lay exposed upon the hill. For seven hours the fight continued. Finally, with his men exhausted by the all-night march and the hunger and fatigue of the engagement, and realising that his position would become more and more untenable as darkness descended, Otter gave the order to retire. The line of retreat was cleared by a charge, and the column, under cover of fire from the cannon and the *machine gun*, made its way over the creek and up the hill on the other side.

That was on May 2nd.

On May 7th, Gen. Middleton's column, which had been divided to each bank of the South Saskatchewan River, the course of which was followed, began to move toward Batoche. The column was attended by the steamer *Northcote*.

The account says that Middleton found the rebel position well chosen. The approach to Batoche was defended by a line of rifle pits or trenches along the edge of the river bank. The main position of the rebels extended along a range of hills running parallel to the river and forming the eastern slope of the valley. The slopes of these hills were fairly well wooded and cut by several coulees, which afforded excellent protection to the defenders. Independent of the main line of rifle pits, which extended along the brow of the hill, were many others placed at various points on the face of the hill, which might possibly become a commanding position. The pits were admirably constructed for their purpose. They were about three or four feet deep, with breastworks of logs and earth channelled for the rifle. The effectiveness of these fortifications is shown by the fact that the Metis sustained no serious casualties during the first three days of the engagement.

Of the first day's battle, the account says, "only the rapid fire of the machine gun offered any covering for the movement of Middleton's force." Towards evening Middleton's men would retire into a *zareba* which had been formed about a mile to the rear of the battlefield. On the 11th the troops, under cover of an artillery barrage, advanced to the edge of the hills, engaged in skirmishes with the rebels, suffered a few casualties and then retired into the fortified *zareba* for the night.

Planning a combined movement on May 12th, Middleton had determined to move around the north-east of Batoche with 150 men, one cannon and one Gatling gun. The main body of troops under Col. van Straubenzie was to attack from the south. Owing to a misunderstanding, this force did not launch an assault as they were misled by the silence from Middleton's flank.

The account of the battle runs:

> Middleton was thoroughly displeased, and the Midlanders and grenadiers were sent to take up their old position on the left flank as on the previous day. But upon this occasion there was no holding the men. Led by Cols. Williams and Grassett, they advanced with a cheer, driving the enemy out of the first line of rifle pits. Pushing on, they dashed down the slope toward the village of Batoche itself, scattering the Metis before them. In the meantime the general rushed forward his support. The 90th, Boulton's scouts, the surveyors, the *machine gun* and the batteries followed the charging line and in a few moments Batoche had fallen. The Metis fled to the woods. Any hope of resistance was at an end.

Although the mention of the machine guns seemed to have been modest enough in accounts of the several actions in which they took part, the weapon seems to have been made the cause of a controversy which must have been waged with considerable bitterness through the columns of the press, judging by fragments it has been possible to gather up.

The Canadian Pictorial and Illustrated War News, picked up at random in a military mess library and idly thumbed through, produced the following gem of early machine gun controversy in Canadian military history.

Quoting dispatches, the *Pictorial News* acidly commented in an introductory paragraph as follows:

> The endeavour to make a hero of Lieut. Howard, 'the man with the Gatling,' is still being perpetrated by sections of the press in defiance of all the facts and of any exercise of common sense. *Voila!* One of the latest attempts to carry on the boom first started by a correspondent of *The Toronto Mail*, who was not present at Batoche but for whom Howard asserts he formed a close friendship:
>
> > Ottawa, July 25.—The Gatling Gun used by Capt. Howard, late U. S. A., with such good effect at Batoche arrived here yesterday and was viewed by a great many. There seems to be a very general belief, based upon reports of those who saw the weapon in action, that it was of little use except that perhaps it served to demoralize the enemy and this even it did not do so well as shrapnel. After Batoche, of all the killed on the field but one could be positively said to have been struck by the gun though thousands of rounds were fired. Much difficulty seems to have been experienced in getting the correct range, eyen when practicing at a fixed target, and the general conclusion come to by practical men is that the Gatling is not suited to bush fighting or rough campaign work, however useful it might be in repelling an attack in close order or in clearing a street or defile.
>
> The above is a dispatch to *The Montreal Witness* from an intelligent correspondent."

The machine gun under these explosive auspices should still have been a highly controversial subject in military circles of those summer camps of 1914 but was definitely not. Possibly the comparative silence of the machine gun in South Africa had had much to do with lack of interest in the weapon. These among Canadian militiamen who had delved into military history at all were too intent upon their own branches of the service to give much thought to the machine gun.

Moving toward the end of the hot, sultry days of July, Canada had almost forgotten Sarajevo and the tragedy there when suddenly, on July 23rd, the Austrian Government presented its demands to little Serbia. Acceptance of the demands of the note meant that Serbia was to submit to vassalage under the rule of the Dual Monarchy. The chancelleries of Europe were startled into tremendous exertions.

Even Canada could not fail to see the seriousness of the situation as it now suddenly developed. But there was yet no thought on the part of Canadians generally that they would be anything other than horrified spectators of a European war.

Events moved with incredible speed.

Canadians were dazed and bewildered by the suddenness of it all.

On July 28th Austria-Hungary declared war on Serbia.

On August 1st Germany declared war on Russia.

On August 3rd Germany declared war on France.

On August 4th Germany declared war on Belgium and on that same day Great Britain, as a consequence, declared war on Germany.

There were more declarations almost daily.

On July 30th General Sir Sam Hughes, on his own initiative, had called an emergency meeting of the Militia Council.

It was the first step taken by the aggressive, dynamic Hughes which was to see Canada, in seven short weeks, assemble an army on the crest of a wave of such intense patriotism as even surprised the Dominion itself.

Time has done nothing to dim the story of those days when Canada was the first of the Dominions to offer its help to the Motherland nor the recollections of that tremendous driving force to which Sir Sam Hughes gave full reign and to which Canadians of all classes responded with a will. The miracle that money and determination combined to bring about in establishing Valcartier as a concentration camp, the way in which the tremendous rush of volunteers was handled and units eventually straightened into some semblance of a Division, all in feverish weeks, will always stand as a tribute to Canadian determination and organising ability.

Through the seeming chaos of the first weeks, order was slowly but surely manifesting itself, but in the welter of this early confusion, the reason why men joined the Battalion machine gun sections must only be surmised. One knows from fragments of information gathered here and there that there was no formula of selection. In those early August days there was a veil of silence over what was happening in France, so there was no inspiration from the echoes of the iron chatter of Vickers guns as in their paucity they might be doing their share of the task in keeping the German hordes at bay.

A number of reasons come to mind why men were selected or themselves selected machine gun duty. But they don't add up exactly. Then, as afterwards, all types were attracted to the machine gun sections and in their variation they offered flat contradictions.

In those early days the mechanics of the gun seemed to demand as a prime essential that the would-be machine gunner should be mechanically inclined. As often as not, the exact opposite was true. Men who had a vast yearning that defied analysis, to be machine gunners oftentimes had an equally vast ignorance of anything mechanical and quailed at the sight of a Colt gun which an instructor with a few expert shakes had dissembled into a heap of what looked to them like a pile of ill-assorted gadgets on a rubber sheet. Hours of assembling practice after parade often enabled the mechanically inept to surmount this nightmare of machine gun parts. The rumour—and one of the few army rumours ever to be proven true—that there were no guard or fatigue duties connected with the machine gun sections no doubt helped swell the ranks of the sections. And as fatigues grew in infinite and irritating variety this immunity became an envied distinction in time.

As early as August 20th, among the many individual offers of aid which had been sent to Ottawa was one from a group of prominent citizens who wished to raise and equip, at their own expense, a machine gun unit. Sixteen machine guns, eight armoured cars, six trucks and four automobiles for the use of the officers was the suggested equipment, and when this offer was accepted by Sir Sam Hughes the unit was designated as "The Automobile-Machine Gun Brigade No.1."

Major R. Brutinel was named to command this unit and by September 9th had the personnel recruited. Equipment was a more difficult matter, but by September 21st the officer commanding had succeeded in obtaining guns and cars in the United States. Twenty instead of 16 guns had been obtained and eight trucks instead of six. When the unit assembled in Ottawa 20 *per cent* of the personnel were ex-soldiers, five *per cent* had experience in the Canadian militia and the remainder had no military training.

By September 29th the unit had embarked for England, thereby missing participation in an event which was as dramatic and symbolic as the war was to see—the sailing of the huge armada carrying Canada's first contribution of men to the Motherland, from Gaspe Basin on October 3rd. Thirty-three vessels made up this armada, the greatest fleet of transports ever to be gathered together in modern history and in themselves a tribute to the faith prevalent in the power of Britain's grey watch-dogs of the Seven Seas to see them safely across thousands of miles of ocean in the face of unknown dangers.

Salisbury Plain, scene of Canada's first great concentration camp in England, has never been included among the battle honours of the 1st Division, but many survivors think it should have been, for conditions there were almost unbearable.

While the weather was making it almost impossible to do any training at Salisbury Plain, the Princess Pats, comprised almost entirely of men who had seen service, moved over to Winchester in November 14, where they joined the 80th Brigade of the 27th Division. By January 4th the Pats were in the line at Dickiebush.

Early in January the weather improved at Salisbury, where a serious outbreak of meningitis had added to the misery and discomfort of the Canadians, and conditions became more tolerable.

Battalion M. G. sections, one surmises, were still very vague on training.

In at least one battalion a Transport officer "David Harumed" his section for the M. G. section. This would seem to argue a disturbing lack of *esprit de corps* on the part of the machine gunners or maybe the David Harums of the Transport section knew a good thing when they saw it and had a persuasiveness that could not be denied.

The number of machine guns per battalion had now been raised to four, but some of the Canadian units had as many as eight, contributed by communities or individuals.

On February 4th the king inspected the Canadian Division, drawn up on Salisbury Plain.

Then, and for many, many months afterward, no drill was laid down for machine gun sections and parade formations were more or less a matter of individual taste. In this connection a major-general of the highest integrity relates an anecdote in which the Motor Brigade figures:

> Major Brutinel, having no laid-down formation for inspection, had extemporised for the event. Men were dressed by the wheels of the armoured cars and generally the formation appeared very striking. However, Major Brutinel had a few spare parts left over, including men, and he popped the surplus men

in the cars. His Majesty, wishing to inspect the cars more closely, guided his charger over to one of them and as he was about to peer within one of the surplus men bobbed up and looked into the somewhat startled eyes of his king. The surprise was mutual and was communicated to the king's charger, which reared. Fortunately the king had a firm seat and was in full control of the situation immediately.

But even if the story lacks a trifle on the side of accuracy in some details, it was highly characteristic of similar predicaments in which M. G. formations were often to find themselves in, on and on into the future.

After His Majesty's inspection, it was only a matter, everyone knew, of the specific day and hour of departure for France of the 1st Canadian Division and all ranks were jubilant. The first movements started on February 7th and kept up until the 12th, the troops embarking at Avonmouth. By the 15th all had landed at St. Nazaire. While the division lay east of Hazebrouck, detachments were schooled in the ways of trench warfare near Armentieres. The line at Fleurbaix was occupied on March 3rd. After three weeks, the division moved back to the Estaires area and thence to Oxelaere and Watou, prior to extending the front 4,400 yards on April 17th by relieving the French in the north-east face of the Ypres salient from Gravenstafel to the north of Keerselaere.

Battalion histories already written have told the stories of those days and the historians have not overlooked the stirring part played by the machine gun sections. Unfortunately, many battalions have failed to find a chronicler and so, except for isolated but extremely outstanding incidents in which machine gunners played heroic roles, we can but sketchily follow the fortunes of 12 battalions and their machine gun sections.

There seems little doubt but that, added to our inferiority in the number of machine guns, sections were subject to widely varying ideas of employment. The gravest mistake in their employment was that too often they were committed entirely to the front line instead of to the supports.

Brigade machine gun officers were already functioning. The co-ordination of machine guns on a frontage greater than that of a battalion in operations fell to the B. M. G. O. But, except for special assignments to come later, there was little opportunity at this time of exercising those functions. The machine gun sections were part and parcel of the battalions. The B. M. G. O. did not have command of the guns in action, except those in reserve or explicitly placed under his direction. He performed a valuable function, however, in co-ordinating training when the sections were out of the line. And the appointment was to be more significant than it appeared when first established.

The Canadians had been on the fringe of the Battle of Neuve Chapelle, which commenced with such high hopes on March 10th. The Canadian artillery had actually taken a part in the preparations for this great push which was to be a test of the new British fighting machine and aimed to capture the Auber's ridge, which dominated Lille. The enemy's outposts had been driven in after a charge following the most terrific cannonade of the war to date.

Sir Max Aitken wrote in *Canada in Flanders*:

But beyond these, their fortified places bristled with machine guns which wrought havoc on our troops and, indeed, brought the successful offensive to a close,

Hailed as a great victory, Neuve Chapelle was soon admitted to have been a great failure. A mile of territory along a three-mile front was conceded small recompense for losses that had been extremely heavy before the battle was broken off on the third day.

Princess Pats had won the honour of being the first overseas troops to take part in a major engagement when they were ordered to co-operate in the early morning of March 15th with the battalion of the Rifle Brigade in an attack on the St. Eloi mound, which had been lost to the Germans a few days before. Pats came out of the engagement with a reputation for coolness and resolution, though enemy machine gun fire was credited with smothering the attack from the onset.

When the Canadian battalions took over the line on Gravenstafel ridge they had marched through Ypres, historic Flemish city, with its great Cloth Hall, beautiful cathedral and truly Old World air, as yet untouched by war. Children played in the streets as the Canadians marched through in the early evening and out past the ramparted walls along the road to St. Jean. Some took the right, turning up the Fortuin road at Wieltje; the others took the left road that led up to St. Julien and on to the brooding trenches, now defined in the gently rolling landscape. These earthworks had not been so much dug as they had been built up owing to the soggy nature of the soil. There was no elaborate support system yet dug and the Canadians spent their first few days in the line starting a program which would develop supporting points in the rear.

The Canadian troops woke up to April 22nd—a warm day in which Mars seemed to have dozed off into a spring torpor; on their second tour of the line, the Canadians felt like veterans. The day before, the Germans had bombarded Ypres, a continuance of the wanton destruction of the Flemish city which had commenced on April 20th. But that day a spring drowsiness reigned over the whole front in an area which had already seen the First Battle of Ypres and the Britons of 1914 win imperishable fame as dogged fighters.

At five o'clock in the afternoon the haze was suddenly rent by a violent bombardment. Huge 15-inch shells roared overhead to carry more destruction to Ypres. Suddenly those in reserve saw a yellowish-green cloud ascending over a width of three miles along the front. Soon, on the left, fleeing Turcos could be seen and the curtain in a matter of seconds was rudely yanked up on the Second Battle of Ypres, and Canada's citizen army was face to face with a test that would have been an iron test for the best professional army in the world.

Something of the supernatural will always surround the Second Battle of Ypres. By all the laws of war, all the known standards of the human will to endure, the Canadians should have been driven back in utter confusion and chaotic rout by the masses of Germans flung at them. But, although a wide breach of four miles was opened, Canadians not only held the line but counter-attacked from the exposed flank of the 3rd Brigade and thus prevented the turning of the British line by the use of this inhuman weapon of war—poison gas.

This battle, which raged for many days, was to see heroism hoisted to new pinnacles and, though much of the story has been pieced together, there will be hundreds of acts of courage and devotion forever locked in the breasts of the thousands who fell.

In that fiery furnace of war, the 1st Canadian Division won for Canada the spurs of nationhood and welded together a Canadian military tradition of what had necessarily been fragments.

And there, too, was born the tradition of the Canadian Machine Gun Corps, even though the Corps was yet to be born, for in those raging, desperate days when deeds of surpassing bravery were the rule, it fell to the lot of machine gunners to provide exploits that gained for three of them the highest recognition—the award of the Victoria Cross—and for many others a record of high valour and grim, tenacious courage which was to shed lustre over the machine gun service in the days to come.

On April 23rd, the epic stand of the 3rd Brigade, with its attenuated left flank thrown back to form a sharp salient, was providing feats of heroism on every hand that seemed to make it a commodity common to the Canadians. But on a day of audacious deeds, Major W. B. M. King of the Canadian Field Artillery added an extra dash when he kept his guns in an advanced position, where he deliberately awaited the approach of the Germans until they were within 200 yards. Into the dense masses of Germans he poured a blasting fire and then, with the help of infantrymen of the 14th Battalion, he got his guns away. It was here that Lance-Corporal Fred Fisher of the 13th Battalion came into the picture, bringing up a machine gun to cover the battery's retreat. All four men of his crew were shot down, but he took men from the 14th Battalion and worked his gun until the battery was clear. When the artillerymen were clear, he pushed on ahead to reinforce our thin but determined front line. But as he was getting the gun into position under a hail of shrapnel, machine gun and rifle fire, he was killed. He was awarded the Victoria Cross posthumously.

The next day, the embattled 2nd Brigade, under Currie, were still continuing their glorious stand on the right, and Lieut. Edward Donald Bellew, machine gun officer of the 7th Battalion, had two guns in action on the high ground overlooking Keerselaere. The enemy's attack breaks in full force on the battalion's right and right flank, the latter being exposed owing to a gap in the line. The right company was soon put out of action but the advance of the Germans was temporarily stayed by Bellew, who had sited his guns on the left of the right company. Sergt. Peerless was fighting one gun and Bellew the other. In defiance of the Germans, Bellew hoisted a loaf of bread on a bayonet and drew a perfect fury of fire from them.

Reinforcements were sent forward, but they, in turn, were surrounded and destroyed. With the enemy in strength less than 100 yards from him, with no further assistance in sight and practically surrounded, Bellew and Peerless decided to stay and fight it out. Sergt. Peerless was killed but Bellew fought on, then was wounded and fell. Again he dragged himself to the gun and sent more bursts of fire at the Germans who were crawling toward him. As his gun jammed he raised a rifle and smashed the Colt and, fighting to the last, was taken prisoner. The 7th Battalion had in the space of three days lost its colonel and 600 of its officers and men.

The 8th Battalion (Little Black Devils) was also sorely pressed on that day and next day still more so. Sergt. W. A. Aldritt was personally operating two of the battalion's machine guns from the front line parapet. One gun was soon put out of action but Aldritt continued to turn a withering fire on all advancing Germans, though machine gun and rifle bullets fell like hail around him. When late in the afternoon, after being many times repulsed, the enemy finally broke through on both flanks and almost surrounded the platoon with which he was operating, Aldritt was heard to drawl that "he guessed they were going to be captured but they would work the gun to the last." He continued firing after the remainder of those who could get away had withdrawn and the faster chatter of his Colt gun could still be heard in action after dark. To him fell the award of the little bronze cross—the first of several the gallant Devils were to earn.

Among the mentions received was that of Pte. Young of the 2nd Battalion, who handled his machine gun so well that he was given credit for stopping the German attack on the battalion on the 24th. Later at Givenchy he was to be wounded, but refused to leave his guns until the action was over.

The worn but undaunted 1st Division, which had had its losses made good by drafts and been joined by a dismounted detachment of the Canadian Cavalry Brigade, 1,500 strong, was billeted south of Steenwerk and Bailleul through the first weeks of May. They could hear the echoing thunder of an attack which the British had launched on May 9th. This attack was designed to divert reinforcements being rushed to the Lens front, where Gen. Joffre had launched a big scale attack and had reached the very outskirts of Lens itself. The British attack beat vainly against the impregnable German defences for several days and then was renewed with redoubled fury on May 16th.

Hardly had the echoes of the May 9th attack come to the 1st Canadian Division than there also came some details of the tragic prelude in which the Princess Pats had figured the day before, on May 8th. A night and a day of intense bombardment were climaxed on the 8th by three determined infantry assaults. Trenches were obliterated in the holocaust of fire that swept over the 80th Imperial Brigade area near Bellewaarde Wood.

Epics of human behaviour were blasted into dust-like fragments as the roll call of the Pats, which numbered 635 on the evening of the 7th, had melted away to 153 by 6 p.m. of the 8th. All the senior officers had been killed or wounded early. For most of that tragic, yet glorious day, Lieuts. Niven, Papineau and Vandenberg were the only officers left. Vandenberg, machine gun officer, had already arranged novel forms of rifle batteries among the ingenious devices used when the Pats had taken up their new line around May 4th, and this officer, who was to become somewhat of a legendary figure in the Machine Gun Corps afterward, was until wounded, with Niven and Papineau to direct one of the most stubborn stands in the whole history of the war to come.

Even though the Pats were mostly English reservists, Canada took this tragic stand of the Pats as its own, which it was when the shattered unit was rebuilt.

And once more the machine gunners had played an outstanding role. Two guns up front were buried early but after hours of labour were dug up again and put in order to deal with sniping nests. This brought such an avalanche of fire that they were buried again. Guns and crews were repeatedly buried as the enemy uncannily discovered them.

An account of the Pats in *Canada in the Great War* says:

> Every individual in the regiment proved himself a hero, but special mention must be made of Corp. Dover of No. 4 Company, who disinterred his gun on three different occasions, took it apart, cleaned it and brought it into action, and thrice succeeded in opening a destructive fire on the charging enemy. Dover was the survivor of many gun crews, but his last stand cost him both a leg and an arm, and late that same day this heroic soldier extricated his maimed and broken body from the surrounding debris and trailed his mutilated limbs across the intervening ground towards the former support trench. His moans attracted the attention of some men of the Shropshire Light Infantry and two gallant fellows came out of their trench and carried the wounded man to the parapet. He was then recognised, but as he was being passed up to the arms of comrades waiting to receive him into the comparative safety, a chance bullet, aimed in the darkness, passed through his brain and wrote *finis* to his story.

On May 19th the battered 2nd and 7th British Divisions were withdrawn and the Canadian Division and the 51st Highland (Territorial) Division took up the fight. And thus Festubert was inscrolled on Canada's battle honours and added glory fell to the Canadians in their first attacking role.

Festubert was another milepost in the long road of futile sacrifice still ahead. Canadian casualties were 2,204 as in days of minor but epic thrusts the Canadians penetrated 600 yards on 2,500 yards of front. Once again the performances of the machine gun sections are wrapped up in battalion histories, written or still untold. One general mention made of them is in connection with the attack on the Orchard of the 16th Scottish on May 20th. On the night previous to the attack, two of the battalion's machine guns were located in a deserted house close to the German lines. Next evening at 7.45, when the attack was launched, these two guns replied to a withering fire from German machine guns which swept the Scottish as they climbed out over the trenches. These two guns were credited with keeping the Germans, who had withdrawn to their support trenches in the bombardment, from rushing overland to man their front system in time to meet the Scottish.

Festubert, while a military failure, had vast repercussions. It demonstrated first of all that the German defences were impregnable against such attacks as had been planned, no matter to what heights of heroism the attacking forces might rise.

Sir Max Aitken observed as Canada's "Eyewitness:"

> They had constructed trenches reinforced by concrete-lined galleries and linked them up with underground tunnels. The battle of the miniature fortresses proved the triumph of the machine gun. The Germans employed the machine gun to an extent which turned even a pigsty into Sebastopol.

Festubert, secondly, brought about the accusation in the *London Times* that a shortage of munitions existed and that nothing but high explosives in greater quantities than were then available would blast the Germans from their redoubts. The crisis which brought about the Coalition Government came almost on the heels of Festubert.

On May 31st the Canadian Division was withdrawn to rest.

Givenchy gets but a brief mention in the report of General Sir John French, but within its scope it again made an urgent call on Canadian determination and heroism which was answered in overflowing measure.

The 7th British Division on June 15th had been ordered to make a frontal attack on an enemy strong point known as "Stony Mountain". The 1st Canadian Division was detailed to attack on the right flank of the Imperials and capture two lines of German trenches extending from Stony Mountain to another point known as Dorchester.

To the 1st Canadian Battalion fell the task of making the actual assault.

Two 18-pounder guns of the 4th Battery, C.F.A., had been moved into position in the front line for the assault and cleverly concealed. Sappers had tunnelled a mine toward the German line. The enemy was answering our bombardment viciously but the attacking battalion, which had been waiting since 3 o'clock in the jump-off trench, escaped lightly. Fifteen minutes before the attack swept over the top, the two 18-pounder guns opened fire as false parapets were suddenly lowered. They knocked out two German machine guns. Then the mine exploded, but our own men suffered heavily from the blast. Just at that instant the leading company leaped forward, accompanied by the Battalion Machine Gun Officer, Lieut. Fred Campbell, a farmer hailing from Mt. Forest, Ontario, and a Boer war veteran. Lieut. Campbell's crews had two machine guns.

A deadly fire met the advancing company with its bombing parties on the flank and one of the machine gun crews was wiped out. Several of the other crew were killed, but the survivors reached the German front line trench and then advanced along a trench in the direction of "Stony Mountain". The machine gunners followed a bombing party which found itself suddenly facing a barricade which had been hastily put up by the Germans. The machine gun crew which reached this portion of the trench was reduced to Lieut. Campbell and Pte. Vincent, a lumberjack from Bracebridge, Ont., the machine gun and a tripod. Lieut. Campbell saw a spot to mount the gun but a tripod could not be used.

Pte. Vincent, it is related, suggested that he lay prone and that Lieut. Campbell use his back as a base. This was done and Campbell ran four belts through the Colt, which was getting hotter every minute and scorching Vincent's tunic. Campbell was hit and crawled out of the enemy trench and was carried into the Canadian trench by Comp. Sergt.-Major Owen in a dying condition. Pte. Vincent saved the gun, dragging the blistering hot Colt over the ground as it was too hot to handle. Lieut. Campbell was awarded the V. C. posthumously.

Canada In Flanders relates another incident affecting machine gunners, which happened on the 18th:

About midday in the neighbourhood of 'Duck's Bill', Lieut. E. H. Houghton of Winnipeg, machine gun officer of the 8th Battalion, saw a wounded British soldier lying near the German trench. As soon as dusk fell, he and Pte. Clarke, of the machine gun section, dug a hole in the parapet through which Clarke went and brought in the wounded man, who proved to be a private of the East Yorks. The trenches at this point were only thirty-five yards apart. Pte. Clarke had received a bullet through his cap during his rescue of the wounded Englishman, but he crawled through the hole in the parapet again and went after a Canadian machine gun which had been abandoned within a few yards of the German trench during the recent attack. He brought the gun safely into our trench and the tripod to within a few feet of our parapet. He wished to keep the gun to add to the battery of his own section, but the general officer commanding ruled that it was to be returned to its original battalion and promised Clarke something in its place which he would find less awkward to carry.

And on such glorious incidents as these does the machine gunners' tradition continue to grow and take on added lustre. The legend outstrips them, for in numbers they are still but a small part of the battalion.

The Automobile Machine Gun Brigade, now rechristened the "1st Canadian Motor Machine Gun Brigade," arrived in France on June 16th, just after the echoes of Givenchy had died down. Even though designed for highly mobile duty and arriving at a time when the. fact that the war had settled into an apparent stalemate of trenches stretching from the Vosges to the North Sea was beginning to be recognised by the Allies, the 1st Canadian Motor Machine Gun Brigade was destined in its personnel, rather than in its purely active role, to have a far-reaching effect on Canadian machine gunnery.

The roster of officers who landed in France with the Motors was as follows:

Lieut.-Col. R. Brutinel, Officer Commanding
Lieut. E. D. Wallace, Adjutant
Capt. J. E. Browne, O.C. "A" Battery
Lieut. W. E. C. McCarthy
Lieut. F. A. Wilkin
Capt. C. F. Hawkins, O.C. "B" Battery
Lieut. F. M. Garrison
Lieut. M. A. Scott
Capt. H. H. Donnelly, Q.M. and O.C. Train

Capt. D. MacClennan, M.O.

Canada's war strength was rapidly gathering. The Mother Country, seemingly so remote in 1914, was now bound to Canada by a living chain of khaki-clad soldiers.

By the end of August, 1915, there were 23,431 Canadians in France; in England there were 57,206 and back in the Dominion were 62,362 more of Canada's citizens training for what every man in uniform realised was no idle adventure but a grim struggle of endurance on which the fate of the Empire balanced.

The survivors of Ypres, St. Julien, Festubert and Givenchy, brought to full strength by reinforcing arrangements upon which a totally unexpected strain had been placed, were now veterans in every sense of the word. They spent an uneventful summer in the desolate salient which was at least dry for once. On September 13th, 1915, the Canadian Corps was formed and was immediately joined by the 2nd Canadian Division. On December 24th the formation of the 3rd Division from units already in the field was announced.

Formation of Brigade Machine Gun Companies, most important step to be taken in establishing of Machine Gunnery as a separate arm with tactics peculiarly its own and intermediate between those of infantry and artillery, was authorized on October 29th, 1915

Companies took their names from the brigade to which they were attached.

The mobilisation of the 1st and 2nd Division Brigade companies began in December, 1915. Machine gun sections from the battalions were to form the nucleus for the new Brigade Machine Gun Companies, which had a strength of 10 officers and 161 other ranks.

Colt guns were to be in use until July 16, but in the transition of battalion sections to brigade companies and the arming of the infantry with Lewis guns, there was to be a shortage of guns that was keenly felt.

There was a contradictory appreciation and an indifference to machine guns in the Canadian Corps, but at least the appreciation outweighed the indifference. Canadians already had four guns per battalion when they felt the first hot breath of war in the Salient and, as pointed out before, some units had more.

Canadians, however, who felt that there were still not enough machine guns and couldn't be for the demands this war was making, could not know at that time what was going on behind the scenes.

There are enlightening passages in a book written by Brigadier-General Baker-Carr, founder of the Machine Gun Training Corps, *From Chauffer to Brigadier*, which paint the dismal picture of the British Higher Command's apathy and indifference to machine guns. It was the same command, by the way, which took great pride in the excellent musketry training of the Old Contemptibles and much satisfaction from the fact that the precision of British rifle fire in the retreat from Mons was such that it was mistaken by the Germans for a preponderance of British machine guns, and yet lost entirely the point and lesson of the comparison.

Touching upon his continued urging that machine guns be increased in 1915, Baker-Carr writes:

> The fighting line, at any rate, had awakened to the realisation of the automatic weapon and many commanders were showing themselves eager to learn anything they could which would help to strengthen their front without increasing their men.
> Already I was urging the advisability of doubling the number of machine guns. I had put forward the suggestion, very tentatively, to G. H. Q. and had been promptly told to mind my own business. The commanders of larger units such as armies and army corps did not at that time appreciate the vast saving in man power that could be effected by the substitution of machinery for brawn and it was only when we got within the danger zone that the proposals drew forth a cordial response.

He describes setting up his machine gun school behind the lines, though with little encouragement.

> Not one single member of the staff of G. H. Q. ever took the trouble to pay a visit to the school during the six months that it was quartered in the Artillery Barracks, a quarter of a mile distance from the General Staff Office.

In the summer of 1915, after great pressure from the fighting line, sanction was given to increase the number of machine guns per battalion from two to four. General Carr-Baker writes:

> Within 24 hours of hearing the news I put forward a proposal to double this amended establishment. G. H. Q. was horrified. 'Look here Baker,' I was told indignantly, 'we've given you two extra guns per battalion. You ought to be satisfied.'
> Vainly I pointed out that the additional guns were not a per-

sonal present to me, but a badly needed increase in the arrangement of the fighting troops. But it was useless to argue.

David Lloyd George, war-time Premier of Great Britain says, in *War Memoirs*:

> It is an incredible story for anyone who had no actual experience of the fanatical hostility displayed by the Higher Command to any new ideas.

Continuing to describe the obstacles he faced in trying, upon the formation of the Ministry of Munitions, to overcome the comfortable complacency of the War Office, Lloyd George tells of an incident in which Sir Eric Geddes, who had been placed in charge of the output of rifles and machine guns, figured with Lord Kitchener on the subject of machine guns. He quotes in Geddes' own words:

> I told Kitchener that rifles and machine guns were the same as shillings and pence; that nine rifles were equal to a Lewis automatic gun and thirteen rifles to a Vickers machine gun in the productive effort required for their manufacture. I wanted to know the proportions of each wanted for nine months ahead, so that I could make my plans. His reply was 'Do you think I am God almighty that I can tell you what is wanted nine months ahead?' I replied, 'No sir. And I do not think that I am either but we have to work it out between us and try and get it right.' Then he gave me the old War Office answer, 'I want as much of both as you can produce.'
> My patience was wearing thin, and I think I spoke fairly definitely. I told him of the weeks I had spent trying to get these elementary facts out of his subordinates. Eventually he said that the proportion was to be two machine guns per battalion, four as a maximum, and anything above four was a luxury. That was the opinion of the Secretary of State, who was looked upon generally as our greatest soldier, on 26th of July, 1915.
> I sat down in the War Office and wrote this down. So elated was I at my success in having, at last, got something upon which I could work that I spelt 'luxury' wrong. I asked Kitchener to sign it. He always had a reluctance to sign documents and said that he gave orders and expected them to be obeyed. I replied that doubtless that was the military way but I had been brought up to accept a signature as an authority for money I spent, and

unless he would sign it, the document was no good to me. He walked out of the room. Girouard caught him in the doorway, and said, 'Geddes is like that; he won't act unless you sign a paper.' So Kitchener came back and initialled the document.

A facsimile is reproduced in the *Lloyd George Memoirs* in the firm, slanting handwriting of "K".

Lloyd George admits that he was so indignant when he read the miserable estimate that he would have torn it up had not Geddes rescued it from him. He says Geddes treasures it still.

Lloyd George says Geddes reports him as declaring.

> Geddes reports that I said to him: 'Take Kitchener's maximum, (four per battalion); square it, multiply that result by two; and when you are in sight of that again, double it again for good luck.

However Lloyd George did not mean, he says, that each battalion should have sixty-four guns but that manufacture should be on that scale to provide for all contingencies.

In October, 1915, some three months after the question of the number of guns to be provided had been settled by him, Lloyd George was to run into another baffling maze of War Office apathy which had to it more than a suggestion of deliberate obstructionism.

In that month the project of forming a special Machine Gun Corps received royal assent. He relates:

> This was a plan which I strongly supported. I had been informed of the very effective methods employed by the enemy to get the best results from this weapon-methods involving the use of special machine gun companies, not permanently attached or allotted to any battalion or division.
> But I was greatly alarmed to hear, shortly afterwards, that although this Machine Gun Corps had been authorized, little was being done to make it a reality and hardly any men were being brought into training for it, out of the millions of men that had been recruited. Orders had in fact been issued that no man should be recruited for it or transferred to it from other units. By this date, my capacity for amazement at professional repugnance to new ideas or new formations had reached the saturation point. The estimated deliveries of machine guns by March, 1916, would reach a cumulative total of more than

10,000, and midsummer of over 20,000. No doubt there were many other demands for men being made upon the War Office, but the machine gun was obviously such a formidable factor in defence and attack that only some curious form of unbelief and opposition could be responsible for this, to my mind, otherwise inexplicable and unintelligent failure to train men to make the best use of it. I determined, therefore, at the risk of once again interfering in something which was not departmentally my concern, to ascertain the exact position.

Lloyd George then quotes from a memorandum he laid before the War Committee on Nov. 13, 1915, urging that Britain might make up her shortage in men by obtaining the equivalent fighting value in machine gunners and stated as his opinion, that 50,000 machine gunners could do the work of 250,000 infantrymen. He pointed to the strategic elasticity the Germans had obtained by this procedure.

In this he was ably backed up by General Sir Archibald Murray, then acting Chief of the Imperial General Staff under Lord Kitchener (at that time away in the Mediterranean). He stated that the general staff had actually started a Machine Gun School at Grantham but that the adjutant-general would not supply the men. Lloyd George concludes:

As a result of my pressure the War Council decided to ask the Army Council to provide for 10,000 men to be put continuously under instruction. Actually some considerable delay occurred before this instruction was carried out but eventually a number of men were drafted from various units to the Corps Training Centre, and even then they were not especially picked men, like the German machine gunners, whom Sir Douglas Haig has described as a *corps d'elite*. None the less they added immensely to the efficiency of our army. Four years later, in November 1918, the strength of this new branch of the army, which had been initiated under such difficulties, amounted to 6,427 officers and 123,835 other ranks.

And yet as criminal, almost, as this neglect of the machine gun seems to have been in high places, those who were connected with the machine gun sections in the battalions in 1915, who were either in England or forming and training in Canada, will recall with what indifference their weapon and their work was regarded by the rest of the battalion. True, the legend of the "Suicide Squad" had reached full blown proportions but there was remarkably little interest manifested in the machine gun itself. Machine gun officers were not pestered by requests of even the mechanically-minded to see the guns at close range. Platoon officers were pre-occupied with the task of achieving precision in forming fours and if there was any envy of the M. G. O., it was that he was allowed to wear spurs and riding boots, rather than that he commanded concentrated fire power equal to a company of infantry.

The machine gun section, so often left to its own devices in training and outside the regimentation of the battalion, in its turn developed an individuality of its own. When battalion sections were later absorbed into the M. G. Corps, they were to find there the individuality of the section merely expanded as to scale.

But if there was a shortage of machine guns, there was no shortage of faith in the weapon by Canadians.

1915 had witnessed the formation of many separate machine gun units in Canada. The Eatons, Bordens and the Yukon came along in fast succession and that same year also saw the 86th Battalion of Hamilton, under Lieut.-Col. W. W. Stewart, (later killed at Vimy Ridge) recruited as the first and only machine gun battalion in the British Army.

The Borden Battery, recruited in Ottawa and the mining areas of Cobalt and the Porcupine, had arrived in France on September 15th, 1915, and during the winter of 1915-16 served with the Second Canadian Division.

The officers serving with it on arrival in France were: Major E. J. Holland, V.C., officer commanding; Capt. P. A. G. McCarthy, Lieut. W. F. Battersby, Lieut. E. H. Holland, Lieut. J. H. Rattray.

The Eaton Battery crossed to France the night of February 24th-25th, 1916, and operated as Divisional troops under the 3rd Division, the battery having been formed from the original Eaton M. G. Brigade, most of which had been sent to France as drafts for other M. G. units. The officers serving with this battery were: Major E. L. Knight, Lieuts. W. A. Holloway, P. McMurdoch and E. Osborne.

The unit first known as the Boyle Mounted Machine Gun Detachment, and raised by Yukon Joe (later Lieut.-Col.) Boyle in Dawson City, Yukon Territory, had been attached to the Eaton M. G. Brigade. They were not on establishment and had no guns or equipment for many months. Through the winter of 1915-16, they remained at Shorncliffe and then 33 of the 50 originals who had not been selected for drafts to France were formed into a battery which later became attached to the 4th Division in training at Bramshott, as divisional troops. The officers who eventually proceeded to France with the unit were: Capt. H. F.V. Muerling, officer commanding; Lieut. R. D. Harkness, Lieut. W. C. Nicholson, Lieut. H. H. Strong.

Although the establishment of the brigade companies had been authorised in October, it was not until 1916 that they came into being, and that was on New Year's Day.

The 1st Brigade Company was mobilised near Mont des Cats; the 2nd near Ploegstreert and the 3rd near Meteren.

The roster of officers in the three companies were:

1st C.M.G. Company—Capt. W. J. A. Lalor, O.C.; Lieuts. J. I. Bundy, A. W. Couler, H. E. Detchon, A. F. Dowling, S. A. Griffin, F. Hotrum, W. H. Scruton, G. T. Scott-Brown.

2nd C.M.G. Company—Capt. T. H. Raddall, O.C.; Lieuts. F. Edgar, J. E. Hetherington, N. E. Kitson, J. E. Mathews, C. G. McLean, J. A. Ptolmy, J. J. Sclater, R. McB. Stewart, B. S. Walton.

3rd C.M.G. Company—Capt. E. H. Houghton, O.C.: Capt W. M. Pearce, Lieuts. F. M. Bressey, L. Buchanan, E. W. Brookfield, A. Denholm, J. Kay, H. A. Kennedy, J. M. McEachern, G. K. McBeth, H. G. Pepall, J. S. Thorpe, H. M. Wilson.

The companies were equipped and made ready for the line in the order of their brigades with the exception of the 3rd Company, which was unable to obtain guns for several months.

The machine gun units of the 2nd Division were formed in the same way.

The roster of officers of the three companies upon formation were as follows:

4th C.M.G. Company—Lieut. J. Edwards, O.C.; Lieuts. J. Duncanson, W. J. Forbes-Mitchell, A. D. Gray, C. H. J. James, J. Mess, H. J. Price, J. G. Weir, J. F. White, R. W. White.

5th C.M.G. Company—Lieut. S. W. Watson, O.C.; Lieuts. L. H. Bartram, A. C. Bowles, C. V. Grantham, W. H. F. Ketcheson, J. E. McCorkell, C. E. H. Thomas, F. H. Duck.

6th C.M.G. Company—Lieut. T. A. H. Taylor, O.C.; J. Basevi, C. L. Beck, A. G. W. McLean, G. G. White, A. Eastham.

The 3rd Division companies were also formed in the line. The units were organised in March and April and on formation, the following officers were serving:

7th C.M.G. Company—Capt. H. F. Cook, O.C.; Lieuts. H. T. Beecroft, G. O. C. Fenton, F. A. Hale, G. T. Scroggie, W. F. Tobey, W. G. Williams, E. H. Ziegler.

8th C.M.G. Company—Capt. W. M. Balfour, O.C.; S. J. Redpath, P. W. Beatty, C. N. Bennett, J. R. Coull, W. C. Ince, C. W. Laubach, W. N. Moorehouse, H. J. C. Morgan, F. A. Ney, A. W. Sine, H. C. Young.

9th C.M.G. Company—Capt. W.H. Bothwell, O.C.; Lieuts. H. D. Browne, G. W. Beresford, R. C. Cordingly, K. Eager, I. Mackinnon, E. I. H. Ings, L. S. Page, G. Rutherford, R. A. Whittaker.

Christmas Day in the sodden trenches of the salient had been a depressing event for the Canadians and the New Year brought only a continuance of the monotony of trench life in weather that was generally dreary. In November, the 5th and 7th Battalions had initiated trench raids, a Canadian invention which was destined to be a feature of the British policy of keeping alive an offensive spirit during years to come of nightly battles in No Man's Land. Better and more deadly bombs, mine throwers, rifle grenades, improved artillery and handy weapons like the trench knife and *knobkerrie* had been added to the refinements of trench warfare.

Routine trench warfare exacted, of course, its daily toll of casualties but there was nothing of major importance occurred to the Canadians until toward the end of March.

During the winter the British tunnellers had wormed their way underground to the support lines of the Germans on the bluff in front of St. Eloi. an March 27, with the 3rd British Division in the line, a series of seven mines packed with thousands of tons of high explosive were fired. The resulting earthquake shook the ground for miles around and erupted seven enormous geysers of earth and stones, leaving huge craters where only a few moments before unsuspecting Germans were engaged in their daily routine of trench life.

The explosion blew out a whole salient along a front of 600 yards and the Imperials advanced to consolidate. The German lines had been obliterated but as the British took possession and sought to link up the craters separated by a morass of mud and water-filled shell holes, the enemy poured such an intense concentration of artillery and machine gun fire into the small area that nothing could live. When the 2nd

Canadian Division relieved the utterly exhausted 3rd Imperial Division on April 4th, only remnants of trenches choked with dead and wounded were to be seen. The 6th Brigade tried to hold the line with patrols and bombing posts while men of the 5th Brigade in working parties attempted to construct new trenches.

Rifles and machine guns jammed with the mud, supplies and rations could not be got up and how any lived to come out of that holocaust of high explosive will always be miraculous. For sixty hours the bombardment went on, during which time the units in the craters were totally isolated. Little detail of the action can be gathered up in the chaos reigning on this tortured ground. Craters changed hands as epic hand-to-hand struggles, which must ever go unrecorded, took place through five endless days and nights but Canadians held grimly to the ground.

The 2nd Canadian Division lost over 4,000 men and the units engaged suffered an agonizing ordeal that was out of all proportion to the importance of the ground at issue. Men who went through it may justly claim that the war, nowhere and at no time, was to produce anything like the concentrated carnage that was the price of these craters.

The historic battle for Verdun had already started on February 21 wherein France was to give enduring evidence of her manhood's will and strength to endure unbelievable hardships and to provide a depth of courage in wells from which Frenchmen may ever draw up revivifying draughts of pride of race.

On June 1st, the 3rd Division was holding a sector in the Ypres salient a few miles south of Langemark and St. Julien. The 3rd Division was on the left with the 7th and 8th Brigades in the line. The 2nd Brigade of the 1st Division was on their right, reaching down as far as Hill 60.

The front was ominously quiet and an attack was more or less expected.

Major-General Mercer, commanding the 3rd Division, and Brigadier-General Victor Williams, commanding the 8th Brigade, were making an inspection when, at nine o'clock, the first deluge of shells came over. Williams was wounded and later taken prisoner by the Germans and as the intense bombardment rocked the whole area hour after hour, General Mercer tried to get back through the barrage. He was wounded near Armagh Wood and his *aide*, Lieut. Gooderham, dragged him into a ditch. When the Huns swept over the 4th C.M.R.'s in their first attack, the General and his aide escaped detection but General Mercer was killed by a British shell burst in the supporting barrage for the fourth attack of eight which Canadians attempted that night to win back the captured ground.

Six hundred of the C.M.R.'s were killed and wounded as the Germans swept over in dense waves following what was said to have been the most intense bombardment of the war to date, over one million shells roaring over and smashing trenches out of all recognition. One whole company of the Pats, in a salient known as the Loop, were blown up by a German mine and the Pats were actually at one time firing into the backs of the Germans surging past them on the right flank. Another company stood off repeated assaults on the front line for 18 hours.

Nine battalions were mustered for a counter-attack on June 3rd but it went badly from the first, even to the arrangements, the 3rd Brigade carrying the brunt of the parried thrust and suffering the worst casualties. It was bitter ding-dong fighting for days and the Canadians planned another general attack but before they got it off the Germans came over in a mass attack against the 6th Brigade, survivors of the bitter fighting at the St. Eloi craters, on the evening of June 6th. The thrust was aimed at the village of Hooge, the village on the Menin road down which the Germans hoped for an opening through the iron ring around Ypres. They came on in dense masses and carrying full equipment as if on their way to the Channel.

Once again it is claimed that the preliminary bombardment which started at 7 o'clock in the morning exceeded in sheer intensity anything the Canadians had been called upon to face. The Canadians suffered heavily but, although losing the debris which had once been Hooge, held their support line solidly. The Battalion Lewis guns were proving their mettle now and with the brigade guns in support, defence in depth was attained though not in those terms.

The brigade companies newly formed and with so many other things to think of had not become historically minded. Their reports as incorporated in brigade diaries in connection with the battles of St. Eloi, Sanctuary Wood and Hooge are terse and devoid of any adornment in the way of description.

One does run into descriptive items in the *History of the Princess Pats,* for instance, in connection with the fighting at Sanctuary Wood as in the following:

> Lieut. D. S. Forbes, who was in command of the brigade machine guns, was hit in the face in Lovers Walk and, although unable to speak, refused to leave the trench and continued to carryon with his men.

In another passage it says:

> Lieut. H. T. Beecroft of the 7th M.G. Company discovered that certain parts of the line were short of food and, not being able to spare his own men, personally carried up on his own back sacks of food after daylight had broken.
>
> Other officers of the 7th M. G. Company also attracted high praise.

An extract from letter from Brig.-Gen. Ketchen, D.S.O., Commanding 6th Can. Inf. Bgde., to Brig.-Gen. MacDonell, C.M.G., D.S.O., Commanding 7th Can. Inf. Bgde., dated 9.6.16.

> ... I am enclosing reports on the various officers you so kindly left to help us out.
>
> They were most useful and your machine gun crews and guns were of the greatest use to us at the 'Culvert' when the Boche came across.
>
> They did excellent work indeed and it was very fortunate they were with us.
>
> We all regret very much that Lieut. Ziegler was wounded, he is a gallant chap....

An extract from report sent in by the 28th (North West) Battalion, C.E.F. and;

> ... Lieut. Ziegler, 7th Brigade Machine Gun Company.
> This officer did valuable work in getting the machine guns into position when the enemy's fire lifted previous to the attack.
> He showed utter disregard for personal danger.
> He gave valuable information of the enemy's advance from a very exposed Observation Post that he was forced to take up.
> He directed the fire of the guns splendidly and caused heavy casualties to the enemy. Unfortunately he was seriously wounded ten minutes after the attack commenced....

And so it must be presumed, lacking more specific descriptions, that all the newly-formed Machine Gun Companies, who with their brigades were caught in those furious German attacks, acquitted themselves much along the lines of the 7th Company.

The 4th Division arriving in France in the middle of August had a sprinkling of veterans, in its three Machine Gun Companies, the 10th, 11th and 12th. It was an odd coincidence that the companies should land in France on dates corresponding to their numbers. Thus the 10th Company landed on French soil on August 10th and so on with the others in that order.

The rosters of the officers of these companies as they landed in France consisted of the following:

10th M.G. Company—Capt. J. Mess, O.C.; Lieuts. C. T. Bowring, H. A. Fowler, C. U. Hebden, A. E. Ladler, G. Sage, C. W. Smith, C. E. Thompson, K. Weaver, H. S. Whiteside.

11th M.G. Company—Capt. B. M. Clerk, O.C.; Lieuts. H. Ward, F. E. Boultbee, F. Bullock-Webster, H. J. Burden, K. W. Junor, T. F. Murray, E. W. Sansom, A. G. Scott, C. W. Stroud.

12th M.G. Company—Capt. H. E. Hodge, O.C.; Lieuts. L. F. Pearce, F. R. Alford, C. C. Drew, I. C. Hall, H. E. Henderson, H. T. Logan, H. A. Peverly, J. A. Riddell, W. G. Williams.

Since the hard fighting of April, May and June, the Canadian Corps had had a quiet time-as quiet as the salient could ever be for raids, artillery shoots and patrols brought constant casualties.

In January, Capt. Muerling had given the first lectures on indirect fire to a class consisting of the officers and N.C.O.'s of the Eaton Machine Gun Battery and also to the officers of the Boyle unit, then attached.

In the summer of 1916, the Canadian Machine Gun School established at Napier and Riseborough barracks was amalgamated with the 86th (Machine Gun) Battalion to form the Canadian Machine Gun Depot. Major (Sonny m'boy) Barnfield continued as Chief Instructor. Before February 1917, 7,000 officers and men were to have received training in the Colt Machine Gun School (started in April, 1915, when Capt. D. J. Johnston, 1st Battalion, the Queen's Own (Royal West Kents), was loaned to the Canadians to instruct in machine gunnery at the Canadian Machine Gun School and finally the Machine Gun Depot.

During this period (1915-16) selected Canadian officers, N.C.O.'s and other ranks were sent to attend machine gun courses conducted by the British authorities at Nisques, near St. Omer, Camiers and in England at the Machine Gun Training Centre at Grantham. There was as yet no Canadian Corps Machine Gun School in the field.

The 4th Division was not long in getting its first taste of warfare and after relieving a division leaving for the Somme, carried out a big raid with remarkable success on September 16th-17th.

In the late fall of 1915, the British had extended their line from Arras to the Somme. British strength had now reached close to the peak at which it was now possible to stage an offensive on a scale greater than that previously attempted on the Western Front.

Most post war accounts agree that the British and French strategy at this stage was not aimed at a sudden break-through and the capture of territory so much as it was to bring the Germans into action and through a preponderance of artillery and a constant and tremendous pressure, blast him out of his field fortresses and destroy them on a cold, calculated mathematical basis of killing two for one.

There was little attempt made to conceal the vast preparations and effort the British were making and so on June 30th, when the sun finally chased away weeks of sullen clouds and rain, the order was given for the 25-mile wide British attack to be launched next morning. From June 24th the bombardment along the whole British front but more concentrated on the Somme had become more intense and on a crashing scale not even envisaged but last year.

On the morning of July 1, the very earth shook as the full blast of the British barrage opened, and along 25 miles, troops went over the top as if on parade. But the counter-barrage of the Germans was even more deadly for, while deep tunnels had saved many German lives, the British troops. walking steadily behind their barrage, literally melted away. The mathematics of attrition were adding up wrong. By nightfall, on the sector from Gommecourt to Thiespval, the attack had everywhere been held and a pitiful remnant of our own troops were back in their jumping off line. Machine guns from pits dug well in advance of the German line had extracted the heaviest toll. To the south, the attack went much better though slower than the rapid advance the French had made. On a combined front of 14 miles from Mametz to Fay, the British and French had won the first German line and captured 6,000 prisoners.

The Canadians, knowing they were destined for this front, could hear for weeks the roar of the giant cannonade as the attack slowed down after the first few days to a matter of keeping up a steady and immense pressure. As their successive treks to the south began, they realised with a start that at last they were to see France.

The 1st Division was engaged in the struggle at Pozieres, north of Albert, on August 31st. Three days later the Canadian Corps occupied 4,100 yards east and west of the Bapaume road.

The 1st M. G. Company reports that this company relieved the 7th and 12th Australian Brigades the afternoon of August 31, on the Pozieres front. On September 3rd, the Canadian machine gunners covered the attack of the 12th Australian Brigade upon Ferme du Moquet with indirect fire.

Rapid fire opened at 5.10 a.m. and was maintained until 6.45 a.m.; 8,000 rounds were expended. Result of attack not yet known. Artillery very active during the day. Weather fine.

This very terse, business-like report is tucked away in the daily summary of the 1st Canadian Infantry Brigade.

The 1st Division was to have plenty of excitement during its tour in beating off German attempts to retrieve lost ground. On the 8th the fighting was particularly bitter after two days of heavy artillery exchanges. The Canadians were temporarily beaten back from Moquet Farm, while the 2nd C.I.B. was relieving the 3rd. Again on the 10th, our artillery and brigade machine guns broke up a threatening German attack on the 1st C.I.B. sector. The 3rd Division arrived on the Somme on this date, having been preceded by the 2nd Division on September 7th.

On September 11th the 1st Division was relieved on the right sector by the 2nd Division and early that morning the 4th C.I.B. was called upon to repel an attempt to rush posts out ahead of the front line.

On September 12th, the 3rd Division took over a new area from the Ovillers-Courcelette Road south to Moy Avenue.

For an impending assault, jumping-off trenches were straightened out or captured in minor pushes.

On September 13th the British artillery started a sustained bombardment and then came Friday morning, September 15th, and perfect autumn weather with a light mist swirling around the slopes. At 6 a.m. the British bombardment reached a new note of fury and at 6.20 the 2nd and 3rd Divisions advanced down the slope and stormed Sugar Trench and Fabeck Graben. Lumbering along with the waves of troops in the wake of the barrage falling like a curtain of iron ahead of them, wobbled queer monsters of iron, which dipped into trenches and huge craters and crawled crazily up the other side. They were almost as great a surprise to the troops they accompanied as they were to the Germans who saw them looming up through the mist.

Despite the vicious fusillade of machine gun fire that met them, the Canadian waves of attackers never faltered and soon they scaled the last ridges to see Martinpuich on their right and looked into the ruins of the Sugar Refinery, which was their objective. The momentum of the whole attack of the Canadians, though set back here and there by stubborn German resistance, had carried, by noon, beyond the objectives set and then it was that the adventure was expanded and the 5th C.I.B., which had been in reserve all morning, was launched against Courcelette itself. The 22nd, the 25th and the 26th made the assault, but it was the impetuous dash of the French-Canadian 22nd which featured this lightning thrust which was hastily improvised.

In one day the British had broken through three of the enemy's main defensive systems on a front of over six miles to an average depth of a mile. Sir Douglas Haig asserted:

> It was the most effective blow, yet dealt at the enemy by British troops.

Machine gunners who took part in the attack hardly recognised in "*Creme de Menthe*" and "*Cordon Rouge*", the two tanks fed into the attack with the Canadians as blood and iron brothers, but the tanks were officially known as "Machine Gun Corps, Heavy Section". Though the tanks did marvellous work in flattening out machine gun nests and spreading terror among many of the German troops, of whom, some were stout-hearted enough to offer battle to the armoured sides of the monsters, the wisdom of feeding them into a battle of such proportions in such small numbers instead of holding them as an overwhelming surprise over more suitable terrain was immediately debated.

On this day, when Canadian arms won new lustre, reports from many of the Brigade Machine Gun Companies seem to be totally missing.

Those that were written were terribly matter of fact.

Apparently the new formations, while they believed they were fighting a war to end all war, had no notion that they were also supposed to do a little writing for posterity.

But we gather enough sketchy material to see the machine gunners' role plainly. Indirect fire which they had been swatting up on is now being used in terms of barrages. Their main role, however, seems to be accompanying the assaulting waves and consolidating the captured ground and with the Germans constantly threatening to counter-attack and time and time again launching them in strength, the Brigade machine gunners had an important task. But already even the first brunt of that role was falling to the Lewis gun teams and they more than met the tests.

As a model of brevity, one could not in an intensive search fare much better than with the account of the September 15th, as reported by the 4th M. G. Company.

Written at 12 midnight, it states:

> At zero hour, eight guns went over in the attack with the fifth wave. Eight guns fired on enemy lines from X. 5. a. 6. 6.

What could be briefer? The 5th Company history reports as follows:

> At 10.00 p.m., a large party of the enemy, estimated at 700, was seen coming down the Bapaume-Albert road toward Courcellette with full kit and marching in fours. Sgt. Hobson ... held his fire. In the meantime, Lieut. Bowles, in charge of "B" section, held his fire until the German officer was within 50 yards. All four guns opened up. Two of the enemy reached the guns but these were quickly despatched by Lieut. Bowles with the butt of an enemy rifle. Another jumped in beside No. 3 Gun but Corporal Houghton quickly despatched him. When Sgt. Hobson heard the guns of "B" section open fire he immediately opened fire, cutting off their only means of escape. So unexpected was this attack that they threw down their arms and surrendered and the prisoners when counted numbered 395 men and one officer.

The 6th M. G. Company reports of this day:

> Weather fine. Attack by 27th and 28th Battalions on German lines. No. 2 section advanced and took up defensive positions in support. No. 3 and 4 sections conducted indirect fire. Approximately 45,000 S. A. A. were fired during the course of the attack.

The 7th M. G. Company does a little better for posterity. Important fragments piece together a more complete picture of their day's work on the 15th:

> Three guns of 'A' and one of 'B' Sections were in action. No. 2 gun of 'A' put out of action when taking up position—one killed, three wounded.
>
> I had issued orders to enfilade first objective but on observation with glasses it was found that western part of trench was occupied by Canadian troops, presumably C.M.R.'s. As a result guns were elevated to fire on eastern part of trench towards Courcelette. No. 1 'A' gun went out of action by shrapnel piercing barrel casing. Good targets were taken advantage of as groups of enemy rushed from eastern end of sunken road trench overland towards Fabeck Graben. (This was at 6.10 p.m.)
>
> At 6.15 p.m. fire was lifted to second objective. Fabeck Graben trench on which frontal and oblique fire was brought to bear. Observation good, showing heavy losses of the enemy inflicted by machine guns as enemy abandoned Fabeck Graben and retreated to Zollern Graben. At 6.30 p.m. range lifted and barrage was placed on Zollern Graben and road in rear.

Again on the 16th, the same company report says:

> At 3 p.m. issued orders re attack by 7th Brigade on Zollern Graben. About 4.40 p.m. fire was opened on Zollern Graben. Our artillery fire was inaccurate and the enemy showed himself in large numbers in trench. Securing excellent observation of fire, we were enabled to bring whole group on trench.

Later the report says that on advice from Royal Flying Corps, fire was ordered on Sunken Road.

The casualty report shows four killed and 12 wounded. Of two men recommended for bravery, one was attached from the Princess Pats.

The 8th M. G. Company report tells of having five wounded as the artillery warmed up for the show two days later.

In part it goes on to say:

> At 6.25 a.m. (five minutes after artillery) our machine guns opened barrage fire as per table. In addition to our barrage, 10 guns from 1st Canadian M. IVI. G. Battery were in position to west of Pozieres firing towards Courcelette. Also four guns of 9th C.M.G. Company in position near R 34.a 4.4.
>
> At 8.15 a.m. about 75 German prisoners passed down road

from Pozieres. All seemed glad to get out, saluted and gave us 'good morning.' Their physique was poor and they seemed a rather low type.

(10.30 a.m.) Caterpillar "Land Ships" passed down road returning from front. They were shelled all the way but undamaged. Our casualties until noon, Company 2 O.R., attached 4 O.R.

The 9th C.M.G. Company tells of having eight guns in a barrage role and two sections up with battalions.

On September 16th, the report notes:

> Hostile shelling has continued heavy since yesterday's attack. German batteries very close to front line and within range of our guns. We are ordered to engage a German 77 C.M. battery. Guns are trained on German front lines at 6 p.m. with orders to fire if S.O.S. goes up.

Bitter stubborn fighting continued day by day and there was hardly a respite in the constant and shattering roar of artillery duels. Attacks were minor in scope but of major intensity. The pressure of the Canadians was inexorably kept up.

Another general attack was planned for September 26th, in conjunction with British Corps on the left. The objective of the 1st and 2nd Divisions was a ridge running northwest of Courcelette to the Schwaben Redoubt.

The attack, preceded by a tremendously intense barrage, was launched at noon on a two-mile front. The Canadians took their objective but not without severe losses. Regina trench was actually entered but this area, to be the scene of further bitter fighting, was relinquished. The 2nd Brigade, on the morning of the 27th, drove the Germans back to Regina trench but lost the most of their gain as a strong German counter-attack swept over. At 6.30 that night, the Germans withdrew from their line and patrols were pushed out to the North and South Practice trenches along the Dyke Road and towards Regina trench between East and West Miraumont Roads. Germans reinforced on the left, drove the 14th Battalion back 200 yards from Kenora trench.

A strange sight met the eyes of the Canadian troops on the 28th when Canadian cavalry patrols pushed out to get in touch with the enemy, when it was learned that they had withdrawn from their main line of resistance to another position. Two patrols working toward Le Sars went over a mile where Germans were located in Destremont

Farm and another patrol, according to an account, penetrated 2,500 yards north of Courcelette, actually crossing Regina trench, before snipers forced them to turn back. The Canadian lines were immediately advanced, the 4th Brigade thrusting 1,000 yards to the northeast of Courcelette. There was ding dong fighting around Kenora trench and German attacks threatened constantly.

Again, in connection with these days of stubborn battle, reports of the Machine Gun Companies are fragmentary.

The 3rd Company, for instance, had two reserve sections firing a barrage under the command of the O.C. 1st C.M.G.C. Brigade from positions northeast of Pozieres. Four other guns supported the attack of the 14th Battalion and excellent results on approaches and sunken roads to the rear of Regina trench were claimed by the eight barrage guns when they moved up after the attack had been launched. On September 27th, these guns kept up an intermittent fire on working and ration parties of the enemy as they were momentarily glimpsed. Suspected channels of movement were liberally sprayed by the machine gunners.

The 6th C.M.G. Company reports very briefly on its activities, though it had six guns up with the 28th, 29th and 31st Battalions. On the 28th this report says the weather is fine and remarks upon cavalry patrols being pushed out and of impending relief by 4th C.M.G. Company.

The 8th C.M.G. Company on the 26th had 10 guns firing barrage in conjunction with the Borden and Eaton Batteries and the 3rd C.M.G. Company.

An officer, who had two guns with the barrage group, reported:

> My left flank gun continued through the whole barrage, but my other gun was put out of action by an H.E. shell after firing for only half an hour. One man was killed and one wounded. At 1.15 the No. 2 on the left gun was wounded and shortly after the new No. 2 had to be taken off duty suffering from shell shock.

The 14th Battalion asked several times for barrages and many S.O.S. calls were answered during a night of heavy shelling by the enemy.

"B" Section of the same company had a very similar experience, but escaped without the loss of any men, but one of the guns was put out of action.

These reports deal only with those machine guns in an indirect fire

Machine Gun Section. Ottawa, 1901
(Lieut.-Col. Birtwhistle, Secretary of the D. R. A., was at that time the Lieutenant commanding the section.)

role and reflect little of the bitter nature of the fighting nor the conditions under which this tide of destruction ebbed and flowed incessantly across the churned-up, tortured earth that had not so long ago been a pleasant enough countryside. Indirect or barrage m.g. sections were suffering heavily, but we know nothing of what was happening the crews which went forward with the dogged waves of infantry, except that in the steadily-mounting lists of casualties, machine gunners were doing their share to tragically prove that attrition had a double edge which could cut both ways.

By October 1st, the 2nd and 3rd Divisions were ready to attack the Regina trench system into which Canadians had at times penetrated. The 4th and 5th C.M.R.'s of the 8th C.I.B. were attacking on the 3rd Division front and on the right, elements of the 5th and 4th C.I.B.'s formed the spearhead for the 2nd Division thrust. The attack was launched in the afternoon and though preceded by days of bombardment and another hurricane barrage, the most heroic and stubborn qualities could not prevail against the hail of machine gun fire, the blasting effect of counter barrages and the desperate, determined German counter-attacks which engulfed the Canadians. The day was a failure with losses that were appalling in the case of many of the units, but with eddies of small scale epic battles never surpassed in the history of British arms.

The 5th M.G. Company report of this day is no more elaborate than those which have gone before. It says in part:

> During the afternoon the guns were used for indirect firing under the M.G.O. of the 24th Battalion, the remainder of the guns were held in reserve with the exception of the two attached to the 22nd and the two in Sudbury trench under the 25th Battalion. The two guns of 'C' section which were put out of action on the night of 28th-29th September were salvaged by a party in the morning and taken to headquarters at Bailiff Wood.

Again on October 2nd:

> Information was received that Lieut. C—— had been shell shocked the evening of the 1st; also that one of his guns in the Sunken Road at r. 24c. 88 (East Miraumont Road) had been put out of action during the night, two of the crew being killed and a third member missing. The gun and spare parts were salvaged during the day and the two men buried.

Later on, after details of the relief, the last reassuring sentence reads that:

The health of the company is very good.

Failure to cut the wire sufficiently on October 1st was blamed for the debacle and more time was taken. Rain had been more and more turning the Somme into a quagmire. It was decided to attack on October 8th with the 1st Division on the right and the 3rd on the left. Each had four battalions attacking. The attack was launched at 4.30 a.m. Here and there remnants of a company or even an individual reached the general objective but a withering machine gun fire met the waves of the attackers, who slithered uncertainly in the treacherous mud and blotted large segments completely out. Of this bitter day, in which the gallant Canadians were finally pushed back to their jumping off trenches, the 1st M.G. Company report says:

"'A' and 'D' Sections took up positions for indirect fire in Sugar trench. 'E' Section was handed over to Lieut.-Col. Brutinel and was also placed in Sugar trench.

'C' Section was withdrawn and remained in reserve. Fire was opened at 4.50 a.m. and a steady barrage was maintained until 6.30 a.m. At 2.50 p.m. Germans were seen assembling in rear of their lost trench and four guns opened fire. At 3.03, Capt. Lalor ordered a steady barrage behind captured German trench. This fire was maintained until 4.30. At 5 p.m. O.C. 4th Battalion requested a barrage in front of his line. A slow barrage was kept up until 8 p.m.

The 3rd M.G. Company had one section covering the attack on the 8th. Its report says:

At 4.50 a.m., zero hour, all guns opened up rapid fire, establishing a covering barrage for the 16th and 13th Battalions. Roads, tracks, paths and junctions of enemy trenches also ranged upon. This rapid fire was continued for two hours. During the remainder of the day and night intermittent fire was kept up on roads and approaches.

(On October 9th), intermittent fire continued during the day, ranging on road and approaches to enemy's line. Two enemy working parties fired upon with good results.

The 4th Division having arrived in the Somme area on October

5th, there was now hope of relief for the exhausted brigades. Unceasingly the artillery battle now raged.

While other divisions were beginning to leave the area, attacks by the 4th Division culminated on November 11th in the 46th and 47th Battalions of the 10th C.I.B. and the 102nd Battalion of the 11th Brigade capturing Regina trench which had cost the Canadian Corps so heavily. The time of attack had been switched to midnight and the barrage for the small frontage attacked was perhaps the most concentrated yet to blast the German defences.

The 12th M.G. Company report most briefly says

> Our guns took part in the capture by 11th Brigade of the portion of Regina trench untaken in the operations of October 21st, furnishing a continuous barrage of fire.

The 11th M.G. Company report is a trifle more expansive in saying:

> ..at 2 a.m. sections 1 and 2 go into line. Canadian infantry make successful attack on enemy trenches. Intense artillery fire by both sides until 5.30 a.m. From 5 a.m. to 5.30 a.m. intense m.g. fire. At 9.15 a.m. enemy observed gathering in Below trench. We at once opened rapid fire with eight machine guns—very effectively. Our signallers repair wire under heavy shell-fire. At 2 p.m. enemy collecting in Below and Gallowitz trenches. Effectively turned m.g.'s on them. Kept this locality under fire rest of day and night.

Canadian trenches were by now nothing but a sea of mud and the occupants had none of the elaborate shelters still available for the enemy. Despite almost unendurable conditions, the attack which aimed at Desire trench was being prepared and the 11th and 10th C.I.B.'s drew the assignment.

Shortly after 6 o'clock on November 17th, the barrage opened and although the 11th Brigade got through with comparatively few casualties and gained its objectives, the 10th Brigade, 50th and 46th Battalions ran into a devastating machine gun fire and suffered heavily. It was another day of epics fought on a minor scale under conditions that are indescribable.

The 11th M.G. Company as a matter of necessary routine reports:

> Eight of our machine guns helped form the usual machine gun barrage. Sergt. Vincent, with one crew, advanced to the attack

in the first wave of the 54th Battalion. Corporal Love with his guns went over the parapet with the 75th Battalion, while Corporal Corrigan and crew operated with the 38th Battalion. We had several casualties.

Canada had paid dearly for her new battle honours won at the Somme.

In gaining 4,000 yards on a front of 3,000, the total losses were 24,029.

The Somme had brought vast strides in the use of indirect machine gun fire. Though it was initiated rather more as area shoots than in the barrage sense as used by the artillery, reports of German prisoners proved its effectiveness. The laying down of S.O.S. lines had been speedily developed and if M.G. reports at this time lacked moving descriptive qualities, they did reveal the growing confidence of infantry battalion commanders in machine gun indirect fire support, both in the attack and as a protection against counter-attacks.

Though the guns detailed for infantry action perhaps suffered the heaviest, the indirect fire groups took much punishment also. In the first attack on Regina trench and in the subsequent actions of the next few days, the Borden Battery had had three guns destroyed and 22 casualties.

Winter was already setting in on the Somme. It only served to add a chill to the sombreness of a scene that had witnessed the greatest British effort of the war to date and, by far, the costliest.

CHAPTER 3

Vimy Ridge

As the Brigade Machine Gun Companies trekked northward somewhere in the wake of their Infantry Brigades, they were perhaps not giving much thought to the larger, tactical or strategic issues of the Battles of the Somme, the desolate scenes of which they were leaving. Theirs was a vast feeling of relief at every step which took them farther away from the still-incessant roar of the much heralded and biggest British artillery effort of the war to date and lengthened the distance between them and the clinging, chalky, muddy wastes of that scene with its always-present misery and always-blasting threat of death and grievous wounds as the price of so little gain in ground.

The threat of death and wounds, of course, lay surely ahead but it would be in a different scene—in a new shuffle of the cards of fate. The in visible cable routes of rumour carried their usual burden of messages in their uncanny but not always accurate fashion. This time the burden of the message was that not only was the next scene to be different—it was to be refreshingly new. This time these rumours happened to be true.

As the now fully-grown corps settled for short spells of rest in the area back of Bully Grenay and Arras, fears that this might only be a temporary halt before the march was resumed back to the torn, hated salient of miserable memories, where through weary, tense, costly months three divisions had gone through the red baptism of modern war, were set at rest.

And in the reprieve from the grisly setting of the Somme and the freshness of the new scene, drooping spirits quickly rose, there was again the rollicking song in the air and once more a buoyant sense of adventure—never far below the surface in the Canadian Corps—began to assert itself.

Vimy Ridge dominated the whole eastern side of this sector, which had been used for some time by both sides, apparently, as a resting spot for tired, worn-out troops. When the German hordes were flung back from the very gates of Paris, Vimy Ridge was among those natural features, embodied in the plans of the German Higher Command for retreat—should it become necessary. It remained a notable, outstanding choice along the front on which the Germans finally turned at bay.

Canadians were not to be there long before the history of the dauntless attempts of the 10th French Army in 1915-16 to capture the Ridge was common knowledge. At no point in the far-flung battle line had there been greater loss—and fruitless waste of French lives. Fifty thousand had been lost in the course of a few days of bitter fighting as wave after wave of Frenchmen charged the de Lorette spur, on up the slopes of the Ridge, only to be driven from the very crest itself. Early in 1916, the British had taken over this front and, except for one futile effort in May of that year, had apparently concurred in the French conviction that Vimy Ridge was impregnable to frontal assault under conditions of modern warfare. Both sides had engaged in extensive mining and tunnelling and from this latter endeavour the Canadians were to benefit immensely when their big moment came.

For the first month, Canadians took the opportunity of the rest that was offered and contented themselves with the normal trench routine, the while they became acquainted with their new sector and its own peculiarities.

Then came a change. Suddenly there was purpose in the air—a sense of something impending. The rustle of an operation order in the hands of a staff officer far back at corps seemed somehow—and very quickly—to magically echo its portent to the occupants of a bay in the front line trench.

The first faint rustle had probably echoed its way up to the front in early December weeks so it was not surprising that the Corps Commander should publish an outline of an entire Operation on December 23rd, just approaching the festive Christmas season. He asked divisions to prepare a detailed attack scheme for their own frontages.

Of vast significance to the future of machine gunnery in this war was the request made to the Corps M.G.O. Officer, Colonel Brutinel, that "proposals for machine gun covering and barrage fire on the front of the corps be submitted.

It was the signal for preparations, by every arm and every unit of the Canadian Corps, unprecedented in their thoroughness of detail and co-ordination, and which were to usher in a new science of offensive warfare by British troops.

In that matter of a month, the Canadian infantry battalions, who had initiated a phase of trench raids and aggressive night patrols, had gained the upper hand in No Man's Land. Artillery fire was intensified and became a still more highly-specialised accompaniment to these almost nightly raids.

Brigade machine gun companies had been doing their normal tours with their own brigades. From their formation early in 1916, this was the normal routine. It meant a long stretch for the companies—a whole brigade tour. The strength of gun crews under the Company establishment did not admit of reliefs being carried out within the company but there had seemed no other alternative. The experience of the Somme, however, had crystallized the severe strain upon the physical powers of machine gunners which an entire brigade tour entailed and relief came in the formation of a fourth company for each division. These additions not only offered a solution to the serious problem of reliefs but provided a divisional reserve of machine guns, which was a much-desired tactical advance.

The new companies of the four Canadian Divisions assembled at Floringhem, near Pernes-en-Artois, and began training on January 18th, 1917, under the supervision of Major W. M. Balfour, D.S.O. The companies were numbered 13th, 14th, 15th and 16th, the 13th being the 1st Divisional Company and so on in order.

The personnel of officers and other ranks were drawn from three sources, *viz*: (1) the existing Machine Gun Companies, (2) Infantry Battalions in the field, and (3) the Canadian Machine Gun Depot newly-established at Crowborough.

As they were selected, the divisional companies had the following officers commanding and serving on March 1st, 1918.

13th Company—Lieut. J. Kay, officer commanding; Lieuts. A. Denholm, G. W. Day, G. H. Dunbar, J. Maitland, D. A. McIntosh, C. G. McLean, A. McKenzie.

14th Company—Lieut. J. Basevi, officer commanding; Lieuts. G. N. Douglas, P. J. Bullock, T. Dick, T. F. O'Flaherty, W. G. Thompson, J. Turner, L. F. White.

15th Company—Capt. W. N. Moorehouse, officer commanding;

Lieuts. J. C. Hartley, F. McK. Garrison, G. E. Garneau, W. J. Hutchens, J. R. McLean, P. C. Mulholland.

16th Company—Lieut. E. W. Sanson, officer commanding; Lieuts. H. T. Logan, L. Gavreau, S. Johnston, B. C. Montagnon, E. L. Rainboth, A. Ritchie, W. H. Watson.

Promotions in these companies were later to be confirmed in orders.

Despite the fact that "Indirect Fire" was being discouraged at British Machine Gun Schools in Grantham, England, and Camiers, France, faith in this method of fire support had been stoutly maintained by Colonel Brutinel and by Capt. H.V. Muerling, already referred to previously as the "gunnery" expert of the Emma Gees. It was not, nor had it been, extensively used but throughout the companies, officers but lately over from England and not a few of the veterans had a good knowledge of the methods of working out these fire orders.

The corps commander's request for "proposals for machine gun covering and barrage fire" brought into being a school at Pernes where special training in an 8-day course was given on Indirect Fire and subsidiary subjects. There began to creep into the machine gun language a lot of new "gunnery" terms. A considerable number of machine gunners were engineers of one sort and another and the simple formulas were merely a light lunch for them. Others wore their pencils to mere stubs as they laboriously worked over fire orders.

Gradually into the sudden eruptions of concentrated artillery barrages that crashed the frosty quiet and comparative stillness of those Vimy nights, signalizing another sudden thrust by impudent raiding parties, there also crept the ringing chatter of machine gun barrage fire. It was somehow noticeable in an undertone of its own, despite the larger volume of sharp, successive barks from the 18-pounders and the more rounded voices of the "Hows."

In addition to thickening up the box barrages of the artillery for these raids, machine guns were given their nightly allotment of harassing fire targets on cross roads and overland enemy carrying parties. While sited in defence positions, machine guns were coordinated day and night on S.O.S. barrage lines, where they filled in gaps left by the artillery.

Thus did Machine Gunners more definitely assume the role of light artillery.

Fifty-five raids carried on during this "quiet winter of rest, in a great many of which machine gun barrages played an important part, not only cultivated a high degree of efficiency among officers and crews in the use of "Indirect Fire" methods but there also grew up in battalions and on into whole brigades, a greater confidence in machine gun covering fire.

The singing whine of a burst of machine gun fire overhead was no longer the signal for the infantryman, several hundred yards off, to duck behind the *parados* and curse a careless gunner under his breath.

March ushered in a program of systematic destruction of dugouts, rearward positions, barb-wire entanglements and a continual rain of harassing fire. As an example of the sort of co-operation that was being built up in roles between the machine guns and artillery is the fact that while the latter pounded and smashed strongly-wired posts with their greater destructive power, the machine guns were given the task of preventing repairs being made and of hindering new work.

For minus 30 days onwards, every effort was made in divisions to increase the number of machine guns working in co-ordinated destructive shoots with trench mortars and artillery. Sixty-four guns by day and sixty-four by night were first employed on this strenuous task.

However, difficulty was encountered by machine guns in meeting this continuous program. The life of a barrel for purposes of accurate overhead fire was 15,000 rounds and since the demands for every sort of conceivable material at this time was so great, the harassing fire program had to be considerably curtailed on toward the end of March.

Prisoners taken earlier in the month had testified that our machine gun harassing fire had kept down practically all overland movement and restricted carrying parties almost entirely to the trenches. After the machine gun harassing fire program had been cut down, Germans captured on April 1st said that reliefs and ration parties were again moving overland as far as Zwischen Stellunge, 800 to 1,000 yards behind their own front line, without suffering any casualties from the reduced machine gun fire. Air photographs on the snow-covered ground confirmed these statements by the prisoners.

The enormity of the whole preparations at Vimy, their marvellous and close fidelity to detail, had never before been attempted nor were they ever to be surpassed on any sector in which the limited offensive idea obtained.

Incessant air photographing, bearings taken on gun flashes and every conceivable method of finding out "what was over the hill,"

Lieut.-Col. A. J. Balfour, D.S.O. and staff of the Canadian Machine Gun Depot, Seaford, 1918

all combined to keep the "Intelligence" picture right up to the very minute. While tunnellers bent nightly to the arduous task of boring three tunnels through the hard chalky soil up to the German front lines, Lieut.-Gen. Sir Julian Byng had a full-scale plan of the battlefield laid out near Houdain, with broad white tapes to mark the trenches, and flags of different colours to mark the boundaries and strong points in enemy defences.

Already it had been decided that the machine guns would play a dual role. On January 19th, an outline of the machine gun scheme had been issued whereby it was detailed that "Mobile Guns" were to be detached to Brigades and operate in close liaison with the attacking infantry battalions, taking on direct targets where they might be found and then forming strong points for consolidation of the ground won. Barrage groups were named, their positions allotted. From then on the positions from which the barrages on the Black and Red Lines would be fired were improved and stored with ammunition. Forward dumps of S.A.A. were filled up.

The Mobile Guns had trained with the infantry over the full scale model of the German trench system. In these exercises, repeated over and over again, every man was shown exactly where to go and what he was to do. The rate of progress was controlled by the artillery and machine gun barrage, represented by mounted men who, carrying flags, impersonated a screen of bursting shrapnel. By battalions, brigades and divisions, they advanced in a rehearsal to a scales that was entirely new to the Allied side of the Western Front.

In this assembling of all the vast supply of materials for a mighty assault, the application of every possible scientific aid to a new phase of warfare, General Byng did not overlook a happy combination of psychology, the human element and good old-fashioned horse sense.

Under him he had 97,184 of Canada's best. He handled them, not as so many regimental numbers, but took everyone into his confidence—as far as lectures, demonstrations and 40,000 especially prepared maps could accomplish that end. It was a recognition of their general high standard of intelligence, their native initiative, to which the Canadians could not help but respond.

The "Byng Boys" were born in that gesture.

As an accompaniment to the dawning of all these new hopes among the Canadians, events were transpiring which were to restore a measure of confidence in the Higher British command—a confidence more than a trifle shaken by events on the Somme. None of the costly efforts there had seemed to have repaid anything like the toll of casualties the Battles of the Somme so greedily took. The bitter disappointment in France was reflected in the dismissal of Joffre and Foch. Before Joffre's dismissal he, with Haig, had planned an offensive to open February 1st with the main blow falling between Loos and the Oise, and a subsidiary operation to the East of Rheims. British Headquarters had visualized a sustained summer offensive which would drive the enemy from his submarine bases in Flanders. Joffre had planned more "nibbling" tactics after the style of the Somme.

General Nivelle, who succeeded to the French command, pooh-poohed such set-piece tactics. The motto of every commander was to be, "violence, *brutalité et rapidité*," and Nivelle's flair and his fluent vision of a German Army utterly defeated after 48 hours of intensive fighting caught the imagination of Premier Lloyd George, since risen to supreme political power on top of the terrific casualty figures which piled up on the Somme.

Sir Douglas Haig, while not convinced by Nivelle's glowing optimism, on the suggestion of the British Premier agreed to a measure of control to be exercised over the British forces by the French and modified his plans. He had decided to attack south of the Scarpe extending down over the old Somme battlefields. When Hindenberg ordered his famous retreat to his new fortified line of Cambrai-St. Quentin, leaving behind a ravaged countryside to be known as the "Hindenberg Desert," 20 miles in depth, Sir Douglas Haig extended his proposed battle line to include Vimy Ridge.

Nivelle prophesied that the Vimy attack would end in failure and disaster. However Haig had his way and Vimy was therefore to be fought for the dual purpose of seizing ground of great tactical importance and providing a large scale diversion which, it was hoped, would draw a great many German reserves away from the impetuous thrust planned by General Nivelle on the Aisne.

Briefly the Canadian plan of attack was that, for the first time in history and the last, the four divisions of the Canadian Corps were to attack simultaneously. On the right was the 17th British Corps with orders to advance while on the left was the 1st Corps which was to remain stationary. The operation was to be carried out in four stages, occupying successively the Black, Red, Blue and Brown lines. Owing to the importance of gaining early possession of Hill 140, it was arranged that the Canadian Corps should push on to the Blue line, 500 yards east of Thelus, with as short intermediate pauses as possible.

The total of machine guns under the Canadian Corps for the operation was three hundred and fifty eight, made up as follows:

16 Canadian Machine Gun Companies	256
4 British M.G. Companies (5th British Division)	64
1st C.M.M.G. Brigade	38
	358

One hundred and four Mobile Guns were detailed to the attacking infantry.

That left two hundred and thirty guns to be allotted for the machine gun barrage, since twenty-four guns were being held in corps reserve.

Owing to the great number of trenches to be captured and on account of the strength and commanding position of most of them, it was decided that machine gun supporting fire should be given the entire corps at every step of the advance.

A creeping machine gun barrage was arranged and fire organisation tables were drawn up to correspond with the artillery barrage. In order to assist the Infantry in warding off possible enemy counterattacks, a protective machine gun barrage was to be established at each definite stage of the operation. Arrangements were also made for a final protective barrage to be fired during the early consolidation of the final objective. Divisions retained control of the guns covering their own sectors and this went down to brigade. Thus, secondary targets could be allotted, when necessity arose, providing the final barrage was in no way interfered with. It was the primary consideration.

The supply of machine gun ammunition alone was a tremendous problem that had been efficiently tackled. Days before the show was to open the following amounts were provided at the gun positions and at forward dumps to be taken forward to the Blue and Brown Line batteries:

1st Division Companies	1,408,000 rounds
	1,568,000 "
	1,000,000 "
	1,000,000 "
Total for Barrage Batteries.	4,976,000 rounds

These amounts were for the first 24 hours of the operation. Mobile guns drew on a basis of 15,000 rounds per gun per day for three days.

The handling of this vast amount of small arms ammunition had made necessary a call on the Infantry for carriers and they were allotted on the basis of 32 per company. They were trained with the crews for three weeks.

On Saturday, April 7th, Corps operation orders announced that:

> Zero hour is fixed for five-thirty a.m. (5.30 a.m.), April 9th, 1917.

Zero had first been arranged for Sunday morning, but when the 17th Corps needed time to complete arrangements it was moved back 24 hours.

Easter Sunday presented a situation hardly in keeping with the traditional spirit of the Resurrection. A false calm brooded over the slopes of Vimy as Sunday night's darkness closed down. Through the darkness units went to their assembly points. There was no confusion—no traffic jams. The attacking brigades lined the front line trenches in dead silence. Supporting brigades were in the tunnels. Mobile machine guns joined their designated battalions. Barrage crews, confident after their long winter of harassing fire, checked up on their night firing posts and' anxiously checked up their watches.

The minutes, then seconds, ticked away.

Four seconds before zero hour, with the exception of the trench mortars, all the guns ceased firing.

One description of this significant pause said:

> As if some giant director had poised his baton at the stop while his orchestra was in the midst of a *crescendo*.

Exactly at 5.30 every gun on the 12-mile front opened up. The earth trembled as the blind ends of the tunnels were blown up. To the German sentries and to gunners behind the ridge it must have looked as if the door of a giant furnace had suddenly been thrown open.

The iron chatter of the 230 machine guns firing their first large-scale barrage in battle was drowned out in the gigantic uproar which shattered eardrums, though here and there, as momentary pauses came, they could be heard.

Into the dawn, on the heels of a barrage which moved ahead with smoothness and precision, swept the attacking battalions of the four divisions, numbered in order from the right of the Canadian attack.

In 35 minutes the first objective on all divisional fronts was captured.

Dazed and rocked by the fury of that first downpour of steel, the Germans made but a feeble reply at first. Artillery allotment per gun was 16 yards of front in the opening barrage. Each machine gun in the barrage scheme had 50 yards.

Snow was falling as the brigades in rear leapfrogged over the attacking units but, despite the heavy going over the churned-up mud, the sweep of the four divisions kept its parade-like aspect—and strictly to time schedule.

By seven o'clock two miles of the crest was in Canadian hands. Two hours later the final objectives on the easterly slope had been reached by all divisions except the 4th, which had been forced to traverse more broken country, where sterner resistance cropped up.

Batter Trench, between Bauble and Black, was defended with tenacity against the assaults of the 11th Brigade. It was not until late afternoon, when reserves were rushed up, that the enemy was finally driven out and back to Beggar Trench near the crest of Hill 145. Subject to vicious enfilade fire, the 3rd Division was forced to form a flank to the north. Trainloads of German reserves were rushed from Lens and Douai to counter-attack on this involved left flank but were repulsed and the 10th Brigade, originally held in reserve for an attack on the Pimple next day, pushed home the attack on Hill 145 at the point of the bayonet.

The mobile guns, jumping off with the Infantry, either in the first wave or the second, ran the gamut of varied fortunes.

All the guns of the 1st Division reached their positions, as planned, in good time and without serious casualties. The 2nd and 3rd Companies operated with their brigades to capture the Red and Black objectives. The 1st Company went through to the final objective. To the 3rd Company each of the battalions had loaned a Colt gun so this brigade had 12 mobile guns for the actual assault. The Colt guns, however, were withdrawn after being used to consolidate the Black Line. They had captured seven German machine guns, however, so still had a profitable margin on the deal.

The 2nd Division's mobile guns had a similar report to make as they swept forward with the attack. The 5th Company was on the flank, watchful for any signs of a counter-attack from Vimy Village and also to cover the Bonval Ravine. The 6th Company were right on scheduled time in their advance and along the way picked up two

German machine guns, along with a large store of ammunition, and as they found numerous targets on the reverse slope of the Ridge during the afternoon these enemy guns came in exceptionally handy.

The mobile guns of the 3rd Division, although not having so deep an advance as the most forward guns of the two right divisions, had much more difficult tasks to do, as it turned out. There was uncertainty on the left flank owing to the stubborn resistance which was holding up the 4th Division and the right flank had the Bonval Ravine. a deep re-entrant into the Ridge, 200 to 300 yards wide, as a potential source of trouble. The ravine's steep sides were fringed with trees, giving excellent concealment, and lined with dugouts.

The 8th Company, working with the C.M.R. Brigade, had two guns sited, covering Bonval Ravine in position, 50 yards east of the Lens-Arras road near the point where it bends eastwards along the north side of the Ravine towards Vimy Ridge. Soon after the guns were in position a group of 300 Germans were seen 100 yards away in the lower ground in front. These were immediately fired on and approximately 100 casualties inflicted. The remainder took shelter in the dugouts along the road beside the steep north side of the ravine. While two guns were trained to sweep the dugout entrances, the Machine Gun officer and seven men went forward and bombed the dugouts, capturing 150 men, including six regimental officers and one staff officer.

Another officer of the same company, with two other ranks, rushed a machine gun post concealed in the wooded high ground of the ravine, capturing the gun and the three remaining members of the crew. They were helped by an Infantry Lewis gun crew threatening from the right, higher up the side of the ravine. During the earlier morning the right four guns of the same company, as they topped the crest of the ridge and got their first full view of the vast Douia plain stretching away for miles to the east, had plenty of live-target practice. They scattered numerous infantry bodies and caused much confusion as German transports made quick dashes up the roads towards them in an attempt apparently to save as many stores as possible.

In the afternoon, when the German shelling thickened up, a direct hit was made on one of the gun crews here and killed four of its members. One officer of this 6th Company trio was the lone officer left on the 4th C. M. R. Battalion front and helped organise the front line of the final objective while using his guns for covering purposes. The 7th Company kept pace and linked up in consolidation phases. As

Headquarters, 4th Battalion C.M.G.C

early as 8.30 a.m. one gun crew of this company overran its selected Strong Point position and got over the crest of the ridge. As they did so they caught several large groups of Germans retreating toward Bloater Trench at the foot of the Ridge and did some fine execution. Enfilade fire from Hill 145 gave the left flank guns of this company many anxious moments. About noon hostile machine gun fire put one of the guns out of action. Two guns were later detached from "E" Barrage Battery to strengthen this threatened point.

Only the mobile guns of the 12th Company were in action during the hard-won advance of the 4th Division. The guns of the 10th and 11th Companies were kept throughout the day in their assembly positions and then at night sent up as defensive guns in rear of the Black objective.

The 12th C. I. B. had two distinct tasks: the capture of the Black and Red objectives and securing of the left flank of the entire Corps attack. During the whole operation the brigade was subjected to a heavy enfilade fire from the flank as well as particularly stubborn resistance from the enemy in front, who were taking every advantage of the many natural features of the cut-up terrain in that area.

The four right guns reached their designated "crater" positions before the Infantry, though leaving 30 minutes after the zero hour. They marched by compass, bearing direct to the spot. Two guns had fine targets as the Germans retreated. They had captured a German gun and 12 gunners before they dug in and got into action and the German gun was turned on its late compatriots. The other. two guns bore too far left and downhill in the direction of Givenchy and suffered heavy casualties. The officer was among the seven wounded on one gun, the tripod of which was destroyed. The left flank guns had an unfortunate time. The officer (Hall) of one subsection received five wounds in the head and body but kept going until too weak to go farther. Both tripods of this section were knocked out by shell fire and four other ranks killed and five wounded.

One of the guns was carried forward by a lance-corporal, who found himself the only member of the crew left when he reached the objective. There he placed himself under an officer of the 72nd Battalion and helped establish Infantry posts. Two guns were sent up at 10 a.m. from "M" Battery to No. 2 crater and did most effective work on targets presented by the Germans, who, fighting every step of the way, made breaks for positions in rear.

The task of the batteries firing the Black and Red Line barrages was comparatively simple, with the exception of "G" Battery. That the barrage positions had been well camouflaged was proven by the few casualties sustained. Five batteries had no casualties.

"G" Battery from the 15th Company had a more difficult task. They were firing a barrage for the capture of the Red Line only and their position was chosen in the German front line up to the right of the sunken road leading out of Bruville St. Vaast in a north-easterly direction over the ridge. This position could not be occupied until after the German front line system of trenches was carried. Also, the guns had to be ready to open fire at zero plus 105. The officer in charge in a skilful reconnaisance discovered a gap in the hostile barrage as soon as it was laid down. Through it he led his battery, numbering 100, and arrived at his barrage position at zero plus 20, with the loss of one other rank, slightly wounded. All guns were in position and ready to fire one hour after zero.

The task of the Blue and Brown Line batteries on the 1st and 2nd Divisional fronts was a most difficult one and called for a very high degree of skill and leadership on the part of the officers and a maximum of determination and endurance on the part of all ranks.

The eight Blue Line batteries, numbering from right to left, Y1, Xl, AI, B1, C1, D1, E1 and F1, had all supported the capture of the Black objective. On completion of firing this barrage they moved forward under cover of our Red Line supporting fire to their Blue Line positions. During the pause of the Infantry on the Red Line emplacements were dug, ammunition was brought up and the guns got ready to fire at zero plus 4½ hours.

Four of these batteries, Xl, AI, B1 and C1, carried out a second move forward to the Brown Line positions, X2, A2, B2, C2, situated about midway between the Red and Blue objectives. This move was conducted in echelon, one battery at a time. The 5th Brown Line battery, Y2, moved direct to its Brown Line positions from the brigade assembly area and in line with the fire organisation scheme, opened fire on their Brown Line targets.

The four batteries fired two barrages and made two moves with equipment over rough, shell-torn ground and under trying weather conditions. It was arduous labour, if not spectacular. The total distance covered from the first to the third positions was between 3,500 and 4,000 yards.

Casualties in these guns were relatively light though the enemy protective barrage was getting reorganised and shelling was getting heavier.

X2 Battery was the most unfortunate. It came under particularly intense shelling. At one spot five other ranks were killed and three guns put out of action. Guns of other batteries were switched on to the targets these guns would have covered and the five remaining guns speeded up their rate of fire to effect a balance for the loss. The efficiency of the communications organised in connection with the machine gun barrage effort was to be proven. And a new elasticity in outlook between the purely infantry and light artillery role of machine guns in several incidents which saw a departure from the precise schedule of the operations.

For instance, during the advance of the 1st Infantry Brigade through the Black and Blue objectives to their attack on the Blue and Brown Lines, considerable enemy sniping and machine gun fire was met with, coming from the 17th Corps front on the right. In order to stop this fire, which was causing heavy casualties, the brigadier, seeing four guns of the 1st Company on their way to Y2 Battery positions, stopped them. He asked for help in beating down this fire from the flank and the four guns went merrily into action. They subdued that fire and then took up the job of getting to their barrage position, where they joined the other four guns, already in position, in time to fire the Brown Line barrage.

Again, when the infantry were halted on the Red Line, a counterattack was threatened from the left of the 2nd Division front at the foot of Bonval Ravine. The G. O. C. 5th Brigade asked for a concentration to be applied to this menacing area and the brigade barrage group commander had the fire of "Fs" Battery switched to this target and engaged it from zero plus 150 to zero plus 200 when word was received that the danger was apparently over. "Fs" Battery resumed its barrage fire on the Red Line protective barrage.

The pack trains organised in each division had done their task extremely well. Far into the captured enemy ground they pushed and by mid-afternoon had established dumps; 400,000 rounds were packed up on the 1st Division front.

In the 1st and 2nd Divisions the employment of infantry carriers, two per gun, and organised in sections, supplemented the work of the pack trains in this arduous, non-spectacular but very useful work.

By nightfall the whole of Vimy Ridge in the areas of the 1st, 2nd and 3rd Divisions were in our hands, but as the units consolidated there was no time to appraise the day's work.

On the 4th Division front the enemy still held Hill 145 and most of the ground between the Black and Red objectives. A protective barrage of artillery and machine guns was established across the entire corps front and answered several SOS calls. Harassing fire was carried out over the frontal areas.

In a gallant night attack the 85th from Nova Scotia and the 47th Battalions attacked Brer Trench on the forward slope of the hill and by 6 a.m. of the 10th had consolidated the hard-won ground. At 3.15 p.m. on the 10th the 10th C.I.B., which had been in reserve the previous day, launched its attack on Hill 145 and swept the Germans off this dominating feature. The 4th Division M. G. batteries fired their original schedule and repeated the experiences on the other divisional fronts, with the possible exception that helter-skelter targets bobbed up less frequently and it was by all means a stiffer show.

The 10th C. I B. had had little more than time to get its breath after the assault on Hill 145 before it was sent against its original objective—the Pimple. The 24th Division, 1st Corps, on the left at the same time attacked Boise-en-Rache, immediately north of the Souchez River. The attack took place at 5 a.m. in the face of a blinding snowstorm and a hail of well-organised fire. Well over their first confusion, the Germans here offered stubborn resistance. Eight mobile guns of the brigade which went over with the attack got through with the loss of only one gun. Targets were not as plentiful for direct fire as they had been on the 9th, but the 10th Company guns made the best of what offered.

On the same day that the Pimple was captured plans were issued for a further attack in conjunction with the 12th Corps on the right. Patrols had ascertained that the enemy was holding Vimy village and the Vimy-Farbus railway line in great strength. The date was not fixed but was likely to be on April 14th.

The Germans anticipated this operation, however, by a hurried withdrawal on the 13th. Our line was advanced and by evening of the same day had been pushed out more than 1,000 yards east of the Ridge along the whole Corps front. The new advance took in the villages of Willerval, Vimy and Givenchy-en-Goelle, a line that at this end of the ridge was not to change very substantially from that day until the word flashed out to some tired British Division, holding it on November 11th, 1918, that an Armistice had been signed.

And that was the Battle of Vimy.

It stood then, and does yet, as a model of preparation and achievement.

After Vimy the Canadian Corps never looked back. It was to have a far greater significance, too, than the exultation of the moment.

The cost in casualties had been, for the whole month of April, 13,477 killed and wounded. At Ypres, in 1915, a single division had lost 6,000 in killed and wounded. For a small and insignificant stretch of ground on the Somme the toll paid by Canadians was 24,000 killed and wounded.

The financial cost alone marked another stupendous stride in war. In ammunition, on the Canadian front alone, $17,000,000 worth of shells were exploded over the German lines between April 4th and 10th, and a quarter of this vast fury was expended on April 9th.

But in the valuation of the time and compared to other previous efforts, the cost was a low one.

Numerically small in the number of men engaged in the whole operation, the Machine Guns came off splendidly when their casualty lists were mustered. Nine officers and 191 other ranks were killed and wounded. Since 51 other ranks were killed, the abnormally high percentage of approximately .26 had been reached.

There at Vimy, up its slopes, on its crest and down the other side, was welded the Canadian Corps into a cohesive whole.

In this welding the work of the machine guns played no small part.

In its turn, the machine gun service itself was to be welded into a new structure. Machine gun methods of the Canadian Corps became at once the object of study by staff representatives and machine gun experts of the British and French armies.

On January 15th, 1917, Lieut.-Gen. Sir Julian Byng had made application for the establishment of the Canadian Machine Gun Corps. The entire personnel of 222 officers and 5,943 other ranks of the machine gun service, undergoing separate and different forms of training from the infantry, were still on the strength of infantry units. Questions of seniority and promotion were settled by infantry lists.

The serious conditions are clearly indicated in the corps commander's letter asking for authority to form a Machine Gun Corps on similar lines to that of the British Service:

> The situation of the Machine Gun Companies serving with the Canadian Corps as regards supply of personnel, condition of service and promotion is highly unsatisfactory and has resulted

in extravagance, inefficiency and discontent.

To remedy this serious state of things the creation of a Canadian Machine Gun Corps should be undertaken forthwith and I attach the greatest importance to this step being taken without delay.

As things are at present, the Machine Gun Companies of the Canadian Corps must inevitably break down during active and prolonged operations.

Therefore Vimy took on especial significance to the Machine Gun Service. For on April 16th, 1917, just a week after the assault on the supposedly impregnable ridge was launched, the Canadian Machine Gun Corps was authorised.

It was to build up a tradition of its own in the stirring, anxious months to come.

But never was the machine gun to present a better-balanced picture of its potentialities in attack than it did as the forbidding, snow-flecked dawn of April 9th broke to bare the outlines of the coveted ridge, against which, in a matter of moments, Canada's assaulting legions were to be let loose.

The echoes of Vimy had no more than died away than it was generally realised that a much deeper advance could have been made, had full advantage been taken of the German demoralisation.

However, the Canadian Corps did not have much leisure time for vain regrets. On April 28th another attack was launched on an eight-mile front by British troops and the 2nd Canadian Division. Canadians captured the Village of Arleux in bitter fighting and penetrated 1,800 yards on a front of 2,500 yards. On the 3rd of May the 1st Division, in an attack which saw both Imperial and Australian Divisions attacking farther south, stormed Fresnoy. Fresnoy happened to be hosts to the 15th Reserve Division of the Imperial German Army, which was contemplating an attack for a later hour that morning, but the Canadians swept them out of the village and held it against repeated counter-attacks. These attacks were designed to create a diversion to aid the French troops still pushing a fruitless attack on the Aisne.

Steady pressure which was to be maintained the next few months was to develop into an investment of Lens by the Canadian Corps and in contrast with the sharp, decisive blow which won them the prized ridge, was to prove a costly business.

On June 3rd, in the moonlight of the early morning hours, the 4th

Division thrust south of the Souchez River from Bois de Riaumont in the direction of La Coulette and Avion. They captured La Coulette, but in the face of determined enemy counter-attacks following a concentrated rain of high explosive shells, they were forced to retreat to their original trenches.

On June 8th and again on June 19th Canadians aided Imperial Brigades in capturing ground and on June 25th made a very realistic feint as the British captured Hill 65. On June 27th the 4th Division captured Eleu dit Leuvette and this set the stage for the same division the following day to go for Avion, southern suburb of Lens. The Canadians used flame projectors for the first time and, under cover of an intense barrage, the attacking brigades faced a driving rain and flooded areas to reach the village. It was tightly-locked fighting, as intensely waged as any fighting of the war, but the Canadians hung grimly on to Avion and registered another 500-yard bite into German territory on a mile of front. Machine gunners sent up to consolidate with the advancing battalions ran into hand-to-hand fighting. In one instance the Germans came over and took two guns, but the officer of the half section organised his own crews and, borrowing some infantry bombers, recaptured his guns.

These attacks were wearing down the Germans, but were also taking heavy toll of the Canadians.

Meantime, on June 19th, Sir Arthur Currie was appointed to succeed Gen. Sir Julian Byng. On July 11th the Canadians were honoured by a visit from His Majesty King George V, who saw the men at their ordinary tasks. To end his day with the Canadians, King George conducted the ceremony of knighting Sir Arthur Currie in the midst of a scarred landscape which bore eloquent testimony of the bitter fighting which marked the winning of Vimy Ridge.

There was a slight lull in the fighting. Towards the end of July and in the first weeks of August an increase in artillery firing was noted. Already an attack was planned, but it had been held up. Finally, on August 15th, it was launched, the 1st, 2nd and 4th Divisions sweeping forward in the direction of Hill 70 under the protection of one of the most intense barrages yet devised.

Machine gunners not only thickened up this barrage as they had done at Vimy but again sent mobile guns forward with the attacking infantry.

It took only sixteen minutes to capture the first objective—a general advance of 400 yards—but it was a bitter hand-to-hand struggle from there on with the German machine gunners from their heavily-cemented pill boxes exacting a heavy price for every inch the Canadians took as they edged their way to, up and over Hill 70.

On the night of the 15th-16th the Germans launched five separate counter-attacks which were beaten off.

On the 16th, as the 4th Division attacked Lens proper, they were met by a German force which itself was preparing to attack at that same time. Reports say the two opposing forces met in the open. boxed in by their own barrages. There was a general melee in which the bayonets of the Canadians came into their own. The Germans fought stubbornly and finally held on the outskirts of Lens itself.

Counter-attacks on almost successive days against the Canadians witnessed bitter fighting but prompt artillery and machine gun barrages presented an impenetrable barrier, though the Germans came on bravely enough.

From the front line to the support lines, from where indirect fire was used back to groups assigned to barrage tasks, the guns of the various Machine Gun Companies were scattered, but reports are sparse in details. Some got off lightly but others suffered severe casualties.

The 3rd C. M. Company report says, in part, of August 15th:

> (12.10 p.m.)—Enemy launched counter-attack. Seven of our guns opened fire with excellent results, enemy being seen to fall in groups. S. A. A. expended by our guns was 4,250 rounds; 500 rounds were fired by the captured German gun. Attack was broken up with heavy loss to enemy.
>
> (7.00 p.m.)—Enemy launched second counter-attack and succeeded in advancing to within 25 yards of one of our guns in S. P. 7 and endeavoured to bomb same but were driven off with heavy loss. Our guns in S. P. 7 had exceptionally good targets."

This company had 12 mobile guns with the 13th, 14th and 15th Battalions and casualties by midnight were approximately 15 other ranks with one gun knocked out by shell fire.

The 8th M. G. Company, after a terse summary, states its casualties were two officers and 29 men, most of whom were gassed. Most of the men were gassed more or less but did not go out. One gun was destroyed by shell fire. S. A. A. expended by the 16 guns was 360,000 rounds.

We'll take a report from the 4th Division, from the 11th Company in this case.

Of the 15th of August this company matter-of-factly reports:

> Enemy projected quantity of his shells from 10 p.m. to 2 a.m., making atmosphere very dense with gas. This was followed by bombardment of H. E. shells from 2 a.m. until 4 a.m. At 4.25 a.m. our guns opened heavy barrage fire in conjunction with the attack of our divisions on the left. At 8.25 a.m. our guns moved forward and took part in the attack by the 11th C. I. B. on the Green Crassier and Aconite Trench. Continuous firing up until 12 noon against enemy counter-attacks.

Another sentence disposes of the events of the 16th.

Here and there in the midst of routine details a report will be varied by conclusions as in the case of a divisional company which had used trench slits. Of these it says:

> Trench slits again proved satisfactory, although the men suffered more hardships than would have been the case if the trenches had been utilized, chiefly owing to the fact that they were unable to move about. After moving into slits before zero hour, camouflage was spread over positions and no movement was allowed during the day. During the 10 days these slits were occupied batteries suffered only two casualties and no direct hits were obtained. On the other hand, a unit of the division on our left in a trench some 150 yards from the slits suffered many casualties in two or three days.

In these hurrying post-war days machine gunners who grow impatient at the momentary delays of life should have an effective brake on such growing impatience if they cast back in memory to the cramped vigils of days and nights in these slits, when only a minimum of movement was possible and that minimum only at the cost of many slow contortions.

In this same report, also, a little *esprit de corps* creeps in. This report mildly exults:

> In all cases batteries answered SOS signals from one to four minutes ahead of the artillery.

This indicates that the machine gunners were beginning to feel far from apologetic about their role as a light artillery in the barrage schemes.

On August 23rd, just before dawn, the Canadians launched their attack on the Green Crassier, giant slag heap which barred their entry into Lens from the south. The huge pile was a labyrinth of trenches and machine gun emplacements, but the Canadians carried these with a rush. The slag heap was a maze of tunnels, too, down which the Canadians bombed their way. It proved a fitting climax to the siege of Lens for there was no quarter asked or given. However, after holding on all night the Canadians were forced to relinquish what they had won next day, as a German counter-attack swarmed over in such strength that it forced a stubborn retreat back down the smashed trenches.

This brought to a close the Canadian attempts to wrest Lens from the Germans. Casualties for July and August were now listed at 10,746. In addition, the nature of the fighting had imposed a heavy strain on all ranks.

CHAPTER 4

Battle of Passchendaele

Warned early in September by Gen. Sir Henry Horne, commander of the 1st Army, that they were likely to be detached and sent to Flanders to take part in the main British thrust being made there, it came as no surprise to the Canadians when by mid-October the 3rd and 4th Divisions were already in the van of the movement which was to take the whole Corps northwards, back to Belgium.

They were headed back to the very salient where the 1st Division had won imperishable fame and to an area that had seen the 2nd and then 3rd Division, each in turn, offered to the holocaust of modern war, out of which they came, maimed but never broken and tempered as with steel to an added hardness which three years and a half had shown the gods of war demanded in ever increasing degree. Even the 4th Division had had its first peek inside the theatre of war as it was gently initiated into trench tours just to the south of the grim salient to which all were now pointing.

Started on July 31st after numerous, unavoidable delays, the Third Battle of Ypres, as this offensive of 1917 was to be known, had been raging with ever-increasing intensity for two months, when the movement of the Canadians to the north began.

Even in the midst of their own immediate and pressing troubles in front of Lens, Canadians had followed the fortunes of the Imperials, Australians, New Zealanders and South Africans to the north in the salient as daily the toll of comparatively shallow advances strengthened the claim of Ypres and its surrounding area as the "Graveyard of an Empire." They had learned to read between the lines of war dispatches as they perused them in trench or billet. They had no illusions regarding what lay at the end of this trek north. The most imaginative and morbid of speculative flights were to fall far, far below the most comfortable, "cushy" levels of realisation.

The fourth British attack had been started on October 4th. Despite another downpour of the rain that had been falling almost incessantly since July and had long ago rendered the whole salient but one vast quagmire, the assault made remarkable headway and British and Australian troops, at a great cost in lives, wrested another 3,000 yards of muddy desolation from the Germans. They captured Zonnebeke, they reached Poelcappelle and the higher land at Broodseinde, and on the right they pushed up the valley, where runs the Weiltje-Passchendaele road, and ran their line of connected shell holes up beyond the Gravenstafel cross roads and Abraham Heights to Berlin Wood. But they were short some 3,000 yards of their original objective, the Village of Passchendaele itself which hung on the crest of the low ridge to which it gave its sombre name—a ridge that looked little more than a ripple in the flatness of this sodden Belgian landscape but yet gave dominance over the plain stretching away toward Roulers, important railway centre.

At a terrific cost in lives, under conditions that were always to remain a monument to British courage, to bulldog tenacity, the line had now been established along the main series of ridges for 9,000 yards from the starting point at Mount Sorrell.

The operations had first been launched with a vision of sweeping the Germans off this system of ridges, sending them pell-mell over the plains approaching Roulers and thrusting on to clear them out of their Flemish bases and cut their communications to their submarine bases on the coast.

What had been conceived in the dry months as a tremendous two-week smash had now prolonged itself into two months of battering against two foes—mud and the Germans. Even had the weather been normal, the newly-devised system of elastic defence based on heavily-armoured pill-boxes, commandingly placed and which were impervious to direct hits by 12-inch shells, would have given the Germans an even chance in the defence of these low, sprawling ridges. With the clinging, slimy mud as an ally the Germans had slowed the operation down to a soggy crawl.

But even if two months of continual rain had shrunken the original conception down to trench raid proportions, yet there were still presented weighty reasons why the British should keep the initiative.

Seemingly overwhelming disasters in Russia and Italy made the grim necessities of the salient, and finally its climax, Passchendaele, look microscopic by comparison but no less forbidding for all of that. The weakened morale of the French further fanned the urgency and a continuation of the "limited operations" were still more necessary to focus still more German attention while the Cambrai "surprise" of November 20th was still simmering.

On October 9th the British had continued their push, reaching Houlthulst Forest, the final objective on the north, but the assault of October 12th, farther south, sent off after 48 hours more downpour, completely bogged down in impassable swamps and was abandoned.

To keep the enemy's attention two more weeks and to shove him out of Passchendaele and off the final ridge were the twofold reasons which diverted the Canadians from their planned attack at Sallaumines and routed them to the north for this final smash at the salient.

And so on October 18th Gen. Sir Arthur Currie took over command of the Passchendaele front. Though he had been represented as offering alternative action for his Corps to the British higher command, once committed to the task, the Canadian Corps commander, as far as was humanly possible and within the limited time at his disposal, made sure that everything that foresight and preparation could do to make the operation a success must be pushed through. Those preparations cost lives but ultimately they saved many.

Plank roads on fascines were pushed out across the slimy terrain; duckboards that were to offer precarious footing but were to be necessarily vital, even if narrow, arteries carrying food and .ammunition up to the front, were assembled in large quantities. Light railways were speedily laid to ensure the rapid distribution of the huge quantities of shells and material needed. All this vital work was carried on under constant shell-fire of the back areas and constantly recurring bombing raids from the air, both day and night, for a new note of defiance. even aggressiveness was apparent from the German side as news of fresh Russian and Italian disasters inspired them to new effort.

The 10th Machine Gun Company (Major James Britton) was the first Canadian unit to take over the line, relieving the 10th and 11th Australian Companies' 16 guns. Typical of many officers who had been fed into the 4th Division as a leavening of experience, it was peculiarly fitting that the O. C. of the 10th should have this honour of leading the first M. G. unit back into an area which echoed the tramping feet of those survivors of the Second Battle of Ypres, of which he was one, as a sergeant in the machine gun section of the gallant 5th Battalion.

By the 22nd the two-division relief was complete. The 4th Division had the 10th and 16th Companies in the line and the 3rd Division were supported by the 7th and 15th.

The preparations for the opening attack, planned for four days later, went on feverishly. Into the comparatively small confines of the ever-narrowing salient were poured supplies of men and material that were staggering in round figures.

In general the plans for employment of machine guns were to be those of Vimy with only minor exceptions. Again they were to assume the roles of barrage and mobile guns but with the addition this time of "Sniping Sections" of four guns each, one or two of which were to be allotted to each divisional front.

Always the "human pack mules" of the front line areas, the machine gunners were to face in the next few grisly weeks, conditions which would seem beyond human endurance and stamina as they struggled with their heavier equipment through dragging mud, plunged into bogs, sprawled into shell-holes filled waist, and sometimes shoulder-high with water and man-handed into position, the ammunition which their weapons so rapaciously devoured. They envied for the moment the self-contained readiness of the more lightly-loaded infantry soldier for instant battle.

In fact there were times the gunners envied the mules.

A No. 1 gunner in a 4th Division Company, for instance, had a one-sided monologue that he used to employ against passing mules and when he caught one standing-well, that was so much the better. "Slackers, conchies," he would spit at them in mock viciousness, as with heavy Vickers tripod slung over his shoulder he might be passing "trains" of the patient "mokes" from whom the heaviest and nearest explosions brought only a protesting twitching of the long ears.

"Think you're carrying a load," he would harangue the mule in a tone of high scorn. "You slacker, you—nice solid roads to walk on—no shell holes to fall into—and call yourself a pack animal!"

"Look at me, moke," showing the unconcerned and unimpressed "moke" the tripod; "how'd you like to lug that through the mud?"

"Come from Missouri, do you? Well, you gotta show me," would be the No. 1 gunner's parting and most withering shot.

This monologue never failed to get a laugh though most of the grins were mud-caked at Passchendaele.

Every unit had these lads, whose drollery kept a balance of saneness in the hottest spots. More often than not they did not wear stars or chevrons. In fact, they were quite often overlooked when the decorations were being passed out. Yet Passchendaele especially needed this spirit, which could pluck a jest out of the very air which was so oppressive and menacing-and death-laden.

As at Vimy, divisional pack trains were again formed and were to do highly useful work. At Vimy, however, they had been able to establish dumps almost at the positions themselves. In the salient, forced to keep to the solid footing of what were once called roads, they could only get up to very definite points owing to the intense shelling. Much of the huge supply of 1,500,000 rounds of S. A. A. assembled for each division had therefore to be man-handled by the gunners and the infantry carrying parties which, once more, had been detailed to this task.

In the few days preceding the attack itself machine guns in the line carried out a program of indirect harassing fire and the barrage positions were completed under conditions that baffle description. The artillery farther back had little or no protection and were dug in in the open. Trying to get a solid platform for the barrage machine guns in the slimy ooze was a hard, trying task.

The battle order for the first attack found the 4th Division attacking on the Canadian right, with the 1st Australian Division on their flank. The 4th was to attack with one brigade-the 10th-while the 3rd Division was using a two-brigade front and employing the 9th and 8th C. 1. B's. On the left flank of the Canadian Corps boundary was the 63rd Naval Division. The Canadian frontage gave the two divisions slightly over 3,000 yards at the jumping-off line, extending roughly from the Passchendaele-Zonnebeke Road to Wallemolen. They had as their objectives Hillside Farm, Heine House, Augustus Wood, Lamkeek, Bellevue Spur, Wolfe Copse and the slightly higher ground to the north-west.

Sixteen mobile guns in all were attached to the divisions for the whole attack and in some cases the infantry had detailed sections for the local protection of the machine guns while in consolidation positions. The 10th Company (Major Britton) and the 9th Company (Major McFaul) provided the mobile guns as well as the new innovation—the three "Sniping Batteries." The 4th Division used only one of these four-gun batteries. The 3rd ordered two up.

Eighty guns in all were given the task of laying down a supporting barrage to fit into the artillery's fire scheme. Five eight-gun batteries were allotted to each divisional front, on the basis of one gun to every 30 yards of frontage. Positions for these extended, roughly, from

Abraham Heights on the right to the northern slopes of Gravenstafel Spur.

In the gray dawn of October 26th, at exactly 5.40, thousands of guns along the 10-mile front rolled out their deafening thunder to herald the attack. Out-gunned as they were to be many times before they left the salient a few weeks hence, the Canadian gunners shouldered their full share of one of the most terrific, most cruelly concentrated and most intense artillery duels in all the history of the Western Front. It seemed as if nothing could possibly live as the gunners from both sides searched up and down whole areas in a scientific hunt for victims. Gradually the volume of the German guns grew perceptibly less and as the attacking brigades pushed off into the sea of shell-churned mud, superiority was definitely with the British gunners.

Waist-deep in mud, the attacking brigades struggled forward. The 10th Brigade wallowed ahead and won their objectives after sharp fighting, especially fronting Crest Farm and Deck Wood, from where a perfect hail of machine gun fire was poured into their struggling ranks. On the extreme right the 10th got as far as Decline Copse and Hillside Farm, Heine House and Augustus Wood were gathered in as the brigade went beyond its objectives to Deck Wood.

But on the left it was a different story. Crossing the swollen Ravebeek stream at "Fleet Cottages," 1,000 yards beyond Gravenstafel, the 8th and 9th Brigades were stopped in temporary confusion by a withering machine gun fire and by the havoc of the German barrage. When the original attack on Bellevue was halted, Capt. Chris O'Kelly of the 52nd Battalion won a V. C. as by his skill and determination he advanced his command over 1,000 yards unsupported by artillery barrage and took the enemy position on the hill by storm and then organised a series of attacks on pill boxes, which resulted in the capture of six and their stubborn, courageous garrisons, together with 10 machine guns. While both right and left the objectives had been reached, one pill-box known as "Snipe Hall" had successfully withstood all concentrated artillery fire and direct assault and here the line between the 8th and 9th Brigades presented a sharp cleavage. All attempts to dent back this salient in our lines were to fail for four days as elements of the 11th Bavarian Division put up one of the stoutest defences ever offered by German troops.

Since garrisons of the pill-boxes fought to the bitter end and even those isolated shell-hole garrisons knew they were hopelessly fastened in the mud, targets of opportunity during the attack for the machine

The machine Guns at Paschendaele

guns were mighty few. But the principle of this elastic defence plan of the Germans was to provide our mobile and sniping batteries with their real and effective role as the elastic defence, giving away before the first onslaught, was bounced back by counterattacks in force and with a determination, lately lacking in German counter-attacks elsewhere.

On the extreme right Lieut. Hugh Aird had placed his two guns in a sunken road 200 yards to the right of the Zonebeeke-Passchendaele Road so as to cover the right flank and the low ground to the left of the railway in the neighbourhood of Vienna Cottage. The other two guns, under Corp. Carey, were sited in front of Hillside Farm in the centre of the 46th Battalion frontage to the left of the Passchendaele Road and looking to the right flank.

Lieut. Aird's guns were handled with the utmost skill and daring and did fine execution a the German counter-attack was launched at 4.40 p.m. As the enemy opened a terrific bombardment on the sunken road where the guns were, Lieut. Aird sent all the gunners to the junction of the sunken road with the main Passchendaele Road, where there was less shelling and more shelter. He himself, along with Corp. Thursby, remained at the guns. The Germans were seen massing for the attack in a field near Vienna Cottage about 200 yards off. Both guns came into action, scattering the Germans and causing many casualties. Lieut. Aird's gun was put out of action as a large shell exploded close to the gun and he joined Sergt. Thursby.

The German counter-attack kept developing and they started advancing in extended order. Shells were falling so close that on hard ground nothing above the ground level could have lived, but the mud proved the salvation in its way of this gun crew, although mud also in the space of a few minutes was to put the gun out of action. It could still fire single shots but Lieut. Aird, realising the danger of being cut off from the left, moved the gun back when the Germans were within 100 yards and mounted it near Hillside Farm. Corp. Carey with the other two guns, having been killed, the three guns were dug in defensive positions. Lieut. Aird was unfortunately killed the same night during one of the frequent bombardments the Germans laid down with so much venom.

On the 3rd Division front, where the fight was more bitter, machine gunners had many difficult moments. Two guns with the 58th Battalion were out of action and only the officer and two other ranks left when the battalion resumed its attack in the afternoon. Two of the four guns with the 43rd were put out of action early, but the other two not only formed a rallying point when the line was withdrawn on the right in the morning set-back but with a little group of infantrymen holding fast inflicted severe losses on the Germans, who attempted to reorganise 250 yards from the gun positions. It was in-fighting with a vengeance. The officer, wounded earlier in the attack, did not leave until the guns were consolidated and No. 1 gunners carried on. At 10 a.m. they caught two companies of Germans on the Weiltje Road in a perfect field of fire and dispersed them and they threw confusion into the Germans assembling for the counter-attack later to be launched at 4 p.m. from Meetoseele and Furst Farm. When the actual counter-attack came these two guns played like a hose on the Germans struggling ahead in the mud in extended order.

Believing as men of the 4th C. M. R. filed back through his positions that they were making an unauthorized withdrawal though they had been ordered by their company commander to swing back their flank, the M. G. officer in charge of the other two guns of the 9th Company collected about two platoons, led them forward to a commanding position and proceeded with consolidation. When two platoons of the 1st C. M. R. were sent up as reserves the position was turned over and, as established and consolidated, was thereafter held. The G. O. C. 8th Brigade asked for four more guns for left flank protection but these didn't have time to get suitable fields of fire before the German counter-attack was launched.

The three sniping batteries met with varying fortunes. The 10th Brigade section were able to support the 3rd Division attack in the afternoon by firing on Meetcheele and Graf Wood. With the nearby battery from the 9th, both were heavily shelled. Two guns of the other sniping battery from the 9th Company were destroyed and in the temporary withdrawal of the morning the remaining two took part. Later they were taken back to the original positions to consolidate a part of the line that remained a danger spot for four days.

The barrage batteries had escaped lightly in the matter of casualties but had had a very strenuous time. On the 4th Division front the M. G. barrage responded to the SOS as the German counter-attack was launched at 4.40 p.m., some minutes before the artillery answer came.

The G. O. C., 10th C. I. B., in his report spoke in the highest terms of the M. G. fire developed so rapidly. He wrote in his report:

The barrage work of all Machine Guns was particularly evident during the counter-attack on the 26th instant, when they responded immediately to the SOS and caused considerable loss to the attacking forces during the period the artillery failed to respond.

One gun was knocked out in the barrage group of the 3rd Division but was quickly replaced from the Advanced Armourer's shop. The forward position of the latter was to be of immense and immediate help in other contingencies that the conditions of the battle were to produce. The Machine Guns covered the afternoon attack, carried out area shoots where the enemy were reported massing and sent during the day half a million menacing, zinging messages toward the Hun lines.

Guns in barrage positions carried out harassing programs on the next three days and nights after reliefs had been made. On the night of the 27th—28th the 4th Division batteries furnished a barrage for the 44th Battalion's successful attack on Decline Copse, an important position on the extreme right flank. Two guns, one from the 12th Company and one from the 16th, went forward with this attack.

On the morning of the 29th the P. P. C. L.I's drove forward over 500 yards of terrible ground to surround and capture Snipe Hall and its garrison and thus straighten out the line which this pill-box had held at bay in the previous operation.

The swollen Ravebeek divided the 12th C. I. B., the attacking brigade on the 4th Division front, from the 7th C. I. B. in the centre and the 8th C. I. B. on the left flank.

Ten mobile guns went forward with the 12th C. I. B. on the 4th Division front, four from the 12th Company and six from the 16th. The 7th Company provided four and the 8th Company two mobile guns for the 3rd Division battalions.

The sky was clear—for once—and the moon full as the attacking battalions assembled for the attack during the late hours of the 29th and the early morning hours of the 30th. The shelling was constant and destructive.

Towards zero hour—5.40 a.m.—the weather turned to a cold, chill wind and rain fell.

With slight variations—tragic especially in the case of the Princess Patricias—the attacking battalions started for their objective. The barrage lift was fifty yards every four minutes—a rate of 750 yards an hour, and even this crawling pace was fast enough. The German counter-barrage came down three minutes after zero hour and exacted the first toll on the struggling attackers.

The 4th Division, after hard, stubborn fighting, broke through the German main line of resistance and by 6.35 a.m. all objectives were taken. The 72nd Battalion by a brilliant flanking movement captured Deck Wood with its German garrison and Crest Farm fell to the men of the Green Patch. Early in the day the G. O. C. 12th C. I. B. called for four more guns for right flank protection and these came from the 12th Company. Two of the guns with the 85th Battalion were discovered by low-flying German planes which swept our planes out of the air this day and were knocked out by direct hits shortly after. Four guns under Lieut. Montagnon of the 16th Company were first used for indirect fire to a flank and then two were taken up for consolidation in a commanding position at Crest Farm. These were in position at 7.30 a.m. They were on the forward slope of the crest with the Germans but 200 yards away.

The officer fearlessly exposed himself, says an account, to enemy machine gun and rifle fire while moving about, cheering his crews. Later he was severely wounded by shell-fire but crawled to a gun and refused to leave it, believing the Germans were going to counter-attack. He was carried out by a stretcher party but died two weeks later in hospital, being posthumously awarded the Military Cross. Command of this officer's guns fell upon Sergt. Crites, who carried on in succeeding days with courage and determination.

The 3rd Division was again to meet with exceptionally stubborn resistance. Meetcheele was the key to the defences fronting the 3rd and in addition to the pill-boxes the Germans had machine guns in shell holes and snipers in pairs in the same cover and they poured a devastating fire into the scattered ranks of the attacking battalions. The 5th C. M. R. on the extreme left, wading through morass and swamp, went forward to Source and Vapour Farms and secured a footing in Vanity House. On the left, the 63rd Imperials could not get ahead and fought with one flank exposed. The Pats added another stirring but sombre page to their marvellous record in their struggle over 1,000 yards of slowly rising ground, for every step of which advance they paid a terrific price.

The 49th, on its left, was sharing that cost, stiffened by the 7th Company machine guns. Headed direct for the fortified positions on Meetcheele Spur, which were spurting a continuous hail of destruction, only two officers were left in the two leading Pats' companies.

Ralph Hodder-Williams, historian of the Princess Pats' vivid history, writes:

> At a moment when it seemed the line must waver or break utterly, appeared Lieut. Hugh McKenzie, D.C.M., of the Brigade (7th) Machine Gunners (himself an old No. 3 Company man) and Lieut. J. M. Christie, D.C.M., and Sergt. G. H. Mullin, M.M., of the regimental snipers. While Christie made a rush forward on the left, found a good position and covered the advance with his rearly marksmanship, McKenzie dashed from shell hole to shell hole rallying the survivors for a last effort and leading them toward the pill-box. McKenzie was killed at the head of the men he had inspired with his own magnificent courage, but while he and his party drew the fire, Mullin was crawling up the slope and he actually performed the incredible feat of taking the pill-box single-handed.
>
> 'He rushed a sniper's post in front and destroyed the garrison with bombs and crawling on to the top of the pill-box shot the two machine gunners with his revolver. Sergt. Mullin then rushed to another entrance and compelled the garrison of ten to surrender. His gallantry and fearlessness were witnessed by many and, although rapid fire was directed upon him and his clothes riddled by bullets, he never faltered in his purpose and he not only helped to save the situation but also indirectly saved many lives.'

So it was that Lieut. McKenzie, D.C.M., and Sergt. Mullin won the first Victoria Crosses awarded the Patricias in the war.

The Pats' claim to Lieut. McKenzie may be well understood.

The account given of the exploit by Corporal T. Hampson of the 7th Company in its essential details tells much the same story. This N.C.O. later established his two guns to the right of the Weiltje Road, about midway between Bellevue and Meetcheele, where he could command the left flank. The two guns under Sergt. Howard (later killed) suffered heavily in casualties as they followed the centre of the attack. At night there were but four men left with the two guns. In fact, the four mobile gun crews of the 7th Company, which mustered one officer and 27 other ranks, had been reduced to 11 other ranks by nightfall, the rest either being killed or wounded. The two guns of the 8th Company on the extreme left got off much more lightly. They dispersed Germans bringing two machine guns into action near Vine Cottage and caught fleeting glimpses of good targets.

Twelve sniping guns had gone over with the general attack, four from the 9th Company and four from the 12th on the 4th Division front and four from the 15th Company on the 3rd Division front. The two right batteries, owing to the smoke barrage of the Germans throughout the morning, were unable to get good targets. The left battery, just after zero, using direct overhead fire, had good shooting on the enemy seen on the skyline of the ridge, running from pill-boxes and shelters. Two guns, however, of this left battery were knocked out of action shortly getting their first targets.

The barrage guns suffered very heavily in this action and no stronger proof could be had of the effectiveness of our barrage fire than the attention the enemy's low-flying planes gave to locating and dealing with them.

Batteries 1 to 4, after losing six guns, managed to move to the rear and take up new positions near Seine. Of these four batteries that of the 16th Company suffered most severely. Lieut. Gavreau, in charge, was killed. He had been wounded before zero hour but refused to go out and was killed by shell fire shortly after. Five other ranks killed, one officer and nine other ranks wounded completed the heavy toll before the guns could be moved. The 10th, 11th and 12th Companies officers did a magnificent job in reorganising and 26 remaining guns were in action in the new positions by 2 p.m., despite vicious machine-gunning attacks from enemy low-flying planes.

Battery No. 5 (1st C.M.M.G. Brigade) was completely disabled in a very short time. Capt. Brotherston, O. C., had been killed while reconnoitring his battery positions on the night before the attack. Two other officers wounded, seven other ranks killed, 14 wounded and five gassed left only 10 men to man the guns.

The 3rd Division Barrage Batteries were running in good fortune for their barrage program but as low-flying planes of the enemy drove our flights back shortly before 10 o'clock they directed artillery which shelled Nos. 7 and 8 heavily with 5.9's and 8-inch shells. The concentration was so heavy and sudden and the condition of the ground on both sides of the batteries so marshy that guns and personnel were greatly reduced before they could be moved. Only two guns were left in action in each battery. No. 7 ("B" Battery, 1st C. M. M. G. Brigade) had only one officer and 11 other ranks left and No. 8 (9th Company) had but one officer and 16 other ranks with the guns

Nos. 9 and 10 Batteries were laid on the whole SOS line while new positions were located, barrage lines worked out and reinforcements brought up and placed in position. By 7 p.m. all four batteries were complete and again in action. About 1 p.m. No. 3 Battery (two guns, 8th; six guns, 15th Company) was heavily shelled and both officers were casualties. Three guns of No. 4 Battery were put out of action but owing to the proximity of the advanced armourers' depot no gun was out of action more than 30 minutes. Stoppages were mostly caused from wet and dirty belts in spite of every precaution taken to keep them dry.

Once more the effects of our machine gun barrage fire drew high praise from the infantry and prisoners taken on the 30th confirmed its terrific execution, especially as it came down on defended shell holes.

And now came an interval of six days. It was a pause that could, audibly, hardly be construed as such.

True, the wholesale horror of the battle operations themselves was over for the moment, but into the rest areas—which were that only in the broad, comparative sense—men of the 3rd and 4th Divisions were to carry unforgettable mental pictures of a living hell of exploding shells, of machine gun and rifle fire that swept whole platoons into the mire; of wounded left helpless and pinned in the pitiless mud; of moments up there, where, if only for short spells, reason and sanity—and mercy—returned so that stretcher parties of the enemy and our own, under the protection of white flags, were able to clear the battlefield. From that momentary gesture the wounded and their brave bearers had still to run the gamut of constant, destructive shelling along duckboards and roads that, to German gunners, were known to a foot.

The back areas, as the 1st and 2nd Divisions trudged in to start the relief of the shattered but still unshaken men of the other two divisions who had borne the first brunt of attacking, presented an indescribable picture. A whole corps was crowded in there and yet it was uncanny the way in which this vast number of men took to ground and seemed utterly to disappear into the labyrinth of warrens. Forward roads were under constant shelling and the unblinking stare of a ring of enemy "sausage balloons" which hung in the gray skies to the east, roughly outlining the salient as it had been further pushed in. The "camps" to the rear, the innumerable "horse lines," with their patient, enduring equine occupants dotting the flat landscape, all presented an inviting target that seeming swarms of Hun bombers could not, and did not, neglect.

Only Passchendaele and Mosselmarkt villages remained to be taken before the ridge would be secure, but that "only" was a four-letter word that was to spell out a demand for heroism and endurance by the 1st and 2nd Divisions to fully equal those qualities which the 3rd and 4th had displayed in such deathless fashion. The German Higher Command had ordered that this last ridge be held at all costs and if lost, recaptured no matter how high and heavy the price. More artillery was rushed up to fill the gaps blown out in the two previous operations by accuracy and concentration of our own gunners. Defences in front of, and in, these two key villages were strengthened in every way German ingenuity could suggest.

On October 31st there had been isolated counter-attacks on the 4th Division and one was launched against the 3rd Division at 1.15 a.m. the same day.

After taking over the line, the 1st and 2nd Division Machine Gun Companies started immediately in on preparations for the impending attack. Just on completion of their relief on November 3rd, the 4th C. I. B. beat off an enemy counter-attack. On November 4th the barrage guns, already in position, responded to an SOS call at 4 a.m., but no enemy attack developed.

The frontage of the attack to be launched on November 6th was considerably shortened for the 2nd Division on the right. Passchendaele itself was included in this Division's objectives. The ground over which the 2nd was to attack was high and included comparatively little marshy ground. On the right flank of the 1st Division large areas of mud and water existed and in front of the centre and left the ground was practically impassable for infantry. The only good ground was the narrow Bellevue-Meetcheele Spur, which was 350 yards wide at its narrowest point west of Meetcheele. The 1st therefore was to avoid the swamp on the left in Goudberg Valley. A subsidiary attack on Vine Cottage by a company and a half of Canadians the night before the general attack was considered one of the lesser epics of the war, since its garrison fought to the end against cold steel.

Corps to the right and left prolonged our artillery and machine gun barrage on their own frontage, simulating an attack at the same time, but in the case of the machine gun barrage the Canadians were to have the barrage help of 26 guns of the 1st Anzac Corps on the right and 9 guns of the 2nd Corps on the left. With our own 80 guns, made up from the Companies and from the 1st Motor Brigade, a grand total of 114 guns were to fire the barrage.

Sixteen mobile guns were to be employed on the 2nd Division front, but there were to be no "Sniping Batteries." Nine of these were to have a purely defensive role. They were to be placed in forward positions prior to zero hour and remain there throughout the operation. The shallow advance contemplated on the 2nd Division front accounted for this decision. The 5th and 6th Companies provided these guns.

Eight mobile guns of the 1st Company were detailed to the 1st Brigade, which was to do the attacking for the 1st Division. Our guns had been deluging the enemy front with shells for 48 hours and only two minutes of intense concentration heralded the attack of November 6th as the Canadians pushed off close behind their barrage at 6 a.m. The attack progressed well along the whole front. By 7.10 2nd Divisional men were in Passchendaele Village itself in large numbers and at 8.45 all objectives had been carried. The 1st Division reached their first objective at 7.45 a.m., the garrison of Mosselmarkt not having offered the expected resistance. They were so dazed by our barrage and surprised by our men following so close behind it that they had no time for resistance.

On the whole, the mobile guns got off rather easily in the matter of casualties, especially those with the 2nd Division. At 8.50 a.m. the enemy attempted a counter-attack with one battalion north of Passchendaele but this attack was beaten off. Three times that morning they were again to attempt assembling for attacks but were dispersed by artillery and machine gun fire.

Six 1st Company guns, under Lieut. Trebilcock, covering the advance of the 1st Infantry Battalion while waiting for zero hour, had three other ranks killed and one wounded and a gun put out of action, but the gun was quickly replaced, and shortly after zero the crews were led forward to positions on the highest ground of the Bellevue-Meetcheele Spur on either side of the Weiltje Road. At 10.05 Lieut. Trebilcock was seriously wounded and died of wounds in the afternoon.

Four sniping guns of the 2nd Company, located at Crest Farm, laid on Meetcheele Spur, failed to get any good targets during the attack and avoided suffering any casualties. On the evening of the 7th, however, when the battery was preparing to leave, two crews, guns and equipment were buried as heavy enemy shelling destroyed the trench.

Four other ranks were killed, one was dug out of the shattered trench, badly wounded, and two could not be found.

Thus went the luck of battles.

If mobile guns came off lightly in the actual battle, the barrage guns did not.

Nos. 1 and 2 Batteries, near Augustus Wood, came in for a lot of shelling and No. 1 Battery was forced out of its position. No. 2 Battery lost five other ranks wounded and one gun but remained in position. Batteries 3, 4 and 5, near Heine House, had comparatively few casualties though heavily shelled. A carrying party for No. 3 Battery, bringing up ammunition, had six killed and four wounded out of 12 as the searching enemy artillery caught them. No. 5 Battery (Bordens) fired 35,000 rounds in reply to the SOS call at 10 a.m.

Batteries 6 and 7 suffered the heaviest during the attack, no less than 23 casualties being counted. These two batteries got off 44,000 rounds in the attack barrage. No. 8 Battery (3rd and 13th Companies) had one gun destroyed early but within 30 minutes it was replaced from the advanced armourer's depot. A second gun destroyed later in the day was similarly replaced.

Once more there came high praise for the effectiveness of the machine gun barrage.

The G. O. C. 5th C. I. B. wrote:

> Our machine gun barrage was perfect and, according to reports from prisoners, caused heavy casualties among the enemy. When the SOS signal went up our machine guns opened up so promptly that they were all firing before the flare reached the ground. This was favourably commented upon by all hands in the infantry.

Prisoners captured on November 6th stated that men of a Second Line battalion coming up in support between 6.45 and 7 a.m. were literally mown down by our machine gun barrage. Captured German machine gunners of the 3rd M. K. Kompanies, 10th Grenadier Regiment, said that owing to our M. G. and artillery barrage and the rapidity of our infantry advance not one of their 10 machine guns got into action.

Owing to the heavy losses suffered by the barrage groups in the intervals between phases and because of the great strain upon the personnel who had to remain in the line, in some cases as long as eight days, the corps commander on representations from the C.M.G.C.

gave orders that these batteries were to be withdrawn 48 hours after an operation, leaving only sufficient guns for harassing fire and dealing with SOS signals.

The elements of the Motors were withdrawn and four guns from each of the Machine Gun Companies in the divisions were left in the line, in pursuance of these orders.

The 2nd Brigade of the 1st Division and the 6th Brigade of the 2nd were assigned the task of carrying out the last operation on November 10th on an extremely narrow frontage.

Considering the small depth of advance aimed at in the operation, no sniping or mobile guns were used on the 2nd Division front. Guns already in position were sited in positions from which they could efficiently handle any tasks. Six mobile guns went over with the 2nd Brigade on the 1st Division front.

For barrage tasks a total of 88 guns were available. There were 24 each from the two divisional "battalions," 24 from the Motors and 16 guns from the 1st Anzac Corps on the right comprising this total.

Rain had fallen during the night and when, at 6.05 on the morning of November 10th, our attacking barrage was laid down and started on its way, it was still raining. By 8 a.m. all objectives of this attack, entirely to the north of Passchendaele Village had been taken. The 2nd Division encountered none of the enemy. In the left sector the 7th Battalion, bothered by machine gun fire from Venison Trench 300 yards beyond the objective, charged forward and capturing a portion of the trench and some prisoners, retired to conform with the rest of the line. The 8th Battalion, after reaching the left objective at 6.50 a.m., found their flanks in the air owing to the inability of the 1st (British) Division to advance in the face of machine gun fire from Vocation and Vox Farms. The flank was bent back to a point 100 yards south of Venture Farm. There the Westerners were shelled heavily and at 2.36 p.m. repelled a determined enemy counter-attack.

Preparations for this small-scale attack took a bigger toll of machine gunners than the actual operation.

Three guns of the 14th Company, 300 yards east of Passchendaele Village, had been destroyed on the day before the attack. Seven other ranks were killed, the officer and two other ranks wounded. As three other guns to replace these were being started for their defence positions at 2 a.m. on the morning of the attack, an enemy bombardment of Tyne Cottage killed two other ranks and destroyed the three guns. Replacement guns did not arrive until 4.30 p.m. on the afternoon of the 10th and shelling was so severe that it was decided to keep them until next morning. Two of them were then started on their way and by noon these two guns had been destroyed, though the crews escaped.

The 6th Company defence guns had also had an unfortunate tour. Two guns were destroyed on the way into the line on the 8th and on November 9th four other ranks were killed and two wounded at the positions of these guns during severe shelling.

Four mobile guns of the 1st Division got forward with the infantry into previously selected positions and had numerous targets during the 10th, but by evening three of these four guns had been destroyed or put out of action by the intense enemy shelling. Lieut. Laing, in charge of these guns, had left the gun he was with to supervise the positions taken 200 yards in rear of the final objective and report his final disposition to the infantry. This was the last seen of the officer, who was first reported missing, then "killed in action."

Lance-Corp. Frost's action as he was left finally alone with the one remaining gun, splendidly illustrates that initiative, even in isolation, of gun numbers. This soldier worked his gun, sniping at enemy parties until his ammunition gave out. He dismounted his gun and put it under cover in a shell hole and went back to get more ammunition. With his new supply he kept his gun in action until the battalion was relieved, though throughout this period he was without food or water.

As if this tragic confusion up front were not enough, the disappearance of these guns caused more than a flurry elsewhere. Four guns were brought up from barrage positions and when orders for their disposal were not forthcoming they were sent back and it was not until the 11th that these defence guns were in position, two at Vindictive Crossroads firing north-east and two north of Venture Farm to assist in the defence of the exposed left flank.

A tale of such an ill-starred venture as these four guns present might well illustrate why war is an art—not an exact science.

The barrage guns had again a story of heavy losses. Eleven barrage guns were destroyed by the intense shelling during the day.

The batteries fired an average of 20,000 rounds each in the attack barrage but after heavy rain started falling at 10 a.m. there was extreme difficulty in keeping the guns in action though every device to keep the belts dry was tried. Six guns of No. 5 Battery (13th Company) had answered the SOS signal in the afternoon. After firing three belts four of these guns went out of action because of wet and dirty belts. Mud thrown over guns and equipment by exploding shells had put all the battery out of action in another 20 minutes.

This was a common experience of the day. One hour after zero No. 1 Battery (14th Company), after having two guns blown up, moved to new positions but not before Lieut. Lyon was killed.

No. 4 Battery (Eatons) had no casualties but thanked the mud for it. At No. 8 Battery (Bordens) Lieut. Kill was killed 30 minutes after fire opened and two guns were put out of action. At 1.30 p.m. three other ranks were killed and three wounded. No. 9 (Yukons) had two guns put out of action and at 11.15 one officer and five other ranks were buried in a section of trench on which two shells fell in succession.

And thus came to an end the attacks on Passchendaele Ridge. There was still holding to be done, however, and since the Germans were still in a venomous, retaliatory frame of mind the task of the 3rd and 4th Divisions which returned to the area and relieved the 1st and 2nd was not to be by any means a "cushy" one.

Reliefs were completed by November 13th and then came a stretch of six days, when merely holding what had been won at such cost proved in itself a costly enough business. In fact on the 13th at 4.35 p.m. the enemy launched an attack against the 3rd Division front in determined fashion, but this was broken up with great loss to the attackers.

The 11th Company had a particularly nasty tour in local defence positions south of Passchendaele from November 11th to November 15th until relieved by guns from the 10th and 8th Companies. The 10th Company lost two of its four crews sent up to the relief.

Guns put out by direct hits in the almost constant shelling, conditions even on the higher ground of the ridge itself which demanded the utmost in stamina from infantry in sodden trenches and machine gunners in their shell holes continued the strain and the stress of what was the final "holding tour" at Passchendaele. Enemy planes still continued to swoop down over the ridge and the Hun airman had time to take a malicious delight in "machine gunning" runners who, in pairs, tried to keep up communication.

For several nights as the relief between the Canadian Divisions was going on there was a reminder to worn troops that a solar system still existed for in the late afternoons the sun broke through the heavy, gray overhanging clouds and went down in a riot of red, throwing the broken, shattered silhouette of the City of Ypres up in eye-catching relief. It was one of the few things that happened in those dreary weeks of misery and strain to remind Canadians that another world than this mangled area in the salient existed and that there people awoke to the expectation of life rather than death.

The 16th and 10th M. G. Companies were the last Canadians to leave the Passchendaele Ridge. The 16th was relieved by the 248th British M. G. Company on the night of the 19th—20th of November. Their relief was completed in the early morning hours.

The 10th Company, which had been the first machine gun unit in the salient, had also the distinction of being the last to leave, for their relief by the 100th British Company was not completed until 7 a.m. on the 20th.

Though filing out in broad daylight from positions in which no movement had been allowed by day, they were not shelled.

Their last look over their shoulders at the rolling plain of Roulers, overhung by a low mist, was not a lingering one. Nor, as with hurried steps which took them back over the ground of the hard-won advance, were they to have any possible way of knowing that in a few months the German tide would once more swirl up and over Passchendaele Ridge with ridiculous ease and almost up to the very ramparts of Ypres itself, nor even yet that a year from this same November that peace would come to torn Flanders and to nearly all the world.

CHAPTER 5

Tense Interlude

The 3rd and 13th Companies of the 1st Division and the 4th and 14th of the 2nd had no rest after Passchendaele as they proceeded immediately upon arrival back in the Lens-Vimy front to the relief of British Machine Gun Companies in the line.

The 3rd and 13th Companies relieved the 177th M. G. Company (British) and 174th M. G. Company (British) in the Lens-Avion sector on the night of November 16th—17th.

The 4th and 14th Companies relieved the 143rd and 144th M.G. Companies (British) on the same night, taking over positions on the Mericourt sector.

But even immediate duty in the line here was a "rest" after Passchendaele and the Canadian Machine Gun Corps was to have plenty of time in which to go through a wide variety of experiences and was to enter upon a period that was to make the Vimy-Lens sector for the Canadian Corps as a whole as much akin to "home" as was possible in a country where war had laid a wide swath of desolation from the North Sea to the Vosges Mountains, 400 miles away to the south.

As the 3rd and 4th Divisions made their more leisurely trek back to Vimy, part of it by marching, the corps was practically settled in its old area by November 23rd and was to continue service on this front which ultimately was to pile up into the staggering total of 33,500,000 man days—days that were to have many new and pleasant features, days and nights which were to see flashes of war return in grim intensity for short periods and days and nights that would add up to months of a new type of strain—that of tense waiting for events of immense, world-shaking portent to happen.

More pressing, however, for the moment to the Canadian Machine Gun Corps was the immediate realisation of what Passchendaele had cost this arm.

It was easy enough for companies, batteries and down to gun crews to realise that they had been hit hard. They needed no details—no compilation of data on the subject—and asked for none. Roll calls that had been sorrowfully shortened were to be a constant reminder of Passchendaele's cost to the machine gunners—until reinforcements filled the gap.

Still a *résumé* of casualties to the Machine Gun Corps during the four phases of the Passchendaele operations was revealing and will probably contradict the impression of the time in regard to relative losses by units.

Compiled by division and corps units, the list is:

Unit	Period	Other Officers	Ranks	Total
1st M. G. Battalion	(Nov. 2nd to 15th)	8	152	160
2nd M. G. Battalion	(Nov. 2nd to 12th)	8	159	167
3rd M. G. Battalion	(Oct. 26th to Nov. 1st)	9	133	142
4th M. G. Battalion	(Oct. 26th to Nov. 1st)	10	125	135
1st C.M.M.G. Brigade	(Oct. 25th to Nov. 15th)	9	86	95
Total Casualties		44	655	699

The above data, however, did not cover the holding tour of the 3rd and 4th Divisions, which, of course, added casualties in considerable numbers to the totals.

The arrangements for the supply of reinforcements had worked splendidly despite the heavy casualty lists. The normal supply of reinforcements in France for active units was 10 *per cent* of the strength but by the end of the first attack at Passchendaele this allotment had been used up. Reinforcements then consisted of men freshly arrived from England, most of whom had never been under fire. In one case a barrage battery was reduced to two gunners per gun and these gunners were fresh drafts. Lieut.-Col. Brutinel, C. M. G. C. officer commanding, in a letter to the corps commander, paid high tribute to these drafts and attributed it to the high standard of training in the Canadian Machine Gun Depot in Seaford, commanded by Lieut.-Col. W. M. Balfour, D.S.O.

At Passchendaele, the rapidly evolving organisation of the corps had proven sound at every step.

The theory of tactical handling which had undergone such radical at Passchendaele had helped very greatly in giving tactical theories a definite form and content. Principles of employment, hitherto in changes since 1914 was now being stabilized and the experience gained a more or less experimental stage, were now established, it seemed, without question.

> Successful co-operation of machine guns with infantry depends as much upon the knowledge of machine gun tactics possessed by the infantry commander concerned, and the interest which he takes in the employment of these weapons, as upon the energy and ability of the machine gun officer in charge of the guns.

—was a conclusion arrived at following the experience of close liaison with the infantry as carried out by the mobile and sniping guns.

The muddy conditions at Passchendaele had served not only to show the scope but the limitations as well of the Vickers guns. The lack of the mobility of the Vickers under certain conditions as contrasted with its lighter contemporary, the Lewis gun, was emphasized and subsequent to these operations there was less and less a tendency on the part of the higher infantry command to confuse the functions of these two weapons.

Relative to the part played in the Passchendaele operations by the infant Machine Gun Corps, Gen. Sir Arthur Currie, in an appreciative letter, said in part:

> I regret that the casualties have been so high but these have resulted from the special efforts made by the enemy to destroy the machine gun crews from whom they suffered so much.
> "All prisoners have testified to the great losses caused the enemy by our machine gun fire, while our own infantry are loud in their praises of the support rendered by our machine gunners.
> "That the men of the Machine Gun Corps kept their guns in action under the conditions experienced testifies in the highest possible manner to their splendid discipline and fine fighting spirit. "I would like to have an opportunity of personally conveying to the machine gunners my appreciation of the splendid part played by them in winning our recent battles.
> Ever yours faithfully,
> (Signed)   A. W. Currie.

He was to take that opportunity in the case of the 4th Division "Battalion," which for the first time, shortly after Passchendaele, was drawn up for inspection as one formation, and to the officers and men of this unit Gen. Sir Arthur Currie was to repeat the appreciation of his letter as he was to prove later by executive action his great and abiding faith in the corps. Reinforcements had not come up at the time of the inspection near Dieval, but even with ranks hardly half strength the formation still a "battalion" only on paper, made a very impressive show. It even impressed the machine gun formation itself, since it had never had a view of itself in one spot.

The Corps Machine Gun officer, Lieut.-Col. R. Brutinel, sent to each commanding officer of the Corps a copy of Gen. Sir Arthur Currie's letter as well as one of his own, in which he said, in part:

> The fine example of daring, initiative and fruitful leadership on the part of the officers commanding mobile machine guns stands out with particular brilliancy.
>
> By their physical and moral endurance, their spirit of sacrifice and absolute devotion to duty, the Barrage Machine Gun Batteries succeeded in keeping their batteries in action regardless of the most adverse conditions of ground and weather and of the awful losses inflicted on them by hostile artillery.
>
> The standard set by the Canadian machine gunners during the operations leading to the capture of Passchendaele Ridge may possibly be equalled—it can never be surpassed.

But while a new corps consciousness was beginning to make itself felt, while the definite jobs of machine guns had been clarified and their potentialities—and weaknesses—were in much better-balanced perspective, the Brigade Machine Gun Company continued to be an entity unto itself. The intimate *esprit de corps* which was so quickly possible to build up in an infantry battalion, never had any counterpart in the machine gun sense of a "battalion." Companies found themselves only infrequently out at the machine gun rest camps, at one and the same time. And even when, as the trench routine of the winter of 1917-1918 became more definitely established, two companies found themselves at rest together they maintained separate messes for the officers.

Nevertheless there was a cohesive corps feeling. The evolution of organisation had brought with it a policy and a more definite, more standardised program of training. And a policy, backed by corps organisation, was to give machine gunners a new feeling of security from tactical whims of the moment; a more pronounced independence of thought and action

The Canadian Corps as a whole settled down to a winter of quiet and rest and into the new and manifold activities of the rest periods the Canadian Machine Gun Corps units entered with a zest.

The excitement of an election on the conscription issue in an atmosphere where bullets—not ballots—ruled gave way to periods at rest where the lighter side of war was given full scope in a wholesome, well-organised way. Concert parties which were to achieve real professional fame, bloomed and blossomed under handicaps that produced many ludicrous angles, but Art was to prove that it knew no limitations in the matter of production facilities. In the realm of theatrical fantasy men lost themselves for the moment from the grim realities that might lie a few days ahead or were a few days behind in the trenches over the ridge or in front of Lens. Machine gunners preened themselves because they had provided one of the most wholesome-looking, charming and wholly captivating "girls" of all the concert parties. "She" had been a No. 6 on a gun and a very willing, conscientious gunner.

A "Khaki University," the establishment of officers' clubs and canteens for the men, many reunions of officers from older divisions and billets that generally were dry, clean and comfortable—these were some of the activities and some of the conditions which were to make rest periods out of the line during this winter memorable for war-weary troops.

Came Christmas and then New Year's. To those lucky enough to be out of the line was vouchsafed an opportunity of putting on the festive dog. To those doing a regular tour the two occasions meant only another day. Christmas Day was quiet. Different sectors had different experiences, but any experiences were bound to be incongruous with the spirit of the calendar date.

The New Year was ushering in one unblinking certainty to the higher allied command and that was the inevitability of the Western Front becoming the decisive theatre of war and that an immense Germanic storm was brewing.

The year 1917 had seen the Canadians win greater recognition as one of the strongest-hitting forces in the British armies. They had started the campaign auspiciously off at Vimy and ended their part of it on a note of sorry triumph at Passchendaele. They knew Passchen-

Christmas Card. 4th Canadian . G. Battalion, France. 1917-1918

daele to be a ghastly reflection of victory even then but they felt the exultation of comradely sacrifice since the British strategy which dictated the futile Third Battle of Ypres had been by now translated into the grim necessity of taking blows which a wavering France could no longer absorb. The lower commands knew nothing of mutinies in the French Army.

In fact the lower commands were not much concerned with the larger implications of 1917 and the campaigns which started out with such high hopes and had ended in an atmosphere of menacing doubt.

Russia, with its tremendous potential manpower, was a disabled giant and out of the fight.

The United States had been unable to make any immediate contribution.

The disaster which had overtaken the Italians at Caporetta, when the suddenly delivered Teutonic blow caused Cadorna's army to reel backward for 70 miles in 16 days with a loss of 600,000 men, had almost put Italy out of the fight in October.

Exultation over Gen. Byng's brilliant victory had been subdued by realisation of its tragic limitations in vision and reserves and died out when the full extent of Ludendorf's counter-stroke with 16 fresh divisions on November 30th had become known.

Caporetta and the counter-attack at Cambria demonstrated what was in store for the Western Front.

From autumn through the winter as unrestricted submarine warfare kept sinking allied shipping at a sinister rate it was realised that a mighty race for time was on—a race which Germany might win if the British and French armies could not withstand the full shock before the Americans arrived in sufficient numbers to restore the balance of manpower on the Western Front.

Coming into February, the advance rumblings of this storm manifested itself on the Vimy and Lens fronts by increased aggressiveness of the Germans, which was met in kind by the Canadians—a trifle more so, in fact.

No one appreciated the menace of the storm more than the Canadian Corps Commander. He had fought the suggestion for forming two Canadian Corps by forming three-battalion brigades and had won his argument for the retention of one corps, but a stronger one. Gen. Currie proposed an increase in personnel of 315 officers and 13,755 other ranks and in these figures the Machine Gun Corps were to loom large.

Vimy Ridge had now become the centre of the British line and it was the key to a rich mining area that was absolutely vital to the war material needs of France.

The Allied Command had tried to gauge the power of the coming German offensive accurately. They realised that their lines would bend—they hoped, and felt sure, they would not break.

Back of the strong main system of defence which had been assiduously repaired and strengthened by the Canadian occupation this winter, defensive works were also completed in rear to take care of the more dire contingencies. Defence in depth was provided for the first shock. On Vimy Ridge alone 72 new artillery positions were built and stacked with ammunition. Machine gun emplacements and barbed wire provided local defences for these. In rear of the front system there had been built during the "quiet" winter:

250 miles of trench,
300 miles of barbed wire entanglements,
200 tunnelled machine gun emplacements.

Machine gun positions were stored with several days' supplies of ammunition, food and water for the garrisons. The explanation of those 200 tunnelled machine gun emplacements is revealed in Gen. Sir Arthur Currie's summary of the defensive plans for Vimy Ridge.

> The completion of the revised corps defences, and the execution of the new army program resulted in the organisation of a very deeply defended area, consisting of successive defensive systems, roughly parallel to the general line of the front and linked together by switch lines to protect both flanks.
> Each defensive system was designed to protect definite topographical features, the loss of anyone of which would considerably handicap the defence by uncovering our artillery.
> As planned, the main framework of the defence in depth was based upon machine gun positions, protected by belts of wire entanglements so placed in relation to the field of fire of the machine guns that they enfiladed over the whole length. The whole area was compartmented in such a way that the loss of ground at anyone point could be localized and would not cause a forced retirement from adjoining areas.

Of these vast measures, machine gunners doing their regular tours were little aware except in a general way. Getting on into March, raiding on both sides had become more aggressive, with the Canadians excelling in daring and ingenuity. The new reinforcements after Passchendaele were now hardened to warfare. In support of our raids, machine gun barrages played an important part. Several brigades relied on a machine gun barrage alone for their raids. One incident out of which the machine gunners got a substantial chuckle came when the Germans, signalling one of their offensive parties to make an attack, used the same flare which notified the Emma Gees to open their barrage. The response from the machine gunners was almost instantaneous and the sad result was that the enemy marched right into a hail of machine gun bullets, causing them severe losses and effectually disposing of the attack.

Nor were machine gunners, generally, aware of the fact that a new organisation had already been approved and was pending reorganisation.

As early as December 25th, 1917, Lieut.-Col. Brutinel had drawn up a new establishment for divisional battalions, which were now to consist of two companies. There was no increase in the number of guns, which was to remain at 64 per division, but the establishment aimed first of all at cutting down the administrative duties and personnel of the individual companies and giving the commanders of the larger companies to be formed by the merger of two brigade companies more time to devote to training and to fighting.

There was to be an increase in personnel of two officers and 288 other ranks, bringing the new battalion strength to 1,039 all ranks. The battalion was to be commanded by a lieutenant-colonel with a suitable headquarters staff. Each of the two companies were to be divided into four eight-gun platoons; each platoon was again to be divided into two four-gun sections. Each gun crew was to include both a sergeant and a corporal, thus doubling the existing strength of N.C.O.'s. The total of eight other ranks on each gun crew, together with the 24 carriers (three per gun) on each platoon strength, was calculated to make machine gun units independent of infantry assistance.

The platoon, subsequently renamed the battery, became the tactical unit. Hitherto it had been customary to view the section (four guns) as the unit for tactical purposes to work with an infantry battalion. Each platoon, in addition, was self contained as regards specialists and transport.

Signallers were almost trebled. Under the four-company plan there had been a total of 16 signallers. The new establishment called for 40.

The new establishment had been forwarded on January 10th, 1918, by Gen. Sir Arthur Currie, corps commander, and in a covering letter he unreservedly recommended it:

> It is my considered opinion, that the employment of the infantry and resulting wastage through casualties and sickness will be directly influenced this year, more than ever before, by the '*efficiency, or otherwise, of the machine gun service*.' It is urgent that the proposed establishment may be completed early this winter.

The urgency note in Sir Arthur Currie's letter did not achieve its purpose for, although the whole tempo of the Corps activities had been speeded up with the approach of spring, the German storm broke in all its fury on March 21st as with unbelievable thrusting power Ludendorff struck at the junction between the French and British armies in front of Amiens.

The end of Machine Gun Company traditions, which had been two years in the building, was lost in the welter of vastly more important matters in the next weeks. There was no time for regrets as old company identities were almost utterly lost in the shuffle.

When the German storm broke, the 3rd Division was holding the Mericourt-Avion sector; the 4th Division was on the Lens-St. Emile front; the 1st Division was guarding Hill 70; and the 2nd Division was out in rest in the Auchel area.

Three days later the 4th and 3rd Divisions had extended their fronts, the 1st Division was in Army Reserve and the 2nd Division was in General Headquarters.

In the line, on the move and at temporary halts, the reorganisation of the Machine Gun Companies into battalions took place. Reorganisation was not "numbered" off in succession from the right. The 2nd and 3rd Division units were reorganised first.

The four companies of the 2nd Canadian Divisional Machine Gun "Battalion" (the 4th, 5th, 6th and 14th C. M. G. Companies) were officially embodied in the 2nd Battalion C.M.G.C. on March 23rd. It was arranged that the 5th and 14th Companies should form No. 1 Company under the new organisation and that the 4th and 6th Companies should form No. 2 Company. Owing to the tactical situation at the time and the threatened imminence of active operations, the G. O. C. 2nd Division decided not, actually, to reform existing Machine Gun Companies into four-battery companies in the meantime.

Accordingly the four Machine Gun Companies of the 2nd Division operated on the old basis until April 7th.

Major J. Basevi became O. C. No. 1 Company and Major W. M. Pearce was appointed to command No. 2 Company under the battalion command of Lieut.-Col. J. C. Weir, M.C. The second in command was Major J. E. McCorkell, with Capt. G. N. Douglas, M.C., completing headquarters staff as adjutant.

The 3rd Division, still holding the Mericourt-Avion line on March 23rd, started its reorganisation on that date.

Though momentarily expecting an attack, reorganisation was effected. On March 23rd the 9th and 15th Companies were formed into four batteries to compose No. 2 Company, under the command of Capt. J. C. Hartley, M.C., M.M. The 7th and 8th Companies were embodied in No. 1 Company of the 3rd Battalion C. M. G. C. on the following day, March 24th, and placed under the command of Major H. J. R. Parkes. Lieut.-Col. W. M. Moorehouse commanding, with Major A. M. McFaul as second in command and Lieut. G. M. Downton as adjutant, made up battalion headquarters.

The reorganisation of the 1st Division did not take place until March 27th at Marqueffles Farm, the machine gun rest camp on the Vimy front between Bouvigny Village and Aix-Noulette. The 2nd and 3rd Companies were united to form No. 1 Company under the command of Capt. E. R. Morris. The 1st and 13th C. M. G. Companies were combined to form No. 2 Company under the command of Major J. Kay, M.C. Two days later Major Kay was evacuated sick and Capt. A. Denholm, D.C.M., took over.

Lieut.-Col. S. W. Watson, D.S.O., became the commanding officer; Major C. V. Grantham, M.C., second in command, and Capt. L. C. Francis, M.C., adjutant. On the day of organisation the new battalion was on the move by way of Camblain L'Abbe to the front south of Arras and the first tour of the newly-formed batteries in the line began the night of March 29th-30th.

The 4th Divisional reorganisation was officially last. On the night of March 28th, the companies had been relieved in the Lens-St. Emile and Hill 70 sectors, and by motor lorries had been moved to Springvale Camp, near Ecurin. On March 29th the 10th and 16th Companies were brought together to form No. 1 Company under Major J. C. Britton. No. 2 Company was composed of the 11th and 12th C. M. G. Companies to be commanded by Major L. T. Pearce, M.C.

Lieut.-Col. M. A. Scott, D.S.O., assumed command, with Major

E. W. Sanson as second in command. Capt. H. Ward, M.C., was appointed adjutant. The newly-formed batteries were sent into the line on the Gavrelle-Arleux front to relieve the battered and shaken but dogged 56th Division Imperials, which had withstood the full force of the Ludendorff blow astride the Scarpe. Captured German prisoners had insisted that the attack, which had only managed to win the outpost line, would be renewed next day by fresh storm troops, whose task was to capture Vimy Ridge from the south.

The attack, however, never developed for it was overcome, aborting, by the massed, vicious fire of our artillery, to which chorus the machine guns in their new positions added their chattering challenge.

At 3.45, at 4.30 and again at 5 o'clock, sparse machine gun diaries report, the entire southern flank of the ridge was aflame. On that date the 3rd and 4th Divisions had again come under Gen. Currie's control.

He found the new front on the Blue Line to which the 13th Imperial Corps had withdrawn in front of the Bailleul-Willerval-Chaudiere-Hirondelle Line as far north as the Mericourt sector.

Gen. Currie's interim report, in part says:

> Any advance beyond the Blue Line, on the 4th Canadian Division front would have brought the Germans within assaulting distance of the weakest part of Vimy Ridge, and the severity of the shelling seemed to indicate that a renewal of their attacks was probable ... to increase the depth of our defences, machine gun detachments were extemporised by borrowing men from the machine gun battalions, who had then completed their organisation on an eight-battery basis. Some fifty extra machine guns were secured from Ordnance and other sources.

Into this tense picture came the three companies of the 5th Division, which had been hastily broken up in England. They arrived in France on March 25th and in a matter of hours, practically, were holding reserve positions. Later they were fed into the line in subsections of two guns each, relieving corresponding elements of experienced units.

The officers listed on the rosters of the 17th, 18th and 19th Companies as they landed in France were:

17th Company—Capt. G. Black, Capt. G. C. Hulme, Lieuts. R. W. Chipman, E. M. C. Goodwin, W. Leary, M.C., J. F. Maclennan, W. Murray, W. G. Radford, N. A. Watt, P. S. Wilson.

18th Company—Capt. C. W. de la P. Beresford (O.C.), Major A. W. L. Butler, Lieuts. F. Adam, W. E. Frame, H. Horwick, W. J. Preston, F. W. Thompson, J. E. Tudhope, M. G. Watts and F. F. Worthington.

19th Company—Major J. H. Brownlee (O.C.), Capt. J. McC. Cumming, Lieuts. G. C. Anderson, F. J. Duck, L. W. Dinnie, MacIntyre, J. H. Morwick, S. G. Rennie, M. M. Robinson and A. H. Wylie.

In the resolve of all ranks to hold every inch of territory entrusted to their keeping, to none had it a more personal application than to the machine gunners, for here was their basic role of defence.

It was true that the Somme, Vimy, Hill 70 and Passchendaele had brought to a high state of development the power of the machine gun in the offensive, especially in its barrage role. Outstripped in mobility by its lighter rival, the Lewis, yet the heavy Vickers had stoutly maintained its right to be considered the most important and stable factor in consolidation of newly-won ground. But in the offensive the role of the machine gunners was essentially more dogged than it was spectacular. Not for them was the exultation of the charge, flashing bayonets and personal contact, except in isolated instances. Pushing up in the front waves of the attacking infantry, Vickers crews were much-sought targets by both German gunners and snipers. They were easily distinguishable. Though they might not bunch as crews, still the habits of hours of gun drill could not be thrown off at will and their formation was sure to mark them down for what they were. even if their loads of guns, tripods, water cans and ammunition did not blazon the fact.

On the defensive, as they felt they would be any moment now, they felt a new pride, a new confidence in their weapon.

For almost a matter of years now the Germans, as they repeatedly met the shocks of French and British attacks on the Western Front, had disclosed their main dependence upon the machine gun. And the machine gun had exacted a terrific toll.

The German machine gunner had invariably shown himself as the pick of the enemy troops—fighting his gun to the bitter end. And it was usually the bitter end, for the qualities of mercy had been pretty well strained to the breaking point by the time attacking troops had reached the source of so much of their trouble and from which flamed forth so much of death in their ranks.

Canadian machine gunners, facing their first large-scale defensive test, therefore were determined that in steadfastness and courage they would have nothing to learn from their German adversaries.

The very air that hung over the ridge seemed tense.

On April 9th, just a year from the day that the Canadians had swarmed over Vimy Ridge in the first of a series of quick, sharp blows which the Allied staff hoped would make Germany ready for the "knockout blow" so vividly analogized by Premier David Lloyd George in his famous speech, found the British armies staggered by a Ludendorff blow delivered on the Lys and aimed at Armentieres.

The first day gave them, among other famous spots, Neuve Chapelle and forced a British and a Portuguese division back three miles and a half. Next day another blow was delivered north of Armentieres for 10 miles and, outflanked, Armentieres had to be abandoned. On April 11th the enemy moved over the Lawe, a tributary of the Lys. By the afternoon the Germans had forced a gap in our lines south-east of Bailleul and British units trying to stem the tide provided some of the greatest epic stands of the whole war. On April 12th Sir Douglas Haig issued his famous "with our backs to the wall" message to the troops.

Bailleul had fallen, however, and the enemy swarmed over the famous Messines Ridge. For four days this line held out stubbornly. but the pressure of sheer numbers was too great and the loss of this line compelled withdrawal from Passchendaele, Gheluvelt, Poelcapelle and Langemarck, all names so deeply graven on Canadian minds and all won at such a shocking price in the ghastly Third Battle of Ypres of 1917.

While Merville fell, the magnificent defence of the 1st Army held the line firm at Givenchy and as it joined the Canadian Corps at La Bassee and on past Arras, Vimy was in truth an anchor.

Canadian anxiety over their own task at Vimy was switched to the north of them as the desperate situation unfolded there day by day over terrain the Canadians had reason to know well.

Gen. Currie says:

> The success of the German offensives emphasised the need of greater depth for defensive dispositions, which depend very largely on the stopping power of the machine gun. Unfortunately the number of machine guns with a division was inadequate to give the required depth of defence on a front exceeding four thousand yards in length. Each of my divisions was now holding a front approximately ten thousand yards in length and

the extemporised machine gun detachments formed previously, added to the machine gun companies of the 5th Canadian Division, in my opinion were far from sufficient for the task.

I therefore decided to add a third company of four batteries to each battalion of the C. M. G. Corps, thus bringing to ninety-six the number of machine guns in each Canadian Division. This entailed an increase in personnel of approximately fifty *per cent* of the strength of each machine gun battalion.

These companies were formed provisionally on April 12th by withdrawing fifty men from each infantry battalion. Of these men a portion was sent to the machine gun battalion to be combined with the trained personnel, so that each machine gun crew would include at least four trained gunners. The remainder of the infantry personnel, withdrawn as above stated, was sent to a special machine gun depot, formed for the purpose, and there underwent an abridged but intensive course of training. Thus an immediate supply of reinforcements was ensured. Twenty three-ton lorries had been borrowed from General Headquarters to supply a modicum of transport to the new units and on April 13th some of the new machine gun batteries were already in the line at critical points.

That was the general picture but on April 10th a letter was addressed by the corps commander to the general officers commanding divisions which, in part, was as follows:

> I propose to form immediately a third machine gun company per division. I shall not wait until such organisation is sanctioned by the higher authorities but shall proceed immediately if I can obtain the guns. Official sanction can come later.
> "To do this I require 2,400 men and I propose that each batalion be asked to give fifty of their best men, who, for the time being, will remain on command to the Machine Gun Corps.
> . . .
> A short time ago the strength of each battalion was increased by one hundred men and, in view of the increased fire power which the new machine gun company in each Division will give, it is considered battalions will be agreeable to allowing these men to go. There are no trained machine gun reinforcements in England available at the present time so that the organisation suggested must be improvised from resources here.

I would like you to take this matter up with your battalion commanders at once. While no doubt they will dislike losing their men from the infantry, I believe they will realise it is for the general good, and I would ask you to urge upon them to earmark fifty of their best and brainiest men for the purpose outlined above.

That is a very revealing letter.

It is a revelation in its way of the initiative and type of leadership Gen. Sir Arthur Currie brought to the Canadian Corps and as a tribute to the dependence the Corps Commander placed upon the machine gun it needs no enlargement.

It would be a pleasure to record at this point that all battalion commanders did earmark their "best and brainiest" but that would be wide of the truth. The big majority did do just that but more than a few who had the old "trench raid" view of the situation, whose horizon was bounded by their flanks and who still, when confronted with a plea for suggestions by machine gun subalterns, would mutter "Oh, stick the damned things anywhere, anywhere out of here." They earmarked the lame and the halt.

Even with the addition of a third company the ratio between machine guns and rifles in the Canadian Corps was not percentively larger.

Previously it had been below that of other divisions in the British Army. In a British Division with nine battalions (9,000 rifles) and 64 guns the ratio was one Vickers gun to 141 rifles. In a Canadian Division with 12 battalions (13,200 rifles) and 64 Vickers guns, the proportion was one Vickers gun to 206 rifles. The addition of 32 guns per division brought the Canadian Corps ratio up to one Vickers gun to 138 rifles.

It was on April 12th, 1918, detailed instructions were issued by Canadian Corps for the supply and training of personnel for the new companies. Each division supplied 12 officers and 600 other ranks. The Canadian Corp Reinforcement Camp supplied 25 officers. Signallers and other specialists were not provided initially but were later drawn, partly from the C. R. R. C., partly from the C. M. G. C. R. D. All personnel found unsuitable for machine gun work were returned to their respective units and immediately replaced by men likely to become machine gunners.

It was not until the 16th that Gen. Currie wrote to Canadian

Headquarters in London stating what he had done and at the same time submitting a revised establishment for the approval of the Overseas Ministry.

The war establishment of a Canadian Machine Gun Corps Battalion as finally approved on May 1st, 1918, was as detailed below:

PERSONNEL

	Off.	W.O.	S./Sgts. and Sgts.	Art's	O.R.	Total
Headquarters	7	2	3	1	21	34
Headquarters (attached)	8	15	2	....	8	12
3 Companies	54	....	114	24	1,299	1,506
3 Companies (attached)	....	....	....	....	6	6
Totals	63	17	119	25	1,334	1,558

TRANSPORT

	Rid.	L. Dr.	Hy. Dr.	Total	Bicycles
Headquarters	5	3	....	8	....
Headquarters (attached)	2	....	....	2	....
3 Companies	30	297	12	339	24
3 Companies (attached)	....	....	....	....	....
Totals	37	300	12	349	24

The nominal roll of officers of the four battalions as on February 22nd (the reorganisation on a two-company basis still awaited official sanction) was as follows:

1st BATTALION C. M. G. C.
Battalion Headquarters

Officer Commanding—Lieut.-Col. S. W. Watson, D.S.O.
Second in Command—Major C. V. Grantham, M.C.
Adjutant—Capt. L. G. Francis.
Quartermaster—Lieut. J. Wylie.
Signalling Officer—Lieut. A. W. Beament.
Medical Officer—Capt. D. A. Morrison, C.A.M.C.
Paymaster—Capt. H. B. Woods, C.A.P.C.

Company Officers

Major J. McKay
Capt. G. C. Ferrie
Capt. E. R. Morris
Lieut. D. S. Bankier
Lieut. C. A. Battershill
Lieut. A. C. Bowles

Lieut. C. C. Drew
Lieut. O. W. Fawcett
Lieut. S. J. Freeman
Lieut. K. B. Hamilton
Lieut. E. Hancock
Lieut. W. B. Henry

Lieut. E. V. Chambers
Lieut. V. R. Davies
Lieut. J. A. Dewart
Lieut. M. M. Dillon
Lieut. D. A. McIntosh
Lieut. J. Maitland
Lieut. L. McEwan
Lieut. H. W. Martin
Lieut. A. C. McFarlane
Lieut. J. A. McPherson
Lieut. W. B. Milner
Lieut. J. R. B. More

Lieut. G. B. Herridge
Lieut. P. M. Humme
Lieut. R. S. Jackson
Lieut. S. R. Jeffries
Lieut. R. H. Morris
Lieut. A. F. Norris
Lieut. A. E. Parker
Lieut. J. E. Ritchie
Lieut. J. E. Robinson
Lieut. C. D. Schwab
Lieut. H. Shaughnessy
Lieut. C. G. Warner

2nd BATTALION C. M. G. C.

Battalion Headquarters

Officer Commanding—Lieut.-Col. J. G. Weir, D.S.O., M.C.
Second in Command—
Adjutant—Capt. G. N. Douglas
Quartermaster—Lieut. J. Stonehewer
Signalling Officer—
Medical Officer—
Paymaster—Capt. T. D. Patterson

Company Officers

Major J. Basevi
Major J. E. McCorkell
Major W. M. Pearce
Capt. J. A. McCamus
Capt. G. W. H. Millican
Lieut. G. W. Comstock
Lieut. P. Cowan
Lieut. R. Edmunds
Lieut. R. Fleming
Lieut. C. G. Frost
Lieut. G. E. Harley
Lieut. G. Hobson
Lieut. D. S. Jackson
Lieut. Francis Layton
Lieut. I. G. MacLaren
Lieut. A. F. Mahaffey
Lieut. H. A. McBurney

Lieut. J. A. McCullough
Lieut. R. M. McKenzie
Lieut. F. L. Much
Lieut. T. H. O'Rourke
Lieut. W. H. Patterson
Lieut. H. J. L. Pearce
Lieut. I. F. Price
Lieut. J. A. Ramsay
Lieut. N. G. Richardson
Lieut. S. E. Sacks
Lieut. H. S. Salisbury
Lieut. H. M. Sibbald
Lieut. W. P. Tozer
Lieut. C. W. White
Lieut. A. B. White
Lieut. L. F. White
Lieut. A. F. Williams

Officers of the 2nd Battalion, C.M.G.C.

3rd BATTALION C. M. G. C.

Battalion Headquarters

Officer Commanding—Major W. M. Moorehouse
Second in Command—Major A. M. McFaul
Adjutant—Lieut. G. M. Downton
Quartermaster—Hon. Capt. C. M. Hall

Company Officers

Major A. J. R. Parkes
Capt. F. W. Burnham
Capt. J. H. Clark
Capt. K. E. Drinkwater
Capt. F. M. Garrison
Capt. J. C. Hartley, M.C., M.M.
Capt. E. I. J. Ings
Capt. B. J. Mothersill
Capt. D. W. Rowatt, M.C.
Lieut. D. A. Blunden
Lieut. B. L. Cook
Lieut. J. D. Clark
Lieut. H. E. B. Coyne
Lieut. G. F. Douglas, M.C.
Lieut. A. G. Fisher
Lieut. J. B. Fraser
Lieut. S. C. Gee
Lieut. A. M. German
Lieut. F. E. Hinds
Lieut. R. M. Hopper
Lieut. C. E. Hulbert
Lieut. W. H. Hutchens
Lieut. C. W. Kern
Lieut. F. W. Landreth
Lieut. A. R. Madgett
Lieut. J. R. McLean
Lieut. A. F. Neatby, M.C., D.C.M.
Lieut. P. W. Newman
Lieut. F. A. Parkins
Lieut. G. V. Raynor
Lieut. H. Rothwell
Lieut. J. G. Searles, M.C.
Lieut. G. R. Smith
Lieut. H. F. Smith
Lieut. W. N. Smith
Lieut. E. G. Spalding
Lieut. J. Thompson
Lieut. C. W. Tubbs
Lieut. A. M. Tudhope

4th BATTALION C. M. G. C.

Battalion Headquarters

Officer Commanding—Lieut.-Col. M. A. Scott, D.S.O.
Second in Command—Major E. W. Sansom
Adjutant—Capt. H. Ward, M.C.
Quartermaster—Capt. K. Weaver
Signalling Officer—Lieut. H. S. Moss
Medical Officer—Capt. J. W. Laurie
Paymaster—Capt. T. W. Seagram

Company Officers

Major J. C. Britton, D.S.O.
Major L. F. Pearce, M.C.
Capt. B. M. Clerk, M.C.
Capt. H. A. Fowler, M.C.
Capt. I. C. Hall, M.C.
Capt. S. Johnston
Capt. H. T. Logan
Capt. E. L. Rainboth, M.C.
Capt. A. G. Scott, M.C.
Capt. W. G. Williams
Lieut. H. E. Anderson
Lieut. P. W. Barber-Starkey
Lieut. A. L. Bourque, M.C.
Lieut. E. S. Campbell
Lieut. F. I. Carpenter
Lieut. G. E. W. Cook
Lieut. W. H. Duncan
Lieut. O. B. Eaton
Lieut. C. J. T. French
Lieut. W. J. H. Gill
Lieut. C. S. Grafton

Lieut. S. G. Gudgeon
Lieut. G. J. Hearn
Lieut. F. W. Hooper
Lieut. C. R. Hopper, M.C.
Lieut. J. T. Hughes
Lieut. W. C. Killop
Lieut. C. E. Ladler
Lieut. N. O. Leach, M.C.
Lieut. H. Lewis
Lieut. W. W. R. Mitchell
Lieut. H. A. Peverly
Lieut. N. P. Pope
Lieut. J. A. Riddell
Lieut. W. Riddell
Lieut. G. T. Roach
Lieut. C. J. S. Ryley
Lieut. J. D. Sharp
Lieut. W. J. A. Stewart
Lieut. E. J. L. Stinson
Lieut. C. A. Young

Among the officers transferred in each division were included one major or captain and two lieutenants, all three recommended for promotion. The remainder were lieutenants and in all cases the date of seniority was unaffected by the eventual transfer of these officers to the Machine Gun Corps. The entire personnel were attached to the machine gun battalions pending authority for the new organisation.

Twelve officers of each division, together with 292 out of the 600 other ranks withdrawn, joined the machine gun battalions at once and were trained in machine gun work in the line.

For the remaining 208 other ranks per division, a total of 832, and for the 25 officers supplied by the C. C. R. C., a special Machine Gun Training Depot was formed under the administration of Lieut.-Col. C. N. Hill, D.S.O., at Tank Camp, Bois d'Ohlah, near Verrelel. The instructional staff was in charge of Capt. .H. R. Levy, M.M., assisted by two officers and 45 other ranks from the C. M. G. D., H. D. After 10 days, the school was moved to Fraser Camp, Bois des Ailleux, near Mont St. Eloy.

The following officers were added to the machine gun battalions upon the formation of the third companies, the majority of transfers from the infantry:

1st Battalion

Major R. Murdie
Capt. L. H. Balfe
Capt. J. W. Maynard
Capt. A. D. C. McDermott
Capt. J. Skinner
Lieut. V. C. Anderson
Lieut. L. R. Anrey
Lieut. A. C. Bowles
Lieut. B. Bryne
Lieut. D. H. Campbell
Lieut. W. S. Carey
Lieut. E. E. Duley
Lieut. H. H. Essex
Lieut. W. R. Hamilton
Lieut. J. Hay
Lieut. W. A. Liddell
Lieut. H. M. Lovell
Lieut. W. B. McMullin
Lieut. J. R. B. More
Lieut. A. F. Wallace

2nd Battalion

Major A. Graham
Lieut. C. H. Biddell
Lieut. C. W. Blair
Lieut. J. R. Burchall
Lieut. A. H. Cameron
Lieut. A. C. Cleghorn
Lieut. H. A. Davis
Lieut. T. H. Dudley
Lieut. S. G. Fildes
Lieut. F. J. G. Garneau
Lieut. H. E. Hopkins
Lieut. W. J. H. Krietzer
Lieut. A. G. Mercer
Lieut. A. D. Roughton
Lieut. W. V. Smart
Lieut. A. R. Switzer

3rd Battalion

Capt. D. A. Galt, M.C.
Lieut. A. A. Atkinson
Lieut. P. M. Bradbury
Lieut. G. H. Brown
Lieut. H. V. Copley
Lieut. R. H. Foulds
Lieut. C. R. Garneau
Lieut. H. E. Gee
Lieut. R. H. Werne
Lieut. W. J. Godber
Lieut. O. C. Hughes
Lieut. K. R. Lindsay
Lieut. P. C. Mulholland
Lieut. L. S. Roe
Lieut. J. D. Shearer
Lieut. H. P. Smith
Lieut. W. F. Tobey

Attached—Hon. Capt. R. F. Pinnington (Chaplain).

4th Battalion

Capt. C. E. Bailey, D.S.O., M.C.
Lieut. W. J. A. Fair
Lieut. W. J. Johnston
Lieut. K. Lorimer
Lieut. F. H. McDonald
Lieut. D. McGillivray
Lieut. C. F. Mandel, M.C.
Lieut. H. S. Moss
Lieut. C. R. Parson
Lieut. J. H. Patterson
Lieut. H. R. Simpson, M.M
Lieut. J. M. Snetsinger
Lieut. W. M. Woodward

All during April the tense situation hung ever over Vimy Ridge, the Canadians continuing their aggressive attitude not only in heavy artillery fire but in daring infantry raids, in which the machine gunners filled their usual role of either providing the barrage alone or thickening up the artillery effort.

The machine gun battalions were inspired by reports of the splendid work the Motors had done in front of Amiens, which must have its own record in these pages.

Along the whole line from the North Sea to the Vosges Mountains it was realised that the Germans were regaining their strength for another gigantic Ludendorff gamble.

On April 24th he gained Villers-Bretonneux.

Every day brought the new organisation of the machine gun battalions to a greater peak of efficiency. Only under the most extreme urgency would it have been thought that infantry could be absorbed into the machine gun service and trained right in the line. But it was done and in the doing the wonderful spirit of the old, compact companies was rebuilt into the larger formations.

On May 7th, a day before the Germans made their final threat at the battered hulk of Ypres and were foiled, the Canadian Corps ceased to function in the front line, and for two months was out of the line— that is all with the exception of the 2nd Division. Gen. Byng had the 2nd under the 6th (Imperial) Corps in the Neuville Vitasse sector and when the 2nd was finally returned to Gen. Currie's command it had been in the line 92 days, during which it had held a front of 6,000 yards and by its aggressiveness and resource had created a wonderful record. It had not only repulsed a series of local attacks but had made 27 raids, captured three officers and 101 other ranks, 22 machine guns and two trench mortars.

It was relieved by the 3rd Division.

An added grimness had entered the war for the Canadian Corps as, between May 19th and 30th, four Canadian hospitals had been ruthlessly bombed by German night raiders. Six Canadian nurses were killed or died of wounds, nine were wounded and hospital staffs and their helpless patients suffered heavy casualties. To many who could not regard war as anything but impersonal, this new frightfulness brought a sharp, personal touch of hatred of the enemy.

One of the first twisted bits of information that facetiously made the rounds was that the Canadian Corps was to be sent to Paris as a permanent garrison. Canadians did not get that assignment but garrisoning the pleasant countryside back of Vimy, untouched by war, was as pleasant a task as had fallen to the lot of the Maple Leaf.

One Infantry Brigade and one Machine Gun Company from each of the divisions out of the line were billeted well forward in support of the Imperial Corps in the line. These units were kept at one hour's notice from 5 a.m. to 7 a.m.

Intensive open warfare training was the daily regime. It was a quick about-turn from the defensive strain under which the Canadians had held Vimy.

There were no tapes here. There was more flexibility, more dash to the daily training as whole brigades, usually supported by a complete machine gun company, moved up to the attack, with tanks setting the pace, smoke bombs providing a screen, planes zooming overhead indicating by flares machine gun strong points and the "A" echelon of machine gun transport developing a "hell for leather" school of getting into action that was in the best horse artillery tradition.

Expanded so greatly and so suddenly to meet urgent defensive demands, the new machine gun formations found this opposite role exhilarating.

The problems of administering a unit the size of a Machine Gun Battalion (1,558 all ranks), possessing several times as much transport as an infantry battalion, were admirably tackled. Major W. B. Forster, M.C., Staff Officer to the Corps Machine Gun Officer, visited each Machine Gun Battalion in turn, introducing a system of administration which would be common to all.

The training was hard, even gruelling at times, but still was rest as contrasted with the line, even if the increased shelling of back areas by long-range German naval guns and nightly bombing raids often broke into the dazzling moonlight nights which bathed this rugged, pleasant landscape back of Vimy.

In this intensive open warfare training it was noticeable that all officers were urged to use their own initiative as machine gunners and it had its basis in a memorandum issued by the Canadian Corps, after preparation by General Brutinel. The memorandum dealt with many questions of command and liaison with the infantry which had been wrapped in uncertainty and had been the cause of a great deal of misunderstanding between the Infantry and the Machine Gun Corps.

Under the heading of "Organisation," this memorandum states that "the battalion is the unit for administration and training."

The company has no administrative function. It is a convenient echelon for co-ordination of the machine gun batteries, the supervision of their tactical handling and the maintenance of good liaison with the infantry.

The battery is essentially the tactical unit and will be the smallest unit detailed for detachment to infantry brigades or battalions. It is self-contained as regards command, transport and personnel, except signallers, who are with the Headquarters of the Company.

There is no similarity between the Infantry Battalions and Machine Gun Battalions with regard to administration of tactics. A Machine Gun Battalion can be more closely compared to Divisional Artillery, both in its organisation and in its tactical distribution.

"Under the heading of "Tactical Employment," the memorandum says:

> The Machine Gun Service must be regarded as a distinctive arm *with tactics entirely its own*. In all respects it is intermediate between the Infantry and Artillery, its tactics being radically different from the former, and approximating to but not being identical with those of the latter.

It must be thoroughly realised that the principle governing the employment of machine gun units is that it is their duty to support the infantry in all phases of the fight and to co-operate constantly with them. But they are not part of the Infantry and must not be considered as such.

Under the heading of "Command" there is established the fact that Machine Gun Battalions are divisional troops and should be employed to support Infantry in accordance with the plans of the G. O. C. Division.

> It is essential that, under all conditions. the machine gun resources of a division should be kept as *fluid* as possible and that their distribution on the divisional front should be based solely on tactical considerations.

Again, in part, the memorandum notes that:

> A Machine Gun Commander should be given definite orders by the Infantry Commander, to whom he is tactically attached,

Officers of the 3rd Battalion, C.M.G.C.

as to what is required of him, but he should be allowed as much freedom of action as possible in carrying out these orders and should be kept informed of all changes and developments of the situation which may affect his action. . . .

Under the heading of "Liaison," which is a *résumé* of the normal requirements between all arms, there are several significant paragraphs:

> In a retirement, the definite stopping power of the machine guns should be utilised by infantry commanders to the utmost. Infantry instinctively reform under cover of fire from machine gun batteries, which are the natural rallying points for them. But under the conditions which make such action necessary it is not likely that machine gun personnel will be available to make the liaison; therefore all infantry commanders, whatever their rank, should be impressed with the necessity of initiating and maintaining liaison with the machine guns in such circumstances.
>
> It is the duty of the commander of the infantry force to. arrange, automatically, for the protection, particularly of the flanks, of any Machine Gun Units which are co-operating with him and, in consultation with the Machine Gun Commander, to make definite arrangements for any advance, counter-attack or other tactical manoeuvre.

Thus it will be seen that the Machine Gun Service had not only grown in stature but as well in status effecting its tactical independence and in the initiative and latitude defined in the employment of the weapon.

Training continued throughout June.

A spearhead was being polished day by day. The Canadian Corps was now almost as numerically strong as an army. Day by day it purred with more power. Two British Divisions, just back from Palestine, were sent to train with the Canadians.

On July 1st came a memorable break, when Dominion Day wag celebrated far behind the lines. It was a typical "back home" program, lacrosse furnishing the purely national touch among the sports. Two squadrons of Canadian pilots droned overhead to prevent any curious German planes from disturbing the day. Thirty-five thousand men, including elements of Scottish Divisions training with them, enjoyed a wonderful program, and among the notables there were the Duke of Connaught and Marshal Petain.

Two weeks later the "rest," which was to be looked back upon as something that must have been a dream, an Elysium of the imagination in contrast to days which brought no respite, came to an end.

On July 15th the Canadians went back in the line, relieving the Imperial 17th Corps.

The Germans, fearful of an impending attack they deduced from the Canadians' presence and sure knowledge of the open warfare training the Canadians had been undergoing, gave them a warm welcome back to the Vimy front. The Canadians returned it and more.

War was back for Currie's men.

CHAPTER 6

Motors off Into the Blue

Four motor batteries of the 1st C.M.G.C. Brigade were in divisional reserve positions on the Lens front and one was in the unit's camp at Vedrel when Ludendorff's legions launched their drive against the juncture of the British and French armies in front of Amiens on March 21st.

By the afternoon of the next day the brigade had received orders to move to the 5th Army front. By 2.30 a.m. of April 23rd the four batteries in the line were at Vedrel and by 5.30 a.m. the entire Brigade was under way, headed south, under command of Lieut.-Col. W. K. Walker, D.S.O., M.C., the genial giant who had, up to March 17th, been in command of the Machine Gun Squadron of the Canadian Corps Cavalry.

The cavalcade, as it left a sputtering exhaust in its wake, was composed of five batteries. "A" and "B" Batteries each had eight Vickers guns mounted on four armoured cars. "C" (Bordens), "D" (Eatons) and "E" (Yukons) each had eight Vickers guns, were designated as Motor Batteries and they were transported in light box cars, from which the crews would fight as infantry machine gunners.

The message received by the Motors from Gen. Sir Arthur Currie just before they pushed off was:

> The Corps Commander wishes you the best of luck and has every confidence that you will do more than well.

The eight armoured cars in the long convoy chugging its way southward were the surviving veterans of many vehicular changes which had seen the motorcycle elements of the Motors discarded except as a means of officers keeping control over the widely-flung units. Like many elements of the Cavalry, the Motors had been forced to

275

Cleaning Armoured Cars, Canadian Motor M. G. Brigade

fight as "dismounted troops," while their metallic steeds were threatened by the rust of inaction. The Somme was the first of the later battles in which the mechanized cavalry role always envisioned for the Motors had been promised. The promised "breakthrough" never came. The Motors were doing their barrage task at Passchendaele when they might have been tuning up for a more spectacular, more fitting task in Gen. Byng's temporarily successful thrust for Cambrai in November and had missed that one glorious opportunity of which the Canadian Cavalry took such startling advantage.

Now as they roared south they were heading right for the type of open warfare for which they had been hoping and praying these last few years—but it was to be the reverse side of the picture they were to see, and it was to be painted on a dark, dismal background of tones when first it burst upon their view.

The convoy chugged into Amiens at 12.45 p.m. and just minutes later were again on their way to 5th Army Headquarters at Villers Brettoneux. There, Gen. Sir Hubert Gough met them, warmly commented upon their timely arrival and, in admitting the seriousness of the situation which had overwhelmed his army, said that the Canadian Motors represented the only available reinforcements. This was at 4 o'clock in the afternoon and just a few hours later batteries had been dispatched to fill menacing gaps which had been opened in the sadly-battered ranks of the 5th Army.

The Eaton and Yukon Batteries, under Capt. H.V. Muerling, M.C., reported to the 18th Corps at Roye and "B" and "C" Batteries, under the command of Capt. Holland, were on their way to Corbie, on which the hard-pressed 7th Corps was based. "A" Battery was held in reserve.

As the batteries moved along the roads to their alloted tasks they had time to reflect why well-conducted retreats get almost as favourable attention in the study of military history as successful attacks. In a matter of moments they were breasting the tide of retreat, with its rumours tossing wildly, gaunt-eyed stragglers showing only too eloquently what they had experienced, on roads choked with transport and refugees.

There is no blinking the fact that by the time the Motors arrived there was definite demoralization among British troops. Garrisons of strong redoubts and strong points had fought with a gallantry never surpassed in the annals of British arms, but the enemy, by sheer weight of numbers, a new infiltrating style of attack and a terrific gas and shell bombardment, aided above all by a dense fog on the morning of March 21st, had realised his hopes.

On the 3rd Army front the defences, though pushed back here and there, had not been broken.

But on the 5th Army front the Germans had broken through and by the end of the first day the whole of Gough's army was everywhere in retreat. The next day the retreat was continued while British and French reserves were rushed into the back areas of the crumbling front. The Germans had made the most rapid and greatest ground-gaining thrust on the Western Front since the fighting had settled into trench warfare. They had pushed the British back from in front of St. Quentin as far as the Somme near Peronne and that in fact two-thirds of the territory out of which the Germans had retreated in 1917 was again overrun and the enemy already claimed 30,000 prisoners and 600 guns.

Volumes have been written on the battle and it would take a bulky volume in itself to describe in detail the fortunes of the Motors in the next hectic weeks as they shifted over 35 miles of front, and so swiftly as to give the enemy the impression of far greater strength than they possessed. We can at best try to get a panoramic view of the Motors as they so spectacularly and heroically fought against tremendous odds and in doing so gained added recognition for the whole Canadian Machine Gun Corps.

As a result of a reconnaissance made by Capt. Muerling in the early hours of March 24th, Capt. Harkness with his eight Eaton guns was to assist in a counter-attack of the 183rd Brigade, aimed at the enemy who had gained a footing on the west bank of the canal north of Bethencourt. Four Yukon guns (Babb) were detailed to the 60th Brigade front which was being hard pressed by enemy crossing at Caniszy, Offiscy and Voyennes and the remaining four guns were to protect an artillery brigade northwest of Nesle. By 10 o'clock the various detachments had left for their tasks.

Lieut. Babb, severely wounded, a few hours later was in the hands of the Germans and the forward gun crew to which he was making his way was knocked out. The 60th Brigade had started to withdraw but the infantry rallied around the other five guns east of Mombleaux Cemetery and this position was held until four o'clock in the afternoon. A report says: The five guns obtained excellent targets, especially on the Ham-Nesle road, where the enemy advanced in column. Several belts were fired at between 200 and 300 yards. They had even scattered enemy machine gunners as they sought to get into action. By four o'clock our infantry withdrew across the west bank of the canal and that night the five guns were covering Bacquencourt bridge. The other Yukon guns saw no action as the artillery they were sent to protect had limbered up and they rejoined the Eatons on the 183rd Brigade front that night.

The Eatons arrived for their task just as the enemy laid down a heavy barrage on Mesnil St. Nicaisse in preparation for debouching from Bethencourt to the west. Infantry on the plateau west knew nothing of the 183rd Brigade's projected attack as six guns (Marshall) got there at noon. The six guns got into action at once, being joined by two other guns which had been detailed to assist a Royal Scots Battalion which could not be found near Fargny. The cars were riddled by shrapnel as the drivers had rushed them one by one through the barrage to off-load the crews. About one p.m., when the detachment commander was trying to get in touch with troops on his left, he found instead in low ground between the battery positions and Fontaine-Les-Pargny a 'large group of 500 Germans sitting on the ground and apparently enjoying a siesta. The eight guns concentrated their fire at once on this most exceptional target and inflicted severe losses on the completely surprised enemy. However, the exultation was short-lived for hardly had our guns ceased firing than the enemy machine gunners in front and from both flanks poured such an accurate fire into the Canadians' positions that 50 per cent of the Eatons became casualties.

Finding themselves alone, the Eatons were ordered to retreat by half batteries and with only two men per gun; it was a slow business. As they withdrew they found no infantry with which to co-operate and halted for awhile 1,500 yards south of Morchais. Here the infantry told them that Nesle and Mesnil St. Nicaisse had fallen. Eventually, together with an infantry captain and 50 men, the seven guns remaining established a line immediately northwest of Dreslincourt behind an old belt of wire. The infantry decided to withdraw but the Gunners remained throughout the afternoon, later finding they were 2,000 yards in front of our line. A British pilot enlivened the afternoon by diving low and spraying them with machine gun fire but, fortunately for the exposed battery, his aim was poor.

Word was later brought up that the 24th Division had established a line to the rear and the Eatons went back to positions "E" and "N" of Hyencourt-le-Petit for night defence. From the O. C. of the division the Canadians wangled a few tins of bully beef with which to top off an exciting, thrill-packed day.

Capt. Harkness' one Eaton gun with the hard-pressed 183rd Brigade had been joined by four Yukon guns and the detachment followed the withdrawal until at eight o'clock in the evening it became evident that the enemy would attempt an outflanking movement on Nesle from the north during the night or early next morning. Positions were finally established in front of the railway at Nesle between the station and the Nesle-Dreslincourt and the Mesnil-le-Petit Manicourt roads.

In the afternoon of March 24th "A" Battery (armoured), in reserve under Major Battersby, had been hurriedly dispatched to meet a menacing situation developing on the right flank of the 19th Corps between Bethencourt and Pargny, where the enemy was endeavouring to cross the Somme between St. Christ and Falvy. At 5.30 p.m. Major Battersby in one car and Lieut. Cuttle in a second went *via* Licourt and Cizancourt. At Licourt they ran into shelling and then turned south along the road by the Somme canal at Sancourt. An enemy plane zoomed down but was driven off. A motorcyclist scout reported a body of 50 Germans near the road junction of Epenancourt and Battersby, warning a body of Sherwood Foresters, darted down the road to dispose of this group. They scattered them under a hail of gunfire and then kept on going until they ran into German bombers. The cars had three hours more of potting enemy parties across the canal and searching Epenancourt and nearby fields with fire.

Meanwhile "B" Battery (Holland) and the Bordens (Nicholson) had reported to the 7th Corps area and been sent on to the 21st Division near Maricourt. They did not reach there until 6 a.m. owing to the congestion of the roads. It was about 8 a.m. when the batteries reached the junction of the Maricourt-Vlery-Hem roads. Heavy smoke clouds were rolling over from the German line as they found their rendezvous, but there was no other activity. However the calm was only momentary for hardly had they looked over the country before the commanders were asked to rally the infantry for the defence of a trench running half way up the ridge back of Clery Village.

Enemy artillery was laying a heavy barrage on the Clery and Maricourt road and masses of the enemy were emerging out of the smoke screen, following up our infantry as they fell back. Two Borden guns obtained good shooting as the enemy entered Clery before a shell blew up one of the guns. Then the other crew was blown up and

Lieut. West and Corp. Johnson manned the gun and with the fire of their revolvers held the enemy at bay until they were able to get their gun out of the village. The guns of the two batteries were now in position on both sides of the Clery-Maricourt road along an old shallow trench in front of a strong belt of wire. From these positions the guns covered the ground to the left of the village and they made excellent use of the view, smashing enemy formations with an intense fire. As the Germans continued to approach the infantry fell back but were rallied by Holland and Nicholson. There was in all a garrison of 100 men, holding 500 yards of trench.

Capt. Holland was seriously wounded as he went out to rescue a wounded man in front of the trench. He could not be taken out. Three cars had been ordered back because of the intensity of the shelling and a fourth could not be moved because of its proximity to a dump of explosives set afire by a shell. Corp. Hicks and Pte. Rymfer were killed as they went up to move the stranded car and then Pte. Henderson of the Bordens and an unknown "B" Battery man volunteered to start and drive the car away. Capt. Holland, with other wounded, was placed in the car, but the former died as he was being moved from the car to a stretcher.

Both batteries were suffering severe casualties and Lieut. Snyder of "B" and Lieuts. West and Waldron of the Bordens, who were observing, were all shot through the head and killed instantly. Enemy snipers and machine guns had made getting ammunition up almost impossible and the Germans were gradually creeping up so close to the guns that they were using hand grenades. Three or four of the guns were out of action. Just then a small party of infantry, by rushes, came up and occupied a trench 50 yards to the rear. At 2 p.m. Capt. Nicholson, the only officer left, decided to withdraw to this trench occupied, it developed, by the 15th Cheshires. By four o'clock Capt. Nicholson had only four guns left and these were asked to cover the withdrawal of the Cheshires to a line between Hem and Haurepas. At five o'clock there were only two guns left.

An account of this epic, says:

> Shortly afterwards the enemy launched a strong attack, breaking through on the left flank and advancing in large numbers from the front. Our infantry had withdrawn but the machine gunners remained in action until practically surrounded. One of the two remaining guns was put out of action a few minutes

after the attack commenced, but the other was fired until the Germans were within 50 yards by Pte. Finlayson. The few machine gunners surviving crawled from the trench and in rushes followed the road in the direction of Hem. During those last wild moments Capt. Nicholson received a severe wound which caused the loss of his right arm. Eventually the survivors under Battery Sergt.-Major Frechette reached the cars at Maricourt.

And thus ended the Motors' first day—a day of high heroism, remarkable initiative and wonderful determination to stem the tide of retreat and demoralization. As a day it offered many variations of machine gun roles and was to be repeated in day after day of tenacious fighting against heart-breaking odds. As a day, too, it had exacted a tragic price.

Early in the morning of March 25th the 20th Division, having been pressed back during the night, was holding the line from Buverchy along the Libemont road as far north as Quignery in conjunction with the 22nd French Division and from Quignery to Mesnil-le-Petit. On the right of the 20th the 30th Division, with part of the 62nd French Division, carried on the line southward as far as the bend in the canal. In spite of the French reinforcements, the situation remained critical and Gen. Spooner, commanding the 183rd Brigade, ordered Capt. Harkness to the outskirts of Nesle, there to gather all stragglers, while undertaking a similar task himself near Froidmond.

The enemy attack, already growing bolder, had as its objective the enlargement of the gap between the 18th and 19th Corps. The four Yukon guns inflicted great damage on the enemy in covering the retreat of the infantry. The machine gunners held their fire until the enemy were within 500 yards and then raked their ranks with fire under which they broke. The Germans brought a whizz-bang battery up against the Emma Gees and, though they extricated themselves, three guns were knocked out, one of them being that lone Eaton gun in this area. Argyle and Sutherland Highlanders aided Lieut. Black and four men work two guns until 8.30 a.m., when they retired through Nesle to a line between Nesle and Herly, overlooking the river at Ighom, established by Harkness with the stragglers he had gathered in.

Over on the right flank three Yukon guns on the high ground east of Cresey concentrated their fire on advancing Germans at 2,000 yards and broke up formations. The enemy, however, kept the pressure up and by outflanking forced the machine gunners' withdrawal. He

Officers of the 1st Canadian Motor M.G. Brigade

occupied Herley and Languevois and made progress to Cresey but could make no advance along the Nesle-Roye road all afternoon.

The 59th Infantry Brigade and the 183rd were now merged around Billancourt but how great was the confusion and how rapidly the situation might change was shown in the experience of a driver of a Napier box car, who, having taken one load of rations and ammunition to a designated spot, went back for a second, only to find the Germans in possession. Under intense fire he turned the car around and escaped.

Not only were the guns doing great execution but they were proving to be rallying points for dispirited stragglers.

By the morning of the 25th the right flank of the 8th Division had been bent back from the Somme towards Licourt. The situation on the front between the 8th Division and Nesle was critical. At 7 a.m. the 24th Division launched a counter-attack from their positions near Ryercourt-le-Petit in the direction of Dreslincourt. The Eaton guns (Marshall) were supporting the 73rd Brigade.

The attacking brigade, after the incessant fighting since the morning of March 21st, was only battalion strength. None of the machine guns in position had to be moved forward to cover the attack. Five were in excellent position along the Fouchette-Ominicourt road and two about 400 yards northeast of Hyencourt-le-Petit. The gunners had a complete view and were set to fire at 2,000, 2,500 and 3,000 ranges. The tired 73rd Brigade made a courageous start but a withering fire broke up the attack half-way between Bersaucourt and Dreslincourt. It halted momentarily and then retirement of small groups grew into a general withdrawal. The gunners then reversed their firing program, firing it backward to cover the retirement. The attacking brigade on the right were themselves heavily attacked at Curchy and retired to their original positions. That day the Eatons conformed to the infantry withdrawals but by noon they were reduced to two men per gun and often one; they had no ammunition, no rations and the men were utterly exhausted, so the detachment commander withdrew them through Chaulnes to Bayonvillers, where the men got some food and a little respite.

"A" Battery armoured cars on March 25th were co-operating with the 24th Infantry Brigade and at 4.30 a.m. left Marchelpot for Cizancourt *via* Licourt. Two cars stopped at a factory to be ready to support an attack by our infantry at 9.15. Two other cars, commanded by Major Battersby and Lieut. Adams, went to Cizancourt and then down the road toward Epenancourt.

But before our attack could get started the enemy launched his at 8.50 and from a sunken road the crews of the two cars fired very effectively, delaying the Germans for a short time.

Three cars were slowly backing up the roads covering our infantry's retirement while one was almost cut off as the Germans entered Marchelpot, compelling its retirement by way of Licourt. While the two cars of Battersby and Adams were withdrawing through Licourt the Germans were entering the village from the south. Both crews put up a splendid fight, firing at the Germans from almost point-blank range until Major Battersby together with the driver and the two crews in his car were killed. The other car tried a daring rescue but was turned back by a withering fire. In another minute this car was hit as well and several of the crew wounded. The cars were then withdrawn to Villers-Brettoneaux to replenish ammunition and reorganise badly-riddled gun crews.

In the afternoon of March 25th all of the divisions of the 19th Corps were ordered to withdraw to the line Hattencourt-ChaulnesAblaincourt-Estres-Assevillers-Herecourt-Frise line. The command of the 18th Corps passed from the 5th Army to the 3rd French Army. The 5th Army now commanded only the 19th Corps, holding the front from Hattencourt to the Somme. Also all troops of the 7th Corps north of the Somme were transferred to the 5th Corps to become a part of the 3rd British Army.

Enemy pressure was maintained against the 7th Corps and Guinchy and Thones Wood were the scene of heavy fighting. During the night of March 25th-26th the line of defence was taken back to new positions between Bray-sur-Somme and Albert.

The 26th was a fateful calendar date for on that day Marshal Foch was appointed to the Supreme Command of the Allied Armies.

On the same day the mixed force of details, cooks, batmen, stragglers and Canadian and American Engineers which had been organised under Gen. Grant, Engineer Chief of the 5th Army, was taken over by Gen. Carey, and as Carey's Force provided such a last-ditch show of aggressiveness and determination that its 2,200-strength—the last thin line of reserves behind the tired, weary, battered British Divisions—was multiplied many times in inspirational effect. It was the line interposed between the driving German hordes and Amiens, their eagerly-sought objective. To stiffen this last line of so pitifully few, a 10-gun machine gun battery was hastily formed and that night was in position in Aubercourt, Marcelcave and Hamel.

The morning of the same day had seen the 20th Division withdraw to the Les Quesnel area and Capt. Muerling with the remnants of the Eaton and Yukon batteries were located on the southern outskirts of the town

The situation west and northwest of Roye was critical. The French 22nd and 62nd Divisions were withdrawing in a south-westerly direction towards the valley of the Avre River and the British troops, after extricating themselves from a bad spot, were marching in a north-westerly direction and thus a gap was ever widening. The Germans had Andechy and were close to Erches and trying to push through a gap south of Rosieres and between Meharicourt and Fresnoy-les-Roye. The 20th and 30th Divisions, supposed to have been relieved the night before, found themselves in the thick of the fighting.

The G. O. C. 20th Division had told the tired, depleted machine gunners that they were to be kept out of the line 24 hours, but 20 minutes after the order was rescinded when it was found that the enemy had broken through and captured Fouquescourt. The detachment had only seven guns, most of them salvaged on the way back from the Nesle-Roye front to Le Quesnel. The guns were mounted on light auxiliary tripods for the heavy Mark IV tripods had been found too heavy in the constant moving of a rearguard action. Capt. Harkness was in command of the detachment which by 12.30 p.m. had taken up positions at Rouvroy and Warvillers.

The defence of Rouvroy had been organised by a Royal Engineer officer, who had stragglers and men from every conceivable branch of the service under him. During the afternoon the enemy made several unsuccessful attempts to advance north and northwest from Parvillers and Fouquescort, but the Motors held them off, inflicting heavy losses. Towards night things had quietened down and an independent patrol established on the Rouvroy-Parvillers road during the night established the fact that heavy tractors were evidently hauling heavy guns up to the front. Capt. Muerling had meanwhile salvaged five more Vickers and one Lewis gun with two-man crews. The Lewis gun was sent up to Rouvroy and just at the first streak of dawn on the 27th it rattled out death to the occupants of a German staff car being driven down the Fouquescourt-Rouvroy road. From 75 yards away the machine gunners tried to reach their quarry but were driven off by a hail of bullets from Fouquescourt Village.

The eight machine guns in front of Rouvroy did magnificent

work as they drove off an enemy attack in the morning. South of the Roye road the situation was menacing, with German cavalry pushing through the woods along the Avre River, driving in the outposts of the 36th Division as they advanced against Querbigny. By noon the guns were withdrawn from Rouvroy but Warvillers was still held. Capt. Harkness, dashing back into Rouvroy for some ammunition left there, was blown off his motorcycle by a shell. Regaining consciousness, he walked back to Le Quesnel to report before being evacuated to hospital.

Five of eight men, manning four guns in Rouvroy, had been knocked out and when they got back to Warvillers reinforcements arrived just in time to help them bring a German attack to a standstill.

Earlier in the afternoon four guns (Vosburgh) in front of Hancrest scattered German cavalry trying to advance southeast towards Warvillers and Hancrest. The Germans were pressing on toward Bouchoir and four guns under Black were rushed by car through Beaufort and Le Quesnel and in half an hour were in action at the crossroads one mile west of Bouchoir. They had been told to hold the enemy at all costs and for an hour and a half they had made-to-order targets as the Germans repeatedly tried to advance. The G. O. C. 20th Division personally thanked the detachment for their work.

With nightfall enemy activity decreased and during the night of March 27th-28th the French 133rd Division relieved the 20th (British). The machine gunners were the last to go, the relief being completed on the morning of March 28th.

From the morning of the 22nd, when they had two hours' sleep and another two hours' brief respite on the 24th, the survivors of the Eaton and Yukon batteries had had no rest; they had been subjected to terrific strain and terrible casualties. They were gaunt and staggering as they found rest at Hebcourt, where the 1st C.M. G. C. Brigade Headquarters had been established.

Meanwhile "A" Battery's three armoured cars operating with the 19th Corps on the night of March 26th-27th, in view of the serious and dangerous situation created along the Somme by the withdrawal of the 3rd Army troops from Bray westwards, were ordered to report to the 16th Division at Hamel in order to guard the crossings over the Somme at Cerisy and thus prevent the enemy from outflanking the left of the 19th Corps front at Proyart. They arrived at 4 a.m. on the 27th. Four guns were placed close to the northern outskirts of Cerisy and two others were placed on the south side of the village to cover the right bridge. The cars were withdrawn a little distance. About 10 a.m. the enemy, who was rapidly following the withdrawal of the right flank of the 3rd Army, appeared to be massing his troops north and northwest of Shapilly, apparently for a thrust southward over the canal. The four-gun detachment just at this moment noticed a large enemy group which turned out to be machine gunners. The Germans were given time to mount their guns and then our gunners opened up a devastating fire from 1,200 yards, killing and wounding many and scattering the remainder. "A" Battery guns remained at Cerisy for three hours, pouring 15,000 rounds across the canal.

The next day, March 28th, the same guns were in Rosieres, Vrely and back in Caix and they covered the withdrawal of British and French troops, fighting side by side, and by way of variety took on a flight of 11 enemy planes, apparently looking for a battery of French 75's. They moved out of their positions to the rear and a rain of German shells fell on the spot they had just vacated. Then they returned, dismounting two guns and using two from a forward armoured car and caught the enemy pushing across country between Rosieres, Vrely and Caix. They had another brush with the enemy on the outskirts of Caix before retiring at 7 p.m., picking up about a dozen wounded on their way to Gentelles.

Two armoured cars were operating on the road between Villers-Brettoneaux and Warfuse-Abancourt, but their chief diversion on that sector during the day was an exchange of shots with several hostile planes which dived at them. Two armoured cars were also operated along the Amiens-Roye road on the 28th and did great execution. One car ran into a ditch as it manoeuvred up and down the road but the crew, despite intense rifle and machine gun fire, succeeded in getting it back on the road and safely away.

The wounding of Lieut. Green and Sergt. Morrison as they went clown the Villers-Breattoneaux-Warfuse-Abancourt road to bring in two cars set the stage for a daring rescue of the officer by Pte. McKenzie on a solo motorcycle, who placed the wounded man on the rear. He went back again for Henderson, but the latter had sought a first aid post himself.

By the night of the 28th the sorely pressed British troops held approximately the Amiens defence line, south of the Somme from Mezieres to Ignacourt and Hamel. The 20th Division held the front south of the River Luce and Carey's Force the front between the Luce and the Somme. On the evening of the 28th the Motors in-

Officers of the 2nd Canadian Motor M.G. Brigade

flicted many casualties on the enemy when he attacked and captured Marcelcave and when pressure was resumed on the 19th Corps on the morning of the 29th and Mezieres had to be abandoned, the enemy attacks east and south of Hamel were repulsed.

In the swiftly-changing picture the 29th brought, reorganisation of the much-battered Motors was effected, remnants of the Eatons and Yukons being formed into a 16-gun battery under Muerling, who gathered up an additional 16 guns from Carey's Force, manned by British gunners. By 7 p.m. that day the 32 guns were in position between the Luce and the Somme Rivers.

At daybreak on the 30th this front became very active and the enemy gradually pushed the French out of Moreuil Wood by sheer weight of numbers and, regardless of losses, he succeeded in driving our infantry off the left bank of the Luce and occupying Demuin.

Fourteen machine guns on the north bank of the Luce did most effective work at ranges of 1,700 and 2,000 against the Germans advancing into Demuin. "The Germans," says a machine gun report in part, "were in platoons marching in fours along the top of the ridge in a westerly direction." With this inviting flank exposed to them, the Canadians had good shooting and made the most of it. Another group of guns on the road running due north from Aubercourt had intermittent shooting gallery practice at German columns moving up a road sunken in many spots. It was a fantastic target in its way, suddenly bobbing up and then as quickly fading into a sunken portion of the road and disappearing from sight. Another detachment was heavily engaged west of Marcelcave.

Two armoured cars co-operated on the morning of the 30th in the Avre sector, when a brilliant counter-attack by the Canadian Cavalry Brigade cleared the Germans out of Moreuil Wood. The gunners guarded the gap between the cavalry and the 20th Division.

The progress of the enemy north of the Luce was definitely checked and in the afternoon of the 30th his troops were finally driven back to about the line of the Aubercourt-Marcelcave road by determined counter-attacks carried out by elements of the 66th Division and the 9th Australian Brigade. Further strong counter-attacks in the evening restored our line south of the Luce and slightly later that night hostile attacks on the both sides of the Somme were repulsed by the 1st Cavalry and 3rd Australian Divisions.

That night Carey's famous force was broken up as it was relieved by the 1st British Reserve Division (3rd Australian) to make an appearance on the 5th Army front, but the machine gunners remained in the line.

March 31st brought a continuance of the fighting between the Luce and Avre, our troops being driven from Moreuil Station to Hangard. One of the armoured cars returning from a sortie ran into heavy enemy shelling just south-east of Hourges and dived into a shell-hole. Three of the crew became casualties as the guns were removed. Later that day a party went back to get the abandoned car, but it had been hit squarely by shells and was just smoking debris.

There were plenty of alarms but no more severe fighting until early on the morning of April 4th, when a series of attacks, while generally repulsed, caused the British line to make hurried shifts.

That afternoon the Motors, who were reorganising preparatory to reporting back to the Canadian Corps, were again called on to "hold Villers-Brettonneaux at all costs."

Twelve guns going up on the left were heavily shelled astride the Warfuse-Amiens road, four other ranks being killed and 26 wounded. An enemy shell exploded on, and set fire to, a lorry filled with ammunition just as it was being unloaded by men of the Yukon and Eaton Batteries on the eastern outskirts of Villers-Brettoneaux. Two charabanc cars were near by and, despite the danger from exploding ammunition, Pte. Wegg volunteered to start them. And start them he did and daringly drove them away. Just before dusk, Lieut. Black, who had no men left, joined the armoured cars and, taking one quick dash down the Villers-Brettoneaux road, poured enfilade fire into enemy positions on both sides of the road and withdrew without suffering a single casualty.

Six Borden crews were sent in as reinforcements about 6.30 p.m. that day and as they took up positions northeast of Villers-Brettoneaux an enemy barrage came down. Expecting an enemy attack, these guns opened fire at 2,500 yards on selected enemy positions and it was later reported that this fire had broken up a large enemy concentration, apparently prepared for an attack.

The situation remained comparatively calm and uneventful until on the night of the 8th-9th the Borden, Eaton and Yukon Batteries were relieved and the next morning the armoured cars were withdrawn. On the morning of the 10th the 1st C. M. G. C. Brigade received orders to rejoin the Canadian Corps.

There was praise everywhere for the gallant Motors and they had richly earned it. Thrown into the confusion and chaos of a retreat and into a strange and unfamiliar front, over which there hung at the time the atmosphere of almost a complete rout, the Canadian machine gunners had shown remarkable steadiness and by their initiative and daring and the ubiquity of their great mobility had produced an effect upon the exultant enemy that was greatly out of proportion to their 40 guns.

The Motors paid a heavy price in a display that will always stand out as perhaps the most all-round performance of its power the machine gun was able to give on the Western Front.

In those days between March 24th and April 7th—days and nights of constant strain, with hardly a respite—the casualty summary of the Motors was as follows:

	Killed	Wounded	Missing	Totals
Officers	5	8	1	14
Other Ranks	20	100	10	130
Totals	25	108	11	144

The total of 144 does include the casualties suffered by the British machine gunners attached to the Canadian Motor Machine Gun Batteries during the same period.

CHAPTER 7

Battle of Amiens
August 8th to 25th

On July 6th, the Canadian Corps was warned to relieve the 17th Corps in the line and on July 15th, the day that the Germans launched two more powerful attacks against the French, the relief had been completed, with the 2nd, 1st and 4th Divisions in the line from Telegraph Hill to Oppy and the 3rd Division, under the 6th Corps, in the Neuville Vitasse area.

News filtered through that the Germans were repulsed with heavy losses east of Rheims in the direction of Chalons, but had succeeded in crossing the Marne south-west of Rheims towards Epernay and then, right on the heels of this news came the sudden crushing counter-blow of Gen. Foch to electrically charge the air with a bristling offensive spirit and new hope instead of the passive, even if determined attitude that had at best these last few months meant "sticking it out" until more American help came.

Between Chateau Thierry and Soissons had come the first great counter-stroke on the western side of the long salient the Germans had driven toward Rheims—and Paris—and then, starting on July 20th had come a four-mile push in six days against the eastern side of the salient—days which dramatically changed the whole fortunes of war and had a significance far beyond what the map could show. Some of that significance was more apparent when on July 26th came news that 35 German divisions within the dangerously-narrowed' salient, to save themselves from complete envelopment, if not annihilation, began a general but orderly retreat. Once more the Marne had interposed.

But with all his troubles in the south, the enemy had reserves enough to move three fresh divisions in to face Vimy, where almost incessant activity of the Canadians in the line puzzled the Germans into expecting an attack. But for all this activity there was time for Canadians to reflect that if war could be lovely at all then it must be at its peak of loveliness in July in France, over which hung a lazy summer haze. A green carpet of grass and foliage covered the most recent scars of war on Vimy and patches of it relieved the brick-coloured landscape that stretched over the plain away on to Douai. By day activity quietened down to drowsiness but at night moonlight reveries might be rudely shattered by sudden, spiteful barrages or the whine and crash of searching, random shells.

As July 30th approached there was no instinctive premonition that big things were impending. However, on that day Canadian Headquarters mysteriously pushed off into the blue. And though the 1st and 4th Divisions then in the line did not know it, the other Divisions were already on their way—somewhere.

On the nights of July 31st and August 1st-2nd the divisions in the line were relieved by the British 56th, 57th and 52nd Divisions, the latter of which had been initiated previously into their first sight of trench duty on the Western Front, as they came to France from Mesop.

And the 1st and 4th Divisions kept moving—but where?

The imaginative optimists knew now definitely that that job of garrisoning Paris would be a certainty beyond every crossroad halt. The realists knew just as definitely that those months of training behind the lines certainly justified no visions of pleasant strolls along Paris boulevards—that through the summer pleasantness ahead there were much grimmer things to come.

To many now, years after, it is a stretch of pleasant, confused memories wherein days merged into days and slumbers were caught in strange places. Those sudden embussings, those train rides that were more like merry-go-rounds because of no known destination; those long treks in summer moonlit nights through a totally different France of winding roads over well-forested countryside; those days of sleep in sleepy little villages that were a warming contrast to the starkness of those farther north-all these things are memorable.

But they were mystifying then, for France had seemingly swallowed the Canadian Corps, whole.

How the Canadian Corps was first committed to "a venture" in the South as early as July 20th; how elaborate plans were concocted to keep the Corps itself in ignorance of the intention; the deliberate fostering of the idea of a push in the North; the sending of the two battalions, the 7th (Winnipeg) and the 4th C. M. R., "secretly" northward, where they did a trench tour and had the "humiliating" misfortune to lose prisoners and carelessly leave evidence of other Canadian units being in that sector for the Germans to interpret, were all factors in a magnificently-conceived bit of camouflage that set a new level for the war to date.

To students of the art of war—and of psychology—the suddenly-found elasticity of staff work and conception which could turn from set-piece attacks, from an oftentimes bewildered defence and from a deep-rooted conviction that months of preparation must precede every attack to fluid developments now taking form every hour, must always prove intriguing.

The Canadian Corps' mission was at first to be a purely local attack to free the Amiens-Paris railway line, but the Allied counteroffensive started on July 18th had had such an effect on the general situation that now the operations of the Corps were to have a much wider scope.

And so it was that the Canadian Corps infantry and machine gunners found themselves, almost magically, assembling on the night of August 7th in areas in front of Amiens city. The Canadian artillery was already in position. In Hangard Wood were secreted 130 tanks and on the night of the 7th more came up, the noise of their coming drowned out by the drone of scores of heavy British bombers. In every bit of available cover, troops and guns and vehicles were hidden while the tremendous task of getting adequate supplies of ammunition for the huge job at hand was, somehow, miraculously being accomplished.

The general front of attack was to extend from Moreuil to Ville-sur-Ancre, approximately 20,000 yards. On the right was the 1st French Army (Moreuil to Thennes); in the centre from Thennes to the Amiens-Chaulnes railway line was the Canadian Corps; on the left was the Australian Corps (Amiens-Chaulnes railway line to the Somme) and over again to the extreme left was the 3rd British Corps attacking in the direction of Morlancourt.

The total width of the Canadian Corps front was 8,500 yards and three objectives set for the first day were the Green Line, Red Line and Blue Dotted Line. The last objective visualized a penetration of 14,000 yards—a trifle over eight miles.

Gen. Sir Arthur Currie in his official account of the battle said:

The general scheme of attack was to overrun rapidly the enemy's forward area to a depth of 3,500 yards under cover of a dense artillery barrage which would begin at zero hour; then, without halting, to seize the Red Line, relying on the help of the tanks to overcome the machine gun defences. At that moment the Cavalry was to pass through the Infantry and seize the area as far back as the Blue Dotted Line (running east of Hangest-en-Santerre-les Quesnel-Caix-Harbonnieres) supported on its right flank by the Canadian Independent Force, which consisted of two Motor Machine Gun Brigades, two sections of heavy trench mortars which could be fired from trucks and the Canadian Corps Cyclists, all under the direction of Brig.-Gen. Brutinel, C.M.G., D.S.O., commanding the Canadian Machine Gun Corps. The Cavalry was to be followed as quickly by the 4th Canadian Division passing through the 3rd on the right and by reserve brigades of the other two divisions. Every effort was to be made to exploit success wherever it occurred.

It was a sweeping, bold conception, utterly the opposite of what had gone before in set-piece attacks and to machine gunners, newly formed into their expanded battalions and with the battery as the tactical unit, it was to provide an especially novel test—in particular for the new "Hell-for-Leather" school which had arisen in the machine gun ranks and pictured, as a result of the earlier summer training, a sort of Light Horse Artillery role for itself. But oddest and most novel role of all machine gunners was to fall to No. 3 Company (Capt. W. G. Williams) of the 4th Battalion which with two added guns from No. 2 Company were to go over in 34 old Mark IV tanks. The boldly-conceived role of these slow, but improved, juggernauts was to proceed straight to the Blue Dotted Line, eight miles away, and there disgorge their crews of Vickers and Lewis gunners to harass retreating Germans and hold the Blue Dotted Line until our infantry came up.

The relief of the Australians still holding the outpost line on the night of August 7th-8th came off without a hitch, and every last detail of the vast, complicated preparations were tightly, magically dovetailed in the August night, the stars being fortunately hidden by scudding clouds. The greater part of our forward area consisted of bare slopes exposed to enemy observation from the high ground to the south of the River Luce and east of Hourges but in which trenches were only loosely connected and of temporary construction. On the right there was one bridge on the Domart-Hangard road over which all traffic had to be pushed to get to the jumping-off trenches. That bridge was a high gamble.

And so, with only the odd flare lighting up the sky, this powerful Canadian striking force gathered up its might. An hour before the 4.20 zero hour a heavy mist rolled up from the marshy ground along the Luce and was to be some compensation for the obstacle this ground presented to the attack.

There was to be no co-ordinated machine gun barrage for the whole frontage of attack. Divisions were to arrange their own. Two batteries 2nd Battalion and the No. 3 Company of the 3rd were thus detailed and were to do a particularly effective job.

And now as we near the zero hour it must be confessed that any historian, even if only trying to keep within the limits of the Machine Gun units in this big adventure about to start, would have to have a complete volume at his disposal. There were 48 machine gun batteries to be set in motion at varying times in this sweeping plan of attack, to say nothing of keeping a wary, alert eye on the Independent Force operating on the Amiens-Roye road in an avenging role, for this countryside was of recent, bitter memory for the Motors. Every battery will run the full gamut of adventures.

And so, in fancy, we'll take a view from a two-seater plane, which will share the air with many squadrons which as the light grows better will zoom down in wild dives, machine-gunning surprised and confused German groups. And we'll concentrate on getting glimpses, if only fleeting ones, of the Machine Gunners' part in this battle.

On the dot at 4.20, the mightiest chorus of artillery fire that ever crashed the accompaniment to a Canadian attack opened up in all its fury, the false misty dawn being stabbed with a continuous, serried flash of flame. The surprise was so complete that no answering roar came from the enemy artillery for, it seemed, whole minutes and then it was only fitful and finally, as the accuracy of the Canadian counter-battery work made itself felt and the infantry advance surged over their areas, died away into broken salvos.

Mist had aided the Germans when they opened their thrust for Amiens in March and now Fate was tossing this same mist against them. But if it added to the confusion of the Germans, it also prevented the covering Machine Gun batteries from affording support to infantry units with which they were moving forward.

White, red and green flares are still going up from the German lines as the 3rd Division storms up the slopes of Hourges with No. 3 Company concentrating an intense barrage fire on Dodo Woods. One other rank is killed and six wounded in the barrage positions. Files of pack mules easily distinguish the machine gunners moving up behind their infantry brigades or in the leading battalions. One battery comes into action 1,500 yards north of Demuin, and again at Wren Copse.

All along the Corps front of attack progress is being made and whole groups of Germans are left to themselves as attacks swirl past. Rapid progress is being made by the 1st Division in the centre, a momentary setback being experienced at the road junction 500 yards north of Demuin. With few casualties, batteries move along in diamond formation and occupied the Green Line to consolidate. There is stiff resistance to overcome in Hangard Wood West but the attack opens and eddies around the flanks as it does in Hangard Wood East.

At the latter place M. G. sections overcome groups which had been overlooked by the fast-moving infantry and "M" Battery of the 1st C. M. G. C. Battalion comes into action 300 yards west of the Demuin-Villers-Brettoneaux road and uses overhead fire to support the 13th and 14th Battalions, who are driving at Croates Trench near the crest of the spur southeast of Morgemont Wood. "L" Battery, operating with the 14th Battalion, can be seen attacking a strong point, one section firing on it and the other half battery creeping up on the flank and using bombs to capture five guns and kill all the crews. The battery is to repeat this performance another 100 yards farther on before occupying and consolidating positions in the first objective, the Green Line.

And roaring on over to the left sector we see the 2nd Division carrying the Green Line with dash even though, an hour before zero, its assembly area had been the target of a sudden, heavy German barrage which inflicted many casualties. The same barrage had given the Corps a bad moment as they feared the show had been given away by some Australians captured on the night of August 6th.

No. 3 Company (McCamus) of the 2nd C. M. G. Battalion didn't run into much trouble as it went up with the 4th Infantry Brigade, until it came under fire from German guns in Morgemont Wood from the right. Then later they can be seen giving covering fire to the 18th Battalion as it captures Cancellette Ravine by assault. Two signallers of "J" Battery are wounded as the Battery personnel captures two German guns, one officer and 10 men and the captured guns are immediately turned on a strong point to a flank. The Company's batteries are in position in the Green Line in plenty of time to secure good targets as pockets of Germans break out of dips in the ground and attempt to escape. Jaffa Trench held up the 19th Battalion on the left. "M" Battery had already lost an officer (Roughton) before the jump-off but got nicely out of the enemy barrage, capturing several German guns and crews as it followed the Amiens-Nesle railway.

Corp. Duffy, observing one gun holding up the infantry, rushed it from the rear and killed its two-man crew. The battery O. C. (McCullough) with three gunners rushed three German machine guns successively, the officer being twice wounded. Two other ranks are killed, two officers and 11 other ranks wounded before this battery is seen settling in its Green Line positions, from where they further harried retreating Germans. "K" and "L" Batteries, detailed for barrage duty, had three killed and one wounded before zero hour and, being mistaken for enemy gunners in the mist, were fired upon by our own infantry.

Now back to the right again just as the morning sun is dissipating the mist and we see the Canadian Cavalry Brigade moving out on the plateau—an inspiring sight—and along the tree-lined Amiens-Roye road are moving the Motors, protecting the flank left open by the rapid advance of the 3rd Division and the planned 45-minute delay in the start of the French 1st Army's attack. Now as the mist clears the greatest panorama of modern battle from the Allied side of the Western Front is spreading out before our eyes. Tanks, lumbering Mark IV's and the fleet little Whippets, Cavalry sabres flashing in the sun and Artillery limbering up and galloping to new positions-a whole Corps in movement extending back to the 4th Canadian Division in reserve—make up a sight that beggars description. Long, broken lines of brown dots are the infantry uncoiling like a long snake across the Canadian front as groups stop here and there to take time off from fighting to frisk files of German prisoners going the opposite way and out of the war.

Now it is the Red Line just east of Mezieres—White House—Camp Vermont Farm and the high ground east of Guillacourt for which the supporting brigades of all three divisions will make. At 8.20 our protective barrage in front of the Green Line had ceased and the enemy artillery fire is down to random shots. His defence is broken up now into strong points and isolated groups which are to provide stubborn opposition as the morning wears on.

Near Demuin two tanks filled with machine gunners go straight for a German 5.9 Battery, which fires at them over open sights. They halt in a hollow and off load the gunners, who stalk up the hill and wipe out the battery. Pack mules are taking "A," "B," "E" and "F" Batteries of the 3rd C. M. G. C. Battalion up with the infantry. "B" Battery had to man-handle its guns across the Luce at Hangard on a foot bridge while the mules were swum across. The delay had brought German shelling down on this area, but the battery escaped with two other ranks casualties and losing two mules. Two more other ranks were wounded and a mule killed as the battery came under German machine gun fire while crossing the valley south of Demuin.

The 1st Division is now moving on to Corcelles and Lette Wood and by 11.30 a.m. are taking the Red Line objective, including the villages of Ignacourt and Cayeux. The speed of advance is so great that "A" and "D" Batteries, in diamond formation behind the 3rd C. I. B., had no opportunity of assisting in fire fights before consolidating at the Red Line.

No. 1 Company (Basevi) of the 2nd C. M. G. C. Battalion cooperated with the 5th C. I. B. on the left and used full limbers moving up to the Red Line objectives. "D" Battery lost an officer and three other ranks near Wiencourt.

The entire Red Line is in our hands by noon and the Blue Dotted Line attackers begin moving on through the Red Line positions. The 4th Division now came into the picture, leapfrogging the tired but exultant 3rd Division. The French advance is now beginning to keep pace and along the whole front the horizon blue of the French on the right and the Canadians and Australians move along at a pace to make history.

The 4th Division had two-thirds of the Blue Dotted Line objectives to take with a corresponding decrease of the 1st and 2nd Division fronts. Recovered from their first surprise and confusion, German troops during the afternoon, fighting in the beaming August sunshine, are to offer increasingly stiff resistance all along the line, with reinforcements beginning to make their appearance.

Now cavalry and tanks are really entering the fight and going on to new adventures as they preceded the infantry at this stage of the battle.

Suddenly topping a rise, No. 1 Company (Britton) of the 4th C. I. G. C., even though it is in Divisional reserve, is to suddenly have a grandstand view of the struggle for Beaucourt Wood. Cavalry squadrons are attacking the wood and being mowed down by machine gun fire. They are broken under a hail of fire, wheel and re-form again and again. An 18-pounder battery has galloped into the fight and blazes away at the wood over open sights and out in the open themselves. Finally cavalry coming up from the right flank are seen to go into the wood and there they were found, dismounted and held up by the Germans, who fought from behind every tree as the infantry penetrated the leafy nest of strong points. The 54th and 102nd Battalions cleared the wood after a stiff fight and by 4.30 p.m. are established on the eastern edge, seeking to hook up with the 12th C. I. B.

The 11th C. I. B. suffered severely from machine gun fire from Fresnoy-en-Chaussee over on the French front and were unable to make any headway over the flat ground toward Les Quesnel. "F" Battery was split up, with mobile guns being attached to the 11th C. I. B. The 12th C. I. B. encountered less resistance and with their accompanying M. G. batteries rapidly reached the final objective on the line Caix-les Quesnel road. The 78th had the most stubborn opposition and it required an infantry company, several tanks, an 18-pounder and a Stokes gun crew to subdue enemy strong points on the high level north of Beaucourt Wood.

It is difficult following the varying fortunes of the tanks, many of which were mired in the Luce at the start. The 3rd Canadian Division had requisitioned four of the tanks.

On the right, the tanks co-operating with the 11th C. I. B. went well until reaching Beaucourt Wood, where, debouching from low ground between Beaucourt and Beaucourt Wood, the fire from an enemy battery sited west of Les Quesnel knocked out all but one of the moving forts. The survivor aided the 54th Battalion attack on Beaucourt Wood by moving along in front of the wood, firing into it and then returning to the dead ground. Another tank (Gardner) got forward to the vicinity of Les Quesnel, where its crew was deposited. The tank was immediately surrounded and survivors of the crew and gun crews were taken prisoner. Hostile artillery and machine gun fire set the tanks afire and their crews and Vickers gun crews were either burned to death or shot in trying to escape. Major L. F. Pearce, acting as Liaison Officer, found five crews from destroyed tanks and these remnants, under Eaton and Henderson, were placed in positions on the edge of Beaucourt Wood.

Of the 12 tanks preceding the 1st Division advance, six reached the Blue Dotted Line but, owing to the right being held up, these were obliged to withdraw their detachments 1,500 yards. Not all the

Vickers guns got forward with these tanks. Some had been unable to stand the heat and the fumes and were unloaded with their guns and followed the nearest infantry. On the way up four of these gun crews succeeded in clearing up machine gun nests for the advance of the 78th. One tank on this sector (McDonald) reached the Blue Line before the infantry on the right of the 12th C. I. B. frontage and surviving members of the crew got their guns into action and held the position until troops of the 72nd Battalion hove into view.

Decades after this August day it is essential that the historian forsake the aerial, sweeping view of widely-spread action for a more intimate, detailed story of what happened to these tanks on their novel adventure—an adventure destined to be a fore-runner of mechanized tactics in open warfare.

Describing the action of the tank which first reached the Blue Line and stuck it out there, Lieut. F. M. MacDonald reported:

> Our crews continued to go forward with the tank and about two hours afterwards we passed through the 58th Battalion after they had captured the second objective. From here we pushed forward to the Dotted Blue Line with the cavalry and ahead of the infantry on the frontage of the 12th Brigade. Continued machine gun fire and bursts of shell fire were encountered during the remainder of the advance. For this reason we had to travel inside the tanks almost all the way. Several of the men became weak and sickened by the fumes inside the tank. By using anti-gas tablets and also a solution which we had for the purpose, most of them recovered. Two, however, had to be left behind to be evacuated. The cavalry were moving with us, or ahead of us, but on many occasions they met with hostile machine gun fire and sustained heavy losses.
>
> We also met with fire from anti-tank rifles and a few bullets from these penetrated our tank. Slight casualties were also caused from splinters from the inside of the tank. By continued concentrated fire on the revolver loop holes in the tank, the enemy succeeded in breaking the loop-hole frames and causing casualties. My tank officer was fatally wounded in the head. His N. C. O. was killed and two of the tank men were later mortally wounded. One of the Lewis gun men and the scout were killed. After a direct hit on our tank it stalled a couple of times and on one of these occasions, about 2 p.m., when we were just to the

right of the woods in 21.d, 1,000 yards in the rear of the Blue Line and 500 yards north of the 12th C. I. B. right boundary, the enemy began to rush us from the woods near by.

Machine gun and rifle bullets were rapping on our tanks from all sides and our only hope was to keep all our guns firing and get the tank started if possible. After a great deal of difficulty in cranking the engine, we succeeded in starting the tank again and with our machine guns we wiped out groups of the retreating enemy. We pushed forward about 1,000 yards farther on until we reached our final objective, where we unloaded our guns and took up positions on some unlevel ground. Our tank was hit and destroyed by a shell before we got all our ammunition and rations out of it. We remained there and held our position against enemy fire until the 72nd Battalion reached us about 6.30 p.m.

Capt. W. G. Williams, acting O. C. No. 3 Company, which provided 32 crews of the tank personnel, accompanied "B" Tank Company's 11 tanks into action and his report reads:

I accompanied 'B' Company with the remaining 7 tanks (4 had been detailed to the 3rd Division at Hourges) which eventually went forward to Cayeux Wood, where we were informed by the Cavalry that they were suffering heavy casualties from machine guns in a small wood at E.12-b. We therefore proceeded to the wood and engaged the enemy. Our casualties in this encounter were heavy caused from splinters from the inside of the tanks.

Shortly after this my tank developed engine trouble so I returned and reported to the G. O. C. 12th C. I. B., who requested one tank to remain on the western side of Caix Wood. I also, at his request, placed two Vickers and two Lewis guns on the same side at approximately E.7c.60.15 and D.12.d.3.4.

Describing the start with other tanks from in front of Gentelles Wood, the difficulty of getting over the Luce and slow progress up to Domart, Lieut. McGillivray's account of his tank's action is as follows:

After passing through the 3rd Division we came into our first real action. Our troops were held up by machine gun fire from a wood. We at once proceeded there and went into action. The fire here was heavy and it was aimed mainly against the doors and turrets of the tank. This engagement lasted 20 minutes to half and hour. We succeeded in knocking out several of the German guns but in so doing both our six-pounders and four of our Hotchkiss guns were put out of action. In the case of the six-pounders, the telescopic sights were blown off; the Hotchkiss guns had the gas chambers riddled with bullets. We had done a good deal of turning and manoeuvring in a small area and, owing to the tank being new, the huge treads began to loosen and pound very badly. The tank officer thought it best to withdraw to dead ground and try to effect repairs. The repairs were effected and we were about to go into action again when I received orders to hold Caix Wood.

Those are the recorded reports but other companies of the 4th C. M. G. C. Battalion who had before the attack plaintively asked why No. 3 Company instead of No. 1 or 2 had been favoured with a nice ride into battle were thankful that no such choice had fallen on them, as they knew the unrecorded story of this novelty added to war.

Of the 34 Vickers guns and crews which went forward in the tanks, four actually reached the Blue Dotted Line and came into action against the Germans in accordance with the daring plan for the operation. Eight tanks were set on fire and entirely destroyed; two crews were entirely missing and 16 crews were unloaded from tanks overcome by the unaccustomed heat and gas and cramped conditions inside the tanks. Thirteen machine guns were destroyed or lost.

The following officers of the 4th Battalion C. M. G. C. were in charge of Vickers crews and in tactical handling of the tanks:

Lieuts. O. B. Eaton, Gardner, Hamilton, Lorimer, MacDonald, McGillvray, Patterson and Riddell. Of these Lieut. Lorimer and Lieut. Hamilton were killed and Lieut. Gardner made a prisoner.

Official analysis attributed the general failure to the fact that tanks were diverted to too many other tasks, became separated and were taken on individually by anti-tank crews, which, owing to these delays, had had time to come up. The original plan of going straight for the Blue Line had been lost, but allowances were thereby made for the hurried way in which the plan was launched.

And now as the dusk of evening approached, Canadians exulted as they never had cause to exult before in a sweeping victory that had brought a penetration of over eight miles into the enemy's defences. Before they had known the limits almost of human endurance of set-piece warfare with its concentrated fury of shell-fire and filth and oftentimes mud. At this moment they realised a new limit to the physical demands of a fighting advance of such depth. They were exultant but tired and weary.

Off to the right, the square church tower of Le Quesnel stood out squarely in a leafy tracery against the darkening horizon—and, temporarily at least, was the one monument of successful resistance of the Germans that day.

As units shifted into defence positions for the night, a strange after-battle quiet brooded over the whole area. In other centuries bivouac fires would have studded the darkness. Here all was eerily silent.

The 11th C.I.B., which had been unable to take Les Quesnel during the day, now prepared for an early morning assault.

The Independent Force which had had an exciting day, operating up the Amiens-Roye road and in helping the French capture Mezieres, performed a spectacular piece of work. When a battery had worked out a plan to co-operate with the French trying vainly to debouch from Mezieres in the face of heavy machine gun fire, it was unnecessary as "C" Battery (French) of No. 1 group on its own initiative swept around the village, outflanked the German machine gunners and infantry and forced their withdrawal under withering fire.

The corps as it faced the night could look back at a wonderful summary of the day's work. It was a bag of 6,000 prisoners in a maximum penetration of over eight miles; the capture of over 100 large guns, thousands of machine guns and the possession of immense stores of engineer supplies, and reserve ammunition parks. Sixteen German divisions had been tabbed that day, eight of which had been thrown in against the Canadians' drive.

Chronologically and actually, the capture of Les Quesnel must be credited to August 9th. The 11th C. I. B. in the early morning hours, accompanied by cavalry, tanks and the trench mortars mounted on trucks which were attached to the Independent Force, made the assault. The trench mortars were of great assistance in this auspicious start to a day that was to contain almost as much adventure but much harder fighting, in spots, than on the glorious 8th.

The general advance was not started until between 11 a.m. and 2 p.m., units starting at varying times.

The 3rd Canadian Division had passed through the 4th on the right, the 1st was in the centre and the 2nd was on the left, all within the same boundaries of the day before. The 3rd was using the 8th Bri-

gade, the 1st and 2nd attacked on two-brigade fronts. The objective was the line of the road Bouchoir through Rouvroy and Meharicourt and Lihons. Vreley, Rosieres and Meharicourt were villages in the 2nd Division objectives; Beaufort, Warvillers and Rouvroy in the 1st's and Folies and Bouchoir in the 3rd's.

There was to be no artillery barrage.

The 3rd Division swept through the 4th at the Blue Dotted Line and out to the attack. Stiffest resistance the division met was for possession of the Beetroot Factory near the crossroads 1,000 yards northwest of Bouchoir. This was eventually taken at 6 p.m., by which time the entire objective was in our hands. The 5th C. M. R. gave the French assistance in the capture of Arvillers as they kept pace with the advance. In the move forward No. 3 Company of the 3rd C. M. G. C. Battalion sent three batteries up with the 8th C. I. B., but used them to consolidate. It was not until Bouchoir was captured that they were rushed into positions, suffering five casualties in the move. Special attention was paid to the right flank, where we were slightly in advance of the French.

The 1st Division advance did not commence until 1.15 p.m. and ran into stubborn fighting. The 2nd Battalion on emerging from Beaufort engaged a German force forming up for an attack and scattered it. Two tanks, a detachment of 11th Hussars helped this unit clear one end of Rouvroy, but it was 9.20 p.m. before the 3rd and 4th Battalions captured the whole of the village and all the Division objectives were in its hands. "B" and "D" Batteries of No. 1 Company (Morris), 1st C.M. G. C. Battalion, kept in close touch with the attacking battalions, with guns in pairs in diamond formation. "B" Battery found parties of the enemy along a light railway 1,000 yards east of the jumping-off line an inviting target, and from the vicinity of the Warvillers-Folies road fire was brought to bear on enemy artillery, observed withdrawing south of Rouvroy, causing casualties to men and horses and much confusion. "D" Battery fired a barrage of three lifts, hastily worked out by Lieut. Dillon, as infantry and cavalry were held up at Beaufort Woods. Quick action was obtained by emptying the gun limbers at Les Quesnel. A four-man crew with gun and eight loaded belts was placed in each half limber. The Battery was then galloped into action under cover of a sunken road. Three belts were fired from each gun; the whole action taking place in twenty-eight minutes.

No. 2 Company (Denholm) saw some of the most bitter fighting of the day by the 8th and 5th Battalions, the O. C. of the former,

Major Haddall, D.S.O., former commander of the 2nd C. M. G. Company, being killed as he led an assault on Hatchett Wood. Determined enemy groups, centred around machine gun nests, offered a stubborn front. "E" Battery scattered a party of 50 Germans emerging from the northern end of Beaufort Wood and a group of retreating Germans were splashed with 500 rounds 500 yards west of Warvillers as they retreated. Enemy artillery wagons moving along the Rouvroy-Vreley road next came into the view and two guns got away several belts at them, hurrying their retreat and knocking out two teams.

Pte. McLeod of No. 2 Section, firing No. 6 gun, was given credit for bringing down an enemy plane in flames just east of the Rouvroy-Vreley road as a gun was mounted in an anti-aircraft role to end an exciting day, at one point of which Lieut. McIntosh took charge of elements of the 8th Battalion, who had lost all their officers.

Nos. 1 and 2 Companies of the 2nd C. M. G. C. Battalion supported the 2nd Canadian Division attack, flanked by the Australian advance. No. 1 Company (Basevi) started out with limbers, but the fighting was of such a dogged nature and so much of it hidden as infiltrating methods were used by both brigades that the Batteries were held to a consolidating role. Major Basevi was the senior officer left at 5th Brigade headquarters when a shell killed the brigade Major and wounded the G. O. C. and Staff Capt. Intelligence. The Company only suffered two other ranks wounded.

No. 2 Company (McCorkell) attacked with the 6th C. I. B., the left of which was badly exposed for a time until the Australians came up. When the advance was held up at Rosieres, "F" Battery and four guns of "H" were placed to cover the gap and when the Germans retired before the Australians, the latter guns, enfilading a sunken road, caught them under a terrific fire. The flanking fire of these guns gave the Aussies great assistance. The Company, however, suffered comparatively heavy casualties with four gunners killed and 20 wounded. No. 3 Company (McCamus), which had borne the brunt of the previous day's fighting, was in reserve.

Away over to the right the Independent Force had again had an adventurous day as they kept in touch with the now rapidly-advancing French. One armoured car was hit near Bouchoir in the afternoon and other car crews had sustained casualties before they were withdrawn. The Trench Mortar section operating with No. 2 Group was brought into action against a whizz-bang battery behind the railway embankment and after 25 rounds had them silenced. "A" Battery, with the Cavalry, pushed on through Folies and from positions east of the village inflicted heavy casualties on the retiring enemy. "B" and "C" Batteries were in Arvullers ahead of the French, capturing a large number of prisoners. Pte. H. McCorkell displayed great courage by rushing the village and capturing 15 Germans single-handed. "D" and "E" Batteries, supported by a platoon of Cyclists, worked their way southeast of Folies and with the infantry entered Bouchoir in the evening.

The average depth of the advance had been four miles with a maximum of 6½ miles at some points. Although the enemy's resistance had stiffened and there was much more shelling, there was no halting the forward dash of the Canadians. which had now carried them into the old trench system occupied prior to the Somme operations of 1916. This area had been the right flank of the British line and the trenches, while in disrepair, lent themselves to a still more stubborn defence.

The night of the 9th-10th brought successive bombing raids and very little sleep for those who just ended a hard day's fighting and for the 4th and 3rd Divisions, who were to carryon the attack the next day.

The general objective of the attack on the 10th was the line of Hattencourt-Hallu to the left Corps boundary. The Australians attacked on the left to capture Lihons.

The 3rd Division attacked with the 8th C.1. B., which had been in the front line the previous day. When the attacking battalions, the 2nd C. M. R. and the 1st C. M. R., had won LeQuesnoy, the 32nd Division (British) passed through at 9.45 a.m. and continued the attack. The machine gunners of the 3rd Division maintained their positions.

At 10.15 a.m. the 4th Division assaulting troops, the 12th and 10th Brigades, passed through the 2nd Canadian Division. "D" Battery of the 4th C. M. G. C. Battalion supported the 10th C. I. B. "A" and "C" Batteries supported the 12th C. I. B. "A" and "D" Batteries were in a defensive role. "B" Battery (Rainboth) moved forward with guns on pack animals and came under severe machine gun fire from positions north of the railway soon after jumping off. At 1.43 p.m. four guns of this battery came into action 500 yards west of the Chilly-Lihons road against enemy machine guns and later engaged parties of the enemy south and east of Lihons.

"A" Battery started out in full limbers and switched to half limbers when the mules could not get the limbers across the railway just east of Rosieres and heavy shelling made haste necessary. The battery came under heavy shelling going up in diamond formation, but escaped casualties and finally, when the trench system was reached, deftly changed to pack mules. The advance, however, came to an abrupt halt near Fouquescourt and Chilly. Although crowded into a shallow communication trench, which had fallen in, with a company of 72nd Highlanders, the machine gunners and the infantry—and the mules—escaped casualties as four German planes machine gunned them and finally dropped hand bombs.

During the night of the 10th-11th a strong enemy counter-attack was beaten off east of Hallu, but because of the pronounced salient, the line was pulled into Hallu and then to the eastern outskirts of Chilly.

From August 10th until the Canadian Corps left the Amiens front, no combined attack was made to break down German resistance. Local attacks, in which epic battles on a small scale were fought, advanced the line from trench to trench. Settling back into trench warfare, the machine gunners in minor attacks were able to contribute some valuable overhead supporting fire, especially in the four days, August 12th-16th, in which the 3rd Division captured a strong trench system 400 yards in length and 2,000 yards wide and enabled the French to enter Bois-en-Z from the rear and so pass through the German main resistance line on the way to Roye, 2½ miles distant.

Amiens will be forever memorable to Canadians for its panoramic view of a modern battle in the open. New successes, just as important to the general Allied scheme of Gen. Foch, were to come to the Canadians, but none were to offer the variety of experiences or such a sense of freedom from the cramping confines of battles as they had known them as Amiens.

The new battalion organisation had proven its merit and so had the battery as a tactical unit.

But the experience had shown that the Machine Gun Battalion was hardly ready for any "Hell-for-Leather" role as many had pictured it from their daily open warfare tactics while at rest behind Vimy during the earlier summer, nor yet was it the immobile, heavily-laden, plodding arm it had been when paced to slower infantry advances of set-piece attacks. It had struck a fair balance between the two schools.

Conclusions regarding tactics, the handling of transport to insure the greatest mobility commensurate with concealment and effectiveness and the other new problems suddenly thrust upon the Vickers in open warfare, it will seem years after, were exceptionally sound, as they were voiced by the four Commanders of Canadian Machine Gun Corp

Battalions following Amiens. Not all agree at certain points but in composite they cover all the ground.

After insisting that batteries, whether in reserve or advancing, must use limbers or pack animals and must not be divided into sections while there is a probability of a continued advance, Lieut.-Col. M. A. Scott, D.S.O., of the 4th Battalion C.M.G.C., observed, regarding general co-operation in the attack, as follows:

> To properly support the infantry advance, batteries need not follow closer than 1,000 yards in rear of the first wave. Their moves should be by bounds and detailed by the Battery Commander, who will advance with the infantry. When the infantry are held up by a point of resistance, they do not require machine gun support if the resistance can be overcome in a short time. From half an hour to an hour is required to determine the situation, by which time batteries can easily come into action at any suitable spot in order to develop superiority of fire.

Lieut. S. G. Watson, D.S.O., commanding the 1st Battalion C. M. G. C. recorded:

> Great difficulty was experienced by some batteries who tried to keep pace on foot with the rapidly advancing infantry, preventing participation in fire-fights unless hold-ups were of lengthy duration.

Lieut.-Col. Watson, continues making a point that will probably be generally conceded:

> Battery commanders cannot fight their batteries and personally be Liaison officers to infantry battalions in rapid open warfare. A battery must be allotted a certain area to advance over, cover the consolidation of their objective and eventually defend the area in depth. Also battery commanders should be allowed to use their own initiative in giving supporting fire on targets coming within range, irrespective of the particular unit which they are following. This method was successfully tried out and proved entirely satisfactory. It was demonstrated during the advance on Beaufort that batteries well under control can fire a supporting barrage at short notice.

Lieut.-Col. Scott of the 4th C.M. G. C. noted:

> As many batteries as possible should remain in Divisional Reserve under orders of the battalion commander.

Lieut.-Col. Gordon Weir, D.S.O., M.C., commanding the 2nd Battalion, observed that the use of limbers in semi-open warfare which followed the initial attack proved very satisfactory in the Amiens area, where there were not many trenches to cross and no wire:

> These can then be dispatched on short notice to any part of the divisional front, either to assist in overcoming strong points or leapfrogging forward batteries or to take up defensive positions.
>
> Pack animals were much more suitable than limbers (a) over rough ground with obstacles, (b) if roads and limber tracks are scarce, (c) if on account of hostile fire it is necessary to choose covered approaches and keep away from roads.

Lieut.-Col. Moorehouse, commanding the 3rd Battalion C. M. G. C., reported:

> Limbers should be used with four up in case of casualties among the animals. Pack saddlery should be carried even when using limbers for moving forward.

All the battalion commanders emphasised the need for motorcyclist dispatch riders. Mounted orderlies when used proved invaluable. It was found unsatisfactory to rely upon Divisional and Brigade report centres for communication between M. G. Company and Battalion Headquarters. And undoubtedly the newly-found mobility of the machine guns was wasted at Amiens in many instances because of lack of quick communication. It was the one particular factor that gave a sense of unwieldiness to the new organisation, many machine gunners probably concluded.

M. G. casualties for the first two days were 75% of the total stay in the Amiens sector, but were extremely light, even when compared to the corps totals for the battle. The following table shows the casualties suffered by the four battalions during Amiens:

Unit	Killed O.	Killed O.R.	Wounded O.	Wounded O.R.	Missing O.	Missing O.R.	Totals O.	Totals O.R.
1st Battalion G. M. G. C......	–	22	5	82	–	3	5	107—112
2nd Battalion C. M. G. C......	–	13	4	83	–	5	4	101—105
3rd Battalion C. M. G. C......	–	10	2	38	–	5	2	53— 55
4th Battalion C. M. G. C......	–	16	2	60	*1	12	5	88— 93

*Prisoner of war.

The transfer of the Canadian Corps from Amiens to the north was quickly effected but with no secrecy this time. The 2nd and 3rd Divisions entrained in the Boves area on the nights of 19th-20th and 20th-21st August, respectively.

On the night of August 24th-25th the 1st Canadian Division entrained for the north and the 4th Division was relieved by the 35th and 34th French Divisions on the nights of August 23rd-24th and 24th-25th. "A" Battery was the last to leave, being relieved in the early morning of the 25th. The battery suffered 13 casualties from enemy gas shelling and long lines of French, blinded by mustard gas, left the trenches at the same time, guiding each other by the tails of their long great-coats.

August 8th was later characterized by Ludendorff as "Germany's Black Day."

But to Canadians it was the first flash of a silver lining to a cloud of defeat that had hung menacingly over the Western Front since those gloomy days of late March.

Amiens held an aura of poetic justice, for the spearhead which the Canadians had driven through Germany's last hopes was to raise those of the Allies incalculably.

According to Gen. Sir Arthur Currie's report, the Canadian Corps and their auxiliaries had fought against 15 German divisions, and of these ten were directly engaged and thoroughly defeated. Five other divisions fighting astride our flanks with Australians and French were only partially engaged. The corps had captured 9,131 prisoners, 190 large guns and thousands of machine guns and trench mortars. The area recaptured was over 67 square miles and represented a maximum penetration in the 14 days of fighting of over fourteen miles.

The Canadian thrust had opened the way for the unfolding of more of Foch's plans. On August 21st the British 3rd Army made a large-scale attack north of the Somme and on August 24th opened up their bid to regain Bapaume.

CHAPTER 8

Drocourt-Queant Line
August 28th to September 5th

And so, in the week of August 20th, the 2nd and 3rd Canadian Divisions found themselves within hailing distance of their old home, Vimy Ridge, and this time there was no mystery surrounding intentions.

Reinforcements had filled up the units as they passed through Amiens and the Corps was in grand fighting trim.

On the nights of August 22nd-23rd and 23rd-24th the 2nd Division passed into the trench line, relieving the 15th Imperial Division in the Neuville-Vitasse-Telegraph Hill Section south of Arras. On the night of the 23rd-24th the 3rd Division went into the line on the left of the 2nd, relieving the remainder of the 15th Imperials from the Amiens-Cambrai Road to the Scarpe River.

The setbacks on the Marne, the continued pressure of the British over the old Somme battlefields had begun to produce effects and up on the north, with the 1st British Army pounding at them, the Germans had begun to evacuate the salient of the Lys on August 25th.

The eyes of British G. H. Q. were now focused on Cambria, but in between the spearhead thrust of the Canadians was the Drocourt-Queant line, important hinge of the famous Hindenburg system and key to the whole plan whereby it was hoped that the Germans would be blasted out of these supposedly impregnable positions and forced out into the open country behind.

It wasn't until August 22nd that Gen. Sir Arthur Currie received details of the operations planned for the 1st Army sector which was confronted with four main systems of defence: (1) the old German front line system east of Monchy-le-Preux; (2) the Fresnes-Rouvroy line; (3) the Drocourt-Queant line, and finally the Canal du Nord line, anyone of which were more formidable than trench systems upon which mighty offensives of both British and French had previously been blunted.

The first task of the Canadians was to capture the British defences which had been lost in March, 1918, and which were intact for 5,500 yards, before tackling the German system east of Monchy-le-Preux, the heights of which dominated the ground over which the Canadians must advance.

This was to be no overwhelming surprise as at Amiens. This was not to be conceived in the heavy, ponderous blows of the Somme and Passchendaele but in the modelled perfection of Vimy—of a succession of Vimys but always with the eyes fixed on far horizons and the possible objectives scaled to miles instead of yards.

The operation was originally scheduled for August 25th, but Gen. Sir Arthur Currie represented that this was only 48 hours' notice and, besides, the Canadian Corps had a superstitious feeling about attacking on the Sabbath Day. The attack was then set for the 26th.

The general objectives for the attack on the 26th were that the 2nd Canadian Division was to capture Chapel Hill, then work south through the old British support system and join up with the British troops on the right on the northern end of the Wancourt Spur, thus encircling the enemy troops in the forward area towards Neuville-Vitasse. They were at the same time to push forward and capture the southern end of Monchy-le-Preux Heights.

The 3rd Canadian Division was to capture Orange Hill and then Monchy-le-Preux. The success of the advance was to be exploited as far east as possible. The 51st (Highland) Division was to cover the left flank of the 3rd Canadian Division.

The 2nd Battalion C.M.G.C. (Weir) allotted its companies to brigades as follows: No. 2 Company (Ramsay) to the 6th C.I.B. attacking on the right; No. 3 (McCamus) to the 4th C.I.B. attacking on the left, and No. 1 Company was to fire the barrage.

The 3rd Battalion C.M.G.C. delegated its companies as follows: No. 1 to the 8th C.I.B. attacking; No. 2 (Drinkwater) to the 7th C.I.B. in close support, and No. 3 (McLean) to the 9th C.I.B. in reserve.

Originally the zero hour had been planned for 4.50, the one element of surprise left open to the attackers, but this was moved ahead to 3 a.m. when final preparations were ahead of schedule. A rainstorm drenched the attack just as it started but did not dampen the determination with which it pushed off into the murky night to the roar and flash of 17 brigades of 18-pounders, 9 brigades of heavies and 30 long-range guns.

There was some uncertainty in the first few hours of the attack. The 8th C.I.B. (Draper) by a baffling encircling attack had captured the town of Monchy-le-Preux by 7 a.m., but the 7th C.I.B. did not get the trenches in front of them cleared until 11 a.m., and then joined up with the 8th. On the right, south of the Arras Road, terrific, close-in fighting all morning obscured any certainty of success. The 6th C.I.B. had to throw a defensive flank to the south, 3,500 yards of which were occupied by the 27th Battalion and 1,500 yards by the 29th Battalion. Guemappe was captured by 4 p.m. and Wancourt Tower and the top of Heininel Ridge by 4.40 p.m. of a long day of heavy fighting, and a big factor in the doubtful last stages proved to be an extemporary barrage laid down by the 2nd Canadian Divisional Artillery (Brig.-Gen. H. A. Panet).

During the night the brigade captured Egret trench, securing a good jumping off trench in which 500 dead Germans were found next day. The brigade had given a fine example of a new-found versatility in attack that was to mark the Canadian Corps in many days of hard fighting to come when it turned directly south in a complete change of direction to sweep up Wancourt Ridge. It was at this juncture that a gap occurred in divisional boundaries and the Canadian Independent Force (Brutinel), operating along the Arras-Cambria road, filled until the situation was adjusted.

The 4th C.I.B. was through the first German line half an hour after zero and rushed Chapel Hill, a machine gun strong point. The brigade's casualties were light and they went on fighting into the night, getting a footing on Heininel Heights, from where the crossing of the Cojuel River could be commanded.

Batteries of No. 3 Company, 2nd Battalion, C.M.G.C., saw plenty of close-up action. "J" Battery went forward with the 21st Battalion and saw no action until reaching Nova Scotia trench and then six guns took on a duel with numbers of enemy machine guns which were soon silenced.

"M" Battery found at daybreak that they had pushed beyond their objective and withdrew to better positions in rear of Minorca trench. The battery had escaped casualties even though the positions came under heavy shell fire all afternoon. "K" Battery encountered heavy machine gun fire from the left about 2,000 yards from the start and did not get forward until two tanks waddled up and put these guns

out of action, killing the crews. During the afternoon the battery fired behind Guemappe while the 18th Battalion was attacking the village.

"L" Battery followed the 18th Battalion and came into action at Nova Scotia trench, where Lieut. Bell on the right of the battalion front rushed an enemy machine gun and killed the crew. He had been severely wounded before this but insisted on carrying on and later in the day was killed. In all 40 prisoners were captured here by "L" Battery crews and bombers. The battery employed direct overhead fire with good effect. Later on the battery was to replenish its ammunition supply from tanks that had been knocked out. At Gordon Avenue the battery guns were finally mounted. Besides Lieut. Bell and two other ranks killed, another officer and five other ranks were wounded and three other ranks were posted as missing.

No. 1 Company, 3rd Battalion C.M.G.C., supported the attack of the 8th C.I.B. "B" Battery moved off with the 5th C.M.R. and at Orange Hill, finding that in the darkness they had got ahead of the infantry, moved south towards the Arras-Cambria road, engaging two enemy machine guns which they caught on flank, and taking 11 prisoners. The battery lost one gun during the day but replaced it with two German guns. "A" Battery got forward without serious casualties and took up positions on Orange Hill for indirect fire into Monchy at a range of about 1,800. "C" Battery moved off with the 4th C.M.R. on the left flank of the brigade attack and took 14 prisoners and 2 machine guns. It too lost one gun by shell fire but used two German guns to pour a hot fire into Monchy.

"D" Battery was with the 1st and 4th C.M.R. in their advance and, when at 10 a.m. a counter-attack developed from the direction of Cigar Copse, brought all guns to bear on the advancing Germans. Many of the enemy were killed by the intense fire and the rest forced to stay in unsuitable ground until the 7th C.I.B., pushing through, captured them. The battery afterwards assisted with overhead fire in the capture of Cigar Copse. At dusk, when an enemy counter-attack was reported developing from the Bois de Sart, this battery expended 5,000 rounds on the enemy assembly area. The attack did not come off. The battery lost a gun before opening this barrage.

No. 2 Company, 3rd Battalion C.M.G.C. (Ings), fired the initial barrage. On completion of firing, "E" and "F" batteries moved back to St. Laurent and Blangy respectively, ready to move up with the 7th C.I.B., but "G" battery moved via Orange Hill due southeast and reported to the 42nd Battalion just east of Monchy. "H" Battery moved forward with the 49th Battalion.

No. 3 Company went back into division reserve in the afternoon. Six thousand yards in depth had been gained on a 10,000-yard front at the end of the first day, but there were signs that the task mapped out for the Canadians was going to be a very formidable one.

The next day the battle was renewed, the Canadian barrage opening at 4.55 a.m. The Germans replied immediately, laying a storm of shells down on the front line the Canadians had just left and then started it creeping backwards. Despite the weight of the explosive downpour, Canadian casualties were not heavy at first. At the first objective, the Sensee River, a halt of 30 minutes was ordered. After this halt our artillery only covered the advance for a short time and then ceased until batteries could be brought forward. The 2nd Canadian Division, doggedly pushing forward through the old German trench system, encountered heavy hand-to-hand fighting but crossed the Sensee River after capturing the villages of Cherisy and Vis-en-Artois.

The 3rd Division met with stubborn opposition but succeeded in capturing Bois de Vert, Bois du Sart, and reaching the western outskirts of Haucourt, Remy, Boiry-Notre-Dame and Pelves.

Immediately the barrage stopped the infantry advance became more difficult. The enemy was using a greater number of machine guns and was seen bringing batteries of artillery into action in the open south of Upton Wood. He reinforced the line with mounted infantry. A prisoner stated that the infantry was in process of relief by a machine gun battalion.

No. 1 Company, 2nd Battalion C.M.G.C. (Hobson) went forward with the 5th C.I.B. Batteries moved up in limbers, but just in front of Wancourt the roads were found impassable owing to trenches and wire and, as it was not possible to go across country, equipment had to be manhandled from this point. "B" and "C" Batteries saw plenty of action and subdued several machine gun nests that were holding up the infantry, whose initial pace from Egret trench had been rapid. "C" Battery (Much) moved two guns up on the flank of one nest and wiped out three German crews as they attempted to bolt. "A" Battery covered a gap exposed when Imperials had withdrawn temporarily from Fontaine-les-Croiselles and neutralised fire from Fontaine Wood.

No. 2 Company (Ramsay) was with the 6th C.I.B. less the 29th Battalion, which remained in support during this day's fighting. "F"

Battery operated with the 29th Battalion and was able to bring fire on Fontaine Wood.

"J" Battery of No. 3 Company, 2nd Battalion C.M.G.C., was ordered to move forward with the 4th C.I.B., and followed closely the advance of the 19th Battalion. Heavy machine gun and direct artillery fire were encountered during this advance. The battery got splendid targets when mounted infantry were seen on the opposite side of the Sensee River. Some of the men escaped the hail of bullets, but few of the horses escaped. Tender-hearted gunners took time out to single-shot the kicking, writhing equine victims out of misery.

"M" Battery supported "J" Battery's advance and came under heavy fire. Sergeants Demerse and Duffy were both severely wounded but led their sections through to the first objective before being evacuated.

"K" Battery, No. 3 Company of the 3rd Battalion, C.M.G.C., moved forward with the 43rd Battalion. No. 1 Section succeeded in getting into good positions after going through heavy fire to the right of Beetle Trench. "M" and "L" Batteries operated with the 116th and 58th Battalions, but the fighting was of such a dogged, uncertain nature that batteries had to move cautiously forward. Infantry battalions were charging enemy artillery batteries, firing at them over open sights and the 43rd Battalion, worming its way through a labyrinth of old British and German trenches, fought groups of the enemy in the open with bayonet and bomb while machine gunners held their fire. The Highlanders from the west went gaily on into open country, half a mile ahead of any other Canadian unit, while behind them was a whole German battalion resting in reserve. They used German machine guns on this group and then tried to crack the town of Boiry but found it held in strength. Two companies were fighting back-to-back at one time in the afternoon. They fought their way back through the Germans, suffering remarkably few casualties. Manhandling their guns, and assigned the task of consolidating in depth for expected German counter-attacks, the machine gun batteries got little chance for spectacular targets.

Canadian artillery had been switched on Pelves during the afternoon, enabling the 51st Division to capture Church Trench and thus continue northwards the new line the Canadians had established after a day of the most sanguinary fighting the troops from the Dominion had ever experienced.

It had been intended to continue the battle on the 28th with the

1st Canadian Division on the right and the 4th British Division, then coming under Gen. Sir Arthur Currie's command, on the left. The latter division failed to get up in time and, Gen. Currie's report says, as it was undesirable at this time to employ a fresh division alongside a division which had already been engaged, the orders issued were cancelled and the battle was to be continued by the divisions then in the line.

The 3rd Division, which had had to refuse its flank because the enemy was still holding the high ground around Plouvain, resumed the attack at 9 o'clock on the morning of the 28th, followed at 12.30 p.m. by the 2nd Canadian Division. The objective was the capture of the Fresnes-Rouvroy line, the possession of which was vital to the success of further operations.

On the left, the 3rd Canadian Division had advanced under a heavy barrage but the enemy barrage opened up almost as quickly, first on our front trenches and then creeping backwards. The 3rd Division captured the Fresnes-Rouvroy line from the Sensee River to north of Boiry-Notre-Dame and had secured that village, Jigsaw Wood and entered Pelves. They had not been able to clear the village of Haucourt.

The severest fighting of the battle was to face the 2nd Division this day. The wire in front of the Fresnes-Rouvroy line was found almost intact and the 5th C.I.B. provided an epic in heroism, especially the 22nd Battalion. The whole advance had been subjected to heavy fire from both flanks as well as frontally, but fought doggedly through for hard-won yards. Only on the right did the 2nd Canadian Division succeed in getting the first objective, but by late afternoon, except for small parties facing the wire of the Rouvroy line, it had to be admitted that the line had been advanced very little.

No. 1 Company (Basevi), 2nd Battalion, C.M.G.C., was detailed to attack with the 5th C.I.B. and in the assembly area near the Sensee Valley had to wear gas masks for hours before the attack. Heavy shell fire took its toll.

At 12.30 p.m. "A" Battery went forward with the 26th Battalion attacking on the right; "C" Battery with the 24th Battalion in the centre, and "B" on the left with the 22nd Battalion. Each battery disposed its guns in echelon; four guns in close support and four at a distance of about 800 yards in rear. "D" Battery was in reserve near battalion headquarters. The attack progressed favourably until the top of the ridge was reached across which runs the Vis-en-Artois-Hendecourt

Road. Here the attacking battalions ran into intense machine gun fire from Upton Wood and the Sand Pits. In "C" Battery Lieuts. Much and Davis went forward to reconnoitre, both being mortally wounded. "A" Battery lost Capt. White and Lieut. Young, both of whom were wounded, and Lieut. Dudley got the battery to Ulster trench finally with five guns left. There the remnants of the battery were joined by an officer of the 26th Battalion and eight other ranks from the South Lancashires Battalion and from this position they repelled two counter-attacks which debouched from Upton Wood.

"B" Battery lost all its officers, Lieut. Bole being killed, Capt. Morgan, Lieut. Tozer and all the N.C.O.'s wounded. Pte. Redmond took command and got to Union trench with only four guns. "C" Battery had also lost all its officers, Lieut. Travis being killed in trying to reach Union trench. Three guns under Corp. McAllister ultimately reached Ulster trench and three under Corp. Thorn finally won through to Union trench. Corp. McAllister took command of the battery and increased his crews by collecting infantrymen to act as carriers and belt-fillers. Corp. Thorn made several trips across the open to bring up ammunition. From here they co-operated with "A" Battery in repelling counter-attacks.

The 4th C.I.B. with the 20th and 21st Battalions attacking followed the artillery barrage at 12.30 p.m. and crossed the Sensee River, heading for Olive trench and Ocean work. Again and again with bomb and bayonet the infantry tried to thrust forward but were halted by a devastating machine gun barrage liberally weighted down with high explosive.

"K" Battery of No. 3 Company, 2nd Battalion, C.M.G.C., supported the advance with a barrage. "J" and "M" Batteries attacked with the infantry and "L" Battery was held in reserve. No. 2 crew of "L" Battery was wiped out before zero hour by an exploding shell. In advancing, this battery encountered heavy fire but one section reached the sunken road southeast of Vis-en-Artois while the other was to the north. From these positions no support could be given as there was no field of fire. When the infantry check became definitely admitted, the guns were withdrawn to the west side of the River Sensee, from where direct overhead fire could be maintained. "M" Battery, supporting the second phase of the attack, eventually took up defensive positions which they held with the help of some scattered infantry groups, after the battalion holding the line had withdrawn.

No. 2 Company (McCorkell) was not engaged this day, being in reserve with the 6th C.I.B.

Over on the 3rd Division sector the 8th C.I.B. and 9th C.I.B. were the attacking brigades and, although battalions were slightly mixed up, the 43rd coming under the 8th and the 4th C.M.R. Battalion under orders of the 9th C.I.B., there was no hitch in arrangements. They attacked under a barrage at 12.30 p.m. after having reached the assembly area in the open.

No. 1 Company, 3rd Battalion, C.M.G.C., was figuring on the same barrage line as the artillery, but the machine gun lifts started 10 minutes earlier than the artillery.

No. 3 Company sent "J" Battery forward with the 116th Battalion, finally placing six guns in Lady Lane and assisting our exhausted, badly-battered but determined infantry to consolidate. One of the guns had been destroyed and the other, owing to casualties, had not sufficient men left to bring it forward. "M" Battery operated close to the 42nd Battalion, and when it was seen that the attack had been definitely checked, took up positions in pill boxes on the northern outskirts of Boiry.

The 7th C.I.B. had already pushed off at 5 a.m. of August 28th to attack Pelves and by 10.30 all objectives had been gained, including Pelves, the trenches to the south and Hat and Kit trenches. At 10.30 the Princess Pats and the 42nd Battalion thrust for Jigsaw Wood and, despite terrific machine gun fire, captured this strong point. The line thus gained was consolidated and during the night of August 28th-29th was handed over to Brutinel's Brigade.

"G" operated with the 42nd and eventually occupied defensive positions in the Bois du Sart while "H" Battery covered the advance of the 49th Battalion from the Chalk Pit. "E" Battery was located in Cune trench ultimately while "F" Battery had been held in reserve. It had been an uncertain day for the gunners, with the situation of the bitter trench-to-trench fighting always uncertain.

The 2nd and 3rd Divisions were utterly exhausted by three days of bitter fighting and on the night of August 28th-29th were relieved by the 4th British Division and, as mentioned before, Brutinel's Brigade.

Minor operations on the night of August 29th had advanced the British line. North of the Scarpe the 51st Division had won to the crest of Greenland Hill. During the night of August 29th-30th the 11th Division, which had transferred to the Canadian Corps, relieved Brutinel's Brigade and passed to the G.O.C. 22nd Corps, shortening the line considerably and relieving Gen. Currie of anxiety caused by the length and vulnerability of the northern flank.

On the 30th, when the 1st C.I.B. daringly attacked under an ingenious barrage arranged by the divisional artillery, three batteries of machine guns took part. The barrage planned by the artillery not only boxed in the whole area but also provided a barrage for each of the 1st, 2nd and 3rd Battalions engaged in the smart manoeuvre. The battalions jumped off at 4.40 a.m. and by 7.30 had effected a junction as planned, though all had met with stubborn resistance.

Three batteries of No. 1 Company, 1st Battalion, C.M.G.C., supported this attack and as the infantry slowly but inexorably worked their bombing way up trenches, these batteries got fleeting targets in small enemy groups breaking overland. Four German guns were brought into action by "A" and "B" batteries and fired thousands of rounds.

At noon, when the enemy attacked between Upton Wood and Hendecourt, six guns of "A" Battery had good shooting and, when our infantry were forced to a temporary withdrawal, "B" Battery covered the move.

On the 31st the remainder of the Fresnes-Rouvroy line south of the Arras-Cambria road, including Ocean Work, was captured by the 2nd C.I.B. In the meantime the 4th (British) Division had pushed doggedly ahead, crossing the valley of the Sensee River and winning the villages of Haucourt, Remy and Enterpigny.

That night, the 4th Canadian Division, just in the area a few days after continuing the fight at Amiens, went into the line on a one-brigade front between the 1st Canadian Division and the 4th British.

September 1st had been set as the date for the final attack on the Drocourt-Queant line. When the G.O.C. 4th British Division reported that he was unable to successfully attack on the front allotted to him owing to heavy losses in the preliminary fighting, General Currie decided to extend the 4th Canadian Division front and a few hours before zero the 12th C.I.B. was ordered into the line. However, owing to the wire in front of the Drocourt-Queant line not having been sufficiently cut, the attack was called off until September 2nd.

During the afternoon of September 1st and in the evening the enemy delivered heavy counter-attacks against the junction of the 1st and 4th Divisions and twice our troops gave way slightly but regained the ground at once. The hand-to-hand fighting for the crest continued until actual zero hour for the attack. "E" Battery, in support of the 12th C.I.B., fired 10 belts with good effect as one of these evening attacks was launched at the 72nd Battalion.

At 5 a.m. the attack swept forward for the formidable Drocourt-Queant line and, although in recent days attacks had been battered down to the crawl almost of set-piece attacks, the corps' vision was still trained into the distance. There were no limits set but there were three definite objectives aimed at and the capture of these would carry the attack over 6,000 more yards and over three separate lines of trenches in addition to the frowning Drocourt-Queant system.

The blast of artillery fire, with 50 *per cent* of it devoted to wire-cutting, added a new intensity to modern artillery fire. Counter-battery work reached a new peak of efficiency as the thickened-up German artillery line was sought out, battery by battery. Up the Arras-Cambria road were later to go Brutinel's Brigade, reinforced by the 10th Hussars (British) thrusting for an opening. Soon from every sector came back cheering news and soon after prisoners, badly shaken, came back in thickening lines.

All machine gun batteries went into the battle with their fighting limbers.

The batteries of the 1st Battalion C. M. G. C. were allotted to brigades on the basis of three to each with three others held in reserve.

The artillery barrage would cease on the Red Line 2,500 to 3,000 yards east of the jump-off and from then on infantry were to depend on machine gun support.

Nine batteries were allotted by the 4th Battalion C. M. G. C. to the attacking Brigades. One Battery from each Company ("D," "E" and "J") were assigned barrage work. Eight guns of the 4th British Battalion M. G. C. were to provide a rolling barrage in front of the 10th C. I. B.

The enemy had never put up a more vari-coloured pyrotechnical display than he did on this occasion but our barrage seemed to drench it out.

It was drizzling slightly and the dawn was gloomy, partly masking our movements. The Canadians seemed to drive as surely forward in the darkness as in the daylight. As the attacking brigades surged on, reports went back that visioned another Amiens, for the enemy, despite all his dogged fighting of the past few days, showed early demoralisation.

"K" Battery of the 1st Battalion C. M. G. C., going over with the 16th Battalion, encountered little opposition until the Drocourt-Queant line itself was reached. Heavy machine gun fire from 1,500 east of Cagnicourt was met here and the battery sent two guns to positions northwest of le Brulle to neutralize this fire. During the heavy fighting between the Drocourt-Queant line and the support line, this battery moved closer to Cagnicourt and kept down enemy machine gun fire coming from southwest of the village. During this time the brigade on the right (17th Corps) had been held up and a wide gap grew wider and in pushing guns up to cover this flank "K" Battery suffered heavy casualties. There were only enough men left to carry five guns when the next advance was made to the Buissy Switch line and these helped consolidate the line.

"J" Battery had jumped off with the 13th Battalion and experienced much the same action, except that it came under the point-blank fire of enemy batteries firing from Cagnicourt Woods. The battery got its revenge moving to positions 1,000 yards west of Cagnicourt Woods, from where it brought direct fire to bear on the German artillery and machine guns. Capt. R. H. Morris was severely wounded, leaving no officers in the battery, and Sergt. E. G. Morey took charge. In order to engage the enemy more closely, some of the guns were moved forward of the Drocourt-Queant line and it was here that the crews became involved in a hand-to-hand fight with enemy machine gunners.

When the 3rd C. I. B's flanks both were up in the air No. 1 Section was sent forward to establish a flank near the Bois de Loison and from there they poured a steady fire into Buissy Switch line. Several times during the day our infantry attacked Buissy Switch but were driven back and crews of this battery were able to cover their withdrawals. Forty-five minutes after zero "L" Battery of the No. 3 Company, 1st C. .M. G. C. Battalion, moved up behind supporting battalions and took up defensive positions in the Drocourt-Queant line.

Three batteries of No. 2 Company, 1st Battalion C.M. G. C., supported the advance of the 2nd C. I. B., which met dogged fighting beyond the Drocourt-Queant support line, where enemy machine guns were thick and artillery and trench mortars were firing over open sights. When stronger than usual opposition was encountered about 4 p.m. in the afternoon near the factory at the eastern end of Cagnicourt, a halt was called until artillery support was arranged and at a normal dinner hour at 6 p.m. the brigade again charged over, clearing the Buissy Switch and the sunken road east of Villers-les-Cagnicourt of the enemy. "G" Battery got plenty of action against enemy machine gun nests and enemy groups. At 5.45 a.m. Sergt. Billington rushed two guns ahead of the infantry and engaged a hostile field battery at a range of 800 yards, forcing the enemy crews to retire in disorder, leaving many dead.

A few minutes later Lieut. Harris silenced another field battery and when the enemy endeavored to remove still another field battery from the high ground east of Cagnicourt all the horses brought over the crest of a hill to limber up the guns were killed or wounded. A mounted *unter-offizier* tried to take charge of the retirement but he was shot down and the German gunners abandoned their guns. Six enemy machine guns were captured by this battery and they were turned on enemy positions north of Cagnicourt with good effect. "F" Battery kept in close touch with the 10th Battalion and around 9 o'clock, when the battalion flank was exposed on the left and could not advance, silenced bothersome machine gun nests. In this episode 5,000 rounds of German S.A.A.A. was fired from salvaged enemy machine guns. When the 10th Battalion, supported by a barrage, attacked the Buissy Switch one section supplied indirect overhead fire and the other section engaged selected targets until the Switch was captured at midnight of the longish day.

"H" Battery was in 2nd C. I. B. reserve, being distributed in defence for the night just east of the Hendecourt-Dury road.

No. 1 Company of the 1st Battalion C. M. G. C. advanced with the 1st C. I. B., which found itself committed to the fight at one stage when the advance of the 3rd Battalion was too rapid. "A" Battery, passing through Cagnicourt, came under heavy fire and when Capt. Ferrie and Lieut. Hancock were wounded Sergt.-Major T. Walker took command. His quick work saved the Battery further casualties though three horses and one limber were knocked out before he extricated the group and then took up positions from which he poured a gruelling fire on the enemy. "B" Battery was forced to off load guns at 10.30 a.m. 1,200 yards northwest of Cagnicourt and the battery's eight guns, together with two captured German guns, were massed against enemy machine gun nests near Villers-le-Cagnicourt, enabling the infantry to advance with minimum casualties. "D" Battery guns followed up the attack and were disposed for the night in the Drocourt-Queant line.

On the 4th Division Sector the attacking brigades, 10th and 12th, despite the difficulty of their last-minute switch, got off to a good start and reached the main Drocourt-Queant line without heavy casualties but from there, where they had charged the heavily-manned trenches with cold steel, they came under galling machine gun fire from the

Dury ridge, which was admittedly the worst the Green Patch had ever encountered.

"M" Battery went over with the 72nd Battalion on the right of the 4th Divisional frontage and had already had a tuning-up when the Germans came across on them the night before. Lieut. Eaton was wounded early as the whole battery was forced to manhandle equipment forward owing to the heavy shelling of all roads.

"L" Battery (Williams) managed to use their limbers right to the Drocourt-Queant line and arrived with few casualties, advancing by sections. Eventually the guns were left there in defensive positions. "H" Battery did not start for an hour after zero by request of the O. C. 78th Battalion. When our infantry were being badly cut up by enemy machine gun fire, guns were rushed to a point south of Mont Dury and 400 yards north of the Arras-Cambria road, from where two guns secured moving targets. One of these same guns silenced a trench mortar battery in action on the right from 1,000 yards range. When German field guns were operating within 1,500 yards of the Red Line, Lieut. Carpenter sent back for two guns, but owing to heavy shelling these could not get through.

The 10th C. I. B. ran into its first real setback when intense machine gun fire from a sunken road south of Dury and immediately north of Mont Dury met its advance, but a skilful outflanking movement captured this position, 120 prisoners being taken together with 9 machine guns. With the fall of this position the defence of Dury collapsed and our troops entered the village, capturing the Area Commandant, his assistant and 100 prisoners.

No. 1 Company (Britton) was operating with the 10th C. I. B.

"C" Battery (Rainboth) came under heavy shelling in the assembly area, the O. C. and five other ranks being wounded. The battery at one time was headed for positions east of Dury after a battalion commander said he had captured the village and was going after Recourt, but fortunately the true situation was found out before the plans were executed.

"A" Battery had lost 50 *per cent* of its strength when drenched with gas as it was relieved by French troops at Amiens and had been reinforced by the first "draftees." It was still running in ill-fortune it seemed, for on the battle eve, as it moved up in the jet-black darkness in a thickening stream of traffic, it halted for just a moment so that the track running across the Arras-Cambria road 100 yards in front of the factory near Crater Bridge, over the Cojuel River, might be identified.

COLOURS OF 1st BATTALION C.M.G.C.
TWO COMMANDING OFFICERS, TWO SECONDS IN COMMAND AND THE ADJUTANT

Lt.-Col. E. Sansom, D.S.O., Major V. Grantham, M.C., Capt. L. G. Francis, M.C. Lieut.-Col. S. W. Watson, D.S.O., Major R. Murdie, D.S.O.

Before the officers could return a sudden, vicious salvo of high explosive and gas rained down on the halted battery. When officers and N. C. O's who had been badly gassed staggered back to the road, now illuminated by a lorry which had received a direct hit and was a mass of flames, they found over half the battery transport a twisted mass of wreckage and men and mules in a wild tangle of harness. While mules, which the battery had come to know as well as the "skinners," were mercifully put out of their misery, one of the skinners, badly wounded himself, searched by the roadside. Suddenly he found the object of his search. It was Lion, a big Belgian police dog, which had adopted the original 10th Company when it first landed in France and had gone through the Somme, Vimy and Passchendaele and had been slightly wounded in the salient when he went up the line with the mules.

Only one other rank had been killed but over 20 were wounded. The "draftees" had come out of their initiatory ordeal splendidly and the battery remnants spent the rest of the night in the open field 200 yards west of the factory. Later in the day when the battery was reorganised and was making its way down into the shallow valley to an old trench in the new rear of the now-captured Drocourt-Queant Line, a random shell searched it out and as the crew of a section was returning to take the rest of their equipment out of a half limber. landed direct and blew the vehicle to bits but failed to even scratch a driver or mule.

"B" Battery also ran into trouble, their assembly area beside the Arras-Cambria road west of Haucourt being shelled by heavies and Lieut. Gill being killed among the other casualties inflicted. The battery was later reorganised and went forward using pack mules. On reaching Dury, it was found that the advance was held up. The 44th Battalion had gone through the other battalions but the line actually held was the first objective and the guns were ultimately placed in depth in and to the rear of the Drocourt-Queant line.

No. 2 Company was attached to the 11th C. I. B. When "H" Battery was going to the assembly area on the night of September 2nd-3rd three bombs were dropped by enemy planes in the midst of the transport, killing one driver and wounding six men. Sixteen out of 20 animals were killed or wounded, five limbers destroyed aria four. guns and considerable equipment lost. This necessitated "F" Battery being detailed to act with the 75th Battalion.

"F" and "G" Batteries both got guns in position and engaged live targets. In all, these batteries expended 16,000 rounds of ammunition in the first few hours of the attack. Lieut. Leach, M.C., in charge of "G" Battery, was killed.

"F" Battery was asked by the O. C. 75th Battalion to push forward to fire on Rumaucourt and the transport came under direct artillery and machine gun fire, which killed six animals and destroyed two limbers, while four guns were put out of action.

Eventually, the batteries were in defensive positions on the forward slope of Mont Dury, with "H" Battery, by now reorganised, sending four guns up.

"D," "E" and "J" Batteries reported to No. 3 Company (Bailey) to join the barrage group. "E" and "D" Batteries found their barrage lines masked by the 72nd Battalion, but "J" Battery fired 22,000 rounds.

On the night of September 2nd-3rd our line was a little east of the Red Line. At places the infantry had penetrated 1,000 yards and even 1,500 yards beyond this line, but a line parallel to the Red Line at a distance of 500 yards would give the approximate jumping-off line for further contemplated action.

That same night the 4th (Imperial) Division, on the left, captured Etaing but that did not halt the enfilade fire of heavies from the left, which ranged up and down the Drocourt-Queant line and in the support line. Their gunnery wasn't very exact and machine gun batteries which chose positions in the open were forced to move several times during the night.

Hard fighting was visioned next day when the attack was to be launched at 5 a.m., but this zero hour was later cancelled. Preparations for an organised attack with a barrage were cancelled also when an early dawn patrol reported that the enemy had seemingly withdrawn across the canal.

The 1st Division pushed forward first in mid-morning hours and met with little serious resistance as they captured the Buissy Switch and thrust forward strong fighting patrols. The 2nd C. I. B. had more resistance on their sector and suffered severely from machine gun and artillery fire from the high ground on the east side of the Canal du Nord. The 4th Division shoved forward about noon and as the advancing units, widely extended, pushed their way slowly down the green slopes from the Dury Ridge they came under scattered but heavy artillery fire and, as they neared the west bank of the canal, intense machine gun fire. Numerous efforts were made to force crossings of the canal but without success. The 102nd Battalion surrounded a small wood north of the Cambria road and disposed of its German occupants, who held out to a man. By 3 p.m. in the afternoon the division had occupied the villages of Saudemont, Rumaucourt, Ecourt-St. Quentin and a large lake on which was a chateau, reportedly used as a German army headquarters. French civilians to the number of one hundred were found in their stone cottages in Lecluse and Rumaucourt and these, mostly the very old, greeted their deliverers with a touching hysterical note. Delicacies they had kept hidden for four years were dug from hiding places and offered the Canadians.

Practically the same picture greeted the advancing troops on both the divisional fronts. On the east bank of the canal was a continuously high ridge, dominated by three eminences that were almost peaks, of which Oisy-le-Verger was the loftiest. These sloped sharply to the canal. Most of the Canadian advance was down a gentle slope of two miles over a green-carpeted terrain that had been untouched by war for four long years. Rifle and machine gun pits here and there and battery positions which had been hastily dug, but even with all that haste sheltered over with boards, offered the only evidence of attempted defence of this slope.

A hot September sun blazed down through the afternoon haze as the troops pushed forward slowly. From the high ground to the south of Buissy, the 1st Division saw evidence of great confusion on the east bank of the canal. Guns, lorries, transport could be seen moving eastward along the roads and parties of enemy infantry retiring toward Bourlon Wood. Mounted officers could be seen, without success, trying to rally their men. But in distinct contrast to this, parties of enemy machine gunners, easily enough picked out for the same reasons as our own were always easily recognizable by the enemy, could be seen moving westward to the canal bank apparently oblivious of the confusion of retreat around them.

First Divisional machine gun batteries had common experiences too. Some remained in the positions they had occupied the night before and employed overhead fire against the canal banks. Duelling with low-flying enemy planes was one diversion for some of the batteries distributed in depth. No. 3 Company was in division reserve.

There was some confusion on the 4th Division front, one battalion having advanced and then withdrawn. The general advance before noon of the 11th and 10th C. I. B.'s met with little opposition and, though the advance down the slopes was in plain sight of the enemy, he didn't have enough guns to adequately take care of all the ideal targets so indifferently offered. Mobile batteries left their transport behind the ridge and man-handled their guns and equipment down the slopes. One battery essayed the advance with pack mules and that did arouse the venom of the German gunners. They concentrated their hitherto scattered firing on this appetizing target and soon the landscape was dotted with mules, standing beside shell holes, out of which could be seen the arms of "skinners," holding fast to their mokes while they sought to blend into the surroundings. The battery escaped unscathed as after the first few salvos the enemy apparently considered individual mules were too expensive targets.

"L" Battery of No. 3 Company had three mules killed when the transport was left in the hollow near the Drocourt-Queant line.

"E" Battery (Hall) of No. 2 Company suffered the heaviest casualties of the machine gunners' advance, its effective strength being reduced to two officers, five N.C.O's and only 17 other ranks when they came under one vicious concentration of shell fire as they attempted to advance down the slopes. Other batteries, those of No. 1 Company, sent crews forward singly or in pairs, though some were unable to take up final positions until near dusk.

When reconnoitring a position for a sniping gun near the canal bank just before dusk, Major Bailey of No. 3 Company was severely wounded. Lieut. Perkins went back and got a stretcher party and covering rifleman and the wounded officer was taken out under heavy fire.

No other day had offered quite the picnic atmosphere to battle that September 3rd brought and, generally speaking, machine gun casualties were light.

The formidable Canal du Nord had been reached and it brought a sudden lull as darkness came down. Sulky batteries threw over scattered salvos in the comparative quiet. Canadians certainly had a wonderful two days of accomplishment behind them. They had penetrated through five separate and distinct trench systems, with a measure of ease compared to other adventures which had seemed less formidable, and had thrust another 6,000 yards forward to the ultimate goal. The prisoner total now reached over 10,000, of whom 262 were officers. Ninety-seven pieces of artillery had been captured and 1,016 machine guns and 73 trench mortars had been counted in the two days' operations. Eight enemy divisions had been thoroughly mauled, one of them a cavalry division.

Attacks against the canal were being planned by brigade staffs that night, but two more bridges were blown up. It was realised that the enemy intended to offer determined resistance with all the terrain in his favour and the corps commander decided that further exploitation of this brilliant success was impossible without thorough and elaborate preparation.

On the night of September 3rd-4th the 2nd and 3rd Divisions relieved the tired but exultant 1st and 4th Divisions to conclude a battle which at the onset had presented obstacles which were the last word in field engineering and, in theory, seemed impregnable.

Though not won lightly, looking back to August 26th and to the jumping-off line now so far to the rear, the whole corps could not escape a sense of bewilderment that the cost had been so low.

CHAPTER 9

Canal du Nord and Cambria

Although the Canadian Corps conducted only minor operations as divisions in the line and did holding tours awaiting further plans of attack, Machine Gunners were kept busy night and day on harassing fire programs. The line was thinly held, since the flooding of the Sensee and of portions of the Canal du Nord by the enemy had made any offensive action by him unlikely and the right flank was the only possible point from which he could launch an attack. Crossings were well guarded, but the divisional defence was in great depth.

Preparations for the coming attack were under the observation of the Germans from Oisy-le-Verger as well as from Bourlon Wood to the right.

On September 11th the 57th British Division attacked Moevres, and the guns of No. 2 Company, 2nd Battalion C.M.G.C., joined the artillery support for the attack which, however, was unsuccessful. All areas were heavily shelled at night and night bombing by enemy planes rendered life on this sector anything but peaceful.

On September 15th, Gen. Sir Arthur Currie received details of the forthcoming attack. The Canadians were to again form the spearhead thrust of operations in which the 3rd and 4th Armies were co-operating and were to cross the canal, capture Bourlon 'Vood and the high ground northeast of it to protect the left flank of the attack. The date of the operation was definitely fixed for September 27th, but on September 22nd the task of the Corps was enlarged to include the capture of the bridges over the Canal le l'Escaut. The 11th British Division came into the corps command for this operation.

The corps commander had always been considered the cautious, methodical type who demanded a perfection of detail before committing his Canadians to attacks, but in the amazingly daring conception of this attack a tremendous gamble was to be taken that provided also a new twist to tactical planning.

On the corps battle front of 6,400 yards the Canal du Nord was impassable on the northern 3,800 yards. That left, therefore, the narrow neck of 2,600 yards through which the Canadian Corps commander proposed to launch two attacking divisions, the 1st and the 4th, with the 3rd following closely behind. When the attacking divisions had gained their first objective near Bourlon the 3rd was to thrust in on the right of the 4th Division and attack in an easterly direction in liaison with the 17th Corps. The 11th British Division was to come up on the left of the 1st Division, which was to fan out as soon as it crossed the canal, and was to advance in a north-easterly direction toward Epinoy and Oisy-le-Verger.

Even though the element of chance is admitted by Gen. Sir Arthur Currie, the measures taken to minimize it are also explained as follows:

> The assembly of the attacking troops in an extremely congested area known by the enemy to be the only one available was very dangerous, especially in view of the alertness of the enemy. A concentrated bombardment of this area prior to zero, particularly if gas were employed, was a dreaded possibility which could seriously affect the whole operation and possibly cause its total failure.
>
> To meet such an eventuality, careful arrangements were made by the counter-battery staff officer to bring to bear neutralising fire on hostile batteries at any moment during the crucial period of preparation. These arrangements were to be put into effect, in any case, at zero hour to neutralize the hostile defensive barrage on the front of attack.
>
> With the exception of the 2nd Canadian Division, which was now holding the entire front and would be in corps reserve at the time of the attack, every resource of the corps was to be crowded into that narrow space.

The Machine Gun Battalions prepared for the coming attack by establishing well-filled dumps of ammunition as close to the line as possible. Half a million rounds were placed in one, 100 yards north of the crossing of the Baralle-Inchy road and the Queant-Marquoin railway; another containing the same number was located at Inchy and a third of 300,000 rounds on the Arras-Cambria road, 1,000 yards west of the canal.

The one minor adjustment made was on the front of the 5th C.I.B., where the 10th C.I.B. commander wished the enemy driven back slightly, and in these operations the 5th were engaged continuously for five days and nights. "E" Battery, in covering a daylight attack by the 25th Battalion, used two guns on the wood southeast of Inchy and when taken 50 Germans were found who had been killed by machine gun bullets. One of the guns was knocked out but the crew escaped.

Constant reconnaissance, both aerial and by patrols, was kept up and all information gathered tended to add to the difficulties which had to be surmounted. Numerous ditches on both sides of the canal, strong nests of machine guns and belts of wire expertly placed on the east side of the canal made the prospect formidable.

No. 1 Company of the 3rd Battalion C.M.G.C. was attached to the 4th Canadian Division for the purpose of firing a rolling barrage in support of the attacking 10th C.I.B.

No. 1 Company, plus "H" and "L" Batteries, was to go over with the 10th C.I.B.; No. 2 Company was to attack with the 11th C.I.B., and No. 3, less "L" Battery, would go with the 12th C.I.B.

In the 1st Division attack Nos. 1 and 2 Companies were to attack with the 1st and 2nd C.I.B's, respectively, and No. 3 Company was to fire the barrage. Each had a battery in divisional reserve.

Rain and a black night added to the difficulties of assembly for the attacking divisions. Although artillery which had been unable to move into position previously jammed the roads and every factor was present for the utmost confusion, the units somehow got into position and as the roar of the barrage seemed to shake the very earth the attacking brigades went over the top at 5.20. A percentage of our barrage was a smoke screen to cut off observation from the high ground. Although the German counter-barrage came down with exceptional rapidity, it thinned out nearly as rapidly, thanks to the counter-battery work of the Canadian artillerists. But it was still heavy and that so many units got through that small neck with so few casualties will always be one of those unexplained miracles of war.

The artillery barrage planned for this show was one of the most ingenious yet created by the Canadian gunners, for it too fanned out to adequately cover the spreading fan-wise manoeuvre of a whole corps.

And in this ringing inferno of sound and shock the chattering machine guns had one of the most complicated barrage fire programs

to fire yet devised.

Twenty-four batteries were detailed to the barrage.

Owing to the depth of the advance contemplated by the infantry and the consequent deep advance by supporting machine gunners, the 4th Battalion C.M.G.C. did not participate in the corps barrage. For the same reason the 1st Battalion C.M.G.C. supplied only two batteries.

On the 4th Divisional front No. 1 Company, 3rd Battalion C.M.G.C., supplied the barrage on a line north to south which rested at zero on the canal bank on the left flank of the 10th C.I.B. and 300 yards west of the canal on the right flank. From that line the barrage travelled eastwards in lifts of 100 yards every four minutes as far as Quarry Wood, roughly 1,000 yards west of the Red Line.

This barrage was the right wing of a barrage which ran west to east as far north as the Red Line. It was continued on the left in the first 1st Division area, eight batteries forming the right subgroup (Trench) and consisting of four batteries each of the 1st C.M.G.C. Brigades.

The left sub-group (Grantham) laid down a barrage which opened at zero plus 20 minutes on the Red Line. The left of the barrage rested on the Canal du Nord and its average width was 2,000 yards. It travelled almost north (*i.e.*, in the direction of the Canal du Nord) in lifts of 100 yards, through Marquoin, until at zero plus 400 it reached Sauchy-Lestree (north of the Blue Line), where it ended. The rate of progress of this barrage varied. For 20 minutes from the Red Line it lifted 100 yards every four minutes, then 100 yards every 10 minutes up to zero plus 180 minutes. From the southern outskirt of Marquoin to the Arras-Cambria road the barrage only travelled 400 yards in 70 minutes. From there northwards to Sauchy-Lestree it lifted 100 yards every five minutes. Batteries Nos. 1 to 12 laid down the barrage running west to east for the capture of the Red Line; Batteries Nos. 13 to 24 laid down the barrage running south to north for the advance from the Red to the Blue Line.

The barrage laid down by the left sub-group was arranged in such a way as to cover the swampy ground extending from just north of Sains-le-Marquoin to the Arras-Cambria road and north of this to Sauchy-Lestree. In depth it extended over the Canal du Nord and the Marquoin Line, which was the main line of defence covering the Canal du Nord.

The attack was planned with a view to leaving the swamp as a pocket and the machine gun fire was to keep down snipers from among the trees and to disorganise the defence while the main attack proceeded south of the swamp over the dry part of the canal. Most of the barrage guns escaped enemy shells, but 90 minutes after zero several enemy machine guns in the Wood 500 yards north of Sains-les-Marquoin caused casualties in "C" sub-group.

In all 320,000 rounds were expended by these sub-groups—and effectively expended judging by reports afterward—and a new adaptability had been marked up for machine gunnery in a barrage role.

No. 1 Company batteries of the 4th Battalion C.M.G.C. manhandled guns and ammunition, six-men crews carrying 4,000 rounds per gun. "H" Battery came into action when the 52nd Division (British), on our right, experienced trouble and from the Red Line expended 7,500 rounds. It then moved forward and denied a sunken road near Anneux to enemy concentrations. Other batteries secured good targets as far east as Bourlon Village and Wood and then as the 12th and 11th Brigades leapfrogged on to Bourlon Wood used direct overhead fire. The 63rd Naval Division was slow in getting up and the 11th C.I.B. battalions suffered heavy casualties. It dealt with a counter-attack assembled by three enemy battalions, crushing the plan in the bud.

No. 2 Company batteries started off at zero plus two hours. "G" Battery (Johnston) used pack mules half way to the north side of Bourlon Wood and came into contact with the enemy at the end of the sunken road on the northern outskirts of the wood. The guns brought into action here caught numerous parties of the enemy as they scuttled over the open. This battery assisted, by flanking and overhead fire, the attack of the 75th Battalion on trenches east of Fontaine-Notre Dame, scene in 1917 of the Guards Brigade heroic stand. "F" Battery operated with the 102nd Battalion around the south side of Bourlon Wood but had few targets.

No. 3 Company (Logan) attacked with the 12th C.I.B. and took quick advantage of several good targets offered. Two guns of "J" Battery from positions northeast of Bourlon Wood scattered confusion in an enemy field gun battery, firing over open sights from a point 1,000 yards west of Raillencourt, but, generally speaking, the situation was too obscure most of the time for the gunners to do more than consolidate in depth as they followed up the general line of attack.

On the 1st Division sector the front was so narrow that the 4th Battalion was assigned the task of effecting the canal crossing with other elements of the brigade leapfrogging at the Red Line. The attack fanned out to a two-battalion front and then to a brigade.

Nos. 1 and 2 Companies of the 1st Battalion C.M.G.C. supporting the 1st and 3rd C.I.B's, respectively, and No. 3 was firing the barrage. "A" Battery of No. 1 Company (Morrison) organised a local covering barrage for the 4th Battalion's attack, firing for half an hour, first on the canal and then on the defence line which was a series of connected shell-holes. Later they moved up with the 3rd Battalion as it leapfrogged through, having no trouble until 1,000 yards east of Sains-les-Marquoin, where they came under intense machine gun fire. Six guns came into action as the 3rd Battalion was held up and excellent targets came into the sight along the Arras-Cambria road as large enemy groups broke for cover. Just as ammunition was running short, the pack mules arrived with an extra supply.

"C" Battery (Dewart) moved forward with the 4th Battalion seven minutes after zero, entirely escaping the hostile barrage fire, but near Deligny Mill came into heavy artillery and machine gun fire. About 1,000 yards west of Bourlon Village four guns of this battery came into action against groups on the enemy near the Arras-Cambria road. All guns of the battery came into action farther forward and during this action both officers were wounded.

At zero plus 15 minutes "D" Battery (Jordan) also moved forward with the 4th Battalion, splitting up into sections to make the crossing of the canal and then later re-assembling. No. 1 Section came into action west of the Marquoin Line from positions in shell-holes and when a field gun was spotted in the vicinity of Deligny Mill Corp. Beattie moved two guns forward, while Lieut. McMullin and Sergt. Coombe worked around the flank, rushed the gun and captured it, together with its crew of 10. No. 2 Section found plenty of targets north of Bourlon Village and saw No. 1 Section salvage two enemy machine guns, from which they fired 3,500 rounds. When just forward of the Marquoin Line an enemy machine gun, strongly entrenched, was causing terrific casualties. Pte. Holloway went forward with a tank, bayoneted the gunner, shot two of the crew and took six prisoners.

The 14th did the single-battalion attack on the 3rd C.I.B. front and suffered heavy casualties as it stormed the canal. Two tanks detailed to cut wire had not come up, the woods on the east bank of the canal had not been cleared of the enemy and direct machine gun fire swept the brigade's attack and also that of the 11th British Division on the left.

No. 2 Company (Denholm), 1st Battalion C.M.G.C., was assigned to the 2nd C.I.B. All elements of the brigade fought stubbornly for every few hundreds of yards advance in the early stages, but the 1st Division swept rapidly forward after the second phase, capturing Haynecourt and crossing the Douia-Cambria road, the 11th Division (British) keeping pace by turning northward and capturing Epinoy and Oisy-le-Verger by evening.

"G" Battery (Maynard) sent No. 1 Section forward with the leading company of the 7th Battalion. As the attack reached the southern outskirts of Marquoin it was held up by an enemy strong point and Corp. Wilson immediately opened fire at point-blank range and as two other guns were rushed forward to hell-holes and opened up Wilson rushed his crew to the flank, from where he inflicted severe casualties on the enemy. The infantry coming up, the strong point was rushed and 50 prisoners, together with 6 light machine guns, were bagged. The section came into action again on the Marquoin line west of Dartford Wood, firing on large enemy groups in the vicinity of Sauchicourt Farm. No. 2 Section pushed up *via* the Marquoin line and from 1,000 yards south of the Arras-Cambria road concentrated an intense fire on enemy positions eastward along the main road.

"K" Battery (MacIntosh) went over with the 5th Battalion. No. 1 Section reached Haynecourt without serious casualties, skirted the village and came into action on the south side against retreating groups. They moved to the north side of the village and got more good targets but were too far ahead and were withdrawn west of Haynecourt. No. 2 Section came into action on the southern edge of Leek Wood, getting many sustained bursts off against enemy parties and two of the guns a few moments later, as they moved along the north of the Divisional boundary, caught an enemy battery moving at a brisk trot north of Epinoy. The gun under Sergt. Kearse caught a wagon moving east from north of Haynecourt. The wagon was turned over in the confusion and Pte. Lumsden and Corp. Ellis pushed out and captured the vehicle and the two drivers, who surrendered. The captors returned in state, riding the captured mounts.

"F" Battery (Herridge) was with the 10th Battalion and when nearing the Arras-Cambria road came under heavy shell-fire. They went into action here against enemy field guns between Haynecourt and Raillencourt and from the outskirts of the former they caught other batteries in movement as well as infantry groups. Five thousand rounds brought results for one battery, which, after cutting loose wounded horses, had to manhandle the guns away.

"B," "H" and "X" Batteries were in divisional reserve and by 7 p.m.

had been moved up into positions east of Sains-les-Marquoin and later were moved up to protect the right flank east and southeast of Haynecourt, which was exposed when the 4th Division did not get quite up owing to the failure of the 17th Corps on the right again to keep pace.

The 4th Division, however, did later attack from the north side of Bourlon Wood and captured all the high ground, pushing patrols as far as Fontaine-Notre Dame, and so the position of the 1st Division was not as precarious as, at times, it seemed. However, the only flaw in the day's operations came when the encircling movement to capture Bourlon Wood could not be put into operation and the thrust planned for the 3rd Division could not be executed.

During the night September 27th-28th the 3rd Division relieved a portion of the 4th Division and the 3rd, 4th and 1st Canadian Divisions and the 11th (British) in that order from right to left were in battle positions. The 3rd and 4th Divisions attacked at 6 a.m. the following day. In view of its advanced position of the day before, the 1st Division did not attack until 9 a.m.

On the 3rd Division front the 9th and 7th C.I.B.'s attacked; the 10th C.I.B. attacked on the 4th Division front and the 2nd C.I.B. on the 1st Division's sector.

The 3rd Division was forced to attack through the 11th C.I.B., which had been unable to capture Fontaine-Notre Dame during an evening and a whole night of stubborn fighting.

The fresh 3rd Division completed the first part of their operation in jig time and by 9 a.m. the 43rd Battalion had won Fontaine-Notre Dame. But it ran into desperate resistance at the Marcoing Line and an attack planned for 3 p.m. was postponed until 7 o'clock in the evening to get more adequate artillery support. By 11 p.m., in the darkness, the 43rd, 58th and 116th Battalions were holding a line facing southwest astride the Cambria-Bapaume road, in the Marcoing Line and one company of the 116th had pushed as far as the outskirts of St. Olle.

No. 3 Company (Burnham) of the 3rd Battalion C.M.G.C. was allotted to the 9th C.I.B. attack.

"M" Battery defended the flank of the 43rd Battalion near Fontaine and "I" Battery went forward with the 52nd Battalion. When the infantry was held up by the Marcoing Line this battery used direct overhead fire, getting off 8,000 rounds and putting two enemy machine guns out of action.

The 7th C.I.B. attack was swept by intense machine gun fire, which caused heavy casualties. No. 1 Company (Fowler) supported this attack. "F" and "G" Batteries accompanied the R.C.R. and Princess Pats and, while the latter did not get into action until later, "F" Battery, reaching a position south of Raillencourt, brought its eight guns into action against the Marcoing Line just south of its junction with the Arras-Cambrai road. Later on in the morning "M" Battery went forward with the 49th Battalion attack, with "P" Battery in support. They took up positions east of Sailly and swept the Arras-Cambria road and the Village of St. Olle, part of Cambrai's wide outskirts, with their fire. "N" Battery also saw action, taking up positions in the Marcoing Line south of Sailly.

In the early stages of the 10th C.I.B's attack little opposition was encountered up to the Marcoing Line, but from here the most intense machine gun fire that the brigade had ever experienced swept the level, open plain on which they finally emerged and which stretched toward Cambrai's outskirts. The 47th Battalion fought its way around the north of Raillencourt and the 50th Battalion reached the Marcoing Line after the severest kind of fighting.

No. 1 Company (Britton) of the 4th Battalion C.M.G.C. went over with the 10th C.I.B. "H" and "L" Batteries were attached from Nos. 2 and 3 Companies and were employed as brigade reserve.

When the advance was held up in the vicinity of the Douai-Cambria road by enemy machine gun nests all the batteries suffered severely and were forced to dig in, out in the open. "B" Battery helped break up a strong enemy counter-attack when the 44th Battalion was driven back 700 yards from the railway line. The 47th Battalion later re-established the line, but the enemy held trenches in front of the 4th Canadian Division between 500 and 700 yards west of the Douai-Cambria road until the organised attack in conjunction with the 7th C.I.B. at 7 p.m. won back the original ground.

Lieut. French, M.C., was the only officer killed but of the No. 1 Company batteries by nightfall all the batteries had lost an officer and in the case of several, including "A" Battery, all their officers. In one case one officer had command of 16 machine guns and a number of infantry who had collected in the vicinity. Another officer had his batman catch a German horse which, with carbine slung at its side, was galloping aimlessly about between sporadic shell bursts. A strongly-built stone barn, part of a *château*-like farmhouse group on the northern outskirts of Raillencourt, seemed to offer a safe haven for the capture, but just a few minutes later when the same officer was wounded and bethought him of his charger to save the pain of walking on a shattered foot, the charger was nowhere to be found.

Nine officers of this company woke up at base hospital two nights later to find themselves side by side.

On the 1st Division front the 10th Battalion was attacking and it was met with a heavy machine gun fire from the high grounds on both flanks where the attacks had not come up. It became apparent that the attack could not succeed, but in spite of this the battalion went bravely forward against the enemy entanglements and calmly commenced cutting passages through by hand. For two hours this unequal fight went on in spite of swiftly diminishing numbers.

Threatened enemy counter-attacks between 3 and 4 o'clock in the afternoon were crushed by artillery and machine gun fire.

No. 2 Company (Denholm), 1st Battalion C.M.G.C., went forward with the 10th Battalion. Lieut. Norris of No. 2 Section, "F" Battery, in a daring attempt to push his guns forward from a sunken road near Sancourt, was killed and then the guns were taken back to higher ground west of the Douai-Cambria road and from there they poured a sustained fire into Sancourt. No. 1 Section had better luck, getting into trenches west of the Cambrai-Douai road without sustaining a casualty. There they remained during the day, getting momentary targets and concentrating on suspected strong points. "E" Battery went up on the left of the 10th and "C" Battery followed later and both consolidated against anticipated counter-attacks which did not, however, develop. Other officers of the 1st Battalion C.:V1.G.C. made a reconnaissance of the area, since their batteries were at an hour's notice to push up into defensive positions against hostile attacks.

The advance had taken a heavy toll in casualties and it was driven home to the Corps that such formidable defence systems as it had conquered earlier in the month did not constitute all of war's worst obstacles.

It had been a field day for the enemy machine gunners. The enemy's artillery fire had been kept well down by our own batteries, but the German machine gunners, thrown into the fight in exceptional numbers, with a flat plain intervening, had a field of fire which meant annihilation to attackers. By the same token machine gunners in the attack were at an exceptional disadvantage as the heavy casualty list of all ranks demonstrated.

Orders that night provided for a continuance of the attack the next day. The 3rd Division was attacking with the 9th and 7th C.I.B's; the

4th Division assigned the 12th C.I.B. to the attack and the 2nd C.I.B. was to do the thrusting for the 1st Division.

The attacks were launched at 6 a.m. and all along the line stubborn resistance was met in addition to heavy artillery and machine gun fire. The 3rd Division pushed the line forward to the junction of the Arras and Bapaume road, the western outskirts of Neuville St. Remy and the Douai-Cambria road. They also cleared the Marquoin Line from the Bapaume-Cambria road southwards towards the Canal de l'Escaut. These trenches were in the 17th Corps area, but it was difficult for the division to advance, leaving this strongly-held position on its flank and rear.

The 4th Division captured Sancourt, crossed the Douai-Cambria railway and entered Blecourt, but later withdrew to the line of the railway before a heavy counter-attack. The 11th Division in two attacks had been unable to win the high ground northeast of Epinoy and this interfered with the progress of the 1st Division's attack, the Red Patches having to give up positions gained earlier near Abancourt Station. So the 4th Division had been in its turn effected.

"K" and "J" Batteries of the 3rd Battalion C.M.G.C. attacked with the 58th and 116th Battalions, respectively. "K" Battery got off 10,000 rounds in indirect and direct fire and two guns helped out the 58th when it was held up in front of the Marcoing Line.

"J" Battery also got off 10,000 rounds and caught many groups of the enemy as they suddenly broke from cover in short retirements. However, two guns were put out of action by shell-fire during the day.

"A" and "B" Batteries accompanied the 1st and 2nd C.M.R. Battalions in their attack. Four guns went up on the flanks of the attacking battalions from each battery and four were kept 500 yards in rear for defence in depth. The guns going forward with the attacking waves used light mounts and these proved much less cumbersome to handle and for the work required were vastly more effective.

One gun of "B" Battery, when 500 yards northeast of St. Olle, was met with heavy machine gun fire from the high ground in front. The officer in charge of this section was killed and all the crew became casualties except Pte. Dick, who pushed forward as far as possible, taking the gun and two boxes of ammunition. He got into a commanding position and opened fire on enemy machine guns, killing over 30 of the enemy gunners.

Both the advanced sections of these batteries did fine work in neutralising enemy machine gun fire, which was intense at the least sign of movement.

"G" and "E" Batteries moved off with the 42nd Battalion on the left of the 7th C.I.B. attack, but this thrust did not progress beyond the Douai-Cambria road, being held fast by wire and such intense hostile fire that it was foolhardy to face it. These two batteries succeeded in reaching the road but suffered heavy casualties in the attempt.

"K" and "M " Batteries of the 4th Battalion C.M.G.C. attacked with the 38th and 72nd Battalions. "K" Battery reached the Douai road, but fell back when it was seen that the attack could not progress. The guns were withdrawn to a trench astride the light railway 1,000 yards northeast of Sailly. "M" Battery had four guns up with the 72nd Battalion, which reached Blecourt but could not penetrate this strongly-held point. The Highlanders retired their line to the railway and later were forced to withdraw the left of that line back to Sancourt. These developments and setbacks forced the cancellation of plans for the 78th and 85th to attack on through and "L" and "J" Batteries took up defensive positions.

"F" Battery, 1st Battalion C.M.G.C., attacked with the 8th Battalion and, though the attack went well just at first, it was stopped and finally had to repel three enemy counter-attacks. No. 1 Section brought all four guns to bear on an enemy battery in the vicinity of Blecourt. "E" Battery, in support of the attack, could not get into action as the situation remained so obscure from the early setback. It was established in a strong defensive position, however, and the imminence of counter-attacks made this role assumed by supporting batteries tremendously important, if not spectacular.

Back again on September 30th went the Canadians into an attack, planned in two phases. In the first stage the 3rd and. 4th Canadian Divisions were to capture bridgeheads on the Canal de l'Escaut. In the second stage the 1st Canadian Division and the 11th British Division on the left were to secure the high ground overlooking the Sensee River.

The attack commenced favourably, the 3rd Division taking Tilloy and the 4th capturing Blecourt. However, heavy counter-attacks with severe enfilade fire from the left drove the 4th Division and the 3rd back again to the general line, Sancourt-Tilloy. The 1st Division, when it found that the 4th had been forced back, concluded the second phase as planned could not be successful and its operation was cancelled.

No. 2 Company of the 3rd Battalion C.M.G.C. supported the attack of the 7th C.I.B.

"F" Battery (Roe) gave covering fire on Neuville St. Remy and at one phase was 500 yards in front of the enemy, where they killed an enemy machine gun crew in a pill-box and from the pill-box got off several thousand rounds before deciding the attack wasn't coming up and withdrew. "H" Battery used indirect fire on the road junction north of Tilloy and from the railway east of the Douai road three guns of "C" Battery brought a deadly fire to bear on parties of the enemy who were dribbling into Tilloy.

No. 2 Company (Pearce) of the 4th Battalion C.M.G.C., was detailed to support the 11th C.I.B. attack behind a smoke screen that unfortunately wasn't thick enough and which was soon blown away by a wind that suddenly whipped up.

Resolute opposition met the attack from the onset. The 75th Battalion, although suffering heavy casualties, did reach and hold the railway south of Sancourt, which had been the centre of enemy resistance the day before. It was dark when the attack pushed off at 6 a.m., but with daylight resistance everywhere increased. "F" Battery pushed up to the railway cutting without suffering undue casualties. despite the density of the fire. From there, this battery got some excellent targets.

No. 1 Company had been ordered up in support but later was moved back and resumed the positions vacated.

On October 1st it was decided that the whole corps would attack under a heavy barrage.

The attack made excellent progress in the early stages. At 8 a.m. the line had been advanced to the canal bank on the right, touching the northern outskirts of Cambria, thence along the canal to Morenchies Wood (inclusive). The towns of Cuvillers, Bantigny and Abancourt were captured.

At 10 a.m. heavy enemy counter-attacks developed from Paillencourt up the Bantigny Valley. Our troops were driven back. The flank on the left of the 1st C.I.B. was exposed and this fact made progress difficult. The 3rd Division was held up definitely by intense artillery and machine gun fire as they attempted to push down the exposed slopes towards the Canal de l'Escaut.

With ten divisions, two regiments of machine guns and special marksmen companies crowded into this narrow front, the reckless use of reserves by the enemy forced the Canadians back but at a tremendous cost to the Germans. Masses of the enemy troops were caught by well-directed artillery fire in the Bantigny Valley and their losses were tremendous.

No. 3 Company of the 3rd Division operated with the 9th C.I.B. on October 1st. "M" Battery laid down a barrage for the attack on suspected strong points, getting off 16,000 rounds from zero to zero plus 15 minutes and then advanced with the 43rd Battalion. The battery was 1,000 yards west of Ramillies at 10 a.m., when counterattacks began to develop. They helped beat off one counter-attack with 3,000 rounds and, ironically enough, the four guns used were German.

No. 2 Company (Pearce) of the 4th Battalion C.M.G.C. again supported the 11th C.I.B. attack, going forward with the 102nd, through which the 87th later leapfrogged. The batteries secured good targets but suffered extremely heavy casualties. The left flank was in a critical condition at one time and the O. C. No. 2 Company received orders to cover this flank. Ten of his guns were out of action, but he placed the others in defensive position facing northward. Ten guns were placed along the railway embankment from 500 to 1,000 yards south of Sancourt, four guns were located 500 yards east of Sancourt and eight guns southeast of the same village. Besides these 22 guns there were 36 guns of the 2nd Battalion C.M.G.C. now in the line, distributed in depth and prepared to give the enemy some of his own machine gun medicine so disastrously ladled out in these last few days.

The 1st Division attacked with two brigades, the 1st and 3rd Battalions of these two brigades suffering heavily as they pushed forward in the face of the most stubborn opposition and under intense fire.

No. 3 Company (Grantham) supported the 3rd C.I.B. and played an important role. "M" Battery pushed forward to positions east of Blecourt and when counter-attacks compelled the infantry to withdraw poured 6,000 rounds at the advancing enemy. Two guns were put out of action by shells and casualties were heavy.

"J" Battery lost a gun in its advance under heavy fire to the south of Cuvillers. When the infantry withdrew, one of the crews was almost surrounded. They held off the enemy with rifles and bombs while they removed the lock and feed block from the gun, for which they had no more ammunition.

"L" Battery got off 2,500 rounds at parties of the enemy assembling in the vicinity of Abancourt. A captured gun was turned on low-flying enemy planes. The other section lost one gun 1,000 yards east of Blecourt and another gun got off 750 rounds at hostile infantry near Abancourt before a shell put it out of action.

The guns of this battery repeatedly covered short withdrawals of our infantry. Establishing positions northeast of Sancourt, four guns fired a protective barrage. The other four guns, in position just east of Blecourt, found seven officers and 125 other ranks of the infantry with eight Lewis guns and helped form a strong point, which was defended for four hours. During the defence Sergt. McCall brought in three enemy machine guns and mounted them. Runners were sent back to get assistance, but when none was forthcoming and with the ammunition all expended, the little garrison withdrew to the railway line just east of Sancourt.

No. 1 Company supported the attack of the 1st C.I.B. on the left of the corps' advance and had, in addition, "B," "H" and "K" Batteries from divisional reserve.

"H" and "K" Batteries advanced with the 1st Battalion, the former encountering an enemy strong point 900 yards northeast of Sancourt and in 1,500 rounds silencing its four machine guns. Two of these captured guns were manned and the fire of ten guns concentrated on Abancourt station and church and numerous targets as they came into view. Lieut. Sheringham went forward to reconnoitre but was not seen again and Lieut. Carter was wounded, whereupon Sergts. Cuthbertson and Boulet took command. Two enemy machine guns firing from a small trench were rushed and the crews killed by Sergt. Boulet and Corp. Collyer. The battery at dusk covered the retirement of our troops.

"K" Battery lost both its officers (Knill and Turk) as the battery was concentrating on a German 7.7 battery firing from north of Blecourt and Sergt. Pell took charge. Two guns of "K" Battery were destroyed by shell-fire at 6.30 p.m. The others remained in position, but before retiring two more had been put out of action by shell and machine gun fire. The remaining guns, with a heavy German machine gun, were organised in a defensive position on the road running north of Sancourt, from where they caught the enemy advancing from Abancourt. During the time the battery was being reorganised, Lieut. More and Sergt. Mabley encountered a party of 40 Germans making I heir way toward Abancourt station and with some men of the 1st Battalion they engaged this party with revolvers and rifles, killing over 20, the rest escaping. A short time after, the same pair charged a small trench 1,000 yards northeast of Sancourt and captured one officer and 17 men.

"A" Battery moved forward with the 4th Battalion through heavy machine gun fire. It was found necessary to form a defensive flank to the left and 4,000 rounds were fired from here. The advance continued to the sunken road 1,500 yards east of Epinoy and here Sergt. Holmes turned a captured enemy field gun around and fired 20 rounds point-blank at enemy targets. When the infantry attack was held up, the guns were moved back 500 yards and from these positions 8,000 rounds were fired at enemy groups 1,700 yards south of Preshies.

"D" Battery advanced with the reserve company of the 4th and both sections were forced to advance by short rushes from shell-hole to shell-hole. Both engaged enemy machine guns in the advance, eventually reaching the sunken road north of Sancourt.

The results of the October 1st fighting were to confirm Sir Arthur Currie in the belief that the point had arrived at which to break off the battle and this he accordingly did.

Infantry reliefs on the night of October 1st had thinned out their strength very considerably and for this reason a very large number of machine gun batteries were distributed in depth, since machine gun units attached to infantry being relieved stayed on and incoming machine gun units brought the strength to double normal fire power.

It was anticipated that the enemy might launch a desperate attack on a large scale to drive the Canadians back on Bourlon and two hours before dawn of October 2nd a terrific Canadian barrage was laid down, which included machine guns and trench mortars. But when day broke the German line was uncannily quiet. To the south the Germans were retreating and the Imperials were freeing town after town and finding little opposition.

In a special order on October 3rd Gen. Currie gave a *résumé* of the corps' exploits. At one point he said:

> How arduous has been the task assigned to you can be judged by the fact that, whereas in the operations of the 1st, 3rd and 4th Armies 36 enemy divisions have been engaged, 12 of these divisions, supported by 11 independent machine gun units, have been met and defeated by the Canadian Corps.
>
> Even of greater importance, you have wrested 69 towns and villages and over 175 square miles of French soil from the defiling Hun.
>
> In two months you have, with three British divisions which have been attached to the Corps, encountered and defeated decisively 47 German divisions—one-quarter of the whole Ger-

man forces on the Western Front.

Until October 8th there was no territorial change on the Canadian Corps frontage, although harassing fire was constant and intense on both sides. The British used a new gas just at this time, which was reported as tremendously effective.

The 3rd British Army to the south was still advancing and by October 8th was ready for its attack on Awoignt. The attack was not a complete success and this complicated somewhat plans for a night attack by the 2nd Canadian Division set for the next day. However, the plans were followed, the 2nd Division to aim for Escaudouevres and the high ground east of there. As soon as the Division had seized these points and Morenchies, Point d'Aire, Ramillies, Brutinel's Brigade was to dash through and seize the high ground east of Thun St. Martin. The 3rd Division was to advance through Cambria, protecting the flank of the 2nd, which was bound to be up in the air for some time after a night attack.

The 2nd Division's attack was launched through rain and jet blackness at 1.30 a.m. and they swept down the glacis which, in daylight, was in full view of the enemy on the high ground east of the canal. Their progress was rapid and by 2.25 a.m. they had won Ramillies. On the right the infantry, assisted by the Engineers, had rushed the crossings at Point d'Aire and after a brief, sharp fight captured the bridge intact. Two cork bridges were thrown across and by 3.35 a.m. our infantry were strongly established on the eastern side of the canal. By 8 a.m. the 2nd Division had captured Escaudoeuvres, had established a line to the north and east and detachments of the 3rd Division had completely cleared Cambria, which had been generally evacuated the night before, and on the east side of the coveted city being put to flame by the Germans, troops of the 3rd Army could be seen coming up from the south. Thus was Cambria pinched out. At 7.10 o'clock that night the 3rd Division was withdrawn, when the 24th Division, 17th Corps, passed through it and joined up with the 2nd Canadian Division, which had continued on, occupying Thun Levecque, Thun St. Martin, Blecourt, Cuvillers and Bantigny. The 11th Division occupied Abancourt and had reached the outskirts of Paillencourt.

On the 8th heavy reinforcements had been reported pouring into Cambria and the attack of the 9th expected stubborn opposition, but the night advance took the enemy completely by surprise and in some cases caught him just before retiring. Until daylight came, machine gun batteries could do no more than follow on the heels of the groping infantry and this they did either by pack mule or using full transport and advancing in jumps.

Casualties were light, with, of course, the inevitable exception. "L" Battery of No. 3 Company, 2nd Battalion C.M.G.C., provided the exception when it was heavily shelled protecting the left flank of the 4th C.I.B. When the order cancelling the plan for the 4th C.I.B. to attack on the 9th came through, but before the machine gunners could get under way, they suffered 18 casualties and had three guns put out of action. Pte. A. Toroux particularly distinguished himself in this affair, returning time after time after wounded through Escaudoeuvres and then finally making one last trip into the gas-filled village without his gas mask, only to collapse when he had brought this severely wounded case back to shelter.

The 2nd Canadian Division resumed the attack on the 10th in conjunction with the 24th Imperial Division, the 4th C.I.B. carrying forward the advance with the 5th and 6th C.I.B's in reserve. No. 3 Company went over with the attacking brigade. In the early phases of the attack, launched at 6 a.m., "K" Battery covered the gap between the Canadian and Imperial Division. "M" Battery was able to bring effective fire to bear on the dump southwest of Iwuy, from where strong enemy opposition was causing heavy losses to the 6th C.I.B's advance in support.

At 1.30 p.m. "J" and "M" Batteries supported the battalions attacking east from the Erclin River. This attack was held up, the enemy positions being too strongly held. No. 2 Company assisted the 6th C.I.B's flank attack toward Iwuy, sending "F" Battery forward. When the infantry were held up in front of Thun St. Martin, No. 2 Section engaged the machine gun nests which were causing the damage. The enemy retired in the direction of Iwuy, the garrison of which was still holding out though nearly surrounded, since the left flank of the division rested on Canal d'Escaut, 1,500 yards northeast of Iwuy.

Orders were received for the continuation of the 2nd Division attack. Its left flank was clear, thanks to the splendid advance of the 11th Division, which had cleared the whole ground between the Canal de la Sensee and the Canal de l'Escaut.

Again the 4th C.I.B. was on the right with the 6th C.I.B. attacking on the left as the attack pushed off at 9 o'clock on the morning of the 11th. The objective on the right was Noyelles and to make good the crossing over the River Selle in that area. The 6th C.I.B. was to attack Iwuy and then advance on Hordain and Lieu-St. Amand, both inclusive. No. 3 Company was again attacking with the 4th C.I.B. and No. 2 Company of the 2nd Battalion C.M.G.C. supported the 6th C.I.B. advance.

As the attack was launched the enemy barrage came down across the whole front, being particularly severe in the vicinity of Thun St. Martin. The enemy machine gun fire also was intense. This lasted for less than half an hour, when his fire slackened and he was reported to be in retirement east from Iwuy. At 11 a.m. the enemy counterattacked in strength with infantry, supported by seven tanks. The 49th British Division was driven back almost to its jumping-off spot and the 4th C.I.B. gave way slightly, at the same time throwing out a defensive flank, and assisted the British Division to reorganise its attack.

The 2nd Division battle narrative said:

> Thanks to the good work done by a battery of the 2nd Battalion C.M.G.C., which engaged the enemy tanks with three guns and the accompanying infantry with four guns at a range rather less than 600 yards, the surviving tanks finally retired to the northwest slopes of the ridge, behind which they took up a defensive position and allowed their infantry to reform.

This referred to "L" Battery (Garneau), the report of which stated that:

> The enemy infantry quickly broke and fled and that the remaining tank fired a few shells and a few bursts from its machine guns and then turned and followed its own infantry to cover.

The battery escaped with two men killed.

Shortly after noon the Village of Iwuy was finally cleared and at 3.30 p.m. the 4th C.I.B., though suffering many casualties, made good the crest of the spur.

The 1st Division had carried out a "Chinese" attack on the 8th after relieving the 4th (British) Division on the night of October 7th-8th, during which No. 1 Company 1st Battalion C.M.G.C. had fired 32,000 rounds. Still holding this front from Pailluel to Biache-St.Vaast and separated from the enemy by the flooded valley of the Trinquis and Sensee Rivers, this division on the 10th pushed out patrols which resulted in the 13th Battalion penetrating the Drocourt-Queant line and taking Sailly. The 15th Battalion, in endeavouring to effect a crossing on the tow path at Biache-St. Vaast, encountered heavy machine gun fire and withdrew. One party of the 13th Battalion had been cut off and overrun by the enemy, two officers and 50 other ranks being taken prisoner.

On October 11th the 1st Division at 9 a.m. heard from the 8th (British) Division, which had started an attack to the north, that the enemy was in full retreat and ordered its brigades to advance. The 2nd C.I.B. sent the 7th Battalion forward, but heavy machine gun fire met this unit's bold attempt to cross the river on the Lecluse-Tortequesme road. This rearguard was soon silenced by our artillery and the advance continued, culminating on the 12th with the occupation of Arleux.

No. 2 Company supported this advance.

The hard-fighting 2nd Division was partly relieved by the 51st Highland Division on the night of October 11th-12th and thus was brought to a close the Battle of Arras-Cambria, which from August 26th to October 11th had seen the Canadian Corps win new and imperishable honours for itself. Sir Arthur Currie in his terse report summed up:

> Since August 26th the Canadian Corps had advanced 23 miles, fighting for every foot of ground and overcoming the most bitter resistance. In that period the Canadian Corps decisively defeated 31 German divisions, reinforced by numerous Marksmen Machine Gun Companies. These divisions were met in fortified positions and under conditions most favourable for defence. In this battle 18,585 prisoners, including 450 officers, were captured by us, together with 371 guns, 1,923 machine guns and many trench mortars. One hundred and sixteen square miles of French soil, containing 54 towns and villages and including the large city of Cambria, were liberated. The severity of the fighting and the heroism of our troops may be gathered from the casualties suffered between August 22nd and October 11th and which are as follows:

	Officers	Other Ranks
Killed	296	4,071
Missing	18	1,912
Wounded	1,230	23,279
Total	1,544	29,262

During this period casualties to machine gunners had been particularly heavy.

The following table shows the casualty totals of the four battalions of the C.M.G.C. from August 26th to October 11th, inclusive

	1st Battalion	2nd Battalion	3rd Battalion	4th Battalion
Officers killed	5	3	2	5
Other Ranks killed	59	58	98	52
Officers wounded	22	12	8	17
Other Ranks wounded	449	389	254	351
Officers missing	1	....	....	....
Other Ranks missing	5	12	5	....
Totals	541	474	367	425

A more detailed summary shows that the heaviest losses sustained for anyone period was the attack on the Canal du Nord between September 1st and 30th. The 4th Battalion C.M.G.C. suffered the heaviest, with five officers killed and 17 wounded and 45 other ranks killed and 319 wounded. The 1st Battalion C.M.G.C. in this period had two officers killed and 16 wounded, while 17 other ranks were killed and 230 wounded.

That stretch of time from August 26th to October 11th had brought every known test of warfare to the Canadian Corps and it had met them all. In retrospect, a fighting advance of 23 miles when compared to the short time before, when battles were computed in hundreds of yards, seemed an incredible accomplishment.

To the Canadian Machine Gun Corps this long advance had brought varying conditions of warfare with which the machine gunners had grappled with ready adaptability.

With memories still fresh of September 28th, when the German defence of Cambria itself depended almost entirely upon a frame work of Special Marksmen Machine Gun Companies, there seemed to be the prospect still of plenty of hard fighting to be done as the Canadian Corps prepared to take a brief breathing space.

CHAPTER 10

To Mons and Apres le Guerre

While an enemy withdrawal on a large scale was the expectation held forth on October 12th, there was no telling what the Germans were up to. Patrols were pushed boldly out by night by the four Divisions in the line—the 2nd (Canadian), the 11th (Imperial), the 56th (Imperial) and the 1st Division on the left, holding the Corps frontage from Pailleul to the left Corps boundary just two miles south of Douai, the clock tower of which city Canadians had watched for many months from the opposite ridge of Vimy.

On the night of October 12th-13th the 11th (British) Division was relieved as the 2nd Division side-slipped. The 4th Division was ordered to relieve the 56th (British) by the night of October 16th. During the early morning of the 13th the 56th Division crossed the canal and succeeded in establishing a bridge-head at Aubigny-au-Bac and capturing the village with 201 prisoners. At 10 p.m. the following night, however, an enemy counter-attack forced the withdrawal of the Imperials. During the early morning of the next day patrols of the 1st Division succeeded in crossing the canal near Ferin. They met with strong resistance and withdrew, but not without a quota of prisoners and also several machine guns. On the night of October 14th-15th the 4th Division relieved the 56th.

It was not until the 17th that the morning test barrages, which were routine, found the enemy uncannily quiet. 1st Division patrols started the big advance of all divisions and, though it was met by determined machine gun fire in spots, kept sweeping forward until by 6 o'clock next morning all the infantry of the 1st and 4th Divisions were across the Canal de la Sensee and several battalions of the 2nd Division were on the other side.

Gen. Sir Arthur Currie's report, says:

Composite Battery, 1st Battalion C. M. G. C., at Leige review by the Belgian Chief of Staff. 1919.

During that day two armoured cars and one company of Canadian Corps Cyclists were attached to each of the 1st and 4th Divisions to assist in the pursuit. These troops rendered valuable service to the divisions to which they were attached, although the enemy's very complete road destruction prevented the armoured cars from operating to their full extent.

As this great surge forward was taking place, few in the ranks realised that they were on their way to a historic rendezvous—a rendezvous that had been pledged by the Contemptibles over four years before and which their overseas cousins were to make good.

There was little to be taken from the attitude of the enemy but that he was taking his own time to get to some line of his own choosing for—probably—a winter stand.

For a time on October 20th the 4th Division was held up just east of Denain by machine gun and artillery fire and it wasn't until late in the afternoon that our troops could make headway there.

Village after village was relieved and, although the retiring Germans knew they contained civilians, they were often viciously—and accurately—shelled.

The 1st Division, which had now been in the line for two weeks without any opportunity to rest and re-fit since crossing of the Canal du Nord, was relieved on October 22nd but on the move for at dawn it had continued the pursuit, later to be leapfrogged by the 3rd Division.

By this date, opposition had begun to get stiffer. A large area northeast of Valenciennes had been flooded and to the west of the city the Canal de l'Escaut had been flooded. To the southwest, beyond the flooded area, the Mont Huoy and the Famars ridge made a natural defence.

The Canadian Corps report also indicates that the 22nd Corps on the right had been held up along the Ecaillon River and the 7th Corps on the left had not been able to make any great advance, not so much because of opposition as because of their own difficulties of supply.

The divisions continued to push forward and by the 25th had reached the canal and western edge of the flooded area along the whole corps front.

Gen. Currie reports:

Our troops had had a very arduous pursuit and the rail-head

for supplies and ammunition was still very far to the rear. It was therefore decided that we should make good the west bank of the canal and stand fast until flanking corps had made progress.

Attempts to cross the canal proved that the enemy was holding in strength a naturally strong position and it was ordered that no crossing in force should be attempted without reference to headquarters.

It was realised that unless the enemy withdrew Valenciennes could only be taken from the south. The 17th Corps on the right had meanwhile succeeded in crossing the Ecaillon River after a hard fight and captured the Famars Ridge. They had, however, been unable to take Mont Huoy, which dominated the city from the south.

The 1st Army commander planned large-scale attacks in conjunction with the 3rd and 4th Armies) wherein the Canadian Corps entered the picture at phase B—that being the capture of high ground overlooking Valenciennes from the south, the date probably being October 30th.

The 51st Division attacked Mont Huoy as a preliminary on October 28th, but it was not a success. After first gaining a foothold, the Highlanders were driven out by repeated counter-attacks.

Later orders were received that the Canadian Corps was to carry out all three of the planned phases of attack in conjunction with the 22nd Corps and, though the time was short and the difficulties of supply very great, the thrust was elaborately planned. Heavy artillery fire was necessarily limited because of the knowledge that the Germans had detained many civilians in the city and surrounding villages.

The time for the assault was fixed at 5.15 a.m. on November 1st. According to the plan, the right brigade of the 4th Division (10th C.I.B.) southeast of the canal was to carry out the attack at zero hour under a co-ordinated barrage in a northerly direction and capture Mont Huoy, Aulnoy and the high ground south of Valenciennes and then to exploit the success by pushing on to the high ground east of the city. Subsequently the troops northwest of the canal, which meant the left brigade of the 4th Division and the 3rd Division, were to force crossings north of the city and encircle it from that side.

No. 1 Company, 4th Battalion C.M.G.C., was detailed to accompany the infantry attack of the 10th C.I.B.

An enfilade machine gun barrage was co-ordinated with the artillery barrage by Lieut.-Col. A. M. Scott, D.S.O., commanding the 4th Battalion C.M.G.C., in which nine batteries were to be used, including the 1st Motors Brigade. Some of the batteries of the 4th Battalion C.M.G.C. were so placed that they expected to see the effects of the barrage fire if conditions of visibility permitted.

It had seemed a considerable time to the troops since they had heard the engulfing roar of an organised barrage, but the one that broke the chilly dawn at 5.15 on November 1st indicated that the Canadian artillery and machine gunners had not slowed down their tempo one whit. The German retaliation to our barrage was prompt and in spots severe, but the reply slackened off quickly after zero. Again the machine gunners of the enemy offered their usual stout resistance, but the enemy infantry gave themselves up in large numbers. The fighting was heaviest in among the houses along the Famars-Valenciennes road and in Aulnoy.

During the advance of the 10th C.I.B., patrols of the 38th C.I.B. and those of the 72nd had little trouble effecting a crossing and by noon the greater part of both battalions was established on the east side of the canal north of the Valenciennes railway station. Batteries of No. 1 Company kept up with the attack but had no occasion to do any firing and selected positions in depth. The 49th Division (British) on the right had been unable to reach the Blue Line phase and in order to increase the machine gun defences of the 10th C.I.B., "E" and "G" Batteries were placed in front of Mont Huoy along the Aulnoy-Poirer Station road in the course of the morning.

"L" Battery of No. 3 Company sent three guns forward with the 72nd Battalion and with the remaining five guns fired a 20-minute barrage for the crossing of the battalion, expending 15.000 rounds.

The 11th C.I.B. relieved the 10th C.I.B. on the right portion of their front in the evening of November 1st and by 10 p.m. their patrols were through Marlay. The advance was continued at 5.30 a.m. November 2 in an easterly direction and a line was reached by evening 1,500 yards east of Valenciennes. 12th C.I.B. patrols pushed into Valenciennes during the night of November 1st-2nd and at 9.50 a.m. November 2nd the 38th and 72nd Battalions joined hands on the eastern outskirts of the city. The Germans were driven out of St. Saulve in the afternoon by the 72nd Battalion and the 12th C.I.B. line was linked up with the 11th C.I.B. on the right and the 8th C.I.B. Division on the left. The 10th C.I.B. was pinched out by the advance of the 11th and 12th C.I.B's and placed in reserve. Two batteries of No. 2 Com-

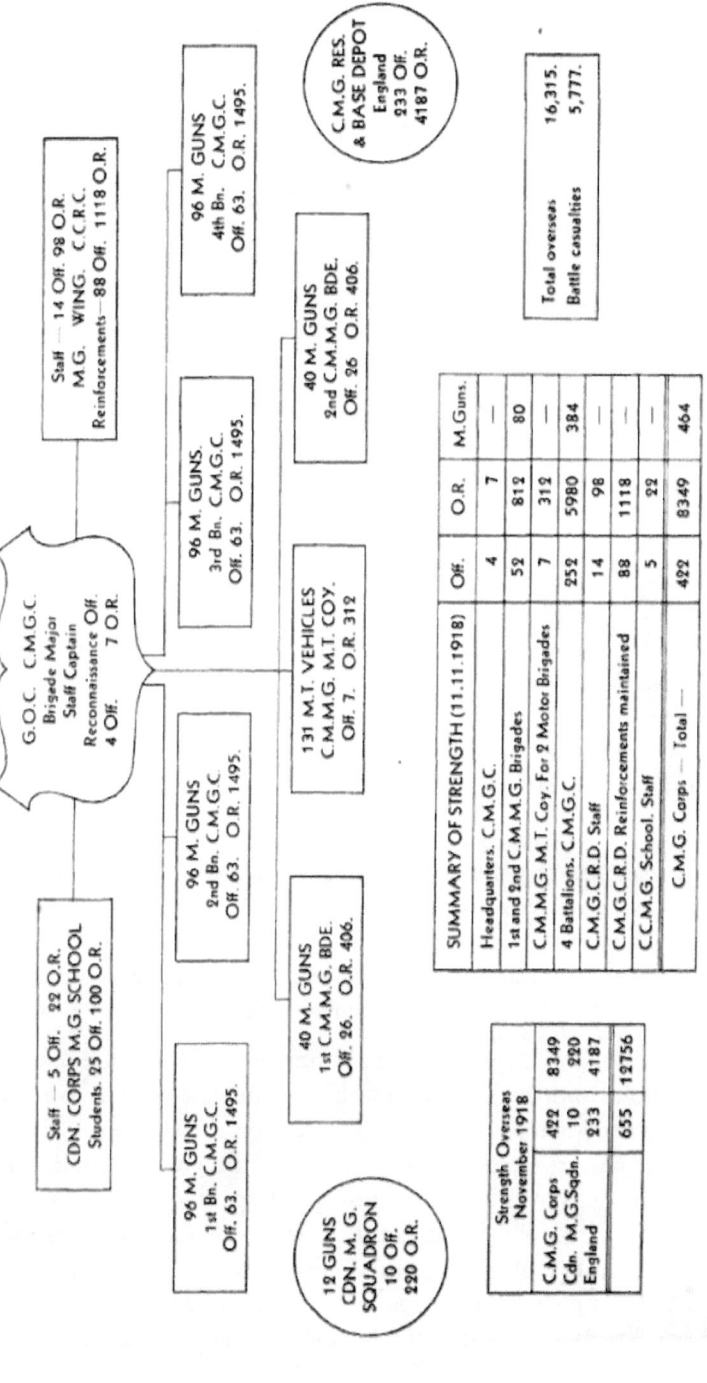

pany advanced with the 54th and 102nd Battalions and No. 3 Company moved forward across the canal through Valenciennes and took up defensive positions in the evening on the outskirts of the city.

The completeness and thoroughness with which the operation was carried out was evidenced in the large number of killed and wounded Germans, which exceeded 2,100. This total was actually greater than the number of assaulting troops. There was abundant evidence of the effectiveness of our machine gun barrage.

Machine gun casualties were small. No. 1 Company had two officers and 21 other ranks wounded and two guns put out of action. No. 3 Company suffered no casualties in the attack.

However, the 1st Brigade Motors, who fired in the barrage, did suffer heavily but not from gun fire. They had one officer and 45 other ranks put out of action by cordite fumes from their own guns which had been placed for the barrage in houses, the confined spaces not permitting the gas to escape before the personnel were overcome. As a result the brigade had to be reorganised into four batteries instead of its normal five—thanks to a lesson which came rather late in the war.

Infantry battalion commanders commented generally on the hearty and quick co-operation of the machine guns in this operation. On November 2nd Lieut.-Col. M. A. Scott, D.S.O., received the following letter of appreciation from Brig.-Gen. J. M. Ross, D.S.O., commanding the 10th C.I.B.:

> Just a line to express the appreciation .of the 10th Brigade for the magnificent work done by your people who were working with us in yesterday's operation.
>
> All my battalions have expressed their satisfaction and I wish you would let those under your command, who were acting with us yesterday, know how we feel about it.

On November 3rd the advance continues, but resistance, if patchy, is still strong and the German machine gunners continue to fight a stubborn rearguard action. Progress is slow on the left, where the 3rd Division finds itself confronted by areas that are entirely flooded, except where railway embankments or slag heaps rear themselves above the ordinary level and afford good cover for the German rearguards. The 11th C.I.B. makes the farthest advance of the 4th Division, the line being advanced 3,000 yards and Estreux captured.

On November 4th the 4th Division inches forward about two

miles and the 3rd Division swishes through its flooded front to make good the Vicq-Thiers railway.

Progress on November 5th was slow, but it was historic, for when patrols of the 4th Division, despite stubborn resistance, pushed across the Aunelle River it marked the first recovery of occupied Belgian territory by Canadian troops.

The advance was resumed on the 6th and the 4th Division crossed into Belgium along the whole Divisional front, capturing the villages of Marchipont, Baisieux and the southern portion of Quievrechain. The 3rd Division pushed on, capturing the railway station and the glass works of Quievrechain and the northern part of the village and also captured Crespin, farther north.

This day had brought the enemy's first counter-attack on the front of the 22nd Corps, elements of which were forced to withdraw to the west bank of the Honelle River at Angre.

The 2nd Battalion C.M.G.C. relieved the 4th Battalion C.M.G.C. on the night of the 6th-7th and the latter unit was withdrawn on November 7th to billets in St. Waast-la-Haut, where it was fated to wait out momentous events.

On the right, the advance was now thrust into the heart of the Belgian coal district, where teeming villages, sprawled cheek by jowl over the flat, sodden landscape in which huge slag heaps rose to offer natural obstacles.

On the 7th the attack was resumed and good progress was made through the soggy going. On the right, the 2nd Division cleared the remainder of Baisieux, captured the sugar refinery northeast of the town, the Town of Elouges and the scattered settlements surrounding it. The two Divisions combined to take Quievrain and in addition, on the left, the 3rd pushed along the Mons road for 4,000 yards. capturing La Croix and Hensies, north of the road.

The 8th Corps, on the left, had not yet been able to negotiate the Canal de l'Escaut and since the left flank was constantly lengthening the 3rd Division was ordered to attack toward the north when the advance was resumed on the 8th. By noon the villages of Thievencelle and St. Aybert were captured and later a footbridge was constructed across the Conde-Mons Canal. Under cover of darkness, patrols crossed and a bridgehead was established. On the right, the 3rd Division pushed as far as the western outskirts of Boussu.

Strong opposition met the 2nd Division but by midnight of these longish days of probing into the unknown ahead the division had captured the important village of Dour and the smaller villages of Bois-de-Boussu, Petit Hornu, Bois-de-Epinois and a portion of the Bois-de-Leveque were cleared.

Signs of increasing demoralisation among the enemy troops were noted in these days filled with intermittent fighting that was wearing on the nerves of all and imposed a constant strain.

On the 9th a general advance of four miles, and at several points of six, carried the 2nd Division clear of the mining area. Numerous towns were cleared, of which Wasmes-Paturages combined boasted a population of 30,000.

The pressure of the Canadians was relentless. Before dawn of the 9th had broken the 3rd Division had crossed the River Haine and later secured a hold on the north bank of the Conde-Mons Canal near Le Petit Crepin. During the afternoon more troops were sent across the canal and the villages of Petit Crepin, Ville Pommeroeuil, Hautrage and Terte were captured.

Also before daylight on the 9th the 3rd Division on its right had pushed into Boussu.

"H" Battery, supporting the Princess Pats on the 7th C.I.B. right, pushed four guns well forward, two on each side of Jemappes. An enemy machine gun nest was silenced by these guns and two prisoners taken.

On November 10th No. 3 Company of the 2nd Battalion C.M.G.C. continued the advance with the 4th C.I.B. Considerable machine gun fire came from Nouvelles on our immediate right flank. "J" Battery kept the area under fire while the 18th Battalion worked around the position.

Here the battery lost Lieut. H. A. Scott, who was killed by a shell as he was directing the fire of his guns.

Lieut. Scott was to be the last officer casualty in the 2nd Battalion C.M.G.C. Actually, the batteries advancing with the thrusting brigades had had few chances to take part in the fighting. The fighting for Valenciennes and Mont Huoy on November 1st-2nd had given the advancing batteries of the 4th Battalion C.M.G.C. a chance to do an organised barrage shoot, but in the daily advances between October 11th and up until now the role of the forward batteries was largely to consolidate as the infantry pressed slowly on, mopping up as they went. Following the infantry as closely as they did put a terrific strain on transport arrangements for M. G. Companies, since the roads were almost totally destroyed and were heavily mined and littered with booby traps. There was little opportunity for the fighting transport echelons to use cross country routes owing to the restricted nature of the country into which the Canadian Corps was now pushing its way.

Brutinel's Brigade, composed of a detachment of cavalry, corps cyclists and mounted mortars, had opportunities for some spectacular dashes into enemy territory and, in the long pursuit, harried the enemy constantly.

On October 8th they had done some fine work along the Cambria-Salzoir road. When bridges were blown up, engineers repaired them under the protection of the armoured cars, and prepared the way for a brilliant cavalry charge.

The destruction of the roads hampered the cars, but they pushed through and from time to time had actual machine gun duels with crack German gunners, who had also been mounted on trucks to give them more mobility.

On October 19th a quick dash by the armoured cars south of Douai prevented the Germans from springing mines on the main road of the Canadian advance. It is recorded that they charged a group of the enemy, mining the only bridge which led through the swamps near the Marais de Beauvages, and drove them off. They held the position four hours until the Canadians came up in force.

On October 22nd a group from the 1st C.M.G.C., consisting of two armoured cars and two batteries. were attached that morning to the 9th C.I.B. with instructions to move forward and get in touch with the enemy.

The detachment advanced beyond the infantry and proceeded into Raismes as far as the sharp bend in the St. Amand-Anien road. The intention was to exploit Chemin Notre Dame. But as the road was reported by a cyclist patrol to be in bad condition, attention was directed toward the Rue de Marais. The civilians in this neighbourhood stated that a party of Germans had once been placed in positions commanding all the exits from it, but on a search being made no enemy was found. The group then continued up the Rue de Marais as far as the railway crossing, where infantry screens came up and established a line of outposts.

After a reconnaisance by motor cyclists, the detachment resumed its forward thrust with the bridge over the canal east of Denain-Anzin as the objective. The armoured cars led the way, followed closely by "E" Battery, with "C" Battery a little way behind. Denain-Anein is a suburb of Valenciennes and a tight cluster of metal factories and mines, with their accompanying mass of closely-clustered workmen's homes. Slag heaps in abundance, railway lines and sidings criss-crossing the villages, made work of this groping but the enemy apparently had decided not to take advantage of this, a set-up perfectly designed for house-to-house fighting. But if trouble didn't bob from around every corner in this area it was in the offing.

The detachment went on down to the end of the Rue de Marais and then turned south along the road south of Marais de Beabrages as far as the "Y" of the roads south of Marais de Arnonville. From this point one road led to Valenciennes. "E" Battery and the cars were now 2,700 yards in front of the infantry and about 1,200 yards from the canal bridge. They were being fired at from the right flank and one party of Germans was seen working on top of the bridge, another group underneath it, apparently laying some demolition dew-dads.

One armoured car was sent to the right to locate and silence the enemy on that flank and the other moved towards the bridge but was unable to get very far owing to engine trouble.

On observing our men the enemy increased the volume of his fire with two machine guns. One was firing from the bridge and his accurate bursts were sending up showers of dust off the rocky road. The other was firing from the railway embankment on the right.

The armoured cars immediately retaliated with their four guns and took time off to Rend groups of the enemy scattering on the banks of the canal. Soon the German guns were temporarily silenced and one of the group on the top of the bridge was seen to tumble off into the canal, while the others clambered down to safety.

The Motors during this duel lost Lieut. T. A. Smith, who in previous actions had done exceptionally fine work, and a gunner was wounded.

It was thus the German rearguards took their toll as day by day the advance pressed forward.

And now back to the 3rd and 2nd Divisions again, exerting their inexorable pressure on the harried Germans and giving them no breathing space in which to properly organise for sustained defence.

During the night of November 10th-11th the two divisions had resumed their advance. On the 3rd Division front the 7th C.I.B. began to close in on Mons. The villages of Nimy and Petit Nimy were quickly captured and before midnight this doughty brigade had effected an entry into Mons itself *via* the railway station.

The famous Princess Pats, first Canadian unit to see service in France, therefore had the honour of being among the first Canadian troops to enter Mons, from which city the Old Contemptibles, under Sir John French, had begun their historic retreat in front of overwhelming German forces.

No. 2 Company of the 3rd Battalion C.M.G.C. sent two batteries over with the attacking battalions. These were "E" and "F" Batteries. At 6 a.m. of November 11th, when word was received by No. 1 Company that the 9th C.I.B. would relieve the 7th C.I.B., "C" and "D" Batteries were detailed for the attack.

Meanwhile the 2nd Division had during the night taken the Bois-le-Haut, a wood crowning a large hill on the south-eastern outskirts of Mons, thus securing the right flank of the 3rd Division. Sir Arthur Currie's report says that the capture of this high ground forced upon the enemy a further retirement and our troops, still pressing on, reached and captured St. Symphorien and Fbg. Barthelmy by 8 a.m.

The report says of those momentous hours of November 11th which was to bring, oftentimes, bitter debate:

In the meantime, word had been received through the 1st Army that hostilities would cease at 11 a.m. on November 11th, the Armistice having been signed in acceptance of our terms.

To secure a satisfactory line for the defence of Mons, our line was further advanced and the Bois-du-Havre, Bois-du-Rapois and the town and villages of Havre, Bon Vouloir, La Bruyere, Masireres, St. Denis and Obourg were captured before hostilities ceased.

Rumours had, as usual, reached the troops of the request for an armistice by the Germans, but for over four years the *Rue de Rumor* that ran its ubiquitous course over every front had run into blank walls of denial and flat contradiction.

The *Rue de Rumor* in this particular area the past two days seemed to be always blocked by masonry that crumbled under the long-range fire of German shells which, if anything, seemed to be searching more intently than they had for weeks past for victims.

Over on the 2nd Division front batteries of No. 2 Company, 2nd Battalion C.M.G.C., had covered the advance on November 11th. Four guns of "F" Battery (Layton) covering the right flank of the 31st Battalion were the last of that Division's machine guns to rattle forth defiance to the enemy on that historic morning. This battery had reached, as the 11th hour of the day approached, Petit Haver, east of Mons, and the left forward battery with the 28th Battalion was on the northeast outskirts of Haver, south of the Canal du Centre. The two batteries in reserve were located in the chemical works on the south edge of the Bois de Haver.

And then the "Cease Fire" sounded.

Strange, uncanny lulls had come in over four years of warfare of intensity such as human nature had never before been subjected to. They were always unreal after days and hours on end of ear-splitting pounding to which life perforce on the Western Front had had to attune itself.

But this lull at 11 o'clock of November 11th?

It seemed ghostly, suddenly peopled, mayhap, to the more imaginative, with those millions of the dead, whose requiem had been sung for so many weary years by the screech and whine of shells, the drone of planes and the *c-r-ru*mp of high explosive and destruction.

Yesterday—German shells screeching over in a spiteful search for victims. and still forms under blankets being stretchered back to the rear. Yesterday—grimy, mud-caked but exultant "blighties" passing those who, with a look of accumulated strain, were trudging eastward. Yesterday—all around the debris of war—the shattered skeleton of a limber—dead horses—huge gouges in the *pavé* road—slashed off trees and poles as gaunt remnants of what a tornado of whistling iron had left—here and there the body of a civilian in an ironic, unlovely sprawl—one who had caught a glimpse of freedom only to have it snatched away by grimacing death.

Last night—the November sun sinking into a red haze—the evening vespers of war merged into the crashing bangs of high explosives—our own at last—but with night's more muffled tone and a broken tempo. Last night—fitful flares piercing the blackness—old Jerry's childish fear of the dark still persisting.

And now today—bleak dawn and war's unending frightfulness apparently ready to go on indefinitely, despite silly rumours of an armistice—the old familiar *staccato* rattle of the Emma Gees—the same damnable game with fate and the Bosche again—and tea sicklier than usual because the rations were hours overdue and the troops hadn't caught up yet with the day before yesterday's breakfast.

And now Peace!

It was too much to grasp. Some wept. Some shouted. Others danced. Some prayed. But few were coherent.

Farther back, mayhap, there was grim disapproval at being robbed of that chance to carry war's lesson right to the heart of Germany itself, but up there, where the last grisly grip of battle had so suddenly been loosened, there was only an immensity of disbelief in the miracle—an unvoiceable immensity of relief when the miracle was understood.

Concluding his account of the operations which had brought about this miraculous denouement, Gen. Sir Arthur Currie said, in part:

> Between October 11th and November 11th the Canadian Corps had advanced to a total depth exceeding 90,000 yards.
> ...
> . . . . when it is recalled that since August 8th the Canadian Corps had fought battles of the first magnitude, having a direct bearing on the general situation and contributing, to an extent difficult to realise, to the defeat of the German armies in the field, this advance under most difficult conditions constitutes a decisive test of the superior energy and power of endurance of our men.
>
> It is befitting that the capture of Mons should close the fighting records of our troops in which every battle is a resplendent page of glory.
>
> The Canadian Corps was deeply appreciative of the honour of having been selected amongst the first for the task of establishing and occupying the bridgeheads east of the Rhine. A long march of 170 miles under difficult conditions was ahead of them, but they ungrudgingly looked forward to what had always been their ultimate objective—the occupation of German soil.
>
> Between August 8th and November 11th the following had been captured: prisoners, 31,537; guns (heavy and field), 623; machine guns, 2,842; trench mortars (heavy and light), 336.
>
> Over 500 square miles of territory and 228 cities, towns and villages had been liberated, including the cities of Cambria, Denain, Valenciennes and Mons. . . .
>
> In the performance of these mighty achievements all arms of the corps have bent their purposeful energy, working one for all and all for one. The dash and magnificent bravery of our incomparable infantry have at all times been devotedly seconded

with great skill and daring by our machine gunners, while the artillery lent them their powerful and never-failing support. The initiative and resourcefulness displayed by the Engineers contributed materially to the depth and rapidity of our advances. The devotion of the medical personnel has been, as always, worthy of every praise. The administrative services, working at all times under very great pressure and adverse conditions, surpassed their usual efficiency. The chaplain services, by their continual devotion to the spiritual welfare of the troops and their utter disregard of personal risk, endeared themselves to the hearts of everyone. The incessant efforts of the Y.M.C.A. and their initiative in bringing comforts right up to the front line in battle were warmly appreciated by all.

In the advance from the Canal de la Sensee the losses of the four machine gun battalions had been comparatively light.

Two officers were killed and four wounded during the long advance, while 20 other ranks were killed and 250 wounded. The 4th Battalion C.M.G.C. suffered the heaviest, having four officers killed and wounded and 222 other ranks killed and wounded.

On November 18th commenced the long trek to the Rhine, the 2nd Canadian Division advancing on the right and the 1st Division on the left. The heads of the columns passed the outpost line at 9 a.m. that day. Each column found its own protection, cavalry screens and cyclists being used.

The 3rd and 4th Divisions were to remain in Belgium for the rest of the year.

As the advancing columns drew farther away from railhead, which was still west of Valenciennes, and the roads became poorer and villages more sparse, the march to the Rhine was beset with more and more difficulties. Added to the scarcity of billets was either rain, which fell intermittently, or fog and a ground haze which was as uncomfortable as rain.

Post-war literature, historical and fiction, has fully pictured the change in outlook on the part of Canadians as they penetrated farther into Belgium.

The better class of Belgians, both farmers and those of the larger towns, were hospitable to a warming degree, but the attitude of the poorer peasants proved baffling to the Canadians, who had been under the impression that at least some of the sacrifices of the past four years had been made on their behalf. Often they were bold enough to say that they preferred the German occupation to victory—they were avaricious, untrustworthy and sullen.

But these were minor considerations in the larger expanse of things and the still almost unbelievable fact that the bally old war was really over.

As the difficulty of maintaining the lengthening line of supply grew more pronounced, troubles resolved themselves into the very primitive one of food for all ranks.

The breakdown in supply reached a climax on November 28th, when the rations for the day before were received just as the day's march was commencing. On the 29th the same situation recurred and the march on that day was cancelled.

Grousing, ever the soldier's privilege and now undisturbed by war's alarms, was given full reign by the troops and was hardly lightened by new scenery, new sights, or the coming thrill of entering upon German soil. The staff's passion for polishing, too, had reasserted itself and altogether, as historians reviewed the trek, it was not a matter of day after day of unalloyed joy. But men who could find humour in the midst of death found amusing aspects to the days of steady slogging through a country which showed no signs of war except as from time to time a grim reminder came in the shape of an abandoned German truck and pieces of equipment.

On December 4th the heads of the two Canadian divisions crossed the German border. The 1st Division crossed at Petit Thier and the 2nd at Beho. They marched over with flags flying and bands playing. Rations were often skimpy as the march through Germany proceeded over roads that were almost impassable at times, but merely to be on German soil was an uplift of the spirit.

The German inhabitants were docile and, in the country, seemed to have ample food.

Approaching the Rhine, the countryside became more beautiful though sombre in the melancholy of autumn and of a nation that had awakened to the knowledge of defeat after a four-year spree of war.

On December 13th the formal occupation of the bridgeheads of the Rhine was marked by the crossing of the 2nd Division at Bonn, where Gen. Currie took the salute, and of the 1st Division at Cologne, where Gen. Plumer, G.O.C. 2nd Army, was at the saluting point.

In Germany and in Belgium then, Canadians were spending still another Christmas. Of this time, Canadians will cherish memories of many strange, many humorous experiences. Gradually, instead of hatred for the hated Hun, there crept in a feeling of pity for a people who could be so blindly led into war and seemed now the antithesis of arrogance and lust of conquest. It was a transformation in a supposedly proud people which Canadians, who had the experience of watching it, will always find utterly baffling.

The New Year brought with it sobering thoughts of the future—of a return to the prosaic ways of peace, of a return to vocations and to picking up the threads of an existence which seemed so far in the past.

The Canadian Machine Gun Corps could review its growth in prestige and status with real gratification as the Emma Gees experienced the common urge now to get back to the homeland.

No single arm, with the exception of the Air Force, had earned greater recognition than the machine guns and, while always tipping a deferential salute to the infantry for their stark heroism, machine gunners had reason to feel that they belonged to a *Corps d'Elite*.

The remarkable growth of the Canadian Machine Gun Corps from the battalion sections in France in 1915 is shown in the following table:

	Officers	Other Ranks	Total
June 21st, 1915	24	567	591
March 31st, 1917	182	3,192	3,374
November 11th, 1918	422	8,349	8,771

Over 16,000 served in the C.M.G.C., of whom 5,777 gave their lives in their country's service.

Infantry battalions, maintained in France, had been able in a large measure to keep their sectional identities and to a certain extent this was true also of artillery units. But when the Canadian overseas forces were ultimately demobilised none was as scattered as the machine gunners.

From the Yukon to the Maritimes, the C.M.G.C. was a cross-section of all Canada, but the ways of peace and the penalty of great distances were to strengthen rather than wither the splendid spirit of the corps.

Recognition of the Canadian Machine Gun Corps' hard-won spurs, it seemed, came on November 3rd, 1919, when authority was given for the establishment of a Canadian Machine Gun Brigade as a part of the reconstructed Canadian Permanent Force.

Too, came the establishment of a Canadian Machine Gun Corps as a part of the Active Militia of Canada. It comprised 12 Machine Gun Battalions (at first styled brigades), two Motor Machine Gun Brigades and a Machine Gun Squadron.

Of these units, of course, only the 1st, 2nd, 3rd and 4th; the 1st and 2nd Motors and the Machine Gun Squadron could perpetuate units which fought in France.

In 1921 a general order set forth that:

> His Majesty the King has graciously approved the grant of the title 'Royal' to the Canadian Permanent Machine Gun Brigade. (then under the command of Lieut.-Col. E. W. Sansom, D.S.O.)

Though the Permanent Brigade had done splendid work, especially valuable in the establishment of the new militia machine gun units, in 1924 came a policy of retrenchment which brought about the disbandment of the Royal Canadian Machine Gun Brigade as a separate organisation. Many of the personnel of the brigade were absorbed into other permanent force units and some years later were to be found filling very important appointments on the General Staff in various capacities.

For many years the machine gun units of the militia were to live under the fear of disbandment, especially since the Imperial authorities had seen fit to abolish the Machine Gun Corps.

If machine gunners in the Canadian Militia became discouraged many times and generally felt that they were the subject of official neglect that was out of keeping with the acknowledged rise of their weapon to pre-eminence during the war, they could scarcely be blamed.

But even if the "war orphan" feeling was prevalent, the corps continued to carry on and generally earned a reputation for efficiency and keenness that was won against heavy odds, especially in the cities where units of other arms were perpetuating, not only units which had won battle honours in France, but had a lengthy tradition in the Canadian Militia behind them.

The Canadian Machine Gun Corps Association was first formed in 1926 and it was to have a tremendous influence in maintaining for the corps the prestige it had gained in France.

Lieut.-Col. B. O. Hooper, D.S.O., M.C., was the association's first president. He was to carry on for three years.

Presidents to follow Lieut.-Col. Hooper were as follows:
Lieut.-Col. James Mess
Lieut.-Col. G. W. H. Millican, M.C.
Lieut.-Col. C. H. Colwell, E.D.
Lieut.-Col. J. A. McCamus, M.C.
Lieut.-Col. George Machum .
Lieut.-Col. J. A. McCamus, M.C.
Lieut.-Col. F. I. Carpenter, V.D.

Throughout Major A. G. Fisher was the efficient Secretary-Treasurer.

While the Association during its many splendid years of service did a great deal to increase the efficiency of the training of Militia Machine Gun units, it succeeded also in keeping the spirit of the old corps alive and the "crossed guns" have always been an open sesame to a comradeship that, to machine gunners at least, seems more characteristic of their service than it is of any other arm.

Perhaps it was the compactness and self-sufficiency of machine gun crews, so often finding themselves in isolated posts, that produced this splendid spirit, which survived the war and thrived through the piping days of peace to follow.

The organisation of central camps for machine gun training, modelled somewhat after the camps in which artillery training had always been pursued, had long been an objective of the Association. In 1933 these camps were established for the first time across Canada.

That point seemed to mark an upturn in the fortunes and the outlook of the Machine Gunners, and so it proved.

When, in 1936, the Canadian Militia was reorganised on a six-division basis, the drastic changes brought about a greatly-enhanced status for machine gunnery.

One hundred and thirty-five infantry regiments were whittled to 91. Of these 59 remained as rifle battalions, six were turned into tank battalions and the machine gun strength rose to 26 battalions—more than double the former strength.

After so many years of seeming fighting for a mere existence in the active lists, the trend toward a mechanised army had returned the machine gunners to first rate importance again in the militia scheme.

Tradition had taken off its epaulettes and donned overalls.

And as machine gunners, because of the nature of their training, had had little opportunity for parade ground smartness—and probably no overweening desire to excel in this side of military training, the

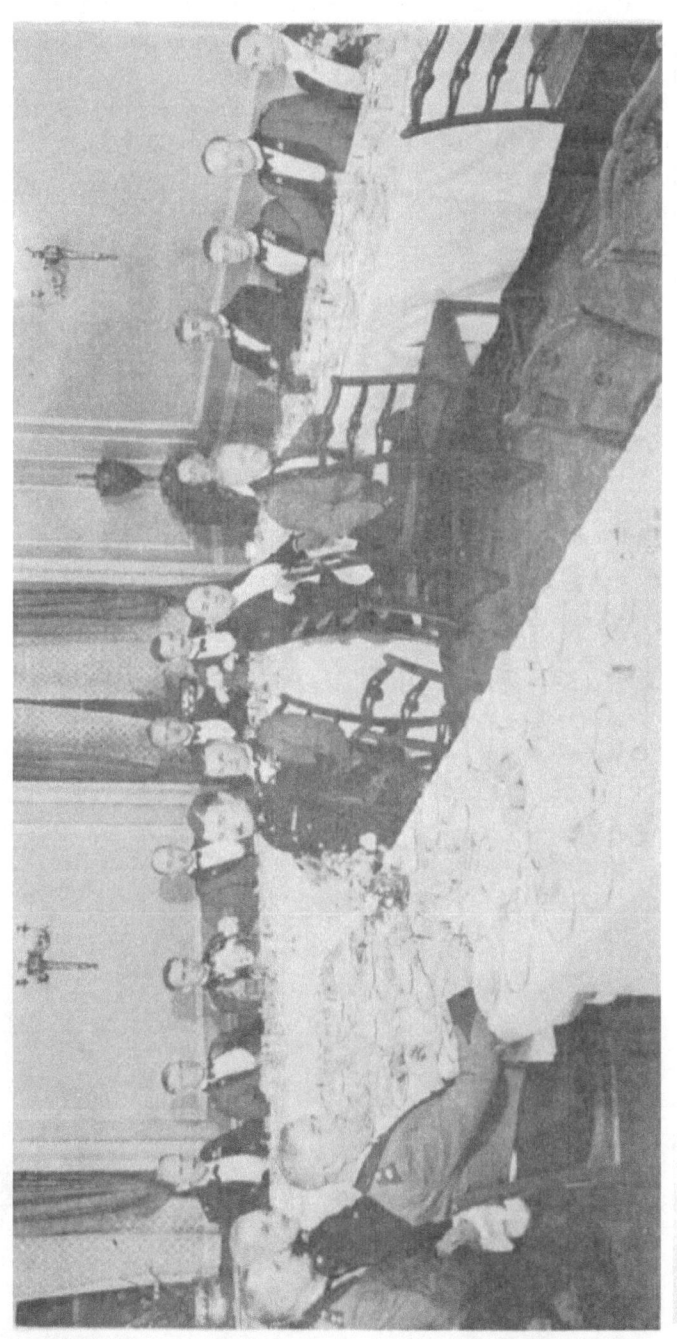

Last meeting of Executive C.M.G.C. Association in Royal York Hotel, Toronto, 1937, to ratify amalgamation with Canadian Infantry Association and to authorize publication of this history.

new order of things found them very much at home.

As this is being written a new generation of machine gunners is all but dominating the scene. With each passing year this domination will become more sharply pronounced.

To this new generation, it may be justly claimed, the old has handed on a tradition of enthusiasm for its arm, heroism and self-sacrifice in battle and further decades of service to the country in peace that is not surpassed by any other arm of the service.

www.ingramcontent.com/pod-product-compliance
Lightning Source LLC
Chambersburg PA
CBHW021959160426
43197CB00007B/188